The Diva & the Rancher

The Diva & the Rancher

The story of Norma Piper and George Pocaterra

JENNIFER HAMBLIN AND DAVID FINCH

Rocky
Mountain Books
Calgary–Victoria–Vancouver

Front cover: George at the Buffalo Head Ranch, late 1920s. GA PD-184-1-244
Norma in costume for the opera "Rigoletto," Milan, Italy, ca 1936. GA PD-184-5-46

Back cover: George and Norma, Milan, Italy, ca 1936. GA PD-184-7-31

Half-title page: George entertaining the Royles and the Runcimans at the Buffalo Head Ranch, ca 1915. GA PD-184-1-9

Title page: George at the Buffalo Head Ranch, 1926. GA PA-2393-14-1-1
Norma in costume for the opera "Barber of Seville," Milan, Italy, ca 1936. GA PD-184-5-21

Chapter heads: The "NPG" monogram is taken from George and Norma's wedding announcement, Milan, Italy, June 18, 1936. GA M6340-194-1

Page 286: Norma in Perugia, Italy, June 1934. GA PA-2393-12-1-3

Rocky Mountain Books
#108—17665 66A Avenue
Surrey, BC V3S 2A7
www.rmbooks.com

06 07 08 09/5 4 3 2 1

Library and Archives Canada Cataloguing in Publication

Hamblin, Jennifer
    The diva and the rancher : the story of Norma Piper and George Pocaterra / Jennifer Hamblin and David Finch.

ISBN-13: 978-1-894765-70-1
ISBN-10: 1-894765-70-2

    1. Pocaterra, Norma Piper, 1898-1983. 2. Pocaterra, George William, 1882-1972.
3. Singers--Alberta--Biography. 4. Ranchers--Alberta--Biography. I. Finch, David, 1956-
II. Title.

FC3675.1.P63H35 2006   971.23'030922   C2006-904179-2

Cover design by Frances Hunter
Substantive editing by Gillean Daffern
Copy editing by Wendy Fitzgibbons
Interior layout by Gillean Daffern
Printed in Canada by Friesens

Rocky Mountain Books acknowledges the financial support for its publishing program from the Government of Canada through the Book Publishing Industry Development Program (BPIDP), Canada Council for the Arts, and the province of British Columbia through the British Columbia Arts Council and the Book Publishing Tax Credit.

BRITISH COLUMBIA
ARTS COUNCIL
Supported by the Province of British Columbia

The Canada Council | Le Conseil des Arts
for the Arts | du Canada

Contents

Photo credits: All photos are from the George
and Norma Piper Pocaterra Collection, courtesy
of Glenbow Archives (GA), with the exception
of 8 photos from the R. M. Patterson Collection,
courtesy of Janet Blanchet.

Acknowledgments

As with any big project, there are many people to thank. First and foremost, a huge thank you to Gillean Daffern for suggesting the project and supporting it through to conclusion. Her familiarity with the subject matter, technical advice and overall enthusiasm were invaluable and sincerely appreciated. Our thanks also go to staff members at Heritage House and Rocky Mountain Books, and especially to our copy editor, Wendy Fitzgibbons.

We would like to acknowledge members of the Piper and Pocaterra families and thank them for their interest and contribution, especially Jack, Julia, Michael and Shirley Piper and Guido Pozza. Norma's youngest brother, Jack, who passed away in 2005 at the age of 99, took a lively interest in the project and provided many intimate memories of his beloved sister, Norma and their early years together.

Many former students, friends and colleagues of the Pocaterras were very generous with their memories during personal interviews. Some of our informants have since passed away, but we would like to extend our thanks to all who participated: Adolf Baumgart, Lois Callaway Brown, Doreen Chinneck, Averil Cook, Louis De Paoli, Cleone Duncan, Eve Zacharias Ford, Phyllis Chapman Clarke Ford, Valeria Gennaro, Shirley Flock Griffin, Molly Blanchfield Hamilton, Dorothy Hawley, Susan Henker, Dale Jackson, Sylvia Jones, Sophie Kok, Jamie and Betty Mackinnon, Faye Macleod, Melody Wilson McMillan, Frances and Gary Miller, Sandra Munn, Florence Musselwhite, P.K. Page, Leona Paterson, Marigold Patterson, Marilyn Perkins, Lil Wilson, Eleanor Carlyle Winans and Susan Milner Woodward. Although we tried our best to relay the information and memories contributed by these individuals accurately, we take full responsibility and apologize in advance for any errors, omissions or misinterpretations.

We are grateful for the financial support provided by the Glenbow Museum's Joy Harvie Maclaren Scholarship Fund and for the generous provision of photographs by the Glenbow Archives. We appreciated the ongoing interest and support of many individuals at Glenbow, but wish to give particular thanks to Senior Librarian, Lindsay Moir and the Director of the Glenbow Library and Archives, Doug Cass for their friendship and advice throughout the project and for their careful reading and comments on the text at various stages. Special thanks to Glenbow Chief Curator Emeritus Hugh Dempsey for providing information on the Pocaterra collection and for graciously writing the foreword to this book. Thanks also to Glenbow staffers Colleen Zetaruk for scanning the photographs; Owen Melenka for producing slides; Ellen Bryant for assisting with photographs; Deepika Fernandez and Aimee Benoit for facilitating access to Pocaterra artifacts in the Cultural History collection; Tonia Fanella for assisting with Italian-English translations; and Wilf Allen for dubbing and enhancing audio recordings from the collection.

Individuals at various institutions were helpful providing background information and confirming details. In particular, we wish to acknowledge the assistance of Arthur McClelland, David McCord, and Sarah Morton of the London Room at the London Public Library, Annie Laflamme of the Canadian Museum of Civilization, and Donna Quinton of the Calgary Kiwanis Music Festival.

Finally, we would like to express heartfelt love and thanks to our families--to Jennifer's husband Tony, and children Lindsay and Graham, and to David's wife Jeannie and daughter Annie--for their patience, love and unflagging support throughout the long duration of this project. It is to them that we dedicate this book.

Jennifer Hamblin, David Finch

Foreword by Hugh Dempsey

My wife, Pauline, and I first met George Pocaterra and Norma Piper in the spring of 1963, when George was invited to speak at a Historical Society of Alberta meeting in Calgary. He and his wife quickly won the hearts of our members, he with his knowledge of the pioneer days and she with her charming personality.

George spoke to our group about his experiences with the Stoney First Nation, beginning in 1904 when he homesteaded at the future site of his Buffalo Head Ranch. His memories were as sharp that day in 1963 as they were when he first met people like Paul Amos, Elijah Hunter and Alex Roll-in-the-Mud. Of his first encounter with the Stoneys he recalled, "As I struck a match and lit my cigarette I suddenly saw five Indians standing behind me in a half circle, every man with a rifle in the crook of his arm. They looked like the Natives of 'Deerslayer' by Fenimore Cooper." This romantic view of the Stoneys never left him. And because of his openness, the Indians responded favourably to him, Paul Amos later becoming his blood brother.

We met the Pocaterras several times after this initial session, sometimes at their home, sometimes at our society meetings and sometimes at the Glenbow Archives. In our social meetings at their Glengarry district home in Calgary there always seemed to be classical music playing in the background and other reminders of Norma's musical career. A piano in the corner of a room was mute testimony to her years as music teacher to scores of young Calgarians over the years.

One thing that impressed us was the fact that the two of them seemed to be as much in love then as they were when they were first married. They sat beside each other whenever possible, held hands and were just like a couple of newlyweds. Yet they seemed such a contrast, for Norma was definitely elitist and refined and her husband was rough-hewn.

George and I were drawn to each other, not only because of our common interest in western history; I think the fact that my wife was of the Blood Nation had a lot to do with it. Her presence seemed to fit in with his romantic ideas. During our visits, we were enthralled by tales of his early days in the

Kananaskis Country and his admiration for the Stoneys. It was clear that he still had a warm place in his heart for the Natives he met when he struggled as a trapper. As he commented about Paul Amos, "We were the closest of friends, until he passed into the happy hunting grounds [in 1960]."

We were very saddened by the death of George in 1972, and I wondered how Norma would fare. I met her on a number of occasions, and one day I asked her how she was able to carry on without him when they had been so close. She replied that there had been so much love between them that it would sustain her for the rest of her life. She missed him, but she knew he was still with her in her heart. It was very touching.

In the spring of 1982 I had a phone call from Norma's brother, Jack Piper, who had come from Montreal to place her in an extended-care centre and to sell the house. Norma had told him to call me to pick up a painting of George that I had admired. When I got to the house, I learned that everything was going to be sold. As I poked around, I found some wonderful stuff and asked if we could have it for Glenbow. Jack checked with Norma and she kindly agreed. When Glenbow curator of Cultural History Ron Getty and I went through the house, we were overwhelmed by the wealth of documents and artifacts. There were George's diaries from 1935 to 1969, letters dating back to 1907, including love letters in Italian between George and Norma and correspondence relating to Norma's career in Italy. To top it off, there were all of Norma's original costumes from her Italian operatic years, brought back to Canada in 1939. And there were many other ranching and pioneer objects that were wonderful additions to Glenbow's collections.

Ron and I worked for three days, packing and bringing to Glenbow these important documents and objects reflecting the careers of two great Albertans. Norma died a year later, but her memory and that of George will live on through the significant role they played in the pioneer and social history of Alberta.

Hugh A. Dempsey
December 2005

Prologue

This is the story of two dreamers who never really fulfilled their dreams but who enjoyed great personal success, nevertheless, and became local legends in their own lifetimes.

The story really begins in 1903, when young Giorgio Pocaterra left Italy and came to the Canadian West looking for adventure. Fascinated with tales of "cowboys and Indians," he settled in the Highwood River valley south of Calgary, where he found a land in transition. Fences were quickly carving up the old rangeland, but the area farther west in the foothills and mountains of the Rockies was still largely untouched. Here there were few signs of white settlement; no real roads, just trails cut through the bush by the Stoney First Nation, whose members still roamed in hunting parties. Making friends with the Stoneys, George explored the region extensively and discovered that the rich resources of the Rocky Mountains remained largely untapped.

For an ambitious man determined to make his fortune the situation was irresistible, and after he established his famous Buffalo Head Ranch, George spent the next 30 years chasing his dreams in the area now known as Kananaskis Country. But his development schemes were derailed by two world wars, the Depression and later by the establishment of protected areas and a provincial park. Still, he managed to create an enduring legacy in his adopted country, indicated today by the widespread use of the Pocaterra name throughout the Kananaskis Lakes area.

In the late 1920s, a young Calgary girl named Norma Piper started taking singing lessons and quickly discovered that her voice had great potential. However, after a promising start her career stalled, largely because of the Depression, which hit western Canada particularly hard. Dreaming of becoming a great star, she moved to Italy in 1934 to study opera. In Milan she met and married George Pocaterra, who became her manager. Quite possibly she was on the verge of international success when the Second World War intervened. Retreating to the Calgary area to wait out the war, Norma began teaching singing, and suddenly her career took flight in a wholly unexpected direction. Beloved of generations of students, Norma found her ultimate success in helping to build and enrich the cultural life of Calgary, her old hometown.

With the encouragement of Hugh Dempsey, director of Collections of Calgary's Glenbow Museum, near the end of her life Norma donated all of the couple's personal papers to the Glenbow Archives. Jennifer was the archivist assigned to organize and create a descriptive listing of the collection, and while she worked my way through the dozens of diaries and hundreds of letters in the collection she fell in love with the Pocaterras, particularly with Norma, whose indomitable spirit and determination was an inspiration. Sometime later, while researching the life of the adventurer Raymond Patterson, David Finch became intrigued with Patterson's irascible friend George Pocaterra, whose ranch and colourful lifestyle were the subject of two of Patterson's most successful books, *The Buffalo Head* and *Far Pastures*.

In deciding to collaborate on the story of this fascinating couple, we discovered a serious gap in the historical record. Whereas the Pocaterra collection at Glenbow provided a rich resource for Norma and for the Pocaterras as a couple (and members of her family and many of her former students were happy to reminisce about the couple's later years), there were very few documents relating to George's early years, mainly because he had moved between continents several times before meeting Norma. Luckily, however, he had saved his photograph albums from the Buffalo Head days and was a prodigious letter writer in later years, filling in many gaps in letters to friends, particularly to Raymond Patterson. Norma's loving tribute to her husband, the unpublished manuscript "Son of the Mountains," was another invaluable resource for information about George's early life and the couple's early years together.

By the time George and Norma met in 1934, George's active life of adventure in the Canadian West had ended. The first two chapters of this book cover that early period; the next two do the same for Norma, who was growing up and developing her talent in Calgary at that time. Once they come together in Italy, their stories merge and the remainder of the book traces their journey through nearly 40 years of happy marriage and into the hearts of Calgarians, who remember them today as a pair of charming eccentrics.

J.H. & D.F
June 2006

MAP OF THE CANADIAN ROCKIES
WEST OF CALGARY

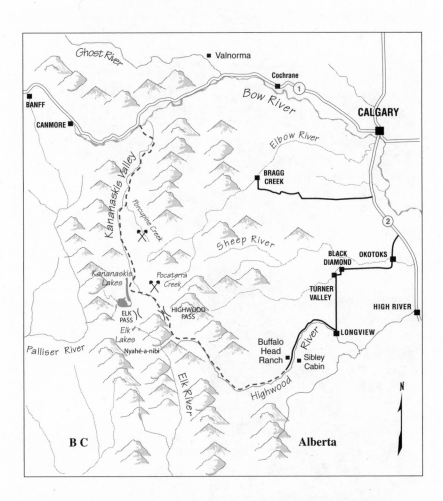

This map shows the roads and trails as they were in the early part of the 20th century when George Pocaterra lived at the Buffalo Head Ranch. The present Trans-Canada Highway did not exist. Highway 1A was the main road to Banff from Calgary. Today's Highway 40 along the Kananaskis Valley was just a trail.

Top: Piovene Rocchette, Italy,
ca 1900. GA PA-2393-1-1-1

Bottom: Giuseppe Pocaterra, Italy,
ca 1930. GA PA-2393-10-1-3

Chapter 1

George: The Buffalo Head
1882–1910

"I love trees too much," said George Pocaterra, "to see them slaughtered to make paper for a book of my life."[1] But he would have approved of a book on recycled paper, written about his passion for the wilderness and the woman he called "my own sweet Norma."

Giorgio Guglielmo Cesare Pocaterra was born on September 22, 1882, in northern Italy. His mother, Ubaldina Talin, was of old Venetian stock, and the Pocaterras were an ancient Roman family with feudal estates in the province of Ferrara, where they were paid an annual tribute by the nearby town of Migliarino. That custom was dropped by Giorgio's father, Giuseppe Pocaterra, but the family continued its long tradition of patriotism and distinguished military service.

This background was a source of pride for young Giorgio. Years later, he recalled an incident when his parents heroically defended themselves and his father's company payroll against bandits mounting an armed ambush: "My Father and also my Mother each one separately were given the highest decoration for civil valour by the unanimous vote of the Italian Parliament, and by the king. I was present as a boy, at the decorating ceremonies ... So I have got to live as much as I am able up to the standard set by my family!"[2]

Like his elder sister, Emilia, and younger sister, Marta, Giorgio was born in Piovene Rocchette, where Giuseppe was an executive in the textile company Lanificio Rossi. The company had built a mill in Rocchette to take advantage of locally available power from streams that poured from the peaks of the Dolomites. Giuseppe was an accomplished climber and later became a director of the Club Alpino Italiano. He sometimes took his small son scrambling and climbing with him, instilling in Giorgio a lifelong love of the mountains.

To ensure a better education for the boy, Giorgio was sent away to school at the age of eight, first to a boarding school in Padua. Then followed six years at the Academy of Commerce in Berne, Switzerland, where he developed a reputation as a practical joker. He once turned off the gas to the lights in the school and forced an early dismissal of classes so that he could attend a soccer match during school hours. Another time, when he was locked into a classroom as punishment and forced to write a misspelled word correctly on the blackboard 1,000 times, he slipped out the third-floor window, pulled it shut with his knife and made his escape along a ledge and down a drainpipe. His athleticism later extended to bicycling, shooting and soccer, and to figure skating with the daughter of a highly placed government official. He also played rugby football (left wing forward) and was one of the founders of the Young Boys of Berne Football Club.

Emilia, Marta and Giorgio Pocaterra,
Rocchette, Italy, ca 1890.
GA PA-2393-10-1-2

A quick study with languages, in Berne Giorgio picked up the local dialect and enlisted in the premilitary forces. While on manoeuvres, he captured the head of the Swiss army, who was disguised as a peasant, and delivered him to headquarters. At a banquet that evening Giorgio sat with the army officers, and the captive revealed that his cane had contained a "secret message" that the young man's actions had prevented from being delivered. But when his true nationality was revealed, Giorgio was relieved of his position in the Swiss army training program.

After finishing at the academy in 1900, Giorgio spent a year at an institute in Bradford, England, to learn more about the wool and textile industries. Afterwards, Matthew Lund provided him with a letter of recommendation on behalf of merchants Daniel & Rudolf Delius: "I have much pleasure in stating that during the 3 months that Mr. G. Pocaterra was in the Wool Sorting Department I always found him a very steady and industrious young man & one that paid strict attention to business." Another company official, Robert Delius, also provided a reference letter: "We have pleasure in stating that during the time Mr. G. Pocaterra has been employed in our Offices, he has applied himself diligently to business & has performed his duties to our entire satisfaction."[3]

Although he returned to work as planned at the mills in Rocchette in 1902, Giorgio's heart was not in the business. He was restless and wanted to explore the world. He had always been fascinated by tales of the South Seas and while in England had ordered a booklet entitled *Travel to Japan, China, Australasia and Round-the-World*. But it was a chance encounter with a Canadian clergyman, Reverend Robert E. Spence, of Glenboro, Manitoba, that determined a direction for his boundless energy and changed his life.

The two men became acquainted in 1900, when Girgio was travelling back to Berne after a visit with his parents. On the train, he offered to interpret for the clergyman, who was having difficulty making himself understood by the authorities. Spence's stories of the Canadian wilderness enthralled the young man, who was intrigued by his offer: "If ever you come to Canada, come to see me." Even after Spence returned to Manitoba, his letters fired Giorgio's imagination. "I like Canada all the better I believe for having seen the other countries," Spence wrote. "I think young men have much better chances for succeeding here than in older countries. Of course there are always some disadvantages to a new country … but still anyone who is anxious to get along can generally do so, if he is willing to work."[4]

A great reader, Giorgio gathered all the books he could on the subject and became captivated by tales of cowboys and "Indians," even producing artwork on the subject while still at the academy. By chance, his time in England coincided with the beginnings of a massive publicity campaign by the Canadian government aimed at enticing British immigrants to settle lands in the newly opened western prairies.[5] Succumbing easily to the seductive advertisements and posters, in March 1901 Giorgio contacted agents in Liverpool acting for the Canadian government and for the Canadian Pacific Railway and ordered information pamphlets on tourist travel and emigration to Canada.

Watercolour painting, "On the Warpath" by Georgio Pocaterra, Bradford, England, ca 1901. GA M6340-193-1

Back in Italy after his English sojourn, Giorgio was given a very good position with Lanificio Rossi, but he was bored. He later told a friend, "My wanderlust was by then so strong and persistent in wishing to go to North America where I felt I could get a large amount of virgin land out of which [to] carve and develop a real home for myself through my own efforts."[6] According to his unpublished biography, "Son of the Mountains," Giorgio

George as a young man, Italy, ca 1900.
GA NA-695-89

finally said to his father, "I know that I cannot go without your permission, because I am not yet twenty-one, but if I have to stay here until I am, I will waste a good deal of time. Let me go, Father, and if I don't like it, I'll come back home and settle down contentedly to life in Italy."

At a family meeting, everyone opposed young Giorgio's plan—except for his father, who said, "I know my son, and I know that if he makes up his mind to do something, nothing will stop him. I am going to give him permission to go, and money to get there." But Uncle Luigi retorted, "Alright, let him go. But he'll soon come back, like a whipped dog with his tail between his legs."[7]

And so, in February of 1903, Giorgio Pocaterra set sail from Italy, stopping for a few days in London on the way to North America. He was accompanied by a classmate from the academy, the son of the station master in Berne, who shared a passionate interest in the Canadian West. But when it was time to board the *The Parisian* in Liverpool for the passage to Canada, the friend backed out, reluctant to travel so far from his family. Giorgio generously lent him funds to return to Berne and boarded the ship alone, landing in Halifax, Nova Scotia, on March 5, 1903. A few days later he stepped from the heated passenger car of the transcontinental train into the searing cold of a winter day in Winnipeg, Manitoba. A stranger alone in a new land, he had just $3.75 in his pocket and no job.

Taking up Reverend Spence on his offer of hospitality, Giorgio found his way to the nearby town of Glenboro and stayed with the minister and his housemate, the editor of the *Glenboro Gazette*, W. T. Shipley. The bachelors treated the young man well and helped him look for work. In fact, even before the Italian had landed in Canada, Reverend Spence had been thinking about a suitable job for him. Several years before, Spence had written:

> … glad to note your progress in the mastery of the English tongue. You will soon be in a position to act as a good correspondent. For that business I do not suppose you would have as many opportunities here as you would in an older country. There is not so much need for those conversant with so many languages. Sometimes, however, in mixed communities of French and English, or English and German, the storekeepers do have a clerk who can speak the dual language. In a case of that kind, you can readily see, that your business combined with that of clerking or bookkeeping would be just the thing.[8]

But George William Pocaterra, as he now came to be known, had not travelled to Canada to work as a clerk. The story is related in "Son of the Mountains" : "I'll tell you what," said Spence, "tomorrow there is going to be an auction sale at a farm near-by and the whole country-side will turn up there. We'll go too, and I'm sure that we will find someone who'll give you a job."

The auction fell on a warm spring day and the reverend introduced Pocaterra to the Steel brothers, Scottish stockbreeders who raised purebred Ayrshire cattle on their large farm. One of the brothers, George, had been a member of Parliament for the district since 1899. Although George Pocaterra was a slight man, only 5 feet 9 inches tall, he pulled himself to his full height and looked up at the tall brothers and said, "If you hire me to work for you, how much will I make a month?" The big men laughed. "Boy," one of them said, "I guess you don't realize that 'greenhorns' like you never get paid in this part of the country. Instead, they pay us to teach them the business. Generally they pay two to three hundred dollars the first year!"

Here George's business training held him in good stead. Admitting that he had no experience, he countered that he was a good worker. "Give me one dollar a month and I'll be glad to come and work for you, but I must have some pay."[9] Impressed, the Steels agreed to give him a try, took him home and gave him a room on the third floor of their large farmhouse. His first job was to clean six months of manure out of a pigsty, an immediate test of the fastidious young man's suitability and resolve.

Other menial tasks followed, and after several weeks the reality of life in the Canadian West got the better of the disillusioned immigrant. "The place and work was very different from the romantic kind I had envisioned of hard-riding cowboys and still real nomad Indian hunters," he later recalled.[10] One Sunday he decided to quit, and he headed for the train station and home. But his uncle's words came back to haunt him as he composed a telegram to his father, requesting money for the trip back to Italy: "He'll soon come back, like a whipped dog with his tail between his legs."

George walked back to the farm, determined to make enough money to leave the prairie drudgery for the Rocky Mountains. At the end of his first month, the Steels expressed satisfaction with his hard work and raised his wages to $8 per month, but he wanted more. At harvest time a neighbouring wheat farmer offered him $15 per month for every binder he could keep up with, stooking the sheaves of wheat as they came off the machine. Working long hours, he nearly wore himself out stooking for three binders and earning "the unheard of wages of $45.00 a month."[11] By the end of the season he had saved $78, so he boarded a train for Calgary, "in view of the Mighty Rockies, which being a mountain-born man suited me 100%."[12]

Prior to the construction of the Canadian Pacific Railway in the early 1880s, the vast prairie comprising what is now southern Alberta and Saskatchewan had been home to nomadic plains First Nations and the bison they hunted. By the late 1870s, a series of government treaties had confined the Native population to well-defined reserves and the bison were nearly gone. The land was then surveyed and subdivided into a checkerboard of plots available for purchase or to homestead.

During the 1880s and 1890s, big cattle- and sheep-ranching operations had claimed much of the land surrounding Calgary, particularly the rich grazing areas to the south that had ready access to markets via the railway. By the time George Pocaterra arrived in 1904, however, the era of the big, open-range roundups was ending and settlers' fences were starting to carve up the land. Ironically, even the Natives participated in this process, building most of the barbed wire fences on contract.

George's plan was simple: to work as a cowboy on large ranches to learn what he could before acquiring a small ranch of his own. Mr. Shipley was related to Ernest Daggett, the general manager of the Lineham Lumber Company in High River, just south of Calgary. Daggett also owned the Bar D Ranch east of High River; George worked there until the spring of 1904, when he moved on to work for Billy Channel at the Domberg Ranch (also known as the Anchor S), a big horse ranch 50 miles downstream from Calgary on the Bow River. There one of his main jobs was building fencelines using cottonwood lumber, work he later described as "gosh-awful" due to the hardness of the cottonwood when dried.[13]

Working for the Anchor S took George into the high foothills of the Rockies, an unfenced land beyond the natural grazing area of the large prairie cattle ranches. "I saw the Highwood country first in 1904," he later wrote, "when I drove a four horse team to help take down, from the upper Ings Creek, a saw-mill belonging to Billy Channel."[14] Several months later, his presence in the area was noted in a diary kept by Fred Kuck, formerly of Redditch, England, who had just beaten the Italian to the valley, filing on a homestead in 1903: "Another summery day, no frost. Two teams with lumber went up and one down; Rhue Kuck driving. Pocaterra wanted us to cut wood for 60 cents a cord. I guess not."[15]

The first white settlers had begun making their way up the Highwood River in the early 1880s, two ruts serving as the first road west from High River, but even by 1904 there were still very few settlers in the area. The John Sullivan family operated the Sullivan Creek Ranch at the creek that today bears their name. Farther east, Fred and Walter Ings operated the OH Ranch, an outfit founded by O. H. Smith and Lafayette French in 1883. Upstream of the Sullivans, there were some seasonal lumber camps but only one settler, Fred Kuck.

It was here, some eight miles northwest of Pekisko, where Flat Creek (Trap Creek) flows into the Highwood River, that George Pocaterra found a country to suit his soul and give him a home for three decades. Described by George M. Dawson as "the most beautiful valley he had ever seen" during his geological survey of the west for the Canadian government in the 1870s,[16] the grassy hills and rocky ridges of the Eden Valley excited the new immigrant. As yet, no settler had claimed the land between the Sullivans and the Kucks, though there was still evidence of previous Native occupation: "All there was on the place then were several sets of tepee poles, standing up, ready to have the tepees rolled around them."[17]

According to the Dominion Lands Act of 1872, a quarter section of land (160 acres) could be had in the Canadian North-West Territories for the 10-dollar filing fee if a homesteader fulfilled the requirements of building, fencing and cultivation within three years of registering a claim. Sometime after he first visited the Highwood in the spring of 1904, George wrote to his older cousin, Arturo Talin, in Italy. Talin, who had lived briefly in Brazil and Argentina, was eager to move to western Canada and arrived later that fall. Afraid that someone else might discover and acquire the land before they could file a claim, the two men tented on the property in January 1905, but George needed more money to fund his portion. This he accomplished with his usual

Highwood River, ca 1915 . GA PD-184-2-43

flamboyance: by winning at cards. He later recalled, "The, as far as I'm concerned, historical poker game took place after I left Billy Channel, at the Pine Coulee Ranch of the Johnson boys (from Minnesota), and the two Allens were there also, and an old Arizona cow-hand, Frank by name."[18]

A lively, probably slightly exaggerated account of the famous game appears in "Son of the Mountains." Apparently, George did not even like poker, but agreed to play one five-hand game and won. The others insisted on a chance to win back their bets and so they played on, through Saturday and Sunday, with short meal breaks. Finally, all the cash was gone and the men put their saddles, bridles, bedrolls, horses, wagons and tents into a pile and bet the whole mess. Still George kept winning.

By daylight on Monday there was nothing left to bet, so George said to Arturo, who was not in the game, "Take away all their six-shooters and put them over on top of the cupboard." He took his own six-shooter and put it on the table. "I've had enough. Here, I'll take away the $2.00 I started with, because I don't want to lose that. Now I'll put every bit of this loot in the middle of the table and we'll have a jack pot—winner takes all."

Each man looked at his cards. George discarded two and drew two more and the others did the same until every tired gambler was satisfied with his hand. Then they turned their cards up on the table. George had three aces and two kings: full house, a winner.

"Once more," he said, "and if I win this time again, it will mean that the Good Lord wants me to have it."

This time George kept the cards he was dealt while the others discarded and drew as best they could. When they revealed their cards, the best that anyone had against George's two queens was two jacks. He collected his winnings, but returned Arizona Frank's saddle, rope, bridle and bedroll, "as they were his tools of the trade and he needed them. To make up for them, he insisted [on] coming up with the cousin and me to the Highwood for a couple of months to help us getting started."[19] At the end of the game George vowed, "This has been my last game of poker. From now on I am through with gambling."[20]

With his winnings, George entered the Dominion Lands Office in High River on February 22, 1905, paid his 10 dollars and registered himself as the homesteader on the Northwest quarter of Section 36, Township 17, Range 4, West of the 5th Meridian. The receipt read, "G. Pocaterra is, in consequence of such entry and payment, vested with the rights conferred in such cases by the provisions of the 'Dominion Lands Act,' respecting Homestead Rights."[21] Soon afterwards, the cousins acquired another section of land "from the railway" (likely the Calgary and Edmonton Railway Company) just downstream at NE-1-18-4-W5. On these gently rolling hills they decided to build their ranch.

Although George eventually named the ranch the Buffalo Head after the bleached skulls found on the property, apparently he also considered other names, possibly searching for something more exotic. In a letter to a Spanish-speaking friend in 1909, he explored other options:

> You know that out west we have the habit to give to some of the ranches a Spanish name, for instance my next neighbour calls his Rio Alto Ranche, a rather liberal translation of High River ... Now, as is the custom with us, I want to get some writing paper printed here with on the one corner a horse and brands and the name of the place; and I would feel much obliged if you, who know Spanish so well, could suggest an appropriate name. I was thinking of calling it "El Nido" as I heard there was such a place in California, then again, as my ranche is almost surrounded by one river and two long creeks, "Tros Rios" or "Entre Rios", but I should like something high sounding. The place is in the hills, in a country which is very much like an English park, little groves of poplars, spruce and pines and nice open reaches and flats, and lots of springs and little brooks; in the Geological Survey they call it Paradise or Eden valley ...[22]

After living in a tent the first winter, George and his cousin began erecting buildings on their new ranch in the spring of 1905. With help from Arizona Frank and "a big Norwegian" who was skilled with an axe, they built a 14-by 16-foot cabin that served for several years as kitchen, living room and bedroom for the two Italians. "This home was mighty different from the beautiful stone and marble mansion where George had spent his boyhood with his family, but it filled his heart with a glow of happiness—for it was his own, his very own home built with his own hands."[23] Later the cousins added a large living room and two bedrooms to the original structure. To meet homestead requirements, they also built corrals and a barn.

George was certainly not a farmer, an occupation he considered below his aristocratic station in life, but to make the ranch more self-sufficient, he planted a vegetable garden. This venture seems to have been a mixed success. Writing decades later, he said, "I remember that in the first years on the Buffalo Head all we could grow were turnips, food fit only for COWS! During the first eight years I could only grow potatoes, at the best, the size of plums."[2]

Top: *Buffalo Head Ranch, 1911. GA PD-184-1-18*

Bottom: *Unknown man, possibly Arturo Talin, and George at the Buffalo Head Ranch, ca 1907. GA PA-2393-14-1-3*

After constructing the home place, George bought enough stock to help make the ranch financially viable. "Next came the buying of a number of brood-mares, and a stallion, followed by acquiring as large a number of cows with calves at foot as I could afford, also a bull."[25] Although he never much cared for the mundane details of cattle ranching (horse breeding was more to his taste), George was a pragmatist and the cattle helped to diversify their income. He and Arturo registered two brands: the XN for their cattle (branded on the right ribs) and a buffalo head-shaped brand for their horses (branded on the right thigh).[26] By 1907 they had acquired another quarter section of land to the northeast along the river (NW-6-18-3-W5), and they had grazing leases and water rights for a number of unoccupied quarter sections farther downstream from the ranch as well as into the foothills five miles to the west. That year, George was appointed voluntary crop correspondent for his township by the Alberta Department of Agriculture.

Later, he recalled his years on the range fondly: "For about thirty years of my early life I averaged seven hours a day riding over my lands, through the herd of cattle and horses, and looking over 30 miles of fences, most of the time alone in hilly country, within less than an hour's easy ride to the

21

higher peaks of the Rockies. Thus I had plenty of time and opportunity for thinking about Life in general and in detail, gradually acquiring a better understanding of the forces which condition human life, and learning to adapt myself so as to collaborate with them."[27]

George had fulfilled a dream in establishing his ranch, but that accomplishment alone would not have satisfied his restless nature. Arriving just as the high country was being settled, he had the advantage of living at the edge of "civilization" in that magical zone between the rich historical past and the promise-filled future. The ranch gave him stability and an income, but most of all, he saw it as a base from where he could explore, prospect and seek adventure. Inevitably, he would have been drawn to the mountains once his ranch was well underway, but this process was hastened by an incident that occurred early in 1906.

In search of more building timbers for his ranch, George headed across the Highwood River—named for the high woods, or cottonwood trees that grew in the flood plain just upstream of High River:

A little over a mile away was a very fine stand of tall and straight-growing spruce trees. It was there that I had gone early one morning, with axe and cross-cut saw, to cut the needed trees, branch them and saw them into the required lengths. After having readied for hauling away a number of logs, I drove my axe into one of the stumps, got out my tobacco pouch, and rolled myself a cigarette of Old Judge tobacco. As I struck a match and lit my cigarette I suddenly saw five Indians standing behind me in a half circle, every man with a rifle in the crook of his arm. They looked like the Indians of "Deerslayer" by Fenimore Cooper. They were dressed in leggings, breechclouts and blanket coats with the capote [hood] at the back, and all had their hair done in tresses, and some had either feathers or ermine skins woven into their tresses. Somehow I managed not to be startled. One living in those early conditions was usually set and ready to meet sudden crises. One had to train oneself for that. I smiled and handing my tobacco pouch to the nearest Indian, said: "Have a smoke with me." All five broke suddenly into a smile, and one of them said to the others: "Ne wahshidjoo tah-ah-ko gheenee-ashin." I started learning foreign languages when still very young, and so I was always keen to grasp the sound of any strange words. I found out that what the Indian had said meant: "This white man is not afraid of anything." [28]

And so began George Pocaterra's long association with the Stoneys. Now called the Stoney Nakoda Nation, the Stoneys were a northern branch of the Dakota Sioux Nation. For decades after signing Treaty No. 7 in 1877, they wintered at the Morley Reserve west of Calgary but wandered and hunted through their traditional home territory at will for much of the year, up and down the Front Ranges from the Highwood River in the south to the North Saskatchewan River in the north. What better place for George

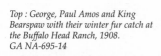

Top : George, Paul Amos and King Bearspaw with their winter fur catch at the Buffalo Head Ranch, 1908. GA NA-695-14

Bottom: George doing laundry at theBuffalo Head Ranch, ca 1907. GA NA-695-80

to dream of adventure than in a teepee with his new friends, the Stoneys, who knew the high country better than any white man. With his natural flair for languages—some accounts say he was fluent in five—George quickly picked up the native tongue. By speaking their language, not only could he communicate more easily with the people who had lived in these mountains for many generations, but he could also integrate himself more easily into their nomadic culture.

Two of the hunters encountered by George that fateful day in the woods were Spotted Wolf and his father, Three Buffalo Bulls. George and Spotted Wolf—or Paul Amos, as he was also known—hit it off immediately, quickly becoming close companions and eventually blood brothers. Paul and his Stoney friends frequently visited George at the Buffalo Head, sometimes staying for weeks at a time, and George, in turn, spent many weeks visiting their teepees in Morley.

Moving into a teepee made George Pocaterra an oddity among whites. Sitting by a small willow-wood fire, he listened as elders recounted the old stories:of mountain passes and good hunting grounds; of victory in battle and ancient rivalries; of the love of the mountains that was their common heritage with George, though their birthplaces were half a world apart. He learned much from them, including how to work with them as partners. As he later explained, "I have had Indians working for me in the mountains many times. Cutting trails, making roads and building bridges with the materials available on the place … I learned early that the only way with Indians is to lead them, NEVER to drive them. One has to be just and firm, and often, generous whenever a principle is not at stake."[29] In this way George gained their trust, a valuable commodity for a man who wanted to ferret out the wealth of his new land. He realized his best chance to capitalize on the potential of the Rockies was to explore them with the people who knew them best, the Stoneys.

And that he did, every year, for nearly three decades. No diary or other organized record exists of these explorations, but we can piece together a chronology of his adventures from "Son of the Mountains," his photograph albums and his letters to friends.

His first trip with the Stoneys occurred a few months after their meeting. Three Buffalo Bulls took him "on a fairly quick trip over the Aldridge Creek pass [Fording River Pass] , over the second range of the Rockies, then down the long, steep slope to the Elk river, up the beautiful valley of that large stream to the Elk lakes, the headwaters of that main tributary of the Kootenay, and over the Elk river pass to the Kananaskis Lakes."[30] He was proud to say, "I was probably the first white man to see the beautiful lake district from the south."[31] Forty years later, the memory was still fresh: "In 1906 I first rode over the Elk Pass late in September, and topping a rise in the ground I first saw spread before me the marvellous Kananaskis Lakes and Valley. You know what sunlight can do at such times? Why, man, that landscape, as I saw it then, as it impinged into my consciousness, was NOT of THIS earth. NO. It was a glimpse of Heaven itself. Never again have I seen the like, never again have I felt the same … and my main quest since has been to fulfill a desire to feel such a virginity of impression (as Stevenson said) again, somewhere else in this shrinking world of ours."[32]

Upper Kananaskis Lake, ca 1915. George labelled this photograph "The finest lake in the mountains." GA PD-184-1-361

This profound experience later prompted him to write a poem inspired by the beauty of two mountain lakes:

Kananaskis Lakes
Carry me back
To Kananaskis shores
Its magic waters
And its changing moods
Majestic mountains
And foaming waterfalls
Enfolded softly
By mystic woods!

There's where I laid
A-gazing and wondering
My soul deeply stirred
By a longing so great!
It was joy and yet pain
The craving to fathom
The innermost meaning
Of such beauty revealed.

Heart of the wilds
Yet friendly its nature
By its visible glory
So fondly providing
A much needed medium
To all who are striving
To an all-satisfying
Spiritual Beyond![33]

*Top: Elijah Hunter en route to the Kananaskis for a winter of trapping, 1906-07.
GA NA-695-12*

*Bottom: Paul Amos, George and Elijah Hunter at Morley after a winter of
trapping, Spring 1907. GA NA-695-13*

Later that year and into 1907, George overwintered with Spotted Wolf and his brother-in-law, Dog Nose (Elijah Hunter), in the Kananaskis Lakes region, trapping, exploring and prospecting in the high country of the Elk and Kananaskis rivers as far south as Upper Elk Lake. Arizona Frank had moved on from the Buffalo Head, but George was able to leave the ranch under the care of Luigi, Gaetano and Ottorino Fedeli, brothers who knew George's family in Italy and had acquired a homestead directly across the Highwood River.

The trapping party left Morley right after Christmas. The snow was not very deep at the reserve, but as the group worked its way up the Kananaskis Valley, they discovered that the snow was too deep and powdery for the pack horses. Stopping for several days at the abandoned buildings of an Eau Claire Lumber Company camp to build three sturdy toboggans, they sent the horses back to Morley. George, Spotted Wolf and Dog Nose continued on pointed-nose snowshoes, specially made at the reserve, dragging behind them the heavy sleds laden with supplies. "Can you realize the heart-breaking work entailed," George later asked, "when you consider the terrible conditions of the old trails, with the many fallen trees obstructing travel that the deep snow did not always manage to cover?"[34]

Cabin at Lower Kananaskis Lake, ca 1906-07. GA PD-184-2-56

The long, hard trek took them to a cabin they had built the previous summer in a meadow where Bolton Creek flowed into Lower Kananaskis Lake, and which they had left stocked with dried venison and pemmican. George was assigned a large trapping territory around the two lakes "and up the valley of the tributary from the east [Pocaterra Creek] that flows into the Kananaskis from the pass leading over it to the Storm Creek ... My two Indian partners took for themselves the Elk River Pass, also the headwaters of the Kananaskis, and over the very high pass from the headwaters of the Kananaskis to the head of the Palliser river, at that time a truly terrific undertaking in the winter."[35] They set up miles of traplines, which they checked on snowshoe every few days.

George had many adventures over the next few months, but the most dramatic was when he was nearly caught in an avalanche:

> I shall never forget what happened once when I decided to set some dead-falls for marten on the south side of the upper lake, where the mountain sides were covered by ancient forest. I snowshoed around the north side of the lake, and after looking carefully over the ground, I noticed several stretches where the trees were all small, a sure sign that avalanches had destroyed the ancient growth. Even though the signs pointed to the fact that a considerable time had elapsed since any slides had occurred something suddenly warned me not to hurry across. I was still standing still trying to decide if I should go on and try my trapping luck in a very promising location on the other side of the lake, when a loud hissing noise suddenly reverberated from high up the mountain. Within seconds an enormous avalanche crashed through the forest not more than 100 yards ahead of me through a part of the forest that had never been hit before. Mighty trees were snapped off, and what surprised me was that the snow-slide seemed to roll contrary to what one would have supposed would be the case. It seemed to roll backward, no doubt caused by the rush of snow to enter the vacuum created by the onward rush of the great mass of snow. Also, to my amazement I saw great trees on the side of the slides being sucked towards it, also by the vacuum, and being snapped off like matches. I do not need to say that I returned to camp the way I had come.[36]

Unluckily, the winter of 1906–1907 was one of the hardest on record and the trapping was very poor. By the end of March, their supplies had run out. According to one account:

> They just got out at the end, & no more—eating moccasins & other what not—& a search party of Indians found them not far from The Wedge, feebly snowshoeing towards Morley. As has happened before & since, the white man's obstinacy had held them on the trail &, moreover, Pocaterra had saved Paul's life. So an old Stoney, Three Buffalo Bulls, the father of these brothers, called the three of them to him before he died & told the Indians that George Pocaterra was his son & a Stoney & no longer a white man to them—that he was to be their brother & that his name should be Mountain Child [in Stoney, Nya-he-taush-kan, or Son of the Mountains]. Then he told Pocaterra of two places where was the black rock that the white men burned & told him to go & stake his claims before the time when men to whom the Indians were nothing should go into that country & find the coal.[37]

George did not follow up on the coal for several years, but later in 1907 he joined his new brother, Paul Amos, on the big fall hunt, a major annual event that lasted until each family had enough meat for the coming winter. Game provided meat for pemmican and the families also took fish, which they dried and smoked, and a few furs. By Christmas, the Stoneys usually had enough food to see them through the winter.

George was deeply impressed with what he had witnessed of Stoney traditions and lifestyle during this and subsequent hunting trips with Paul and his family. Aware that he had been privileged to experience something unique among white men, 50 years later he shared his memories with members of the Historical Society of Alberta:

About the third week of September, the Stoneys of the Bearspaw band arrived at the large meadow near where Whiskey Creek plunges into Sullivan Creek. A great number of lodges were soon up in a half circle, and the places was dotted all over with about 1,000 head of horses, to the consternation of the neighbouring ranchers, who thought they had the right to all the grass for miles around their places. They seemed unable to realize that they were actually the interlopers and not the Indians, who had been accustomed for hundreds of years to think that the country was theirs. The Indians, Paul and his family were amongst the band, remained on that same camping grounds for a few days, during which time each family group acquainted the others of the country they were going to hunt over. The group of a few related families I belonged to usually started hunting soon after they had arrived between the first and second range of the Rockies, on the upper Highwood River. From there they moved a short day's ride every few days, depending on what luck they had had. If the kill had been abundant, it was imperative for them to stop long enough for the women to cut all the fresh meat up into long, thin strips for drying.[38]

As George later explained, the hunting parties sometimes roamed over a large territory in search of game:

In the early years of my hunting with the Stonies, they still honored a sort of loose agreement by which certain families had priority rights to hunt in certain valleys. My Indian brother Paul (Spotted Wolf) and his Father used to hunt the upper Kananaskis, the upper Elk, and Nyah-a-nibi, and only once in a while did they go as far as the Kootenay and the White River, by the Palliser. But, like most more or less primitive races, the Indians were tolerant, and did not always stick to such loose agreements, and only resented repeated and deliberate abuses.[39]

When travelling, the eldest and most respected man usually led the way, followed by the other men and then the women and children, all trailing several horses. After two years of his accompanying them on hunting trips, George's Stoney friends were so impressed with his horsemanship and leadership skills that one day the party's elderly leader, Isaac Roll-in-the-Mud, called him up alongside him and said, "Mountain Child, from now on you will be the chief (leader) on the trail. Go on!" And from then on, whenever he had travelled that way before, George Pocaterra assumed the honoured position at the head of the pack train.[40]

From the Stoneys George learned much about Native ways that was mostly unknown to Europeans. He found their family life "admirable," and,

contrary to "some wrong notions accepted by most white people," found them very conscious of cleanliness; they frequently bathed in rivers and lakes, and cleansed their mouths after each meal. He admired their hospitality to friends and strangers alike—they always shared food with anyone in camp, regardless of whether or not that person had helped with the hunt.

He defended them against accusations of laziness. He knew first-hand the hardship of the hunt, the travail of bringing a kill back to camp, of travelling on snowshoes around traplines, in cold conditions. "And what about the crossing of rivers raging in full flood, and the heavy work connected every year with their fall hunting trips, in some cases hundreds of miles away, when the trails were obstructed by numerous fallen trees after the wild winter's storms?"[41]

Top: Paul Amos, 1927. GA PD-184-1-256

Bottom: Making a new trail through forest devastated by fire the previous year, the Kananaskis Valley, 1911. GA PD-184-2-139

George loved these hunting trips and other expeditions with his Native friends and recounted many exciting adventures. One of his favourite destinations was Nyahé-a-nibi, a beautiful Stoney name that translates to "Go-up-into-the-mountains-country" and refers to Cadorna Creek, a west fork of the Elk River. For George Pocaterra it was always "the hidden valley, the valley of youth." A future friend, Raymond Patterson, was later to write of the Stoney name: "No better name could be found for that great, silent meadow six thousand feet above the sea, ringed around by glaciers and by mountains that rose to 11,000 feet, shut off from the world by passes that were no better than goat trails, by drowning rivers, a wild torrent and a tangle of huge, fallen trees ..."[42]

George recalled, "I first went to Nyah-a-nibi in the early fall of 1908, after the passing of my cousin. We stayed there until December, and it was raining THEN there ... but we had a really terrible time getting over the Aldridge Creek Pass [Fording River Pass]. The snow was a good five feet deep for too long a stretch, until we got over to the Alberta side, where a wondrous Sun was shining brightly, and the snow was, soon after, only lying in patches. On that trip I had with me Spotted Wolf and Dog Nose. It was during that trip, that I carried a mountain goat for about half a mile, and so earned the Indians' respect."[43]

His fearless courage also put him in good stead. "One of those Stoneys was my very dear friend Red Coyote, whom I saw take on an immense silver tip grizzly with a 44 Colt [revolver]. I saved his life that time, by taking a chance of hitting him, and shooting a heavy 34 soft nosed bullet into the bear already standing up to kill him. And believe me, Coyote was NOT A BIT FLUSTERED, when, terribly anxious, I got up to him. I NEVER took such chances in my life as that time, both in shooting and running like mad down that mountain side. I could NOT tell exactly what had happened until I joined with my friend."[44]

George's best friend and most constant companion in his many adventures was always "my wonderful Stoney blood brother Paul Amos, Spotted Wolf ... We were the closest of friends for 52 years, we lived for months on end, often the two of us alone, exploring, hunting and trapping in the wild mountains, we were in great danger together many times, and we NEVER spoke a word in anger to each other. He was a MAN!"[45]

When Arturo Talin died in 1908, George assumed his cousin's interest in the Buffalo Head Ranch. Early the next year, he was granted full rights to the property when he was able to prove to the Canadian government that he had fulfilled all homestead requirements for the grant of free land. Having now been domiciled in Canada for more than the requisite three years, George also applied for naturalized Canadian (at the time, British) citizenship, which was granted by the district court of Calgary on September 9, 1909. Coincidentally, that very day he boarded a twin-screw passenger ship in New York for his first trip back to Italy in more than six years.

During the week-long crossing, in which SS *Moltke* voyaged via the Azores to Gibraltar and Naples and finally into Genoa,

George, dressed in Stoney clothing, on board the SS Moltke off Gibralter, September 1909. GA PD-184-1-5

31

George became very friendly with a few of his fellow second-class passengers, in particular Clarence Smith, Margery J. Moore and Mercedes White. One day, he amused and impressed them by donning full Stoney regalia so they could take photographs. After the voyage, Miss Moore wrote complimenting him on how good he had looked: "The pictures are all splendid I think. You look quite like an Indian warrior in all your Indian togs."[46]

Always a passionate man, George apparently became involved in a shipboard romance with Mrs. White, an attractive married woman who was travelling alone to visit her sisters. It was understood by the other passengers that Mrs. White suffered from some kind of illness, so they were shocked to discover that her husband had remained in Vancouver to attend to business. George's ready sympathy led him to become deeply infatuated, though her letters seem to indicate that she simply viewed the "affair" as a pleasant holiday interlude with a charming young admirer (he was 26).

Although his sense of propriety restrained George from declaring his love to Mrs. White, he relieved his feelings by unburdening himself to Clarence Smith and Margery Moore. They were sympathetic, and each wrote to George expressing their admiration and support. Mr. Smith told him, "Allow me to repeat what I said that night that I think that your attitude throughout toward 'Her' was one of chivalry, delicacy and nobility. You certainly acted the part of a man and not only that but of a gentleman and I feel proud to count you among my friends."[47]

Margery Moore wrote several times at length, attempting to counsel George and perhaps unconsciously revealing more than a little interest in the romantic rancher herself:

> I am glad you told me what you did and I want to thank you for your confidence. You can trust me, Mr. Pocaterra, and you can always feel that I not only appreciate your confidence, but I respect it also. I wonder if you will be surprised when I tell you that I already knew that you loved Mrs. White before you wrote me about it. Of course no one told me, but I simply knew it intuitively. I knew it when we were all on the boat together, and I knew it more certainly when we said good-bye to her in Gibraltar, and during those days and nights on the boat between Gibraltar and Naples—I admired you immensely those few days ... You love Mrs. White—that I know. And you love her with all the intensity of a strong man. She belongs to someone else—and as you say she is beyond even the thought of a possibility of winning. You are such a thorough gentleman at heart that you will not allow yourself even to think of her—except loyally. Mr Pocaterra, I believe you will stick to that resolution whatever it costs you. You must—it is the only thing to do. But it won't be easy. Nature is a mighty big factor to reckon with and you have no easy task before you ... Please write to me then, for I count it a privilege to know such a man as you.[48]

Top: George (standing) with his parents Ubaldina Talin and Giuseppe Pocaterra at the family home, Rocchette, Italy, September 1909. GA PD-184-1-3

Bottom; George in Italy, September 1909. GA PA-2393-10-1-1

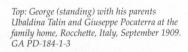

And again, even more tellingly, "I do enjoy hearing from you—for you give me such a strong vigorous breath of your own strong life and personality."[49]

After Mrs. White left the ship at Gibraltar, she and George entered into a friendly correspondence that included an exchange of photographs. In return for photographs from George, Mrs. White wrote, "I am enclosing a tiny snapshot of myself ... I thought perhaps you would like to have it in remembrance of our passage across the Atlantic ... I think the snap shot of your Father and sister very good and I think your sister very pretty."[50] Pleased when George told her she resembled his beloved sister Marta in every detail, she replied, "Fancy your sister being so like me."[51]

Although the two continued to correspond for several years, they never met again. In the spring of 1910, when she was returning to Vancouver from Europe, Mrs. White wrote nostalgically, "I am afraid of not being so lucky this time and getting such nice company as I did on my last voyage 2nd class with the Americans and you."[52] Still smitten, when he learned of her travel plans George met transcontinental trains in Calgary for several days in a vain attempt to see her. But her plans had changed and they did not connect. Soon after, the Whites relocated to England.

Emotional turmoil aside, George had mixed feelings about his visit to Italy in the fall of 1909. Shortly after he arrived, he wrote to tell Mrs. White that his family were "certainly happy to see me again and are only just now getting over the thought that it was really all a dream."[53] But he also missed the freedom of life in the wilderness and was longing to return to his ranch. "When the Red Gods call ... as Kipling has it ... I must go ... Just two months ago now was I tramping the snow on top of the second range of the Rockies, trying hard with my two Indians to break a trail for the pack ponies through the deep snow over the pass to safety, and the remembrance of those days and struggles makes me long for the wild places again."[54]

Admitting that he would be sorry to leave his family, he said: "I try my best, though, not to show to my father that I long for the time of return as he loves me so, I would be afraid to hurt his feelings."[55] But it was clear to him that Italy was no longer his home: "Apart from being glad to be with my people I can't be truthful and say that I enjoy myself; the curse of the West; its peculiar fascination to the people who have lived its life long enough to get used to it, pursues me even here, and makes me restless, so that nothing seems to satisfy me."[56] It was with a sense of relief that he left Italy in early January, 1910, to return to his beloved Alberta foothills.

Chapter 2

George: Dudes and Coal
1910–1933

The winter of 1910 was short and mild, much like that of 1905–1906, and the lack of snow contributed to a cataclysmic forest fire that swept up from the western United States through to Jasper in Western Alberta, charring the high country all along the Rockies. Evidence of this firestorm lingers to this day where huge, blackened stumps are all that remain of the forests of massive trees. George regretted the change: "The range is being over-grown with young poplars, and I remembered it previous to the 1910 fire as practically all good grass range (bunch grass, then) with some large spruce and few cotton-wood and poplar groves, and hundreds of prairie chickens (pinnated grouse) and partridges (ruffed grouse)."[1]

After his long visit to Italy, George was anxious to resume his travels with the Stoneys and told Mrs. White in March, "the 'Red Gods' call is upon me, and I must go as Kipling says; I mean to go through the Rockies right on to the Kootenays in B.C. to hunt grisslies [*sic*]." He also told her that during the trip he intended to "stake several claims I have found or have been shown by the Indians, during my wanderings."[2] He was referring to the coal seams shown to him several years earlier by Three Buffalo Bulls.

According to "Son of the Mountains," as a reward for saving his son Spotted Wolf's life, Three Buffalo Bulls not only told George "I'm going to show you the black rock" but also took him on horseback through a canyon up to a high valley where "there amongst the rock and shale were great chunks of shiny black coal, big as pianos. The rock and shale had eroded but the coal was so hard that it had not weathered."[3] George had become very excited at the time, realizing that this gift from the Stoneys might make his fortune, but he was sensible enough to postpone this dream until he had secured his homestead.

Now, in 1910, he was finally ready to proceed. He started looking for backers in Calgary but inadvertently revealed too much to an unscrupulous opportunist, who decided to stake the claim himself. What followed was classic George Pocaterra, the stuff of legends:

To beat another party in to stake this mine Pocaterra was warned by two Indians who came right in to the hotel lounge. He left Calgary by train & at Morley an Indian was waiting for him with two good horses. Pocaterra ran straight from the train to the horses & they rode four hours till the snow became too deep & the horses played out. The other party had 8 hours start but made camp at night & slept—an error in dealing with a man like G.W.P. Pokey got off his horse & put on his snowshoes, travelled light without food or blanket, crossed a mountain pass, staked the claims & got back to the Indian in 23 hours—27 in all. An awful man—a sort of Burning Daylight ...[4]

Perhaps it was incidents like this that gave rise to the Stoney names for areas associated with George's coal-mining activities: Wasiju Wachi tusin ta Waptan ze and Wasiju Wachi tusin ze Ipabin Oke Na Ze translate to "Crazy white man creek" and "Crazy white man ridge."[5]

With his claim secure, George persuaded some backers to go into partnership with him to form what came to be known as the Mackay and Dippie syndicate. In addition to George, the partners included Calgary taxidermists and fur buyers Walter G. Mackay and George Frederick (Fred) Dippie, and three Millarville-area ranchers Alfred P. Welsh, W. H. King and Francis Wright. Sometime just prior to their agreement dated August 9, 1910, George led the group up the Kananaskis Valley to stake five coal claims totalling 3,615 acres. Of particular interest to George was 640 acres staked in his name: Lease No. 82, located in the Highwood Pass.

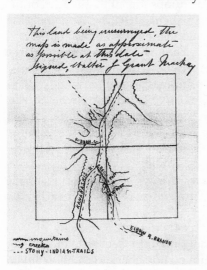

GA M-6340-169

Francis Wright's family owned extensive collieries and ironworks in Derbyshire, England, and through this connection the Mackay and Dippie syndicate attracted the interest of a large coal company in England, which sent out mining engineers to assess the project in 1912. They were impressed; apparently, the chief engineer told George: "If I were asked to draw a design for a perfect coal mine, I would design it exactly like this one. If you had told us it was like this, we would not have come, as we would have thought that it could not be true."

The engineer's report, which was very detailed, included the following comments: "We find that the coal is hard & compact, of the smokeless variety, analogous to the best of the Welsh steam coals & that of Pennsylvania. Twenty seven seams ... aggregate thickness of 196 ft." Apparently, anthracite and steam coal appeared in equal portions in the samples, with at least 100 million tons of coal, 75 percent of which appeared easy to mine. The engineer suggested relying on just the best seams: "These 10 seams alone carry 60,000,000 tons of workable coal ... 100 years at a daily output of 2000 tons." The accessibility of the coal would have made for low labour costs—less than $1.50 per ton loaded into railway cars at the mine site. Grades were easy for a rail line, and a good site for a camp was nearby, with "a plentiful supply of good water." Markets for this coal would extend to the west coast and as far east as Winnipeg. The report concluded that this Kananaskis anthracite coal would certainly become the fuel of choice for the Canadian West.[6]

On the strength of the engineer's report, about 6,000 dollars was subscribed in London, England.[7] George hired a number of Stoney workers and set to work readying the sites for development. It was an exciting, exhausting time, as he reported to Mrs. White in the fall of 1913:

> Outside of a few weeks at haying time I have been practically away in the mountains since the middle of May ... the coal took me til haying time. I made four trips to it, had it all surveyed and had also a big gang of Indians cutting a good foot trail to it, at one time I had up to 70 pack-ponies packing through the mountains for us ... all the prospecting and climbing up and down the mountains devolved upon me as all of my partners are either businessmen in Calgary or ranchers not given to much walking ... And now I have work ahead of me for at least two more years, prospecting and recording several mines I already know of. Three I know to be good, others are mere guess and chance work.[8]

The syndicate tried to sell the mine to the English company for a million dollars—George's share was to have been 30 percent—and a spur line was planned from the mine to the Canadian Pacific Railway main line in the Bow Valley at Seebe. But just at this crucial juncture, when "everything was arranged, including financing," the Grand Trunk Pacific Railway ran into difficulty in Canada: "the London Stock Exchange removed Canadian securities from its listing & the deal fell through." As one of George's friends later remarked, "I have never heard anything to equal the bad luck which has dogged the selling of this mine."[9] Later, George received a letter of regret from the buyers along with a copy of the engineer's report.

The syndicate tried in vain to attract other investors, but again their plans were stymied, this time by the outbreak of the First World War. Hugh Stainsleigh, manager of the Hawkeye Ranch near Hussar, Alberta, tried recruiting for George but eventually had to admit defeat. He wrote regretfully:

> While there were many who would like to take up the proposition, they all have the same cry "Afraid to do anything before the end of the war" or "What spare cash I had I invested in Liberty Bonds." One party took it up pretty keenly and I was expecting him up day after day but in the end he had the same story. They are all afraid of what the unsettled state of the labour market at the end of war will mean and until that arrives and is over one cannot seem to get these Americans to do much investing. [10]

*Top: George looking down
on the Mangin Glacier
above Aster Lake, 1911.
GA PD-183-3-196*

*Bottom:: George named this
feature Waka Nambé
(The Hand of God) during
his explorations above
Aster Lake in 1911.
GA PD-184-3-195*

The timing of the syndicate's failure to attract investors is ironic. During this period, hard, semianthracite coal was in great demand for its clean-burning qualities because ships fuelled with it were hard to detect, owing to an almost complete lack of smoke. Unfortunately, the depression after the war caused the coal market to slump and most of the underground mining operations in the Canadian Rockies closed, though the profitable operations at the Canmore mines continued until the 1980s. Probably, it was this tantalizing local success that prompted George, ever tenacious, to pursue coal mining in the Kananaskis until the end of his life.

During the years before the war, whenever he could spare time from the ranch, George not only worked on his coal claims but also continued his exploration of the mountains. In one of his last letters to Mrs. White, he had written: "I am sorry that you should dislike Canada so; of course it isn't a woman's country but for a man, where is the equal?"[11] In 1911, he travelled with some Stoneys to "the perilous High Pass above Upper Kananaskis Lake [South Kananaskis Pass]." From there he clambered on foot to the top of one of the peaks and looked southwest down the Palliser River, "a country of burnt timber and hanging glaciers, and on the other side of the Valley a chain of very high mountain peaks." Down into this fascinating country they went, investigating a land that was new to George. Once back at the ranch, he wrote to the geographer general in Ottawa, describing the terrain of this part of the west that to date was unmapped. The next summer, Ottawa sent a survey team that George guided into the area. After their return, the geographer general wrote to George, asking him for suggestions for Native names to attach to the peaks. Replying that most white people would not be able to pronounce Native names, and pointing out that poor translations of those were inaccurate and misleading, George suggested that English names be used instead. As a result, Ottawa attached the name "The Royal Group" to the newly mapped peaks, calling them Mount King George, Mount Queen Mary, Mount Prince Henry, etc.

George's photograph albums give hints of other adventures in the years before the Great War. Images dated 1911 show work on a road up Pocaterra Creek toward Highwood Pass and George's coal mine in that area. The Royal Group and Aster Lake also appear in photographs, as well as the mouth of the Palliser River where it joins the Kootenay River in British Columbia. Harry Pollard, well-known southern Alberta photographer, accompanied George on this trip to the Kootenay valley. Companions on other trips included Francis Wright, Johnny and King Bearspaw, Jonas Rider, Paul Amos and the Fedeli brothers.

Rocky Mountains Park warden Bill Peyto and other unidentified persons apparently were involved with George in 1912, pictured as they are in a horse camp with teepees near Upper Kananaskis Lake. Most of the images from that year are of surveying lines to George's Big Twins Seam, Pocaterra Coal Claim No. 7 Seam and Spruce Grove Seam coal claim up Pocaterra Creek. Other pictures show a camp associated with the Mackay coal claim, Fred Dippie

Top; Camp below the Pocaterra Creek coal claim, September 1912. L-R: Johnny Bearspaw, Dan Coyote, George, Gaetano Fedeli, Luigi Fedeli, Walter Mackay. GA PD-184-3-113

Bottom: Fred Dippie at the Pocaterra Creek coal claim, Spruce Grove seam, ca 1912. GA PD-184-3-65

and mining engineer James Ashworth at a winter camp at Pocaterra Creek Coal Claim, and the No. 4 lumber-camp site on the Kananaskis River. Other photographs show George the rancher at work and play with neighbours during roundups, brandings and gymkhanas.

Although snows never arrived some years, George recalled other winters when they came early. "I was talking the other day with King Bearspaw about the big snow of the first of October 1914. Four feet of snow on the level on the Eastern slope. I was caught at the head of the Oldman [River], and I had to find my way over two fairly high passes, and visibility: Zero. I made the Buffalo Head Ranch in three days, my two horses were done for for months. The Stonies stayed in camp in the mountains. King came to the ranch three weeks after, certain to find that I had not turned up. Somewhat the same thing happened years ago, and the cowboy got lost, and was found in the summer, huddled up at the very head of the Livingstone. He had missed the turn."[12] However, the photo albums from those years also show scenes of winter fun, with George and friends skiing and being towed behind horses while "ski-joring."

George ski-joring behind Gentleman at the Buffalo Head Ranch, 1913. GA PD-184-3-25

Photographs in 1915 from a timber-cruising trip suggest George might have been working for a logging company. Others show him with local fish and game warden Sam Smith and at Lower Kananaskis Lake with his sister Marta and friend Ruggero Bozzi, both visiting from Italy. In 1917 he explored the Cataract Creek area and also travelled again to the Old Man River Gap region. Images of Elbow Lake, King's Creek, the Upper Spray River, the Upper Kananaskis, Lower Kananaskis Falls, King's Creek Falls, Mount Paul and Mount Kidd attest to frequent roaming through today's Kananaskis Country.

During these wanderings, George named a number of physical features, including Mount George (later Gap Mountain) and Mount Paul, officially named Elpoca Mountain in 1920. In 1914 a Dominion land surveyor found stakes marked "Pocaterra" along the creek by George's coal claim and, unbeknownst to George, named it Pocaterra Creek. Some two years later, Harry Pollard surprised George with the information that his name appeared on the map of Alberta in two places in the Kananaskis (Pocaterra Creek and Pocaterra Valley).[13]

Despite his relative isolation on a ranch in the Alberta foothills, George corresponded regularly with family and friends and was well aware of events overseas and the First World War. As he later explained, "I had answered the calls of my military class from Italy in the fall of 1916 and spring of 1917, both times having been exempted on account of strong short-sight and lock-knee (on left knee) or Sinovitis ..."[14] In spite of his Italian exemption, George tried to gain commissions with both the British and the American forces. In January of 1918, Hugh Stainsleigh reported on his unsuccessful attempts to get George "a position with the Military forces." Although Stansleigh and his partners had recommended George as of great potential assistance to the Allied war effort because of his facility with languages, when the American authorities investigated, they discovered that George had already applied "to serve under the British colours ... but had been declined on account of defective eyesight." Or, as Stainsleigh suspected, perhaps because he was Italian.[15]

With active service out of the question, George contributed to the Canadian war effort by supplying horses to local mounted regiments and serving on the executive of the local Pekisko Patriotic Fund. When his lack of military service in the First World War was questioned by the Italian government during the 1930s, the Italian Consular Agency in Edmonton vouched for him based on an agricultural exemption: "He has worked during the war years 1914–18 at work, which according to the Canadian Government Military Authorities gave him the right to be exempted from military service, that is by being a breeder of horses and cattle and doing his own work."[16]

A ready market for his stock during the war years rescued George financially. In his enthusiasm to develop coal, he had channelled too much

Marta Pocaterra on Tiger, Buffalo Head Ranch, 1915.
GA PD-184-1-23

money into mine development to the detriment of his ranch, and by 1915 he was desperate for cash. He turned to his father, but Giuseppe had little to spare after helping Marta with the (unsuccessful) development of her acting career, treating her to a holiday in Canada to visit George and paying for an expensive society wedding.[17] His father's inability to help during a period of crisis surprised and upset George, and although Giuseppe finally managed to send "a big amount" in 1917 (600 lire, about 115 Canadian dollars), George was forced to borrow from the Fedeli family and others to keep the ranch afloat. His financial situation gradually improved, but the experience left him with a nagging grudge against his younger sister.

For George the 1920s were busy, with ranch expansions and improvements. Never very interested in cattle, he concentrated on breeding horses, convinced by his success during the war that the demand for them would return. His shifting emphasis is shown in several government documents of the period. Applying for grazing leases in 1907, George reported 120 head of cattle and 89 horses, but by 1921, in an application to divert water for the purpose of irrigation, he claimed ownership of 100 horses and only 70 head of cattle.[18] Unfortunately, George was wrong; horses could never compete with automobiles, and the market declined steadily. His focus on horses meant that the cattle business was never developed to its full financial potential, a situation viewed with some amusement by his more practical neighbours: Johnny "Rabbits" Brown at the OH Ranch, the Bews at Sullivan Creek Ranch, the Hansons at the Chinook Ranch, and the Sheppards at Riverbend Ranch.

In fact, George Pocaterra — or "Pokey," as some of the old-timers had taken to calling him — was considered something of an eccentric by the locals, and not just because of his intimate friendships and travels with the Stoneys. The ranch was home to a menagerie of well-loved dogs, and George was seldom seen without a horse (according to a friend, he operated on the principle "Where I go, I ride"[19]). He was usually dressed in cowboy attire: fringed buckskin jacket, big silk neckerchief, sheepskin chaps, boots or moccasins, and a tall, slightly dilapidated cowboy hat. He had a quick temper and could (and frequently did) swear fluently in at least five languages. With no running water or electricity at the Buffalo Head, his bachelor life was spartan, even primitive, yet he loved to socialize, read widely and engaged in deep philosophical discussions with Paul Amos and others.[20] His life on the ranch was "a curious mixture of old-world aristocracy and wilderness roughness, often winding up his fluted grammaphone [sic] and listening to Italian opera while he washed his dishes by hand outside his cabin."[21] Once, when he had erected a warning sign on his fence advising Beware of the Mad Stallion, a witty passerby mended it to read Beware of the Mad Italian.[22]

George was not considered the only eccentric in the area. Up the valley, showman Guy Weadick and his glamorous wife, trick rider Florence "Flores" LaDue, had the Stampede Ranch (formerly, the Kuck place), and upstream from that was the Eden Valley Ranch, owned by New York writer and associate editor of Cosmopolitan magazine Frazier Hunt; local opinion was that Spike Hunt had been encouraged to buy the ranch in 1926 by his employer, Hearst Publishing Company, to report on the activities of the Prince of Wales whenever he came to visit his nearby EP Ranch. These characters, and many others, possibly gave rise to the Eden Valley's other, unofficial names: Looney Lane and Mad Valley.[23]

Because he was not running many cattle, George's grazing land stayed in good condition. Philosophically, he did not believe in exhausting the grass in any case: "What right has anybody just because he has a man-made deed of property ... to utterly spoil land, which future generations will need?"[24] But he still had to provide year-round for the few cattle he had. In the high country, haying has always been an important summer chore to provide insurance against the inevitable winters with snow so deep the animals cannot graze for feed. To that end George dug a ditch in 1922 to drain the big swamp at the Buffalo Head to create a larger hay meadow. That year he went on a hunting trip to the Elk River with Mr. Bennis, manager of the Round T Ranch.

George had acquired some land directly across the Highwood River from the Buffalo Head when the Fedeli brothers sold out and returned to Italy in 1920. When he resold "the Fedeli quarter" in 1921, George not only made some money but also began a friendship that was to last for decades. A short article titled "Recreation Land Purchase" in the *High River Times* informed the public that George Pocaterra had just sold to Harper Sibley of Rochester, New York, 65 acres on the south side of the Highwood River; "It will be used as recreation grounds for his family and friends." Sibley, a wealthy businessman, planned to build a log cabin and maintain riding ponies on the place "so that trips may be made from that point through the foothills country." He had already purchased 2,000 acres on the Round T Ranch nearer High River and intended to build a large summer home at that location. The editor concluded: "When a gentleman of Mr. Sibley's standing shows this kind of faith in Western Canada, it is about time for those of us here to awake to a sense of realization that we have here in High River district a land of great promise."[25]

In 1922, George diversified his ranching operations in another direction. "Pocaterra Establishes Camp Grounds at Buffalo Head Ranch," read the headline in the *High River Times*. After fencing off 80 acres along the river, he put up signs to direct visitors to the campsites and to his ranch, "where all information regarding the camp site is available." Though the camp was located at a spot where the banks were steep, a trail led down to the river, "making it ideal for hiking and climbing." Obviously, George had sold the venture to the editor of the paper very successfully: "The spot is one of the prettiest in the foothills, commanding a magnificent view and accessible to some of the finest fishing holes of the river."[26]

Another opportunity came knocking at the ranch house door in 1924 when Allen Seymour of the tourism department of the Canadian Pacific Railway visited George and Guy Weadick (then general manager of the Calgary Stampede) and asked them to start dude ranching. Guest ranches were popular in the United States, and the CPR saw an opportunity to expand its passenger business by transporting "dudes" — as these paying guests were known — to ranches in the high country of the Rocky Mountains.

The *High River Times* featured a story on the tourist opportunities in the area in 1924 under the title "Up the Highwood." "The foothills have not looked prettier for many years than they do at the present ..." it boasted, "with the entire country in various shades of green and the mountain flowers in profusion." Tourists were coming to the foothills area from many places, the article continued, and "George Pocaterra's 'Buffalo Head' ranch offers excellent inducements for the many tourists who have been visiting there. George has four cabins, comfortably furnished and situated in sightly spots on the hillsides, and two more are in the course of construction ... In time, our foothills will be

Top: George on Don, Buffalo Head Ranch, ca 1911. GA NA-695-1

Bottom; George with MacDuff, Buffalo Head Ranch, ca late 1920s. GA PA-2393-14-1-2

alive with summer tourists, as the number of visitors seems to be increasing each year."[27] It was probably with his guests in mind that George added a long veranda to the ranch house, which was comfortably furnished and decorated with hunting trophies and Native curios. He also created a beautiful approach to the buildings from the road that he called "the Avenida."

Dudes at the Buffalo Head Ranch, 1931. L-R: Daisy Mamini with MacDuff, Eleanor MacDonald and Laura Mamini. GA PD-184-1-82

George hosted dudes, mostly from the United States, until the early 1930s. His illustrated brochure was very appealing. It promised, "A Playground for people who wish an outing amongst the most beautiful of scenery, in a ranching country, with its picturesque, care-free life and customs, and where, besides riding, one can go hunting and fishing during the open season ..." For a weekly fee of 50 dollars (equivalent to 600 dollars per week today), guests were housed in cabins and teepees, provided with meals, given exclusive use of a "saddle pony" (i.e., a horse) and taken on numerous guided trips into the Front Ranges. There was a special reduced rate of 35 dollars per week for those not intending to ride.

George's love for the area shines through in his brochure, which outlines some of the many expeditions available to guests: "There are abundant short trips one can take on horseback from the ranch; for instance, the E.P. Ranch of H.R.H. the Prince of Wales, and the well-known Bar U Ranch are only a few miles away, or one can make the round trip to the upper reaches of Flat Creek with its wild mountain scenery, or of the Sullivan Creek valley in a short day's ride. Longer trips, lasting from a few days to several weeks, can be arranged beforehand at the ranch.

"One such trip through some of the most wonderful mountain and lake scenery to be found anywhere in the world is the round trip to the sources of the Highwood River and over the Storm Creek Pass, to the Glorious Kananaskis Lakes.

"Then over the Elk pass and the Great Divide, where the waters flow on the one hand to the Hudson Bay, and, on the other, to the Pacific, to the Elk

River Lakes, which look for all the world like mirrors in a setting of lofty mountains and glaciers galore; down the Elk Valley for a couple of days and over the Aldridge Pass, with its gem-like lakelet; back again into the Highwood Valley, and down to the Home Ranch."

The brochure concluded: "Buffalo Head Ranch is not an hotel, but the simple home of nature-loving, outdoor-living people, who, though familiar with the acknowledged best of European scenery, the splendors of Alpine Switzerland and picturesque Italy, have chosen to locate here in the heart of Sunny Alberta and believe it second to none in the world. A hearty welcome awaits congenial guests who appreciate sunshine and smiles, sport and rest and true Western hospitality."[28]

To assist him in hosting the dudes, George entered into an arrangement with Eugene and Marie "Mimi" de Palezieux in 1924. The de Palezieux, who had two young daughters, had been ranching somewhat unsuccessfully in the Millarville district for some time and were happy with George's business proposition. In fact, George considered that he had "rescued them from their awful place … when they actually had not sufficient to live on decently."[29] Because he foresaw that much of his summer would be taken up guiding dudes on mountain trips, George needed the de Palezieux to help him manage the business in return for a share of the profits. Mimi was to oversee the cooking and housekeeping, and Eugene would manage the accounts. During tourist season, the de Palezieux would pay half of any housekeeping expenses, but in the off-season they would be responsible for two-thirds (because there were four of them to feed).[30] This arrangement lasted four years with mixed success, but in that time George grew very fond of the de Palezieux children, particularly young Isamay.

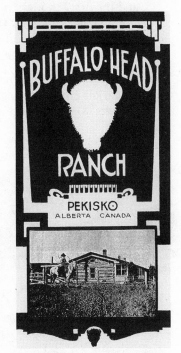

Buffalo Head Ranch brochure, mid 1920s.
GA M6340-198-1

The Buffalo Head guest book and receipt book show that some of George's first dudes in 1924 were three members of the Sibley family from Rochester, New York, and four others from that area. Visitors from Calgary also signed the guest book that summer. The next summer the list included dudes from Calgary, New York and Chicago and even from overseas. Guests from Ireland wrote in the guest book: "This is our first impression of Canada—of ranch life, we certainly could not hope for a better one."

Some of the guests that summer experienced the danger and excitement of mountain expeditions first-hand. As George later recalled:

I was coming out of the Elk once (1925) with Paul and a party of New York Wall Street people. Hunters. We had got our limit already. Just before starting over the pass a sudden blizzard blotted out everything. Paul and I were taking turns to lead. You know how open it is in places. And at a certain point, for no apparent reason, the trail takes a very sudden turn to the east, right, going north down a narrow coulee. Paul missed it. Something seemed to tell me, and I called to Paul to stop. He said: "Nyenno, konnah" so I led on from there. It was the right turn, but at the time I could not tell you rightly why I had wanted to turn, Maybe it was instinct. Anyway we made the Lakes. There we found the Duc de Nemours, with his party. They had not tasted venison nor fish yet … but oh!! Now, plenty of bottled cheer. We had a grand time that night in Johnny Curran's cabin. Everybody sang one or more songs. When my turn came they all wanted me to sing a French song in honor of the duke … and the first I thought of, of several I knew, was "La Marseillaise" … the song Monsieur le Duc's ancestors had heard last in their lives … And you know, (he was a good sport) he joined in! I asked his pardon after, but he said: "Mais mon ami, c'etait bien une chanson de ma Patrie!"[31]

Photographs from 1925 show Dr. Halford J. and Mrs. Morlan atop Survey Hill, or Marker Hill as it is called today, just above the Buffalo Head Ranch headquarters. Very satisfied after her three-week holiday, when she signed

Dr. Halford J. Morlan on Midnight with Isamay and Jacqueline de Palezieux, Buffalo Head Ranch, 1925. GA PD-184-3-221

the guest book Mrs. Morlan called the ranch "a utopian resort." Dr. Morlan, a successful Chicago physician and world traveller, had come to the Buffalo Head to fish along the Highwood River. A good fisherman himself, George was impressed with the congenial doctor's expertise, "how he could drop a fly away across the river, under the cliff, in some small pool,"[32] and the two became lifelong friends.

George was a charming host and many other visitors over the years became his personal friends. Now in his 40s, his dancing hazel eyes and salt-and-pepper hair made him a favourite with female guests, many of whom fell "slightly in love"[33] with the attractive foreigner during their visit. An entertainer at heart, he amused his guests by singing during their trail rides. Years later he recalled "the Spanish (Gaucho) song I used to sing": "Yo tengo un ranchito—Assombrado de flores—Todo lindo y chiquito—Y en el es el mi amor—Es Linda como estrella—Suave como el mie—Na e otra asi bella—VIDALITA!"[34]

Good returns on the business from 1925 allowed George to pay back some debts, with enough remaining to purchase new beds, blankets, saddles and horses, and to construct three new cabins for the 1926 season. That year, visitors came from Bristol in England as well as from Edmonton, Toronto, Pennsylvania, Virginia and Chicago.

Amelie de Vauclain, Buffalo Head Ranch, 1926. GA PA-2393-17-1-1

The Pennsylvania group—Mrs. Samuel M. de Vauclain Jr. and her daughters, Amelie and Patricia—stayed for 10 weeks. The older daughter, Amelie, was an attractive 20-year-old, scheduled to begin studies at exclusive Bryn Mawr College in September. But during the summer she fell in love with George, or at least with the notion of being in love with the handsome, rugged mountain man. Flattered, and irrepressibly romantic himself, 44-year-old George fell in love right back. As he later remembered: "I soon noticed that Amelie was becoming rather fond of me ... We had so many things in common. She was quite a linguist, and we used to switch from English to French and even Italian quite easily. She was traveled and so was I, and she was exceptionally cultured and, spiritually, developed beyond her age."[35] They began spending more and more time together, sharing their dreams for the future and discovering a mutual interest in travelling to the South Seas.

Eventually the pair pledged their love, and by the end of the de Vauclains' holiday at the Buffalo Head, the two were secretly engaged. George was ecstatic, but sensible enough to realize the dangers:

Though I could not help but be pleased at seeing how she liked me, I was *always* and from the *very first* conscious of the obstacles in the way. She was 24 years younger than I, and had been raised within a very wealthy family, and though all my relatives are well-off and some very wealthy, I had chosen to blaze my own Path in life away from them and from my native land … I insisted on an extremely tough condition, that she should go back with her people, go to Bryn Mawr for three years, and after that length of time if she still needed me I would be willing to marry her.[36]

Amelie left the ranch a young woman gloriously in love, perhaps for the first time, but she also appreciated the difficulties and worried about the time ahead: "Three years in which we shall both have to work for our ultimate happiness. I return to my world there to test the strength of my love. It is hard, how hard, for me to go, and yet it is best, I suppose … I have promised you to tell you in case I stop loving you, and I will keep to my word. I respect you too much, my husband, to come to you without a worthy return for what you offer me."[37] Understandably, once she was back in her own milieu, busy with friends and schooling, young Amelie's romantic notion of life as a rancher's wife began to fade. Even by the end of September, she was writing George with a tinge of remorse, "Like you, I should have restrained my feelings somewhat."[38]

Amelie's absence only strengthened George's attachment. Her letters were affectionate but full of the details of her schoolgirl life, whereas his letters betray the intensity of the love affair experienced by this most romantic of men. They had promised their hearts to each other in the teepee, and as soon as she left—leaving him several love letters to tide him over until new letters arrived by mail—he wrote to his family in Italy with the good news. In mid-October, he reported their reaction: "They are tremendously pleased and are keen to see your photo now and yourself later on."[39]

But he was struggling financially and in view of his changed circumstances gallantly offered to release her from the engagement, though he had no real idea that she might accept:

Ever since you went from here everything has gone against me, no matter what I tried … When I asked you in the teepee, love, my great love and longing for you carried me away—I thought at that time that matters were not at all bad, and the prospects good. I've been trying to make good ever since, but when I went over things I soon found out that de P. did not keep the accounts right up-to-date and that if the de Ps went, the strain would be hard to bear financially. On account of the late harvest etc, I have not yet been able to put through any of my summer cottage propositions, everybody thinks it a splendid idea with a great future, but in the meantime …

And so has gone everything else. So dear heart, my last hope to make good and weather this storm is from my coal-claims interests.

Even here I have just received a terrible slam! I have just got a letter from the Syndicate in which they state they wish to drop one of the best claims, as the burden is becoming too heavy for them. I'm going to write to them to hold on a wee bit longer, but dearest one, the heart is almost breaking for what I must in fairness say to you. You see, Amelie, now how hard and difficult it will be for me, not only to make good in the way I would like to for your sake, but even hard for me to keep the integrity of that which I fondly have hoped could be our happy "home"! I am, as a last fight, going to sell all or almost all my cattle, and in the spring another bunch of horses, and if I can have a good concourse of tourists next summer I may pull through and have a good chance then to fight it out. [It] will take years before I could be in a position to give you the life you are entitled to and I would wish to see you have, and dear, oh dear one I just simply can't bear it! . . .

So you see Amelie dearest, I am really not good enough to become your husband, even though it is certain to break my heart and my whole life's ambitions. I have to tell you the facts as they are. I cannot hold you, my own, however much I long for you ... Amelie, Amelie—whatever happens—remember that always, always I shall have my heart full of my love for you. My own, think well of your heartbroken,

George.[40]

(The reference to troubles with his coal-mining partners stemmed from a letter George had received from Fred Dippie of the Mackay and Dippie syndicate in late 1926 to explain why they wanted to drop the coal leases. Dippie wrote: "I cannot blame you for not favoring the cancellation of the Mackay Claim, as your position is so different to the rest of us, but the fact of the matter is that Walter [Mackay] and I have been paying the greater part of the rentals for so long that it has come to the point where we simply cannot spare the money any longer ..." The furriers had been paying hundreds of dollars each year in rentals—the total was in the thousands by this time—and with no returns they feared even greater losses in the future. "You are the only one who has made any money out of the adventure so [you] should not kick."[41])

In late October, Amelie wrote to break off their engagement. She did not refer at all to George's financial problems, but focussed instead on the disparity in their ages and the fact that her family disapproved; her mother had tried to cool the relationship even while they were still at the Buffalo Head. In his sad reply, he returned most of her pictures and tried to rewrite the events of the summer to lessen his profound grief: "Amelie, I have tried to think over your decision, and I must, even though it just kills all the Best in me, come to the conclusion that the real reason, even though you may not be conscious of it, is that 'your Love was not what it did seem to me to be.'"

Bitterly, he told Amelie that Mrs. de Palezieux had tried to warn him against her, had even begged him not to go on the "fatal" mountain trip with the women, "with tears in her eyes … But already I was blind and lost. She begged me again before I left for the Kananaskis trip, to send somebody else in my stead—oh God! would that I had done so!" He said Mrs. de Palezieux could tell—"woman's intuition," he called it—that the relationship with Amelie could not last and that his heart would be broken by the beautiful youngster.

"You will never know what agonies I have gone through these last few days," he continued, "as I lay deep in the pool of misery, like a drowning man trying to fight my way to the top, and hardly knowing which way to try for it. When I first came to the conviction that the Love you bore me was really lacking in strength, I thought my heart would actually break, the physical pain was so great."[42]

Although both expressed a desire to remain friends, George and Amelie had ceased to correspond by mid-November, just five months after their first meeting at the ranch. George worked through some of his feelings and frustrations in letters to his closest correspondents, Dr. Morlan and Josephine Bedingfeld. (The Bedingfelds had become close friends when they ranched at Pekisko Creek. In 1919 they had retired and returned to England. Soon after, their old property was acquired by Edward, Prince of Wales and renamed the EP Ranch.)

Over the next few years, George had news of Amelie from former dudes who moved in the same social circles. In the fall of 1927 he heard from Dorothy Doane, who was acquainted with one of Amelie's best friends and, it is clear, knew all about the abortive love affair. Dorothy wrote with the news that Amelie was engaged to a young man. Several years later, Dr. Morlan, wrote to say that while visiting the de Vauclains in Philadelphia he had been informed that Amelie was happily married.

By the fall of 1926, George was having trouble with the de Palezieux family, particularly Mimi. He complained to Mrs. Bedingfeld:

Mrs de Palezieux, though when normal, one of the nicest women I've ever met, is of a *very* high strung disposition, and at periods given to terrible hysterics. I did not find out for the first six months, and after always hoped against hope … Mrs de P. I noticed used to be jealous if even I was nice to an Indian, Sam Smith or almost any of my friends; so much so that I became almost stiff with everybody, just for the sake of peace … Then Amelie came, and as soon as Mrs de P. noticed that we began caring for each other she showed her very jealous disposition; making all sort of cruel insinuations as to my motives, and trouble all around, so that every tourist felt and noticed that something was wrong.[43]

In December, he told Dr. Morlan:

I think that I shall have to carry on the tourist business mostly alone; Mrs de P. will probably help me for two or three months during the rush season but the rest of the time I shall be alone as far as management is concerned … Mr de P does not like the business, and has absolutely no enthusiasm for it, and Mrs de P all too often shows her likes and dislikes, and it is hard for her to get along with the help. She is unbeatable when 'normal' but unfortunately she is not that very long, and always worries herself and everybody until one is almost frantic with the strain. I have had four months I would hate to repeat … So the best, though it does come hard for me that I shall carry on mostly alone, and let them keep an interest in the business.[44]

Although the de Palezieux actually remained with George that winter, the situation was very tense. "On looking things over I found a terrible mess," he told Mrs. Bedingfeld, "… and all I can make out is that after having paid for almost $2,000 worth of improvements and back debts out of this years tourists business, instead of being clear of other store debts as I was given to understand we will still owe almost $1,000 in that line. It seems that they have spent more than was ever told me." He also blamed bad fall weather for having lost them "between $1,500 and $2,000 worth of business that would have put us through till next summer."[45]

Luckily, the summer of 1927 was a good one, with visitors from Calgary, New York State, Chicago, Toronto, Massachusetts and the United Kingdom. This was the summer that Dorothy Doane was a guest, and she wrote to George that fall to express her appreciation and admiration: "I just had to write and tell you what a perfect summer you helped me have. Although the scenery was heavenly and the situation ideal, it would not have been anywhere near complete without you."[46]

Buffalo Head Ranch dudes riding above Flat Creek in the Highwood, 1926. Mount Head in the distance.
GA PD-184-2-225

One of George's chief pleasures in running a dude ranch was guiding his guests on expeditions into the high country. He was surprisingly generous about sharing its pristine beauty with appreciative visitors and was realistic about the area's potential for recreational development. During the summer of 1927, he shared this vision with a young dude from Ontario, Irving Hollinrake, who later wrote enthusiastically about "that Kananaskis Lake hotel idea of yours," and said encouragingly: "I should like to see that summer resort on the Kananaskis developed and if only some good connection could be made with the railroads it would be a great step on the way."[47]

The de Palezieux remained with George for the summer of 1927, but "Life with the de Palezieux, already a rather difficult matter, became more and more impossible, until in September 1927 I managed to get rid of them. There is an old adage in Italy, which says: 'E meglio soli, che male accompagnati.' (It is better to be alone, than badly mated) and I certainly found it to be true in the case of the de P."[48] Unfortunately for George, he did not have the cash to pay the de Palezieux the 3,000 dollars owing for their share of the business. So, to be free of them, in November 1927 he signed a mortgage secured by the goods and chattels relating to the tourist business, everything from saddles, bridles, cots, chairs, blankets, towels and dishes to cabins, teepees, a chicken house, a dairy house, four saddle horses and the 1919 Dodge touring car.

With the de Palezieux finally gone, George was a little worried about spending the winter alone. Dorothy Doane was sympathetic: "I remember what you said about the helpless state a man was in who has lived alone and then after having had people with him for a while is left alone again but I do hope that you can find some competent and congenial person to stay with you this winter because I can readily sympathize with you, having to be isolated out there at such an ungodly time of the year."[49] Years later, George reported that everything had been for the best: "Though already suffering from something that later turned out to be acute appendicitis, I felt like a new man, with my old enthusiasm, self-reliance and determination to win through. I kept up my Dude business on the ranch besides doing everything else in which I could see a means to get me out of the financial difficulties that the de P. had left in their wake."[50]

A *Calgary Herald* article in 1928 reviewed the facilities offered to tourists in the High River area: "… The two tourist ranches—the T.S. of Guy Weadick and the Buffalo Head of George Pocaterra—each year draw an increasing crowd of eastern guests, enraptured with the ever-changing vistas of mountain scenes."[51] Buffalo Head guests that year came from Rochester and Calgary.

In 1929 there was a special guest. "Prominent Hunter from Europe Enjoys Hunting in Foothills Country" recorded the *High River Times*. Roger Malraison, a Parisian living in South Africa, had visited the Highwood Valley in search of big game. After two months with Guy Weadick he spent more than three months with George. "He has just returned from a five weeks' hunting trip in the mountains with one of Mr. Pocaterra's outfits," the newspaper reported. "He secured beautiful mountain sheep and several deer. But he says there is no comparison between the abundance of game in Central Africa and the relative scarcity in Alberta. However, the five week trip to the mountains was an exhilarating experience for a South African." While hazards in South Africa included fever and other strange illnesses, "an African coming to Canada should be forewarned of the cold of the mountain

Adolf Baumngart.
Photo R. M. Patterson Collection

district. However he considers the Canadian climate extremely healthful."[52] Malraison was pleased with his visit and wrote in the Buffalo Head guest book: "Un ranch dans un cadre merveilleaux avec un rancher charmant."

In 1930 there were guests from Calgary, Edmonton, Ontario and Minnedosa, Manitoba. That year George acquired a new ranch foreman, Adolf Baumgart. Born in East Prussia in 1903, Adolf had arrived in Alberta in the late 1920s, lured by tales of the mountains much as George had been 25 years earlier. This created a bond between the two men, who got along well, although Adolf sometimes questioned his employer's continued obsession with horse breeding and apparent disinterest in the more profitable cattle business.

Adolf had been hired as animal foreman and general superintendent of building projects and sometimes found the tourists "distracting" and "a nuisance."[53] Nevertheless, he often accompanied George on pack trips and apparently enjoyed other adventures as well. The poet and author P. K. Page, who visited the ranch a number of times with her parents, vividly remembered an incident when Adolf helped George build a boat christened the *Vellita*,[54] which they dragged by horse and cart through the bush to a nearby slough:

George sailing the "Vellita,"
Buffalo Head Ranch, ca 1930.
GA PA-2393-7-1-1

Pokey put on a bathing suit that was enough to make a girl of sixteen blush. It was an old-fashioned one that came down to about his knees but because the moths had eaten all the crotch out of it, he had to put a sort of a pair of canvas drawers underneath it. I've never seen such a sight in all my life. I was slightly in love with Pokey until that event and that put me off him. He got into the boat and the boat promptly sank. He and Adolf were in it and it promptly sank. They ignominiously came out covered in leeches.[55]

That summer of fun was one of the last for tourists on the Buffalo Head. Dude ranching in the West depended heavily on the holiday trade of wealthy businessmen, and the financial crash of 1929 and subsequent economic depression during the 1930s dealt the business a severe blow. The final entries in the Buffalo Head guest register are for 1931, when visitors came from Chicago and the United Kingdom. One lighthearted entry read: "Yours 'til you put jam (strawberry) on bread!" to which George replied, "Ok to that, Ed." Laura Mamini, a widowed friend from Calgary, also visited the ranch that summer with her two young daughters. After that, the business seems to have died. The only guests in 1932 appear to have been local children. An account in the *High River Times* reported that the Boy Scouts had been out into the mountains, touring and learning the ways of the wilderness. "While at the Buffalo Head, George Pocaterra gave the boys lessons in rope spinning which they thoroughly enjoyed."[56]

George tried very hard to interest former dudes in return visits, but without success. As Irving Hollinrake candidly replied from Ontario in June 1932, "Things are pretty hard down this way as I suppose they are in your part of the country. I am very sorry I can't do anything for you as regards to the Ranch but it is awfully difficult to interest people in anything at the present time … for the most part people are cutting down on vacation costs and it makes it all the harder. I think your rates are very reasonable and if I can influence anybody to come out you may certainly depend upon me to do it."[57]

But this proved impossible, and without the dudes George turned to other ventures. Even before the business collapsed, his interest had begun to shift. He later recalled, "In the spring of 1929, we had an oil boom of some magnitude. As I knew from investigations done in 1913–14 quite a bit of the geological side of the oil structures in Alberta, I jumped into it, and did a lot of field exploration work, making good money, besides getting out of it also a 25% interest in 10,000 acres of oil-bearing lands."[58] On May 10, 1929, D. P. McDaniel wrote to George from the Palliser Hotel in Calgary to thank him for his assistance with a development that might have benefited the rancher: "It is our intention to form a Company of million and one-half shares of no par value to exploit 3000 acres of oil and gas leases which we have just secured in the vicinity of the Buffalo Head and Stampede Ranches on the High River. In consideration of your valuable services in assisting us to locate these leases, it is our intention to give you credit of 2000 shares, if as and when issued."[59]

In 1930 George himself filed a claim and tried to get in on the booming Turner Valley petroleum-development process. A letter from the Department of the Interior informed him that his application for a lease of the petroleum and natural gas rights on land in Township 16, Range 3, west of the 5th Meridian (southwest of Pekisko) was incorrectly staked. However, "as you made a bona fide effort to comply with the regulations and have apparently gone to a great deal of trouble and expense to secure a lease of the land staked by you, it has been decided by the Department to grant you a further period of sixty days from the nineteenth instant within which to restake the location in accordance with the provisions of the Regulations, and in the meantime your present staking will be protected." Careful instructions on the proper staking of the claim were included.[60]

All this feverish activity ultimately came to nothing, but George had a wonderful few years nevertheless:

> Then came the Crack of September 1929 ... Anyway I had made some cash, as all the interests went West in the depression years that followed; and besides I had a grand time working like a fool, day and night, in the hills and in the mountains with a bunch of my old trusted Indians, staking and exploring and surveying the claims, running lines through some of the most God-forsaken country you ever saw. There was a week, I remember yet, when I slept just FIVE HOURS in the whole week, matters were growing so hot, was on the go all day and all night. During the day with the Indians in the field, and at night traveling to Calgary with my Ford, and back again before daylight, then all day long again with my men. It was a marvellous experience. What matter that the whole thing blew up financially, that was not MY mistake. My part, I DID IT.[61]

Though George participated in the quest for oil and was always looking for a way to develop his coal claims, he derived most of his pleasure in life from mountain expeditions with Adolf and the Stoneys and, increasingly, with a British adventurer named Raymond M. Patterson. It is unclear when they met—perhaps at a Calgary Stampede in the mid-1920s—but by the late 1920s Patterson and his wife, Marigold, were regular visitors at the Italian's ranch. They had many areas of common interest, including a passion for the story of one of the great Europeans: Napoleon Bonaparte.

"My Great-Grandfather," wrote George to a distant cousin in Venezuela, "was the officer commanding the Silver Hussars (Usseri d'Argento), the bodyguard of the Vice-roy of Rome, at the time of Napoleon, prince Eugene de Beauharnois. He fought at the crossing of the Beresina, when he and his men standing in the freezing waters of that Russian stream fought to hold back the onrushing charges of the Cossacks, who were trying to prevent the French army, retreating from Moscow, from getting across. He was a great breeder of horse and a wonderful rider, and knew Napoleon Bonaparte well."[62]

This story impressed Patterson, who was himself in the thrall of the great emperor, the subject of his studies at Oxford before he emigrated to Canada. In fact, though he would eventually write five books about his adventures in the Canadian West, Patterson's final and unpublished book, *The Emperor's Horsemen*, would tell the tales of Napoleon's dispatch riders.

But it was a shared passion for the Canadian wilderness that really drew together Raymond Patterson and George Pocaterra. Patterson had come from Britain in 1924 to homestead in the Peace River area and had pursued adventure in the Far North, most notably in the South Nahanni region. By 1929 he and his bride were running a sheep ranch west of Calgary and enjoying their rustic cabin on the Ghost River northwest of Cochrane.

During the next few years, Patterson joined George and his friends at every opportunity to travel into the high country, and the two men came to know each other very well. Although their personalities were quite different, they shared a certain arrogance, impatience and self-absorption that made them similar enough to cause frequent friction. Patterson later wrote: "Each one of us was (and possibly still is) utterly unpredictable. We each had enormous patience when it came to some long-enduring physical feat—and yet every shred of that patience could fly to the winds over some absurd trifle."[63] Although their relationship was often stormy—for example, they saw themselves on opposing sides of the issue at the beginning of the Second World War—it was never dull, and their letters help fill the gaps in many stories as well as provide much of the detail for George's early days in Canada.

A description of George written by Patterson in 1930 reveals the depth of his admiration and affection: "He had become a great friend of ours although we live 90 miles apart by road. Our real interests are similar & we have the same imaginings. Also it is very pleasant to meet out here an Italian gentleman. He came to the West 27 years ago & saw the country when it was young & open range as I saw the prairies on the Peace. And the same kink which drove me to the South Nahanni, sent him, the first white man, into the far hunting country of the Stonies. A most interesting man & a good bush companion ... A northern Italian from the Fennarese, quick, humourous & with a wonderful gift of narrative. Educated in Padua, Berne, Frankfurt & Paris. A horseman by birth ... Founded the Buffalo Head on the winnings of a night & a day & a night of solid poker. I give you these odd details because he is one of most remarkable & most likeable men I have ever met ...[64] This affection was mutual. George visited the Pattersons at every opportunity and was godparent to their daughter, Janet, born in May 1930. After one memorable visit in 1930, Patterson recounted to a friend an example of George's notoriously bad driving habits:

> Pocaterra spent a couple of nights with us just after Christmas. He arrived a little late for dinner as we are 89 miles from door to door & he had made a sporting effort to do it in three hours. This includes the trail into the Highwood hills which is rocky & has numerous gates & about six miles driving through Calgary. Consequently he broke his neck as the excessive speed with which he proceeded to warm up the main north-south trail when he reached it caused some portion of his near front wheel to crystallise just south of Midnapore. The said front wheel reached Midnapore first & tried to get into the little wooden pioneer church there whose bells came from England a long time ago—as time is reckoned in a new country—& a little while after that Pocaterra & the rest of the car arrived at the church door in a bang & a great cloud of dust. He waited a time, & the car & the wheel were married again in Midnapore—not, Pocaterra said, as would have befitted the occasion, in St. John's of Midnapore, but humdrumly by the high priest of the Fish Creek Service Station ...[65]

Through his friendship with George, Patterson came to know some of his Stoney friends, in particular Paul Amos, who often accompanied them on mountain expeditions. At times, this new cultural contact was a source of amusement for the Englishman:

> I bought three mountain horses from the Stonies—two saddle, one pack. Muhtanga rode them over the other day from Morley & one Tom Powderface drove a vintage flivver over to take him back home. Pocaterra was still with us & shepherded them along to the bathroom to wash the dust off before tea & they had a hell of a time there turning taps & pulling plugs & approving quietly of everything but the real gem was the departure.
>
> Incidentally the Stonies have three words for a car, & these, in their historical order, really give the history of motoring from its infancy.

The first was Sijamna cha oommama, which means skunk wagon, & searching me earliest memories, I give this full marks. The second is Yéjenayaga—he goes by himself. An advance in efficiency. And the last, Perperrangen, which is simply the noise a well behaved car should make—on its day.

The owner was proud, but terrified of the thing. None of us knew anything about it & for a long time we couldn't get it to start. The Indians regard a car as rather human—either it "wants to go" or it "doesn't want to go." What split us up to start with was the absurdity of the remark which came periodically from T. P. in Stony, "He-goes-by-him-self doesn't want to go." It was awful. Pocaterra, Muhtanga & I were sobbing behind the car like little schoolboys—to laugh out loud would have been bad manners. We made one last inspection & a deep voice from the covered wagon said "I think he wants to go now." He went suddenly, in reverse to a board fence & stopped dead. Tom Powderface started the engine again & the four of us made an inspection of its tail end for possible damage—Pocaterra & I crimson & hiccupping into our handkerchiefs—when suddenly the thing got itself into gear somehow, churned across the yard with Tom Powderface after it & gave one of my nice creosoted gateposts a mark that it will carry to its dying day.

That finished me—I came all adrift after that. After considerable fooling I towed them up to the Banff road & to the top of the Cochrane hill where we gave them a shove & sent them rolling down. The hill is 600' so we know they reached Cochrane—unless the car fell apart altogether—but the last we saw of them was the red tail light winking madly on & off—causes unknown. We were just able to point out this fresh phenomenon to each other & wag our heads feebly.[66]

During this period, Raymond Patterson was just embarking on his lengthy writing career, and perhaps it was his interest in George's stories of early adventures with the Stoneys that encouraged his friend to do some writing too. During the early 1930s, George wrote down a number of the stories and legends he had been told, as well as other tales of the early days. To his great pleasure, two stories related to him by David Bearspaw were published in the *Calgary Herald* in 1932: "The Last Buffalo Hunt, as told by a Stony Chief" and "Lone Warrior Defies Tribe for Revenge".[67]

At first, George may have seen in Patterson a possible investor in his coal mines. As Marigold Patterson said later, George "was looking all the time for somebody with money to develop them. He thought we might fill the bill: we didn't."[68] There is no evidence that Patterson ever invested directly in the properties, but he certainly offered a lot of encouragement for the project. During a mountain trip together in September 1930, George had related the history of his coal claims and eventually had taken Patterson to Porcupine Creek to see for himself. He was worried that Mackay and Dippie were losing heart, with no investors in sight, and told Patterson "he personally was coming to the end of his resources & that holding his coal might mean losing his beloved Buffalo Head if their present deal falls through."[69] Claiming that he was "frankly amazed" at the development potential, Patterson offered to promote the project among friends in Britain, for which George agreed to pay a commission.

Patterson's confidence rekindled George's enthusiasm for the project and soon the pair were hard at work. Patterson wrote details to a friend: "We decided promptly to get out & return with Pocaterra's Indians & two or three men, cut out good trails, build comfortable cabins at Porcupine Creek & Pocaterra Creek so that in case of bad weather the stay of a party of investigating engineers at the mines wd. not be a cold, wet hell in a sodden tepee (psychologically & economically wrong & prejudicial to efficient sales-manship), & open up the seams by digging & tunnelling so that a quick, easy & obvious survey cd. be made."[70]

Because neither George nor Patterson was an expert on coal mining, they relied on the informed opinion of others. "We took in three Scottish miners. One of them—a Glasgow man—cried when he first saw & realized what was there. For the rest of the trip he talked of nothing else until one of the Indians said 'White man give him headache.'" Eventually, they had surveyed a total of 16 thick coal seams, from 5 to nearly 50 feet thick. On this trip George "distinguished himself by killing two mountain sheep with one bullet & caught a trout 3' long (photographed & head preserved) which nearly pulled him into the Kananaskis."[71]

Curiously, considering his deep love of the Kananaskis Valley, George was quite philosophical about the effects mining would have on the mountains southwest of his ranch. "Of course this development will mean the passing our OUR ERA," he wrote to Patterson. "But we can do nothing about stopping it, so … we might as well try to make enough out [of] it to make it possible to go in search of other places, appealing to us. And I'm afraid that with all the people who will be swarming in that country, even the Palliser and the Elk will not long be inviolate. So, I think, the sails are beginning to pull with a new, fresh trade wind … what I have longed for for so long. But still it hurts to remember all the old landmarks, tramped over, yes, just THAT, by unconshionable [sic] people. People who will never again taste the exaltation of seeing such a land as the good Lord made it …"[72]

George and his partners entered into a short-term contract with the "Scottish engineers," who "tried in vain to find someone to develop the coal properties."[73] The price on the mines was 200,000 dollars for the Porcupine Creek property and 15,000 for a six-month option and on the Pocaterra Creek land a total price of 100,000 dollars with a 5,000 dollar six-month option.[74] George and his backers were willing to take two-thirds of the price in shares and the remainder in cash or bonds. The London "mining engineers & financiers" were cautious in a time of "monetary stringency,"[75] and no deals were forthcoming. Arguing against further delays, Patterson suggested he approach his English friend Edwin Fenwick to try to entice

Top: Paul Amos and George at No. 1 post, Porcupine
Creek, 1931. Photo R. M. Patterson Collection

Bottom: George returning to The Buffalo Head from
Porcupine Creek, 1931. This meadow area of the Kananskis
Valley was known to the Stoneys as "Tchan-shé-tinga."
Today, the area is occupied by golf courses and the trail
overlaid by Highway 40. In the distance is Mount Lorette.
Photo R. M. Patterson Collection.

him into considering the development of the coal. With that prospect in mind, the syndicate did not renew the engineers' contract when it expired at the end of January 1931.

Patterson's enthusiasm for the project was evident in his letters to Fenwick:

> If this thing can be proved to them workable in a big way the C.P.R. have shown themselves favourable to the construction of the branch line. It wd. pay them & be in accordance with past policy & govt. demands. Personal pull plays a big part out here & I can get the ear of my Uncle Edward (E. R. Peacock) who has taken Revelstoke's place as head of Barings, is financial adviser to the King & the Prince & is director of the C.P.R. R. B. Bennett [then Canadian prime minister] is a personal friend of his & I have met him & his sister at the Peacock's house in town [London, England]. Bennett is anxious to give all possible support from Ottawa to affairs like this. The slump on the exchange & commodity markets has knocked us all but there is no despondency in Canada ... There is a calm & confident opinion that good times will return to the country as soon as to any in the world.[76]

Pushing hard, Patterson told Fenwick: "These people wish me to point out to you that they are not Americans (there is a certain dislike of Americans & American methods amongst the majority of Canadians), that they have tried steadily to interest British capital & not American & that they will do anything to help you or to meet you half way. If immediate development is impossible, they suggest considering a holding company until conditions (financial) improve. They show their faith in the thing by wishing to take the bulk of their interest in shares."[77]

Over the spring of 1931, letters flew back and forth between Fenwick and Patterson. Fenwick worried about the costs, the markets, the weather and especially the fact that no one else had decided to back the project in 20 years of promotion. Frustrated, Patterson tried to explain the local situation as he (and George) saw it:

> Do me the justice to say that I anticipated that & answered it roughly before you ever made question. I can only ask you to believe what I told you. Things are intensely personal here ... Just read & consider again all that I told you & think of the power a millionaire like Pat Burns has in a young country. He has a comparatively damned poor coal property 45 miles from existing railroads. He has all the chances of the game. He can't sell his coal but he can take thundering good care to poison the chances of a small group of men whose only active & brilliant member is rarely in Calgary. If only I could talk to you for a few minutes ...[78]

Having exhausted all his arguments, Patterson could only say, "My honest opinion of this to you, as my oldest friend, is that it is a very big thing going cheap."[79]

By March 1931 it was clear that Fenwick was not going to invest, and the matter was dropped, although Patterson continued to inform him about George's activities. As the recession had deepened into a depression, politicians had stepped in to try to mitigate the effects of the worsening international financial climate. In 1931, Prime Minister Bennett, a Calgarian, had put a duty on imported American coal and lowered the freight rate of western coal bound for Ontario factories. This had led to American interest in Canadian coal and might have provided investment funds for George and his partners. But, as Patterson explained to Fenwick, "Pocaterra & his partners have hitherto not hunted American capital. There is too much of it already & thinking Canadians don't want to see a thing with the possibilities of Porcupine & Pocaterra Creeks fall into American hands. By means of it they hope to make less work & money for Americans & not more. Pocaterra worse than the rest—his family having a strong tradition of pro-English sentiment owing to English help in the wars of liberation in which they took a prominent part."[80]

With this background in mind, Patterson reported to Fenwick on an amusing incident that occurred in the summer of 1931:

> … owing to coal duties—an American outfit came to Calgary to hunt for a mine. They came out to the Buffalo Head when we were there & the deal was queered in about three hours by Pocaterra who can't abide the noisy, quacking, city type of American. Everything was fine & beautiful until they came to arrange the details of their visit to the mine, when this bird began to orate through his nasty eastern nose about the comforts he desired should be taken for him & how he had never fallen so low as to travel on a half-Percheron mountain horse—why hadn't they a road good enough for him to go in in his Cadillac? Pocaterra rose up & told him that for all he cared he could hire a b— — mountain goat & a length of tow rope & get himself skidded up the Kananaskis trail on his half Percheron backside. He personally was going down to the swimming pool & if the Americans wished to look at the mines he had no doubt that they were exactly where he had left them in January.

Patterson continued, "He was not feeling in the mood for American easterners as he & I & Marigold had ridden, the day before, out of British Columbia & over the backbone of America home to the Buffalo Head in not many hours. We certainly travelled."[81] This long trip was just one of many that Patterson and Pocaterra enjoyed together during this period. Although many of their exploits went unrecorded, Patterson wrote about his irascible friend and some of their adventures in a book called *The Buffalo Head*, which he published in 1961. He dedicated the book to his old friend, "seeing that it was you who made clear for me the intricacies of the diamond hitch & so opened the mountain trails for me."[82]

Their half-dozen years of intense personal friendship created a lifetime of happy memories, occasionally recalled by George during their decades of correspondence: "Yes we had some real fun together on our trips. Remember the time I so carefully covered up our tracks at the turn-off into the Nyahe'-Yannibee [sic] trail, to have dear old Adolf tramp his horse right into the muddiest part of the crossing, where even a blind man would have picked them up on a foggy night! And the sudden bursting into view of the valley and flats, on emerging out of the bush and into the open. The larches had just turned, and the sunlight painted them with gold. Well, I can recall many, many wonderful moments."[83]

Unfortunately, George did not record many of these memories, so it is mainly through Raymond Patterson's books (he later wrote a second book that included their adventures, entitled *Far Pastures*) and through Patterson's correspondence with his friend Edwin Fenwick that tales of the Pocaterra-Patterson exploits survive. In March 1930 Patterson gave Fenwick a particularly vivid account of what was probably a typical expedition:

> Herein enfolded you will find photos of Bronzo's [Patterson's nickname] latest outbreak—a tearing expedition with Pocaterra up the Highwood, over Storm Creek Pass, down Pocaterra Creek, into the Kananaskis country, up onto the British Columbia divide, & back again over different trails & with side expeditions. We travelled like hell for nine days & on six of these we had rain, more or less, with intervals of most gorgeous colour—no words can describe it, but simply in the fall the whole of the hill & mountain country of the West is Light. I expect I have tried to tell you about it each one of the six autumns before this one, & failed every time. We crossed the Highwood Pass going out in a thunderstorm & coming back, on the last day, in a snowstorm. In the course of that day we rode over fifty measured map miles which included climbing up & crossing one mountain range in snow & coming through another— hard trails all the way & two packhorses with us. The Stonies were full of unbelief when Pocaterra told them we had made it from Pocaterra Creek to the Buffalo Head in one day.[84]

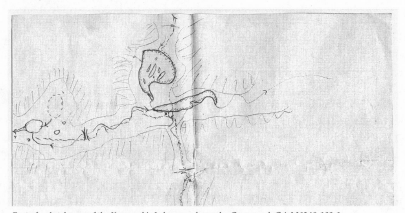

Part of a sketch map of the Kananaskis Lakes area drawn by George. nd. GA M6340-189-1

Upper Kananaskis Lake in 1930 showing Schooner Island. Photo R. M. Patterson Collection

They travelled together again in September of that year, with Adolf accompanying them to Upper Kananaskis Lake. A similar trip was made with Paul Amos in January 1931, "up in the Porcupine Creek mountains," camping "below the Tchan-shé-tinda by the Kananaskis."[85]

George had often done a little prospecting with the Stoneys during their rambles together in the foothills and mountains. An early, undated photograph shows him panning for gold in a tributary of Joffre Creek, itself a tributary of the Palliser River. In 1931 he became involved in an actual gold rush. Ever since its supposed discovery in the 1880s, prospectors had hunted in vain for the Lost Lemon Gold Mine, reputedly located somewhere between the Crowsnest Pass and the headwaters of the Oldman River. According to legend, Stoney chief Jacob Bearspaw had known of the location but had cursed the spot and sworn his band to secrecy because of the violent circumstances surrounding the discovery of the gold. But 50 years later, one of the most persistent treasure seekers was Jacob's grandson, King Bearspaw, who had grown up learning the legends and was determined to make his fortune.

In October 1930, while prospecting in an area 40 miles west of Nanton around North and South Twin creeks, the Livingstone River and Dry Creek, King found a piece of quartz near the summit of Flattop (Plateau) Mountain that seemed to indicate a rich vein of ore nearby. Further investigations yielded nothing, so he moved on. However, his activities had been monitored for some time by fellow prospectors Jack Hagerman and Billy Windiate, of High River, and when Bearspaw showed them his "gold" sample in mid-December, Windiate staked a claim in the Twin Creeks area. News of the claim leaked out, and by early February a number of other claims had been staked in the area. When the Calgary *Albertan* got wind of the activity in mid-February, it created a frenzy by reminding readers of the old legend with its headline, "May Be Lost El Dorado." The rush was on, and within days, hopefuls by the hundreds were heading to the Twin Creeks "goldfields," many totally unprepared to survive winter conditions.

The *Calgary Herald* decided to send reporter Fred Kennedy to cover the stampede, and George was contacted to guide the party into the area. Several days later, Kennedy set out from the Buffalo Head with George and King Bearspaw, who had been hired to assist with packing and making camp. They rode over Sentinel Pass to the head of the Livingstone River, where they joined an estimated 400 prospectors who had converged on the area and were camped at the instantly created and soon-to-be abandoned "Twin City." Privy to King's version of events, George was skeptical about the likelihood of finding gold, but he fulfilled his contract with the *Herald* and Kennedy got his story, which proved instrumental in helping to cool the rush. Thirty years later, George reminisced: "King and I climbed the short way, no more than a quarter of a mile, to the location of the supposed gold-bearing seam, and I broke off about twenty pounds of samples with my prospector's hammer. Those samples were the ones that THE HERALD, later on, had analyzed and had found to be worthless." When nothing of value had been found after 10 days, the rush of '31 ended as suddenly as it had begun.[86]

Later that spring, on the last day of March, George and Raymond Patterson took a float down a relatively easy stretch of the Bow River and managed to turn it into an adventure:

Yesterday Pocaterra & I ran down the Bow from the mouth of the Ghost to Bearspaw in my canoe. We had lunch on an island & landed at Peter Dewhurst's for tea. It was a lovely warm spring day—perfect—& the views every now & then back up the blue-green, tossing river to the mountains was wonderful. It was exciting—in places the canoe bucked like a horse & once I let it graze a big rock that the spray & white water hit till we were close onto it. We swung as we hit & the undertow almost laid us broadside to the waves which rose high above the canoe. It was one of my narrowest escapes from the spill that I have never yet had, even on the Nahanni. I can't swim, but anyhow in that place swimming wd. not have been of much avail—I always trust the canoe to get me out of a mess. A scared Border Terrier sat anxiously in the canoe nose.[87]

In 1930 Patterson had written to Fenwick:

There is a country, not far from here, called Nyahé-a-nibi—The Up in the Mountains Country—harder to reach in a sense than the South Nahanni. That was a matter of distance & time & care—this is barred on the Alberta side by passes which may be 15 ft. deep in snow in early July, & from B.C. by drowning rivers, in flood at that season, such as the Palliser & the Kootenay. It is very very near but is still an untrodden country, & we hope to joust with it a little next year—ourselves & two Indians … if nothing else, it would add one further memory of a pleasantly barbarous physical effort in country as God made it. Tea with the spruce needles in it & porridge & bacon with a touch of wood smoke over them, I find, still beat the home production.[88]

Of course, it was only Patterson who ate porridge on these trips together. George would turn his head away "with a gesture of disgust," telling Patterson "you know I loathe the beastly stuff," and instead make himself bacon and eggs.[89]

They did take that trip the next year, in September of 1931, and both wrote about the experience—Patterson in a letter to Fenwick and later in *The Buffalo Head*, and George for publication in Italy. In his usual breezy style, Patterson described the camaraderie of the adventurers to Fenwick: "Pocaterra, his henchman Adolf Baumgart from the Masurian Lakes, & I, recently made a successful raid into British Columbia. The three of us were a riding commentary on the silly idiocy of the late war. Pocaterra's lands in the Val d' Astico were fought over. The Russians went backwards & forwards over Adolf's farm near Tannenburg, & I did time in Schweidnitz. And we were so dammed happy together."[90]

The plan had been to "pass unnoticed into British Columbia via an abandoned Indian trail through Elk Pass known only to Pocaterra because of his association with the old Stoneys." However, plans went awry in Highwood Pass, where they met a recently appointed forest ranger, an Australian named McKenzie who clearly did not recognize George. Annoyed that they would be forced to take the long way around on the main trail by way of the ranger station, George bristled when McKenzie asked without preamble, "Are you the guide of this party?" Seething, "Pocaterra stared at him with all the anger of an old-timer who is questioned by a newcomer. 'Guide?' he said. 'I don't know about that, but I am George Pocaterra. Those are my coal claims down there—that ridge between the two mountains—and this creek was named after me by the survey. And this is a private party.'" When the ranger insisted on accompanying them, George, "in a gust of fury, leapt on his horse and set off at a lope across the open meadows of the pass," never letting up on his furious pace until they left McKenzie behind at the ranger station. Only then did the tension ease and the threesome settle down to enjoy their trip together.[91]

"We travelled westwards by Stoney trails over six mountain ranges far into the Kootenays & then came into this jewel of a valley," continued Patterson to Fenwick:

I give you its Stoney name. It was wonderful—like living in a zoo. There was a certain goat hunt—I'll tell you about it & other things later. These photos are, as far as I know, originals. Pocaterra wished to name one of the lakes we found after Marigold—he said in memory of much hospitality. We found silver. The best catch of trout was—one man— 5 minutes—20 lbs. of fish, cleaned weight & minus the heads. The worst—Pocaterra & I one too sunny afternoon—7 fish—14 lbs cleaned weight. We always fished with rifles slung ready—grizzly, lots. What a country![92]

George's account of the same expedition was published in the Milan Section newsletter of the Club Alpino Italiano in March 1932. Of necessity more formal than Patterson's accounts, it is interesting because it is one of few descriptions by George himself of an expedition. Although it has been translated from the original Italian, it still reveals George's poetic turn of phrase.

In the Rocky Mountains of British Columbia

At the end of September, 1931 with Mr. Raymond Murray Patterson, an English friend who for years was involved exploring the Canadian Subarctic and with Adolf, my cowboy friend, I set off to explore a series of beautiful valleys, surrounded by high mountains that are part of the Rockies.

I had visited that area, for a short time, with two Indian hunters, twenty years before, in 1908, when the maps still left all that area blank.

After the Great War the Canadian authorities attached the names of important Allied captains and generals to various alpine massifs of the Rocky Mountains, situated partly in the province of Alberta and partly in British Columbia.

Many of these mountains had never been visited before, but their approximate position had been calculated with photographs taken by specialized equipment from aeroplanes in the service of the Topographical Survey of Canada.

In this aforementioned area I found the Cadorna River, which springs from a lake of the same name and whose source in turn lies at the foot of a glacier filling that area between three peaks who together bear the name of a count and Italian general.

A large torrent, a tributary of the Cadorna River, emanates from a mountain called Abruzzi, a huge mountainous "massif" rising 10,700 feet above sea level.

The man after whom this mountain was named was of illustrious heritage and this provided a great incentive in deciding to make this journey.

"The country in the heart of the mountains," Nyahe'-ya-nibi [sic] it is called by the Stony Indians, a mountainous tribe of the Sioux race; and is certainly a name that well describes that place.

After a week of hard travel on horseback we arrived at that place where the Indian path, after many years of disuse and nearly invisible, opens from the dark forest into the broad, open valley of the Cadorna River.

The grassy plain itself extends several kilometres and is one and a half kilometres wide for several hundred metres; it is surrounded, in turn, by dense woods of spruce, pine and larch, then by magnificent dolomite limestone rock mountains; which, in fact, remind me nostalgically of my native Venetian Dolomites.

We passed about two weeks encamped in the area of the point of land captured in the photograph.

Each day we conducted explorative excursions in quite a few of the valleys that flow into the plain of the main river.

On one excursion we ascended the Abruzzi watercourse all the way to its source, and further on to its highest and most dangerous pass that drops off to westerly slopes where another torrent and river form, through an absolutely uninhabited pass, draining towards the great Kootenay River.

Each day we saw herds of wild Rocky Mountain goats ("Oreamnos Montanus"), with long snow-white hair, and with small black horns, pointed, in contrast to the recurve of the mountain sheep.

We saw frequent tracks and signs of grizzly bears, black bears, moose, elk and Bighorn sheep.

In rivers, torrents and lakes, we fished for magnificent trout, while the woods were thick with "spruce grouse" — a dark coloured species with a red semi-circle over the eye. A vast rocky amphitheater at the foot of Mount Abruzzi is occupied by a glacier and a vast moraine.

From the source a little torrent pours down a low slope forming Lake Marigold,[93] named thus in honour of my friend Patterson's wife. It is a little more than a kilometre long and surrounded by high woods of magnificent spruce, and further down, after a continuous succession of rapids and waterfalls, the stream joins the waters of the Abruzzi torrent.

To get to Cadorna Lake, we had to go back to the river, then head north on horseback for several hours, first through grassy plains, and then through dense woods that were almost impenetrable.

The route was at times very difficult due to an entanglement of trees that had been knocked down by the terrible winter storms, that rage in this nordic climate.

The lake is in a harsh place, almost gloomy, surrounded like everything else by high rocky mountains that overhang the area and deny it much of the warmth and radiance of the sun. To the North, a steep grassy slope was punctuated by the white spots of wild goats, among which one can distinguish the more agile she-goats.

A mountain to the west of the central plain with a characteristic form of the prow of a ship of war has been therefore named "The Warship."

We would have prolonged our stay but our schedule for departure was informed by the danger that is always imminent in that season of a heavy snowfall that could block the alpine passes that separated us from my house at the Buffalo Head Ranch, so we decided to return.

We left the Cadorna Valley with real regret, with a firm resolution to return for a longer visit in 1932.

January, 1932

Giorgio Pocaterra[94]

"Giants above Cadorna Lake," Nyahé-a-nibi, 1931. Photo R. M. Patterson Collection.

Sadly, the friends did not return to Nyahé-a-nibi in 1932 as planned. After a quick winter camping trip to the Kananaskis (visiting Fossil Falls), George fell ill with appendicitis that spring and then spent much of the summer fighting to keep the Buffalo Head. Owing to the downturn in the tourist business with the onset of the Depression, he had been unable to repay the de Palezieux and apparently also owed money to the Kucks. By the spring of 1932, they were tired of waiting for payment.

Years later, George recalled six months of turmoil:

One bright afternoon in early May 1932 I was picked up by a good friend of mine on 6th Avenue in Calgary and rushed to the hospital, where I was at once operated for appendicitis. I came out of it right side up, and within nine days I walked out of the hospital alone. And that hospital business gave me back my Faith in human nature. EVERYBODY was kindness personified to me, most everybody who had ever known me, the papers published every day bulletins about my progress, and my room was so full of flowers that they overflowed into the adjacent rooms, besides dozens of books and stack of letters. And all day was a procession of visits. By Jove! That did me a lot of good. While I was in the hospital, incapacitated, other persons took advantage of that fact to bring the matter of a mortgage on the place I had had to take upon myself, to the courts, so when I finally woke up enough, I found that I had until September 30th to GET OUT! After all those years of work! Don't forget that those were the worst years of the depression, when nobody could get any money, least of all a person in admittedly straightened circumstances. I could perhaps have got what was necessary from my Father, but he was then 82 years old, and to let him know that his son after almost thirty years of work was on the point of losing everything might have brought on a very serious relapse, so I at once had to exclude that. To make a long story short at six o'clock p.m. on September 30th, 1932, I walked into a certain lawyer's office with a certified check in my hands for the amount due. I accomplished that by taking a partner in with me, who, of course got the lion's share out of it. But better that way. Of two evils always the lesser one.[95]

George's new partner was Raymond Patterson. The Pattersons, having grown tired of sheep ranching, had fallen in love with the Highwood during their many visits over the preceding years and were contemplating a move to the area. Familiar with George's financial difficulties, Patterson had even discussed the possibility of taking over the Buffalo Head during their epic trip to Nyah-a-nibi in the fall of 1931.[96] With the loss of his ranch imminent, George was relieved when Patterson assumed the de Palezieux mortgage (for a discounted price of 500 dollars, because the original goods had depreciated over five years) and also his debts to the Kucks and others.

The partnership was of short duration. As George recalled, "In March 1933 my Father passed suddenly away. That is suddenly for me, as I only knew of his illness when all hope was lost, being informed by one cable gram first of his precarious health and two day later, by another, of his passing. I tried hard to settle somehow satisfactorily my affairs on the ranch, and finally I came to the conclusion that the best way was to sell my remaining share to my partner."[97]

After one last summer adventuring in the mountains, including a trip to the Elk River with Frazier Hunt, George finalized the sale of his ranch.

Frazier Hunt and George, Elk River trip, 1933.
GA PD-184-3-148

In an agreement dated October 14, 1933, Raymond Patterson paid George Pocaterra 700 dollars in cash (roughly ten thousand dollars today) and gave him clear title to his Ghost River property northwest of Cochrane in exchange for clear title to the Buffalo Head Ranch. The sale included all of George's cattle (only 17 by then), along with the XN cattle brand, and 20 horses. George kept back a dozen horses, their harness and tack and his famous buffalo head-shaped horse brand, which he allowed Patterson to use for 18 months but never sold to him. The Pattersons already owned everything on the ranch connected with the tourist business and intended to revive that business at some point, but George kept everything else, including personal furnishings and "all pictures, trophies, Indian curios, books," etcetera.

Both parties were satisfied. The Pattersons now had their ranch in the Highwood, albeit one in rather poor condition from years of financial neglect and indifferent bachelor housekeeping. Marigold Patterson later recalled the dilapidated state of the ranch outbuildings, the grease-spattered walls of the kitchen and the number of horses inherited from tender-hearted George that were "just pensioners," too old to be of any use.[98] The couple also inherited Adolf Baumgart and with his help as foreman were able to run a successful cattle operation on the Buffalo Head for the next decade.

For his part, George was finally free of debt and had cash to spare for the first time in years. An optimistic, forward-thinking person, he never expressed any regret in selling out to Patterson. In fact, he felt it was the right time to leave, before the Highwood changed forever. He had never achieved financial success with his ranching or coal-mining ventures, but he was satisfied, As he told Raymond Patterson years later, "You and I, let us remember, and hold on tight to all the wonderful memories of places and happenings we were blessed to know, since we came to this virgin land. Few have been, of the first comers, who have gone out into the blue, and tasted the Spirit of this land, when it still was as the good Lord had created. I am humbly grateful for the experience I was granted by the Gods, it has left a deep, deep, mark, it has coloured all my life, and will always be with my innermost self."[99]

After selling the ranch, George's immediate plan was to return to Italy to visit his family and settle his father's estate, but his long-term plans were less certain. As he later explained, one of the deciding factors in selling to Patterson had been "so as to feel free to go anywheres [sic]. Perhaps the South Seas ... I ha[d] never given up on that, just as I never give up any dream. They are only here to be realized. Never the lost endeavour, never the lowered banner."[100] The Pattersons agreed to pasture his horses and store his furniture for a year, until his plans were more settled. Then, in December 1933, George left the foothills to embark on what he called "MY GREAT ADVENTURE."

Chapter 3

Norma: Life at Home
1898–1926

Writing to her father in 1938, Norma Piper Pocaterra grew sentimental. She had been away from him for four and a half years, living in Italy and trying every way she knew to fulfill their joint dream of her becoming an international opera star, "the Melba of Canada." Away from home, she had discovered an excitingly different life, found first love and experienced the thrill of pleasing onstage. But she also missed her home and sometimes yearned for a simpler time, and so she took comfort in sharing reminiscences with her father, her link with childhood, with who she was and what she had become. She wrote to him fondly, "Life has been very sweet and full of sweet memories. I love to look back."[1]

Norma Mill Piper was born on October 29, 1898, in Leamington, Ontario, the first child and only surviving daughter of William and Maud Piper. Her Piper grandparents had emigrated from Devonshire, England, travelling on the same ship with their separate families and arriving in Canada West (now Ontario) in 1843.[2] William Piper was 23; Ann Mill was 18. For both the Piper and Mill families, who seem to have known each other in England, the final destination was Port Stanley in Elgin County. Soon after they arrived, William and Ann married, living at first in nearby Southwold Township and later moving to Westminster Township in Middlesex County. They settled southwest of London, Ontario, on a farm near Lambeth, and William became a successful farmer and stockman. The marriage produced five boys and three girls: the youngest child was Norma's father, William Abraham Piper, born on October 30, 1863.

After graduating from London Collegiate Institute, William A. "Will" Piper headed to Toronto to become a dentist. In 1887 he received a licence to practise dental surgery from the Royal College of Dental Surgeons of Ontario. In 1891, a few years after the college affiliated with the University of Toronto, he was granted the degree doctor of dental surgery and headed back to southwestern Ontario to open a dental practice in Leamington. There he met Maud Gertrude Johnson. Fourteen years his junior, Maud was the daughter of John Enoch Johnson and Melinda Scratch, of nearby Kingsville,

Ontario. Johnson was a well-respected local citizen, a major in the 21st Fusilliers, a magistrate and the mayor of Leamington. He owned and edited the *Leamington Post* and, after Will and Maud married in 1897, he encouraged his son-in-law to do a little reporting and to contribute occasional articles. Two children were born to the Pipers during the busy Leamington years: Norma in 1898 and Henry "Harry" Johnson Piper in 1900.

After a decade of successful practice in Leamington, Dr. Piper decided that a bigger centre would provide more scope for his ambitions. In 1901 he moved the family to London, Ontario, into a spacious home just a few streets away from the busy city centre. The big, rambling house had huge rooms and 12 foot-high ceilings and was located on a corner lot across from the armory. It accommodated both Dr. Piper's dental practice and his growing family: dental patients entered the office off Waterloo Street; family visitors entered off Dundas Street. Advertising himself as a specialist in "gold and porcelain work,"[3] Dr. Piper found his London practice very successful and lucrative. As a respected professional, he played an important role in the community and further built his network and reputation through active involvement in the Freemasons. (He had held several high

Dr. William Piper, Calgary, ca 1926. Studio portrait by W. S. Park. GA PA-2393-9-4

Masonic offices in Leamington and became a 32nd degree Mason during his London years.) During this period, he also served for several years on the board of examiners for the Dental School at the University of Toronto.

While Will was establishing himself in the community, Maud was busy on the home front. Four more children were born to the couple after their move to London: Richard Lloyd in 1901, Edith Maud in 1903, Lawrence Stafford in 1904 and William John "Piper, William John (Jack)" in 1906. Sadly, Edith died at birth and little Harry the same year at age three. Norma grew up to resemble her mother both in appearance and temperament. Maud was a "sweet, lovable, even tempered" woman, "as true as steel," known for her common sense and her "unassuming and gracious" manner, and was well liked in London by a large circle of friends and acquaintances.[4] Her death just before Christmas in 1908 was a crushing blow to Will, who had lost his mother the previous spring and his father only three years before.

Distraught and overwhelmed with the task of raising four young children, he decided to break up the family. His older sister, Susan Davey, childless and two years a widow, came to keep house for him and became a substitute mother for 10-year-old and little Jack, who was just two. Lawrence went to stay with his maternal grandparents in Leamington, and Richard was taken

Top: The William A. Piper family in front of their home at 421 Waterloo St.,
London, Ontario, 1907. L-R, seated at back: Maud, William, William's mother,
Ann Mill Piper, Susan Davey holding Jack.
Seated in front: Lawrence, Norma, Dick.
GA PA-2393-9-2

Bottom: Dr. William Piper in his Model T Ford, Drumheller, Alberta, ca 1914-16.
GA PA-2393-9-3

in by Will's childless brother, Richard Mill Piper, and his wife, Miriam (Aunt Min), who had inherited the old Piper family farm near Lambeth.

Heartbroken and restless, Dr. Piper went in search of a new life away from London. He travelled first to Chicago, where he took several postgraduate courses at the Chicago College of Dental Surgery. Probably he was attracted to the college by the reputation of the long-time dean, fellow Ontarian and Royal College alumnus Dr. Charles Nelson Johnson. It is possible that Dr. Piper was related to the dean by marriage. In any case, he probably knew him personally before heading to Chicago, as Dr. Johnson was a well-known figure in dental circles, editor of the *Dental Review* since 1902 and a popular speaker at dental meetings and conventions.[5]

The two dentists remained lifelong friends, but Dr. Piper grew interested in tales of western Canada and soon moved on to Vancouver, where he stayed only briefly. In about 1911 he connected with J. F. "Frank" Moodie, an acquaintance from Ontario who had discovered Calgary some half-dozen years before and was excited by its frenzied growth and economic potential. Variously described as a mining operator or oil broker (or both), "JF" spent the next two decades in Calgary developing, managing and promoting various businesses including Big Bend Mica Mines Limited, Rosedale Coal and Clay Products Company Limited and Turner Valley–based Sentinel Oils Limited. His boundless optimism and get-rich-quick attitude, which were typical of the booster mentality that infected Calgary during the boom period prior to the First World War, excited gullible and greedy listeners during his frequent promotional trips to eastern Canada.[6]

Eager to believe there was a fortune to be made in the West, Dr. Piper headed to Calgary and handed over 1,000 dollars for the charismatic Moodie to invest in Big Bend Mica Mines. After several weeks of living with JF and waiting in vain for a quick return on his investment, he finally came to realize "JF is alright as a friend but not as a business associate."[7] However, he was hopeful that given more time a fortune might still be his. In the meantime he needed to earn some money, so he bought a used dental engine, a case of dental instruments and an old Ford car and started life as an itinerant dentist, serving small towns in the Calgary hinterland by practising dentistry a few days in each town in turn. His fraternal interests led him to seek out fellow Masons and attend local meetings wherever he went, and these connections quickly helped him to build a network of clients and friends. Dr. Piper's roving practice eventually included such places as Acme, Three Hills, Carbon, Strathmore and Drumheller.

Although his sister Susie teased him, saying that he spent half his life on the train travelling east or west, Dr. Piper usually managed only one annual visit to his family back in Ontario. He was smitten with the West and had no desire to resume his London practice; he always returned to Alberta after an all-too-brief visit of several weeks. This left his children to grow up without him, although he stayed in touch through letters. That his family stayed close to him and to each other was mainly through the efforts of Aunt Susie, who made sure Norma and Jack had frequent visits with their brothers and their many other relatives in the London area. As a result, Norma was always very affectionate with her brothers and throughout her life referred to them by their childhood nicknames: as well as John being "Jack," Richard was "Piper, Richard Lloyd (Dick)" or "Kardo" and Lawrence was "Larry" or "Tass." Norma was often called "Sister" or "Sis" by her brothers and even by her father.

After a lifetime of farming, Aunt Susie was happy to live in a city and the children under her care in London shared her pleasure. Norma and Jack attended nearby Princess Avenue Public School, liked watching concerts at the armory across the street and enjoyed living close to the bustling downtown core. To help stretch the money her brother Will sent home, Aunt Susie took in "paying guests" (the Macdonalds, from 1913 to 1917). In 1910, Dr. Piper joined them for a particularly happy family holiday at their Johnson grandparents' shooting lodge on an island in Oxtongue Lake, north of Huntsville. The family stayed for two months, and Norma, then aged 12, loved everything about the experience: bouncing over corduroy roads in a lumber wagon, sleeping on spruce bough beds, trawling for fish and eating venison. For many years, the family displayed a picture of the cabin that she drew on a piece of fungus.

Top: Norma and Jack Piper and unknown child feeding ducks and chickens, possibly at the Piper family farm, Lambeth, Ontario, ca 1914. GA PA-2393-9-2-3

Bottom: Susan Davey, Dr. William Piper and Norma, Calgary, ca mid 1920s. GA NA-4390-445

Norma remembered her childhood as very happy, though later regretted her disinterest in piano lessons; she preferred roller skating and reading to practicing piano and stopped her lessons when she went to high school. Described by a friend of the family as "very sweet and very pretty, as well as being clever at school,"[8] Norma was very close to Aunt Susie, and the two were considered inseparable. Norma also developed a close relationship with their neighbours, Dr. and Mrs. Nelson George. Dr. George rented office space from Dr. Piper, boarded with the family before his marriage and afterwards lived next door. Norma enjoyed answering telephones at the doctor's office after school if he was out on calls. Occasionally, Dr. George took her with him on those visits and often he helped her with her worst school subjects, arithmetic and algebra.

In her midteens Norma joined a girls' group formed by Mrs. D. C. MacGregor, wife of the family's Presbyterian Church minister. Mary Esther MacGregor (known to her readers as "Marian Keith") was a popular local author who enjoyed a long career writing mainly sentimental fiction with social and religious overtones.[9] In 1917 Norma served as president of this group, which was known as the Marian Keith Club of St. Andrew's Church. In that capacity, she spoke to a "vast" audience on the work of the club as part of a big rally of organized girls' clubs held in London, Ontario, that year. She loved school, and at the London Collegiate Institute she discovered a facility for languages. When she graduated in 1917, she was class valedictorian, earned two medals for general proficiency and received firsts in French and German. However, her graduation coincided with Dr. Piper's decision to reunite the family, which effectively short-circuited any plans she may have had at that time for further education.

When Dr. Piper left his children with family members after Maud's death, he had no idea that it would be so many years before they were reunited. He started offering rural dentistry in Alberta in 1911 and in 1912 started a part-time practice in Calgary as well. For the first few years he shared a Calgary office with fellow dentist Dr. Frank E. Sandercock, first in

The Piper family residence, 227 Scarboro Ave. S.W., Calgary, 1919. GA NA-695-73

the Bruner Block and then in the Royal Bank Chambers. For several years the two men also shared an office in Didsbury, and Dr. Piper maintained an office in Strathmore as well. But it was his Drumheller practice that really flourished and gave him a firm foothold in Alberta. In 1917 he transferred his practice wholly to Calgary and established himself in the Herald

Building downtown. Many of his rural patients continued to write to him for advice and visited him in the city for occasional dental work. By 1918 he felt his Calgary practice was solid enough for him to purchase a substantial home in a newly developed area known as Sunalta, on Calgary's west side. That year, he brought his children back together and moved them, along with Aunt Susie, to 227 Scarboro Avenue.

The house, built in 1914 for Dr. Murdoch W. Macaulay, was a large, red-brick two-storey. At first Norma and Aunt Susieie found it very small in comparison with their London home ("so tiny that there was no room to turn around"), but soon they came to love its cozy atmosphere and large veranda.[10] Later, Norma also fondly remembered "the rich dark colour of the wood and the rugs," and the statues placed on the newel posts by Aunt Susie.[11] When real estate was booming in 1928, Dr. Piper had a chance to sell the house and move them to a small bungalow, but by then the women had grown so fond of the house that they would not hear of the plan, no matter what the profit.

The Pipers' part of Sunalta, now known as Scarboro, had been established in 1912, but was slow to develop and still had a very spacious feel to it when the Pipers arrived in 1918. In fact, for some time they had an unobstructed view across fields to Sunalta School several blocks away, and it was 17 years before a house was built on the vacant lot next door. After downtown London, Sunalta felt like country living and Dr. Piper found he could keep a horse, which he did for a short period in the early 1920s. Norma had finished school, but the boys, who were aged 17, 15 and 12 when they moved, all settled into South Calgary High School. Frank Moodie and his family lived across the street, and many other near neighbours became lifelong friends, in particular the Eneas McCormicks, the Sam Nickles, the George M. Browers and the T. Morton Carlyles.

When he moved the family to Calgary in 1918, Dr. Piper was one of only three dozen dentists in a city of about 60,000 people. As a professional man, he was virtually guaranteed a comfortable income and solid social position, which was aided and enhanced by some of his early friendships. He was active and social and enjoyed memberships in the Alberta Dental Association and the Calgary and District Dental Society. His leadership of the latter group—he was one of the founding members in 1913—earned him the epitaph "pioneer in his profession in Calgary" in his obituary a quarter of a century later.[12] Continuing his involvement with the Masons, in Calgary he was active in the Scottish Rite and became the first Most Wise Sovereign of the Rose Croix Chapter.

Dr. Piper's arrival in Calgary during a boom period was fortuitous; like himself, many businessmen and professionals were flooding into the city, eager to develop new connections and networks. He made many locally influential friends and one of the most powerful was Richard Bedford Bennett, Calgary lawyer, a former member of the Legislative Assembly of Alberta, by 1918 a former member of Parliament but a future prime minister of Canada. In Calgary's small society of the time, it is not surprising that two "bachelor" professional men should meet and socialize, but the two also had a number of other interests in common, including their Methodist faith and their membership in the Masons. Their mutual regard seems to have been sincere and enduring, with R. B. Bennett often expressing admiration for Dr. Piper and his family and Dr. Piper occasionally drawing on that interest for assistance in times of trouble. Through R. B. Bennett, Dr. Piper also met Leonard Brockington, a lawyer in Bennett's firm who became city solicitor in 1922, played an important role in the development of Calgary musical life and was appointed chairman of the board of governors of the newly established Canadian Broadcasting Corporation in 1936.

Rather shy and not given to easy friendships with other young people, Norma limited her socializing mostly to friends of the family and to neighbours. She loved the quiet domesticity of life in Sunalta and later remembered Calgary as "a very nice little town then, with streetcars down the main streets and a lovely class of people that we were fortunate to be associated with."[13] The Sunalta line of the streetcar stopped only a few blocks away, so transportation was easy and Norma and her aunt delighted in their weekly shopping excursions downtown. Aunt Susie was a simple, generous soul who was a little unconventional and loved to have fun. Her philosophy was "Laughing keeps you young."[14] She loved to cook, made Christmas a special time and especially enjoyed family outings in the car. On these trips, they usually headed to Turner Valley or to Banff to visit friends, but one memorable summer they made a longer expedition to visit a relative, Aunt Josie, who had a farm at Islay (just west of Lloydminster). Aunt Susie prepared sumptuous picnics for these outings and over the years treated the family to many thousands of dollars of extras in holidays, clothing and treats.

The 1920s (and her own 20s) passed uneventfully for Norma, who was content to stay at home and help with the housework in spite of Aunt Susie's encouragement to take a stenography course or go for teacher training. Later Norma questioned the wisdom of her decision, wondering if "so much church going as a child with the Macdonalds" had made her feel she should sacrifice her own happiness to that of others.[15] But at the time, she was happy to help out at home, and the family applauded the self-sacrifice that eased the budget and allowed Dr. Piper to concentrate on educating the boys. A product of his time, he was not concerned about Norma's lack of further education; he simply assumed that eventually she would marry and her husband would take care of

Norma on the back steps of the family home, Calgary, ca 1922-23. GA NA-695-95

her. On the other hand, he felt it was very important that the boys be given a good start in life, and he told his sister-in-law, "My pleasure in life is in endeavoring to guide them in the right way and to aid them in attaining a successful career."[16] Although his dental practice gave him a comfortable income, his mineral and oil stock investments often fluctuated in value, which dictated sacrifices at home in order to meet the cost of raising the boys and giving them the advantages he felt were essential.

Top: Lawrence Piper, Edmonton, 1925. Studio portrait by McDermid Studios. GA PA-2393-11-2

Centre: Dick Piper, Calgary, ca 1926. Studio portrait by W. S. Park. GA PA-2393-9-1

Bottom: Jack Piper, Calgary, 1926. Studio portrait by W. S. Park. GA PA-2393-11-1

Aunt Susie and Norma contributed greatly to the success of this scheme at a time when most women from the comfortable professional class would have enjoyed a busy social life and employed domestic servants to manage things at home. Aunt Susie was assisted by a woman who came in twice weekly to help with the heaviest housework, but she and Norma handled the rest and all the cooking themselves. Dr. Piper worked evenings and Sundays to boost his income, and that, along with Aunt Susie's economizing, meant there was extra money available for the boys to buy new suits for dances and to participate in sports. Lawrence played on the south Calgary rugby team and later at the University of Alberta, and one of Jack's fond memories was of the homemade football helmets created for Lawrence and himself by Norma and Aunt Susie. Recalling those years, Jack remembered with gratitude that Dr. Piper had given his boys "every opportunity to make something of themselves."[17] And in return Dr. Piper was proud of his sons, glad to say in 1928 that unlike "the majority of young men," his boys were not "Jazz Hounds and Imbibers."[18]

In 1920 Richard headed to the University of Toronto for a year and then to Montreal to attend McGill University, where he obtained an engineering degree with a specialty in mining and metallurgy. In 1922 Lawrence and Jack both attended Calgary Normal School for teacher training. The next year, Lawrence headed to the University of Alberta to pursue a chemical engineering degree, but Jack taught for several years in the communities of Acme and Standard, where Dr. Piper had connections from his itinerant dentistry days. In 1926 Jack followed Richard to McGill for a commerce degree. Although he had all three sons in university for a short period in the late 1920s, Dr. Piper's financial burden probably was eased by small legacies left to all four of his children when his brother Richard Piper died in 1926. In any case, his careful financing held out until two of the boys were established in jobs. In 1928 Lawrence started with Consolidated Smelters in Trail, British Columbia, and the same year Jack left McGill to take a position with Montreal bond traders Drury and Company.

But Dr. Piper ran into financial difficulties before his son Richard was able to finish his interrupted degree. As was the case for so many people, the stock market problems of 1929 greatly affected Dr. Piper's financial position, although he was philosophical and determined to hold on until stock prices improved again. He told his sons that year, "I am not surprised as I knew that history would repeat itself. I have seen four pronounced depressions . . . two of which were real panics."[19] Fortunately for Richard, when his father revealed that he could no longer afford the university fees, Aunt Min, who still felt like a second mother to "the lad," generously sent money to cover his final year. Although both Jack and Lawrence felt the effects of the Depression (each experienced pay cuts), they managed to keep their jobs in the 1930s. Richard, on the other hand, unluckily graduated in the spring of 1931 during the worst years of the Depression and did not find suitable work in his field until the economy finally improved with the start of the Second World War.

The Pipers all enjoyed music and made every effort to attend the many musical events that occurred in the city. In addition to internationally famous musicians and touring groups like the British D'Oyly Carte and American San Carlo opera companies, which included Calgary in their regular tours of western Canada, the Calgary Women's Musical Club hosted monthly recitals at the Palliser Hotel that featured talented local and visiting artists.[20] The family also enjoyed the superior musical and dramatic entertainment provided by the touring Dominion (later Canadian) chautauquas, which were based in Calgary. Two of the Piper brothers were employed as tent boys on the chautauqua's Haultain School grounds for several summers during the 1920s.

Family music making was a common pastime in many households in the days before other forms of home entertainment, and having a piano was considered a sign both of refinement and relative affluence.[21] When the Piper children were young, they were all given piano lessons, but as they grew older Dr. Piper encouraged them to learn other musical instruments. These accomplishments led to many hours of happy family entertainment, and one of Norma's fondest memories was of one Christmas when Jack came home from Acme and Lawrence from university in Edmonton, and they spent the entire Christmas Day singing and playing their instruments. Apparently, one of their favourite melodies was the lovely Hawaiian song of farewell, "Aloha Oe."

Always enterprising, Dr. Piper soon saw the potential provided by his talented family. Sometime in the early 1920s they formed a little band known as the Piper Orchestra. Norma played the piano, Dr. Piper the cornet, Lawrence the saxophone, Jack the saxophone and clarinet, and

The Piper family orchestra, Calgary, September 15, 1926. L-R: Jack, Dr. William Piper, unknown (possibly George Bell), Aunt Susie, Norma, Lawrence. GA PA-2393-9-2-2

unconventional Aunt Susie played the drums (by this time, Dick had gone to Montreal). In 1925, when Dr. Piper was elected president of a group of transplanted western Ontarians known as the London-Middlesex Old Boys and Girls Association, he suggested that the Piper Orchestra could play for the popular association's "At Home" dances. These dances attracted as many as 300 former Londoners, and the little band, enlarged with a few additional members now that Lawrence had gone away to university, became known as the "club's own orchestra."[22] Although Norma's piano playing was rather indifferent, everyone agreed that she sang beautifully and might have talent worth cultivating. So it was no surprise that when a retired opera singer made Calgary his home, Dr. Piper was more than happy to indulge his daughter with lessons.

Chapter 4

Norma: Calgary Songbird
1926–1934

Rudolphe Brandli de Bevec's arrival in Calgary in 1926 was entirely bychance, but it changed Norma's life. Born into an aristocratic Swiss family,Brandli had studied opera in Italy under Carlo Carignani and had a modest European career behind him when he and his wife (also an opera singer) decided to try the New World. He later told Norma that he had a cousin in New York who was a journalist or music critic, and his original intention had been to immigrate to the United States. However, he had been born in Turkey while his father was Swiss consul there, and the Americans would not let him into the country. The couple headed to Canada instead, first to Montreal and then to Toronto, and they were on their way to Vancouver by train when Mrs. Brandli suffered an attack of appendicitis; they were forced to stay in Calgary for medical treatment. Apparently, the doctor treating Mrs. Brandli convinced her husband that there was scope in Calgary for another singing teacher and the pair decided to stay.[1]

Maria Brandli de Bevec, whom Norma described as "a real, old-fashioned prima donna and quite a character," led her husband "a Devil of a life" according to local gossip.[2] But although she disliked Calgary, the couple remained there for three or four years before completing their journey to Vancouver. In that brief time Brandli established himself as a teacher of the bel canto style of singing, an older form that had never really gone out of style in Italy; it emphasized beautiful, melodious singing and focussed on the operas of Bellini, Donizetti and Rossini. For Calgary this was a novelty, and Brandli managed to attract a number of students. However, he was never really accepted by the local musical community, which was dominated by musicians and teachers trained in England. These talented immigrants had long been the arbiters of local musical taste and included the singing teacher Dorothy Ellis-Browne, longtime *Calgary Herald* music critic Annie Glen Broder and Calgary Women's Musical Club president Mrs. Herman Hooper (Jeanette) Sharples.

Although she was Australian, Mrs. Sharples had implicit confidence in the superiority of English training. In the mid-1920s, she persuaded the Women's Musical Club to use profits earned from sponsoring concerts to create a special scholarship fund for local students. Because the bulk of the fund was raised by sponsoring the famous Italian soprano Amelita Galli-Curci in a gala performance at the Grand Theatre in 1926, the scholarship was named in her honour. In her capacity as resident Alberta secretary, Mrs. Sharples supervised the annual examinations offered by the associated board of the Royal Schools of Music, entertained the British examiners and superintended the annual scholarships awarded by the board so that talented Canadian musicians could receive expert professional training at the Royal Academy or the Royal College of Music in London, England. A number of Calgarians received these scholarships over the years, and many returned home after their studies to participate in the musical life of the city and to perpetuate further the English tradition.[3] As a result of this early bias favouring English methods and training, Brandli's reception in the local musical community was guarded, if not actually hostile.

Because the amateur Piper Orchestra was the extent of their musical involvement in the city at the time, the Pipers may have been oblivious to the nuances in the musical community and simply viewed Brandli's arrival as a good opportunity for Norma to get some professional training. The fact that Brandli taught in the traditional Italian bel canto style may have been the main attraction for them. In 1910 Dr. Piper had attended a concert in Detroit by Australian soprano Dame Nellie Melba and had been enchanted with her pure voice and ornamented style of singing. An opera lover, Dr. Piper made sure his family attended the regular performances of touring opera companies, and it seems quite likely that they attended Galli-Curci's recital in Calgary in 1926. Norma certainly admired the singer's "liquid sound" and "bird like notes." It is interesting to note, however, that Annie Glen Broder gave the Italian singer a very cool review in the *Herald* and particularly criticized her Italian pieces.[4] Significantly, both Melba and Galli-Curci were coloratura sopranos, who specialized in "grand opera" roles requiring voices with wide singing range and the acrobatic agility necessary to perform runs, trills and cadenzas. This style also seemed to suit Norma's unusually sweet and flexible voice and her romantic temperament. Consequently, when Norma showed an interest in singing lessons, Dr. Piper may have encouraged her to pursue training in this style in preference to all others.

It seems clear that Dr. Piper's flourishing financial state in the mid- to late-1920s was the determining factor in allowing Norma to begin lessons with Brandli. His dental practice was well established, but more importantly his oil stocks were booming. Although Norma had inherited money from her Uncle Richard Piper, her father did not seem to require this to fund her singing lessons; he probably viewed the bequest as a safeguard for her future. It was only later, when the lessons became a financial burden, that Uncle Richard's legacy was used to pay for the lessons. But in the mid-1920s, on paper at least, Dr. Piper was a wealthy man looking for ways to invest.

As the son of a successful Ontario farmer, Dr. Piper considered land a good investment, especially after 1924 when prairie crop yields increased year by year, as did worldwide grain prices.[5] He purchased a quarter section of land at Youngstown, Alta., that was farmed for him for nearly a decade by James S. Knudsen.[6] During this period, he also invested in mortgages on properties in Vancouver, but it was oil stocks rather than land that attracted most of his investment income. Not surprisingly, the frenzied excitement of the Turner Valley oil craze in the mid-1920s appealed to Dr. Piper's entrepreneurial nature. A promoter at heart, he determined to join the rush of big and small investors who were naively convinced that speculation in oil stocks was a no-risk method of making a fortune. In 1926 he and a young accountant friend, George Bell, formed a copartnership to act as "brokers for the sale of stocks, bonds, lands and leases of lands, and mineral rights" that they called the British Canadian Investments Company. The main purpose of this short-lived private company seems to have been to manage personal investments and those of family and friends also eager to "get-rich-quick."[7]

Dr. William Piper on horseback, Calgary, 1928. GA NA-695-76

Not content merely to speculate, Dr. Piper also hoped to make his fortune as an oilman. In 1927 he incorporated Canadian Western Royalties Limited, a private company capitalized with 50,000 shares, with himself as president and family members as directors. He had missed the initial boom in Turner Valley, but secured acreage in various other likely oil fields, had test wells drilled and attempted to attract investors from among his network of friends in Alberta and Ontario, even approaching his old friend Dr. C. N. Johnson to see if any of his "millionaire friends" in Chicago might be interested in investing.

Meanwhile, Dr. Piper also hoped to make a fortune from his profession, not as a working dentist but as the promoter of a new dental product. In the late 1920s, he and George Bell formed a small company to promote a dental antiseptic known as Lactis-Ora. They made strenuous efforts to attract stockholders and to promote this product among dentists in

Alberta, British Columbia and Ontario, but without the coveted approval of the American Dental Association, Lactis-Ora was a non-starter and the company soon disbanded.

Sadly for Dr. Piper, not one of these businesses was a success. The changed agricultural and financial climate of the 1930s no doubt was greatly to blame, but his own miscalculations may have contributed as well. As his son Dick so aptly observed after his father's death, Dr. Piper "shone chiefly in his profession. He had no business head."[8] However, in the late 1920s he had been an active member of the Calgary Stock Exchange for more than a decade and was considered a solid and respectable businessman, prominent in his community. The boys were nearly finished their education; now it was Norma's turn to take advantage of his improved financial position. He may also have realized, rather belatedly, that Norma's quiet life at home was not advancing her marriage prospects, and that she not only needed to develop an interest to take her out into the public, but the attainment of a refined accomplishment, such as singing, also could only enhance her social desirability.

Norma started lessons with Brandli in December 1926. She had natural ability, worked hard and progressed very well, although her lack of self-confidence meant she often felt overshadowed by other students, notably Isabelle Logie. On February 8, 1928, the Calgary Women's Musical Club sponsored a program of Italian music featuring five of Brandli's students, including Norma and Isabelle. Although Brandli was complimentary and her family supportive, Norma jealously noted that Isabelle enjoyed the real triumph of the concert. Whereas Isabelle was "mobbed by the audience" and "ran away with all the honours," Norma viewed herself as looking on, with only her family and a few close friends to offer congratulations.[9] This scene affected Norma deeply, and her undeclared jealousy of Isabelle Logie lasted for years, with uncharitable comments popping up in her diaries and letters well into the late 1930s.

Another of Brandli's students was Dr. Piper's sometime business partner George Bell. Bell had served with the Canadian Expeditionary Force in the First World War and was decorated for conspicuous bravery at Vimy Ridge. He arrived in Calgary in the early 1920s, boarding at that time with the Moodies while serving as JF's accountant. By the mid-1920s he was practising chiropody (podiatry) in an office near Dr. Piper's in the Herald Building, was boarding with the Piper family and was involved with Dr. Piper in various business schemes. Although the Pipers may have met him through JF, it is also possible that he had been acquainted with them in London; he certainly seems to have known Aunt Min, was a member of the London-Middlesex Old Boys and Girls Association in Calgary and sang with the Piper Orchestra for a number of years.[10]

The Pipers grew very fond of George, and Norma later joked that her father was talked out of selling their house in 1928 by Aunt Susie, who worried that the new, smaller house would not accommodate George, "who was a fixture immovable in the family."[11] Aunt Susie liked "Geordie" and tried unsuccessfully to encourage a romance between the two young people, reporting to Norma that the "poor Old Boy" was very lonely whenever she went away from home. But although he and Norma had singing in common, Aunt Susie schemed in vain and they formed a couple only when they delighted friends and family with their Sunday evening concerts at the Piper home and occasionally at musical soirees sponsored by the Moodies. Although his business partnerships with Dr. Piper were uniformly disappointing, George's "magnificent dramatic bass voice" earned him a gold medal at the Alberta Musical Festival and he sang with the Detroit Civic Opera Company for the 1930 season.[12]

Norma continued to worry that her voice was inferior to that of some of Brandli's other students, but her nature was such that disappointments made her more determined than ever to succeed, and she persisted with her lessons. She found Brandli to be a "stern ... yet ... sympathetic and inspiring" instructor,[13] and she, in turn, was a conscientious and serious student. He expressed the opinion that her voice was worth the cost and effort of training, but it was not until he began giving her daily lessons that the family finally realized she might have significant potential. Both father and daughter were therefore disappointed when the Brandlis finally completed their cross-country trek by moving to Vancouver in June 1929. To please his daughter, that summer Dr. Piper decided to make a holiday out of a business trip to British Columbia to promote Lactis-Ora among his dental colleagues. Norma, Aunt Susie and George Bell accompanied him to Vancouver, and they spent several weeks visiting and touring the area and listening to Brandli's grandiose hopes for his former student. After that, it was not difficult for Norma to convince her father that she should follow her teacher to Vancouver in the new year to continue her musical training.

After all her years spent quietly at home with Aunt Susie, this was a big step for Norma, but her admiration for Brandli and confidence in her own ability made her unusually determined. Aunt Susie was very upset about the loss of "her little girl," but "after many heartaches" she was reconciled to the idea by her brother, who said that the break would be temporary; although Norma was leaving for Vancouver in February 1930, her father and aunt were planning to join her there in the summer. In fact, Dr. Piper was hoping the move would be permanent: his oil stocks were doing so well that it appeared he could afford to retire from dentistry. He had been suffering knee problems for several years, and in the spring of 1929 had invited a newly qualified dentist, Dr. Roy Thorpe, to share his practice. Soon after, he reported happily to his sons that his new partner was "a very agreeable young man [who] knows his work" and was "getting along splendidly and will I am sure be able to carry on with the majority of my patients."[14] This was a big relief to Dr. Piper, who intended to sell the practice outright to Dr. Thorpe. Realizing the vagaries of Calgary oil stock prices, however, Dr. Piper had a fallback plan: if his current financial position declined, he could always establish a dental practice on the coast.

Although Dr. Piper grandly informed his sister-in-law Min, "We want her to develop her voice to get into Oratorio, Concert or Radio work," he confided to a friend that he felt Norma's training "will be good for her whether she is

Norma at Vancouver, ca 1930.
GA PA-2393-9-2-1

before the public or not."[15] He justified the expense by saying that she had stepped aside in favour of the boys for many years, and now it was her turn. Also, he was anxious for her to have "something to fall back on, should she so desire" in order to make a living in the future. He told Min he was glad Norma "has been persuaded to show what is in her in the way of talent" and, possibly thinking of her age (which was now 32), said, "It is her opportunity which cannot be put off much longer."[16]

In spite of her age, Norma's sheltered life had made her relatively inexperienced and unsophisticated. A petite, fair woman, her sweet, somewhat childish features perfectly suited the "curly headed moppet" look popular in the 1930s,[17] and her dependent, rather clinging manner brought out all the protective instincts in the men in her life: father, brothers and, later, husband. Naturally, Dr. Piper took charge of her move to Vancouver following the procedure that had worked

so well when the boys left home for school: register at the university and find lodgings nearby in a respectable private home.

In January 1930 he wrote to the principal of the University of British Columbia, telling him that Norma wanted to do "special work" in French, Italian and "other subjects bearing on dramatic art."[18] When he wrote to Dean Buchanan at the university a few days later, he elaborated, saying that although Norma had no interest in taking a degree, she would take courses at the university for two years while doing vocal training with Brandli. His fond pride in his "exceptional girl" was evident:

Norma has been with her Auntie all her life and is not of the flapper style as you will see when you meet her. She has a good brain lacking only opportunity to develop. Her ambition being to make the best possible use of her voice and to that end acquire the education necessary to reach that goal . . . Norma has never been away from home and knows very little of what many people have to go through. I am persuaded that I cannot do better than to send her to you direct and let you have full charge of her University training.[19]

They were disappointed to learn that Norma could register only in English Literature and French at the university, because it did not offer courses in Dramatic Arts or Italian. Worried that in the 10 years since Norma had graduated she had "naturally forgotten most of the detail" of her languages, Dr. Piper hit upon an interesting solution. He suggested an informal course of studies to Brandli: could he please teach Norma Italian and his wife review French with her—in addition, of course, to the five weekly singing lessons already arranged? With Dick still in university, Dr. Piper was trying to save money and told Brandli quite frankly that this solution was more economical for him than finding additional tutors to cover these aspects of Norma's education. No doubt he hoped that Brandli would feel obliged to give extra value in return for his high fee—$2.50 a lesson (later $3.00), which translated to $50.00 (later $60.00) per month. Satisfied that he had done his best, Dr. Piper admonished: "Now, Mr. Brandli, [I] place this girl in your hands as if she were your own daughter. Do the best you can. She will appreciate all you and Madam[e] do for her. I am confident that Norma will do her best to attain the high standing you have set for her and when she has reached the top it will be a 'Brandli production.'"[20]

They were fortunate to place Norma with friends in Vancouver, "a musical family" with whom she could board for 35 dollars per month until the summer. Then, the plan was for her father and aunt to join her in an apartment until she finished with Brandli in the summer of 1931. Norma moved to Vancouver in early February 1930 and settled in quickly. She was very busy with school and lessons ("a hard old grind," as her father put it[21]) but also enjoyed meeting a few new friends through Brandli's studio, particularly Margaret Lattimore, a "lovely girl" with a "beautiful voice" who worked as a stenographer while studying singing. Perhaps seeking a substitute for her dear Aunt Susie, one of Norma's best friends in Vancouver became Loni Middlemass, an older woman who lived at Norma's first boarding house, took a maternal interest in her and became a lifelong friend. Although Mrs. Middlemass was not successful promoting a match with her son, Norma was confident of her "great affection" and later said, "We shared many pleasures and sorrows together."[22] (Near the end of her stay in Vancouver, Norma attracted the unwelcome attention of another young man at the studio. He appeared to suffer from the delusion that she secretly returned his affection but was leading him on, and eventually he wrote her a suggestive and upsetting letter. Uncertain how to handle these attentions, Norma turned to her father and let him deal with the situation.)

It was during her periods of study in Vancouver that Norma developed her habit of taking long daily walks as her main form of exercise. Although her days were very busy, still she managed to write home weekly to her lonely family. Aunt Susie told her, "Your Father looks for the letter as much or more so than his meals," and she closed her own letters with "I am still your lonesome Aunt Susie."[23] She was a little jealous of Mrs. Middlemass but loved entertaining Norma with local gossip, including frequent references to the roller-coaster business and financial life of their friend and neighbour, J. F. Moodie ("poor Old Boy," she always called him). Sometimes Aunt Susie was frustrated by the prim nature of Norma's replies, which was dictated by their joint fear of upsetting Dr. Piper when the letters were read aloud at home. She told Norma quite frankly, "How I do hate to have all your letters to me cencered [censored]."[24]

Norma appreciated the unusual freedom of living away from home with a fairly generous budget. In addition to the costs of her room and board, piano rental, accompanists and lessons, her expense books record a series of small luxuries: new dresses, hats and gloves, haircuts and permanent waves, candy, makeup and skin creams. She was vain enough about her looks to follow fashion dictates and advertisers' exhortations, and she spent significantly more than most Canadian women at the time on beauty products that promised to clear her skin, make her attractive and keep her looking younger as she aged.[25] While many young women worked hard teaching, nursing or doing office work to earn far less than 100 dollars per month,[26] Norma's allowance from home allowed her to live a rather privileged life: she spent that amount or more each month on herself and her vocal training.

Had he realized just how long and deep the financial depression would be, Dr. Piper might never have agreed to her continuing with Brandli. Even before Norma left for Vancouver, her father's financial position had begun to change, and over the course of 1929 he watched his oil stocks decline in value. Too late, he sent out a warning to sons Jack and Lawrence, who had followed his investement lead: "The stocks are sure getting knocked about these days. I am not surprised as I knew that history would repeat itself ... I would be very careful in dealing with stocks in the rather unsettled conditions of finance."[27]

By February 1930 he suspected that recovery would be slower than usual and told his sister-in-law Min that his Turner Valley acreage was where he now hoped to make big money. He had signed a drilling contract to start June 1 and was hoping to strike oil (unfortunately this plan never materialized). Relatives who had given him money to invest became anxious, but he advised calm, telling his niece Bertha Reid, "The Oil prospects are a bit gloomy but I believe if we stick things will come out alright." To some extent, his was only a paper loss, but although he was philosophical, he was bitterly disappointed and told Bertha: "I could have taken more than One Hundred Thousand Dollars out of it, had I sold at the right time, however, I have the stock yet and it will be much higher some day than it is at present ... I have 645 shares [of Royalite Oil Company Limited] which some day I beleive [sic] will be worth real money."[28]

There were other signs that all was not well in Alberta by the early 1930s. After the apparent recovery for agriculture after 1924, Dr. Piper was disappointed when a return to hot, dry conditions at the end of the decade resulted in a series of very small crops on his Youngstown farm, "hardly sufficient to pay the expense of seeding and harvesting."[29] His dental practice, which brought him into contact with many people, some of whom still came to him from the surrounding rural area, soon felt the effect of worsening financial conditions. Jack warned Norma, "Father writes that things are pretty slack at the office. Unless some way of disposing of our wheat crop is evolved, I guess the farmers won't have much money to spend on teeth, except getting something to put between them to eat."[30] One desperate patient wrote to Dr. Piper in 1930 that he could not pay his bill: "I wish I could do as you ask but I cannot. I have been out of a job for some months and am just about up against it. Have borrowed from friends and on my insurance to keep going."[31] Dr. Piper's situation was not unique; a survey by the Alberta Dental Association revealed that most dentists were forced to extend credit during the Depression years.[32] As he told a friend in 1932, "I like dentistry as a profession and have a good practice, but we get very little cash these days, in fact as I tell the Nurse we are running a Clinic."[33]

As a consequence of all the uncertainty, Dr. Piper quietly cancelled his retirement plans, and although Dr. Thorpe had already purchased his dental practice, he arranged to stay on with him indefinitely and share the office space. Nevertheless, compared with many during this period, he was still comfortable financially and was able to carry out an earlier promise to take his sister and daughter on a memorable cruise to Alaska in July 1930. On the boat, Norma had one of her first musical triumphs when she astonished and delighted the passengers and crew one evening with an impromptu recital. After the trip, the Pipers returned to Vancouver and established Norma in an apartment

Top: Norma in Vancouver, May 12, 1930.
GA PA-2393-12-3-4

Bottom: Norma on the Alaska cruise, July 1930.
GA NA-4390-447

where she could enjoy more privacy for practising. The Depression had pushed down rental rates, and Norma was able to get a very nice furnished apartment with a fireplace on Pendrell Street near Stanley Park for only 23 dollars per month. Originally, Aunt Susie had planned to make an extended visit to her niece in Vancouver, but after a short stay she decided to return to Calgary. She could see that Norma was very busy and had become quite independent after six months away from home, and she decided that her brother Will was more in need of her mothering skills and cheerful company.

Norma's first opportunity to do radio work came on August 27, 1930. Unfortunately, it aired on a local Vancouver station and the family in Calgary could not tune in to the broadcast. Gaining confidence, in October Norma decided to collaborate with another student and do a little concert tour in addition to Brandli's regular studio concerts. Dr. Piper was relieved that Norma had a chance to earn some money but offered the following advice:

> You must not be easy. Make your bargain and when it is decided have an agreement drawn … stating your percentage of the net profit etc. … You have had considerable expense to get what you now have and you must look to the business and as well as the *professional* . . . do not accept *taffy* in exchange for good services—always get the money—do not (ever) neglect the financial end. You have not had much training in that but start it now . . . there has to be ready money to finance this before you start. Let us see what kind of a business girl you are in your first deal.[34]

Fearing that he might have put her off, Dr. Piper wrote again a week later encouraging her to take any paid singing work that offered itself. For the first time, he disagreed with Brandli: whereas the teacher was trying to focus on developing Norma's voice to its full potential and did not like to see her distracted with financial concerns, Dr. Piper now wanted to see some return for his investment. He said that although he was not sure what her area of specialty ultimately might be, "in the meantime, we must get some money and perhaps concerts is the quickest way to get in. Radio would be alright too and perhaps surer and not much risk attached." Worried that Brandli might be filling her head with unrealistic dreams, he cautioned Norma that "it is not yet been determined that you have a voice for Grand Opera, and it's a very hard life also."[35]

Invitation to Norma's debut concert in Vancouver, December 18, 1930. GA M6340-214-v2-p1

We request the pleasure of your presence at the debut Concert of

Norma Piper
Soprano Leggero

Artist Pupil of R. Brandli de Bevec

in the Oak Room of the Hotel Vancouver

Thursday Evening, December eighteen

at eight-thirty o'clock

(Under the Patronage of Mrs. E. O. Cornish)

Assisting Artist : Frank Leland, Violinist

Accompanist : Frederick Nelson

Donations accepted at the door in aid of the Province Santa Claus Fund

However, Brandli prevailed, and Norma's first concert was a benefit at the Girls' Corner Club in Vancouver on October 17, 1930. She did well and was praised as having "a most pleasing coloratura voice, fresh in quality and flexible."[36] Brandli decided that she was ready for an official debut and persuaded Mrs. E. O. Cornish, president of the Women's Musical Club, to act as patroness for a benefit concert in aid of the *Vancouver Daily Province's* Santa Claus Fund. The concert was held at the Hotel Vancouver on December 19, 1930, and was a gratifying success, with many Calgary friends in attendance. Norma was described as "charming, youthful, fresh" and the audience as "warmly appreciative." Sympathetic reviewers claimed that her "well-trained" voice was "of unusual texture and colour" and also of "scintillating brilliance and extremely wide range." She "quickly captivated her audience, investing her singing with artistic charm and a warmth of feeling that was quickly contagious," and based on her initial appearance, the *Daily Province* predicted "a very promising future."[37]

Norma in Vancouver., ca 1933. Studio portrait by Artona. GA PA-2393-12-3-5

Privately, Dr. Piper was ecstatic, but he wrote sedately to Norma "You sure went over big . . . you have made me very happy for Christmas."[38] Now, with such glowing reviews, he could see a professional career ahead for Norma and advised her to "try for something on the Coast for one year then take a few months with Brandli again then I believe you will be ready for the Big try."[39] He immediately set to work planning Norma's Calgary debut, which was to take place on February 19, 1931, at Central United Church. Drawing on his resources as a clubman, he was able to interest the Men's and Women's Canadian Clubs in jointly sponsoring both the Calgary concert and a follow-up in Edmonton on February 25,1931, at the MacDonald Hotel. The tie-in with the Canadian Clubs seemed obvious: as he explained to the executive, he wanted Norma to be known "firstly as a Canadian singer" when she did her coast-to-coast tour after graduation. By being first to sponsor a rising star, the Canadian Clubs would receive a "big boost" in the future and would have the additional advantage of sponsoring her while she was still relatively unknown and therefore inexpensive.[40]

Dr. Piper invested a lot of time and money to make the Calgary debut a success ("a small fortune," Norma later recalled[41]). There were 1,200 invited guests, and he made sure to invite every Calgarian he could think of who had musical pretensions or pull. His old friend R. B. Bennett consented to be honorary patron, partly out of friendship for Piper himself, but also because

Top: Norma surrounded by bouquets after her Calgary singing debut at Central United Church, February 20, 1931. GA M6340-214-v2-p10a

Bottom: Norma, Calgary, early 1930s. GA PB-589-4

his own beloved sister, Mildred, had impressed him with her high opinion of Norma's ability.[42] Taking no chances with the "customary tribute," Dr. Piper had his Scottish Rite lodge associates (who were also doing usher duty) parade in at the intermission with 18 huge bouquets to decorate the stage. Norma later remembered, "It looked just like a funeral. I had never seen so many flowers in one hall in my life!"[43] He paid for advance publicity and was assured that the reviews in the Calgary newspapers would be friendly.

Norma's friend and popular local pianist Helen Boese was engaged as accompanist; there was also to be a string trio, and the assisting artist was to be George Bell, who had finished his season with the Detroit Civic Opera and planned to be in Calgary for the annual meeting of the Lactis-Ora stockholders. Since George had been a gold medallist at the Alberta Musical Festival and had sung professionally, Dr. Piper thought he would be a "good drawing card" and might also take some of the critical pressure off Norma. The event was eagerly anticipated by friends as "one of the highlights of [the] musical season,"[44] and although her brothers could not attend, they were excited. Lawrence, the rugby enthusiast, wrote, "Sis, you have a whole family of rooters you know. Sounds kind of sporty doesn't it, well then admirers instead of rooters."[45]

The *Albertan* gave Norma its full support with an in-depth interview a week before the concert and an enthusiastic review afterwards: "Singing smoothly, easily with a voice of appealing loveliness, soaring into some beautiful high passages and carrying her audience with her through every mood, Norma Piper, coloratura soprano, sang her way into the hearts of hundreds of Calgarians . . . While she has not yet perfected her truly lovely voice, she is well on the way to becoming a leading singer in this Western Canada." Two weeks later, the *Albertan* further endeared itself to the Pipers by announcing in its social notes that the executive of the Women's Musical Club was hosting an open house to honour Norma, "who made a brilliant debut in this City a few evenings ago in a very delightful recital."[46]

In contrast, the *Calgary Herald* review was charitable, but restrained. Editor Charles Haden was on the Canadian Club executive and Dr. Piper had naturally assumed that his influence would assure a glowing review.[47] But the *Herald*'s doughty music critic, Annie Glen Broder, had never been impressed with the Italian school of singing, nor with Brandli or his pupils. Whereas the *Albertan* titled its review "Song Recital Thrilled Hundreds of Guests," the *Calgary Herald* termed it merely a "Notable Event." However, the review took into account that it was a debut, and it was not unkind: Norma's personality was described as "charming," her stage presence "excellent" and her voice one of "sweetness and purity, and of excellent range."[48]

The concert at the MacDonald Hotel the next week was a gala affair sponsored by the Canadian Clubs and under the patronage of Lieutenant-Governor and Mrs. W. G. Egbert, Premier and Mrs. J. E. Brownlee, members of the legislature and the University of Alberta and their wives, and others from the local musical community. Dr. Piper networked assiduously prior to the event and was able to assure Norma that "many of the high [government] offices are filled by personal friends, who will gladly help you."[49] The concert, which featured the same artists as in Calgary, was well received. The *Edmonton Journal* admired the "astonishing power" of Norma's voice, her "rare personal charm," her "marked dramatic ability" and even her Italian, which the reviewer judged to be "perfect."[50]

However, unlike for the debut concert in Calgary, Dr. Piper was not prepared to pay all the expenses (although Aunt Susie contributed 60 dollars), and the Edmonton Canadian Club was forced to charge admission to recover costs and to pay the performers. The admission was only one dollar, which may not have been significant for the Edmonton gala, but it did make other local Canadian Clubs pause to think. The Depression was well underway in 1931, a dollar was a significant amount for many ordinary people, and the clubs worried about attendance. As a result, Dr. Piper was not able to interest other Canadian Clubs in sponsoring similar concerts and could not persuade his friends in the Calgary Club to sponsor a second concert with paid admission. Even a strong letter to Graham Spry, son of an old Ontario Masonic friend and now national secretary of the Canadian Club, proved fruitless. Dr. Piper was disappointed. In his initial enthusiasm, he had foreseen a Canadian Club tour of other western cities and towns culminating with a gala concert in Victoria under the patronage of the lieutenant- governor of British Columbia and other social leaders. Instead, somewhat anticlimactically, Norma headed back to Vancouver in March to continue her studies with Brandli.

Nevertheless, Norma's success in Edmonton with a paying audience convinced Dr. Piper that she was a marketable commodity. Of an optimistic, "booster" mentality, much like his friend J. F. Moodie, he delighted in getting behind worthy schemes and promoting them to a successful conclusion. Now he saw a way to recoup some of her expenses, but more importantly, he became sure that Norma's talent would take her to the top. He told his London friend Reverend R. J. Bowen, "Norma is getting on wonderfully with her singing. I want to make her an outstanding Canadian coloratura soprano and firmly believe it can be done."[51]

In April 1931 Norma and some classmates went to Seattle to attend a three-concert series put on by the Chicago Opera Company. While there, a friend of Dr. Piper's arranged for Norma to attend a tea in her honour at the Women's Musical Club and to sing a solo at the Sunday service of a local Baptist church. She also auditioned with a local radio station, which apparently offered her a position at 55 dollars per week. Mindful of keeping Norma's name before the public, Dr. Piper gave the details to the *Calgary Herald*, which dutifully reported "Norma Piper Much Appreciated in Coastal Cities."[52] Although he was flattered by the interest shown in Seattle, Dr. Piper had higher ambitions for Norma and told Reverend Bowen, "I have kept my boys in Canada and intend to do the same with Norma until she has established herself a Canadian singer of note, The Melba of Canada."[53]

Still believing that the Canadian Clubs should be interested in promoting Canadian talent, and anxious that Norma become known in eastern Canada, Dr. Piper was "disgusted" when Reverend Bowen reported that the London Club was prepared to pay her only 35 dollars for a concert because she was as yet unknown. Certain that London would be "the key of her success in the East," he turned to the London IODE (Imperial Order of Daughters of the Empire) but was surprised to learn that there was no interest, even though he had counted on support from his many friends and had pointed out that Norma was London's "very own daughter."[54] He was disappointed. With Brandli's encouragement, he had begun to think of an eastern tour as a fundraising precursor to study in Europe.

Giving up on the Canadian Clubs at last, Dr. Piper turned to the Rotary Clubs. He was aware that service clubs had a long history of sponsoring young musical talent and was anxious to interest the Rotary Club because he believed that, once it took on a cause, it put great care into "the putting of it over," which would relieve him of many of the details normally handled by an agent.[55] Over the spring and summer he therefore arranged for Norma to entertain at meetings of the Vancouver and New Westminster Rotary Clubs, and she also sang at a benefit concert sponsored by the latter.

He contacted his old friend Chester Bloom, editor of the *Regina Leader*, who not only invited Norma to sing for Regina Rotarians at a private recital at the Capitol Theatre but also ensured that the event had enthusiastic newspaper coverage. Mutual friend Harry Hutchcroft, who was a Rotarian and promoter of musical entertainment in western Canada, attended the recital and reported to Dr. Piper, "Norma completely captivated her audience and made an exceedingly good impression." He was taken with Norma's lovely voice and pleasing personality and said, "I can only say that I have fallen head over heels in love with her."[56] However, Dr. Piper was frustrated by the timidity of other smaller Rotary Clubs, which worried that they would lose money. Noting that there still seemed to be money available for popular entertainment such as wrestling matches, he reluctantly conceded that no doubt the clubs were right to be cautious: "Where she is not known the people will not be so likely to turn out, during these times of depression."[57]

By September 1931 Norma's lessons with Brandli were becoming a serious financial burden, and Dr. Piper could no longer afford to keep her in Vancouver without some kind of an assured income. In addition to the Rotary Clubs she had sung for the local Kiwanis and Lions clubs, but neither was willing to take on official sponsorship, and shy, modest Norma was unable to promote herself sufficiently to elicit the financial support of other locally influential people. Dr. Piper found it frustrating trying to direct his daughter's career from a distance and wrote to R. B. Bennett, "Norma is experiencing considerable difficulty in getting away to a good start in Vancouver, for there she has no one to help her . . . It is most difficult, as you know for a young artist to get a start, especially now." Although he acknowledged that the prime minister had much to occupy his time, he thanked "R.B." for past kindnesses and asked if he would "mention [Norma] to the right parties" the next time he was in Vancouver, as "it would help tremendously."[58] With great faith, he wrote to another friend, "It is a dreadful time to attempt to bring out a new Star, but the goal is worth striving, for I am sure Norma has the ability to get there."[59] Of course, his own straitened financial position was a major hindrance, and in frustration he revealed to Bennett, "The only time in my life that I [have] really wanted money is at the present time, to help this little girl [to] where I know she could reach."[60]

As a fundraising enterprise, on September 11, 1931, Norma sang a "Farewell Concert" in the Crystal Ballroom of the Hotel Vancouver. As usual, comments on her voice were favourable, but one reviewer regretted the small attendance that resulted in a "devastating echo" in the large ballroom.[61] Music critic Rhynd Jamieson ("RJ") of the *Vancouver Daily Province* claimed she had "made a complete conquest of her listeners," and although he made several critical comments, he praised her rendition of the Mad Scene from *Lucia di Lammermoor*, saying "the enthusiasm which greeted its performance was honestly earned."[62] As "RJ" was known and feared as a severe critic, Norma was pleased with his approval.

Publicity before and after the Farewell Concert revealed some confusion over the singer's future plans. Various newspapers had her heading to Calgary, to eastern Canada, to Italy for further study and to Paris for an international debut. In fact, she was simply saying goodbye to Vancouver, but the idea of European study and an international debut tantalized both father and daughter. In 1931, Dr. Piper first mentioned Italy to his friend Dr. C. N. Johnson, of Chicago: "I would like her to get the finishing touches in the Old Country as there is no doubt about there being a something the singer receives in Italy that cannot be procured elsewhere."[63] That year, an agent with the *Musical Courier* in Paris replied to his inquiry, claiming it could orchestrate a Paris debut for Norma, suitably reviewed afterwards in the *Courier*, for 150 dollars, with an additional tour of French provincial cities for a similar amount or higher (depending on the amount of publicity). For a price it could even arrange an operatic appearance at one of France's largest opera houses.[64] Of course, Norma would have required some months of training in Paris before making the debut, which made the cost seem prohibitive at the time. The idea was dropped, but the dream of international study persisted.

Meanwhile, Dr. Piper had talked the Calgary Rotary Club into sponsoring a concert at Knox United Church in mid-September. Made up of hard-headed businessmen, the Calgary Club only agreed to the sponsorship "on the understanding that we were to be under no financial obligations, and would receive a percentage of the profits."[65] Encouraged, Dr. Piper tried to persuade president D. E. Black to propose Rotary sponsorship for a series of recitals throughout the Fourth District (western Canada). He first suggested that Norma be paid a fixed fee of 3,000 dollars but later prepared a sample circular letter to be sent to other clubs proposing recitals "on the basis of fifty-fifty." However, the Calgary Club was reluctant to take on a more dynamic role and only agreed to assist Norma in securing other engagements by personal word-of-mouth promotion.

Undeterred, Dr. Piper next suggested that Norma could best achieve that end by singing at the Fourth District's annual presidents' meeting in Brandon, Manitoba, in mid-August. To secure Norma's name on the program, he wrote to John Nelson, director of Rotary International in Montreal, soliciting his support with the assurance, "I know of no organization I would prefer her to be connected with."[66] Nelson, who had been "a very warm friend" of Norma's grandfather, Major J. E. Johnson, was happy to comply with Dr. Piper's request. But although Norma pleased the Rotarians in Brandon, the North Battleford and Saskatoon clubs in Saskatchewan were the only others that agreed to sponsor recitals. Dr. Piper was disappointed but well aware of the reason. Regarding the Manitoba clubs, he wrote, "conditions are so terrible in that province they hesitate to take on any new obligations."[67] In retrospect, the trip to Brandon had been futile. It had cost 150 dollars to send Norma to Brandon, but when expenses were deducted the Saskatoon and North Battleford concerts together netted only 45 dollars.

In September 1931 Norma finally sang at the long-awaited concert sponsored by the Rotary Club of Calgary. Although she had preferred singing at Central United Church (she found "an echo in Knox and in some places rather a jumble of sounds"), the event was a success and "people were delighted."[68] However, this was not a beginner's debut. Commenting favourably on the "lively sympathy" which her "unspoiled presence" created between the audience and herself, Dr. William Hackney wrote in the *Albertan*: "Miss Piper has a larger voice than she is yet conscious of." He also expressed the hope that the "very young artist" might, with experience, develop "vocal colour," "depth of feeling" and better diction.[69] The *Calgary Herald*'s reviewer, "MJA," described her as "promising" and, commenting on her "attractive naturalness of manner, coupled with an evident sincerity," termed her a "painstaking vocalist possessed of a voice of remarkable possibilities."[70] Attendance was poorer than expected, and the $1.00 admission netted only a disappointing profit of $62.72, which was then split between the club and the Pipers. Sympathetically, the club invited Norma and her accompanist, Helen Boese, to entertain at its next regular meeting but beyond that felt unable to do anything further to promote her career.

Realizing that despite his best efforts he was unable to convince the service clubs to take on a wholesale official sponsorship of Norma, Dr. Piper came to rely on a more personal approach. Now that she was home again in Calgary, with successful concerts and positive reviews to her credit, she was considered something of a celebrity, and it was easier for her to gain the support of local musical people. In February 1932 she was invited by conductor Grigori Garbovitsky to be guest soloist with the Calgary Symphony Orchestra. It was a major social event at the Grand Theatre that included Lieutenant-Governor and Mrs. Walsh, the Honourable Vincent Massey, Lady Isabella Lougheed and a roster of other local notables. At a reception at the board of trade rooms after the concert, Vincent Massey praised her, reportedly saying, "Miss Piper, Calgary is a nice town, but this city is not big enough for you. I am delighted with your voice, it has great possibilities. If you were in Toronto, in less than two years the world would know of you."[71]

True to form, the *Albertan* gave a sympathetic review, praising her "excellent" singing and noting two encores (but it expressed a definite preference for the one English song on the program).[72] Also true to form, *Calgary Herald* reviewer Annie Glen Broder commented sourly on the "cordiality of her reception by a remarkably representative audience" (i.e., the many family friends in the audience) and gave a caustic review: "The attractive singer who has a pleasing appearance and ingratiating manner evidently gave enjoyment to those not over-familiar with the florid devices of Italian opera which are now in little or no demand in the great world centres. It seems a pity that Miss Norma Piper, who has a light, high soprano voice cannot find a better medium of expression than these outworn forms."[73]

Annoyed with her comments, Dr. Piper wrote to Reverend Bowen that Mrs. Broder "took a great dislike to Mr Brandli and the spiteful old dame is taking it out on poor little Norma ...Annie Glen Broder gave a very severe criticism of Galli-Curci when she was here a few years ago, so that will give you an idea of what she thinks of a Coloratura voice ...What this old dame likes is Dramatic. Tearing the hair and clawing at the breast."[74] No doubt Dr. Piper had gained this impression from the critic's enthusiastic championing in print of her former student, dramatic soprano Odette de Foras. However, he was gratified when Robert Somerville, editorial writer at the *Calgary Herald* and a warm admirer of Norma, said that he was "very much displeased with the criticism Norma received, [and] that he would like to put all critics in a bag and throw them in the river."[75]

The family was further delighted when "A Poetic Reproof to the Hoi Polloi" by Peter A. Moodie (no relation to JF) was published in the Letters section of the *Calgary Herald* the following week:

> The soloist sang. What a thrill of delight
> To that audience spellbound she gave!
> Applause was spontaneous—shattered the night—
> A boisterous way to behave!
> She did extracts from op'ra Italian—outworn—
> The crowd thought she sang brilliantlee;
> Yet never a soul knew enough to think scorn
> but the Musical Censor—and me![7]

Dr. Piper's "personal approach" proved relatively productive and resulted in many other engagements for Norma. She sang with the Edmonton Male Chorus at McDougall Church in March 1932, for which she earned 50 dollars plus expenses. In this concert, one reviewer praised her as being part of the "brilliant group of younger Canadian musicians" and another, in opposition to Mrs. Broder, claimed that "she was at her best in the more florid numbers."[77] She also sang several times in short programs on radio station CFAC, Calgary, for the Vesper Hour broadcasts from Christ Church in Elbow Park. In September 1932 she sang two solos at the IODE's afternoon tea at the Palliser Hotel for its honorary president, the Countess of Bessborough (wife of the Governor General), who reportedly asked that Norma be presented to her and then complimented her on her voice.[78] In a production of a Passion Play at the Grand Theatre in March 1933, Norma's "flute-like voice," heard offstage, was enjoyed in a "sympathetic rendering of Ave Maria."[79]

During this period Norma indulged in a fad popular at the time and had her horoscope prepared by local practitioner "Darius," who used one of Norma's rings to make astrological predictions. Probably Darius knew Norma's identity, because the reading was arranged by a mutual friend and many of the remarks were very personal, including "influence that of father or mother, but not both," and the statement that the subject was "obviously surrounded with strong and loving influences which will always seek to encourage and guide." Norma was thrilled with the prediction "success will undoubtedly be the subject's. It is one of the most outstanding characteristics of this subject's whole reading . . . there is no doubt whatever that a glorious future awaits . . . most assuredly, without any question whatsoever, the subject will sit among the mighty." Over the years Norma often reminded her father of these predictions, although usually she did not refer to Darius's stated qualification about her career: "It will most assuredly not be operatic, however, for several reasons. The subject has not the strong histrionic influences that opera requires nor has she, in sufficient strength, the gift of languages. It is there and quite strongly, but in my opinion, not quite strong enough. The concert stage, however, and the microphone both await a new star."[80]

Newspaper advertisement for Norma's guest appearance as soloist with the Calgary Symphony Orchestra, February 9, 1932. GA M6340-214-v2-p38c

Several months later, Norma defied Darius's prediction by revealing a very creditable acting ability in a local musical production. In November 1932 she took the lead role in the Calgary Light Opera Society's production of *Miss Hook of Holland*. It was performed at the Grand Theatre under the musical direction of Clifford Higgin, with Max Bishop as assistant producer. Norma shone in the role of Sally Hook and afterwards gave full credit to costar Frank Hemming and other cast members for the success of her first acting role, for which she earned high praise from both of Calgary's daily newspapers. The *Albertan* found that "Miss Piper revealed a fine acting ability

*Top: Norma as Sally Hook in the Calgary Light
Opera Society production of "Miss Hook of Holland,"
November 1932. GA NA-4660-4*

*Bottom: Newspaper advertisement for the Calgary Light
Opera Society production of "Miss Hook of Holland,"
November 17-19, 1932. GA M6340-214-v2-p56*

surprising in such a fine singer," and the *Calgary Herald* said, "She made Miss Hook a very appealing young lady, indeed. She showed excellent stage presence as well as a beautiful voice."[81] Happily, her old rival, Isabelle Logie, also received praise as "the flirtatious Mina." Very pleased with Norma's success, the Pipers hosted a cast party in their home afterwards that included a musical program by Norma, Isabelle and several others, a dance in the decorated basement and a "splendid lunch" prepared by Aunt Susie.

Anxious to keep her name in the public eye, the Pipers accepted engagements for Norma whenever and wherever they could. In this way she sang for Calgary organizations as varied as B'nai B'rith, the 31st Battalion Association, the Freemasons, the Elks Club, the Lions Club benefit concert for the unemployed, and the Women's Conservative Club. This last engagement was particularly important for Norma, as she finally received a nod of approval from local musical maven Mrs. H. H. Sharples, who introduced her as "our Norma Piper and we are all proud of her."[82] Norma also appeared on the program with local violinist Jascha Galperin, who remained interested in Norma's career over the years and proved an invaluable friend in the 1940s when he was director of the Conservatory of Music at Mount Royal College in Calgary. Various friends active in the Women's Musical Club ensured that Norma appeared in afternoon programs they arranged: violinist and Sunalta neighbour Olga Nickle included her in an afternoon program in October 1932, and her friend and regular accompanist Helen Boese included her in a program called "Singing Gardens" in March 1933. As Mrs. Boese had intended, "the birdlike qualities of her pretty voice" were much admired.[83] As might be expected, earnings from these appearances were relatively modest.[84]

While most of Norma's singing engagements were in Calgary, Dr. Piper made great efforts to promote her around the province. Drawing on his professional and lodge connections and an extensive network of friends and colleagues from his itinerant dentistry days, he contacted individuals in various towns, suggesting that a concert would be a welcome cultural event that could be a money-maker for whichever local group became the sponsor. He often suggested the name of a service or church group that he knew played a dominant role in the town. As long as they might support a concert, Dr. Piper was encouraging, reasoning that "while there has not been much change in [economic] conditions, the people will have entertainment of some sort, so why not give them something good?"[85]

The proposed arrangements varied only slightly from town to town. The suggested fee was $25.00, if expenses were paid, or $50.00 if Norma had to cover her own expenses. The usual arrangement was for Norma to supply and pay $5.00 each to the accompanist and the assisting artist (often Richard Seaborn, winner of the open violin competition at the Alberta Musical Festival in 1932), while the local group paid for the hall and the advance publicity (examples of which were supplied by Dr. Piper, who also wrote to friends in the surrounding area to encourage their attendance). Generally, admission was $0.50 or less for adults and $0.30 or less for students, and the profit was split on a 50-50 basis. Depending on the size of the town and the popularity of the concert, Norma earned anywhere from $15.00 to $50.00.

Dr. Piper was well aware that Norma often competed for an audience with radio, which now dominated as a cheap source of entertainment.[86] He understood that their promotional material had to convince people that a live concert was money well spent. Accordingly, in the days leading up to Norma's concerts, he had the local organizing committee place little newspaper advertisements such as "Radio Good—Voice Better" and "You will enjoy it immensely—the Norma Piper song recital." Although financial times were difficult, and Dr. Piper himself admitted "the illusive [sic] dollars are hard to capture,"[87] in Alberta this approach resulted in concerts in Sylvan Lake, Nanton, Vulcan and Didsbury in 1932 and 1933. Norma acknowledged her father's hard work and gave him full credit for his crucial role in promoting her career during this stage. She later said, with a hint of regret, "Triumphs I have had, but they have been due to the efforts of Father instilling the notion in people that I sing well and that I should sing in their particular town. I have never on my own merits won any engagement."[88]

In retrospect, some of Norma's happiest memories related to this period of her singing career. Later, when she was struggling to establish herself in

Italy, she remembered the "lovely little trips . . . by train or car" with Aunt Susie (and sometimes Dr. Piper) as "jolly times when I was treated like a visiting queen."[89] Small towns like North Battleford, "off the beaten track of coast-to-coast celebrities,"[90] rarely heard such concerts, and as a result audiences were enthusiastic and uncritical. Norma loved singing at the Normal School in Saskatoon, because the students were "music-starved and therefore appreciative."[91] Money for entertainment was scarce, but at least a few local music lovers realized they had received a rare treat by attending a live concert. In 1933, a letter to the *Didsbury Pioneer* stated, "The Masons are to be congratulated on bringing into our midst these talented artistes. People even in times of depression are hungry for such splendid musical concerts."[92]

But in spite of Dr. Piper's best efforts in 1932–33, they could not seem to get Norma's career launched beyond the level of church halls in western Canada. Gradually he came to believe that Brandli was correct: Norma needed more professional training to qualify for the international or even national career her father envisioned. His financial position had not recovered, so Dr. Piper hit upon the idea of approaching his sons for monthly contributions to Norma's training as a sort of investment that would reap rewards when she became famous. Jack, who worked in the investment industry, was supportive and wrote to Norma, "[Father] told me the conditions and needless to say, I am only too glad to be able to help out. Goodness knows you certainly sacrificed yourself for us boys and now it's our turn to help out. I am enclosing $25 and will send a similar amount each month as long as you require it. We are all very proud of you and I sincerely hope that all your hard work will result in something extremely satisfying."[93] Also single, and working at a good, steady job, Lawrence agreed to monthly contributions as well, but Dick, who was married by this time, was not asked to help.

With financial help from her brothers, Norma headed back to Vancouver in April 1933 to resume her training with Brandli. He had never approved of the concert circuit devised by Dr. Piper and had feared that Norma was squandering her talent. For the past several years, he had been trying to give her singing advice by mail, which he found to be "almost impossible," and had pushed her in every letter to take her career more seriously. He welcomed her back, glad that she could "dive into the stream . . . [and] shake off the Calgary influences which are by no means bad but doubtless not helpful," give up concert touring and focus on perfecting her voice in preparation for "a glorious opera career."[94] In fact, his prediction for Norma's future quite dazzled the Pipers; with proper training, he said, she would some day become a greater artist than even the famous darling of Metropolitan Opera Company in New York, Lily Pons.[95]

Brandli's celebration of Norma's new focus was somewhat precipitate, as Dr. Piper was still anxious to see Norma earn something to supplement money from home. Thanking him for his kindness in "boosting the girl," he asked his friend Dr. George D. Stanley, Calgary MP in Ottawa, to put in a good word for Norma with Hector Charlesworth, chairman of the recently formed Canadian Radio Broadcasting Commission.[96] Charlesworth was sufficiently interested in what he heard to ask his friends Leonard Brockington and Robert Somerville to introduce him to Norma during a subsequent visit to Calgary. He visited the Piper home and apparently enjoyed Norma's singing very much. In June 1933 Dr. Piper reported to Dr. Stanley that his "good work on Norma's behalf" had borne fruit, and she had been given an audition at a local radio station in Vancouver (a CBC affiliate).[97] Over the next six months, while she studied with Brandli, Norma sang over the radio about a dozen times, earning 5 to 10 dollars each time. Generally, she sang with an orchestra for an hour, broadcasting from the Hotel Vancouver, or in 15-minute time slots broadcasting live late in the evening. Her accompanist for these sessions was pianist Magdalene Moore, who admired Norma's voice and became a lifelong friend. Norma enjoyed the work, but later she recalled the loneliness of returning to her apartment late at night with no one to share her success.[98]

Soon after Norma returned to Vancouver, her beloved Aunt Susie died of heart failure. Although this news naturally saddened the family, the small legacy that she left to her brother and his family (the children each received 2,000 dollars—current value more than thirty thousand dollars) allowed Dr. Piper to re-examine the dream of European training for Norma. In October 1933 he told her, "It is definitely decided now that you will go to Europe . . . I figured 3 mos. Italy Milan; 2 mos. Paris and 2-3 mos. London— or whatever you like depending somewhat on the amt of money we can get hold of but this is sure you are going to have a look at Europe."[99] Fearing that this scattered approach would lead to disappointment, Brandli advised them to focus on a year of concentrated study in Milan only.

Others disagreed with Brandli's promotion of European training, warning the Pipers that the scheme would only lead to disappointment. Years later, Norma remembered that "Mr Brandli encouraged me when all others discouraged. He . . . realize[d] the possibilities in my voice, that no one else dreamed were there."[100] Dr. Piper chose to ignore the skeptics, even among his own children, and told Norma that the boys were delighted with the idea. He was as eager as she to try the next step and encouraged her to take some lessons in conversational Italian from a Vancouver teacher, Evelina Usigli Montalban. Then he advised her to "put the shoulder to the wheel as it were. We know you can do it and reach the top. You have now the right foundation on which to build and Europe is the place without doubt for the finishing touches."[101]

They organized farewell concerts in Vancouver and Calgary, hoping to raise upwards of 250 dollars toward the trip at the Calgary concert alone, which was billed as a fundraising effort. The first performance was at the Hotel Vancouver on December 19, 1933. While the *Vancouver Daily Province's* music critic, "RJ," said that "she acquitted herself with more than ordinary credit" and "gave evidence of finer things yet to come," he also commented on the coldness of her voice and took the opportunity to give her some advice on tone, diction and expression.[102] After the glowing and effusive comments in the local presses of small-town Alberta, this constructive criticism affected Norma deeply and she brooded over his words for many years.

In contrast, the "Goodwill Concert" held in Calgary 10 days later at Central United Church was akin to her debut there two years earlier, with a sympathetic audience, many floral tributes and local excitement about the progress of her career. It was an important social event, with patrons and patronesses including Prime Minister R. B. Bennett, Lieutenant-Governor Walsh, Mayor Andrew Davidson, Lady Isabella Lougheed, senators Patrick Burns and Edward Michener and numerous others active in the social and cultural life of the city. Reviewers were generous, commenting only on the "happy thought" that hed led to inclusion of a selection of lighter songs for which Norma's voice was "admirably suited."

Norma left Calgary by train in late December 1933. She stopped for several days in Montreal to visit her brothers Dick and Jack and to secure letters of

recommendation to influential musical people including Giulio Gatti-Casazza, manager of the Metropolitan Opera Company in New York, and Edward Johnson, Canadian tenor with the Met whom she had met in Vancouver in 1930.[103] Letters were forthcoming from Dr. Piper's Rotarian friend John Nelson (who knew the tenor well) and from Morgan Powell, who was the music critic at the *Montreal Star* and a friend of the *Calgary Herald* editor Robert Somerville; although she was unable to book an interview with Gatti-Casazza or Johnson during her brief stay in New York, Norma did manage a short telephone conversation with Johnson. At last, on January 6, 1934, she set sail for Italy on the *Rex*. Her great adventure had begun.

Norma on the SS Rex en route to Italy, January 1934. GA PA-2393-12-3-2

Chapter 5

Norma & George: Milano
1934–1935

"Many here wish you a bon voyage." With typical understatement but an unusual disregard for economy, Dr. Piper sent "heaps of love" in a lengthy cable to his "little girl" bound for Italy on the *Rex*. Surprisingly exuberant and chatty, in the telegram he reported on the weather and his excellent health and then recommended reading "Innocence [Innocents] Abroad."[1] He must have regretted missing the opportunity for a last piece of advice, because a second telegram quickly followed in which he cautioned Norma, "Be careful in choosing teacher not necessary first one interviewed."[2] Good advice, which Norma took seriously, but even so she struggled for many months before finding a suitable replacement for her beloved teacher, Brandli de Bevec.

During her concert tours, Norma had travelled around western Canada but always with the companionship of her father and Aunt Susie. Now she was on her own, in a foreign country and with only rudimentary language skills. Before she left Canada, she had worried about her slow progress in learning Italian, but her father had said, "Courage my dear, Fortier et Ferosi—'Brave but not Fierce.' You have done remarkably well to even get a start in Italian . . . you'll pick it up in Italy so go slowly—and don't worry."[3] Characteristically, once she realized that Italy was a real possibility, she allowed nothing to stand in her way: not the fact that she had to proceed on her own, nor her lack of language skills. No longer was she the timid girl of a decade before; her experiences on the stage and on her own in Vancouver had increased her self-confidence amazingly, and she discovered not only the strength and determination to pursue her dream, but also an unsuspected craving for excitement and adventure.

The *Rex* docked in Genoa on January 12, 1934, and after Norma changed her money (with no idea of whether or not she was given the correct exchange), she hired a car and interpreter to take a sightseeing trip to Naples before travelling to Milan by train. Once there, she booked into the Continental Hotel, where she spent a lonely evening in her room feeling homesick while she listened to the music and dancing below. The next day she toured the city and its great cathedral and then went to see the Canadian trade commissioner, A. B. Muddiman, who was duly impressed with her letter of introduction from Prime Minister Bennett.[4]

Muddiman assigned an assistant to help Norma find "decent lodgings," which turned out to be a "splendid boarding house run by a countess" in reduced circumstances at Bianca Maria 10 in the centre of Milan.[5] Norma was impressed to learn that the Amodei family's other boarders included an aristocratic Romanian lady, an officer of the Bank of Italy and his family, and a professor at the University of Milan and her mother—"all of them very nice, although they spoke not a single word of English between them."[6] However, the Amodeis welcomed Norma as an interesting addition to the mix, and their children helped her with conversational Italian. As her language skills advanced, she found the dinner table discussions fascinating and often wrote to her father about the high degree of culture among ordinary Italians.

Norma standing in front of Bianca Maria 10, location of Amodei pensione, Milan, 1934.
GA PD-184-6-2

Muddiman had been requested to find a good singing teacher for Norma, so he contacted his counterpart at the United States Trade Commission, who introduced Norma to a group of American students studying opera in Milan. Norma learned that there were about 2,000 of these students in Milan at the time, and although she was glad to be welcomed as a fellow North American, when she accompanied them to lessons she was not impressed with their teachers. Anxious to begin her studies, she signed up for 10 lessons with one teacher, though later admitted that she had been more impressed with the big mirrors and chandeliers in his house that with the teacher himself. Next, she tried 10 lessons with a Signor Cattone, but she was dismayed to learn that two American friends had studied with him for two and seven years respectively with no sign of an Italian debut for either. Hindered by her reliance on other foreign students and their limited connections, she was surprised to discover "remarkably few gifted teachers" in the city of music;

after Signor Cattone, she tried a Signor Pais and then a Signor Bergman. She was discouraged when none of her teachers measured up to the high standard set by Brandli

In spite of these disappointments, Norma was enjoying life in Milan. She sent her father a book of views and frequently told him to take it out so that he could enjoy vicariously her lively descriptions of excursions around the famous old city. For his benefit, she often compared what she was seeing to familiar sights back home and was very candid in her opinions. After visiting one local attraction, she wrote: "Being used to places like Stanley Park or even St George's Island it was a rather pitiful attempt at a park. The whole place lake and all are about the size of P[at] Burns home and garden—no bigger—about like Central Park in Calgary. The tearoom was a lovely old house about the size of the Library at home."[7] However, after sightseeing for several weeks, she was critical: "Milano is really the ugliest city I ever was in and the noisiest."[8]

A small-town woman with a WASP background, she shared many of the prejudices and parochial opinions of the times. Some of her early comments regarding minorities, particularly Jews, were thoughtless and ill-informed. After visiting the home of a new acquaintance, she wrote, "I don't know whether they are Jews or not but really I never, never, never, in all my life was in a house so cluttered with trinkets," and then compared their home to "Goldenburg's Grand Second Hand Store on 8th Ave E in Calgary."[9] On another occasion, she wrote that "there were too many Jewish names [on the guest list] to suit me," and, with regard to a fellow student, "perhaps hanging onto Ollendorf's kite I may soar—Jews have a use in the world."[10] Perhaps the experience of living in a big, cosmopolitan city and associating with the many Jews involved in the musical life of Milan eventually modified some of her attitudes, or perhaps the increasingly hostile official attitude toward Jews demonstrated by the Italian government near the end of the 1930s shocked her into silence.[11] In any case, her early habit of referring negatively in her letters to the ethnicity of her colleagues and acquaintances ceased after 1935.

Norma wrote to Dr. Piper frequently, giving detailed descriptions accompanied by little drawings to illustrate new sights and unfamiliar gadgets and foods. She was very open to these new experiences but sometimes missed small comforts: "I would love an honest-to-goodness piece of apple pie, with some nice, mild, Ontario cheese. The cheese over here is horrid, and we have it every day."[12] When her father worried about the effect on her health of "rich foreign foods," she quickly assured him "the food is wholesome. Nothing is greasy,"[13] and, in response to his repeated inquiries about the availability of Roman Meal bread, she extolled the virtues of the Italian diet, saying "I don't believe I need it. My health is absolutely perfect."[14] In fact, she came to believe that her new diet had relieved her of many former complaints, including indigestion, headaches, pimples, catarrh, constipation and even dandruff. She also was very impressed with the moderate drinking habits she observed in Italy and compared Italian restraint favourably with the excesses she had witnessed at public social occasions in Calgary, "where even the finest people lose control of themselves . . . and even the ladies have to be carried home."[15]

Dr. Piper was quite delighted with these detailed letters and, after judicious editing (mainly to take out gossip and family news), had them typed up by his nurse-receptionist and circulated to a number of Calgarians who had expressed an interest in hearing news of Norma's progress. Since his mailing list included many prominent people who had supported Norma's fundraising Goodwill Concert prior to her departure, these updates were an effective way for Dr. Piper to continue promotional efforts on his daughter's behalf while she was overseas. Norma understood and appreciated his tactics, telling him, "you surely are doing a great work, keeping the home fires burning, and preparing the way for my return. It is wonderful to have you behind me . . . gives me the courage to go on working. Believe me, one needs courage in this game."[16]

Once she was settled with the Amodeis, Norma rented a piano for her room so that she could accompany herself for her singing practice. Although most of the boarders enjoyed hearing her practices, she amused her father with tales of one she called "the Hooter," who disliked Norma and competed with her musically. Norma confessed to taking "a spiteful delight in trying to outsing" her through the thin walls but was relieved when her rival left the boarding house in March.[17] To gain experience, Norma attended operas at the cheaper theatres ("the voices are not good but I get to hear the music and see the acting which is good for me"[18]). Even these limited experiences gave her a new perspective, and when her father confused the San Carlo Opera House in Naples with the San Carlo Opera Company (which they had been thrilled to hear in former times), she dismissed the latter as "the 3rd rate touring company that used to come to Calgary."[19]

Anxious to make musical connections, Norma called on Carmen Melis, a faded soprano who had been at the same studio as Brandli de Bevec in the early 1900s, had sung with Caruso in New York in 1913 and was delighted with the opportunity to impress an admirer. Searching for ways to fill her time, when a play called *Canada* opened in March, Norma attended to see what Italians thought of her country (though privately she feared it would simply be a "snow, Eskimo and mounted police play"[20]). Although she gradually made friends among the American students, she was very glad of the news from home in her father's weekly letters. Especially welcome was local "musical" gossip, and she followed former rival Isabelle Logie's budding musical career with jealous interest.[21] Norma was touched and pleased by a "lovely sonnet" dedicated to herself by Elaine M. Catley, well known in Calgary for her clever compositions.[22] Very lonely at times, Norma wrote to her father that "being in a foreign land is a very interesting but rather dreadful experience. You would give anything to see a familiar face."[23]

SONNET

TO NORMA PIPER

Remembering a golden hour of song,
    And all the cadenced beauty of your voice ,
Now soaring up exultant, rich and strong,
    In harmonies which made our hearts rejoice,
Now low and tender like an ebbing tide -
    I oft recall your vivid, mobile face,
Where joy and rapture, pity, deep and wide,
    And human anguish, met in changeful grace.
You have a heritage of sunny skies,
    Of gem-like lakes, and mountains snowy-crowned;
And loving hearts await to see you rise
    To heights of high achievement, so renowned
That Canada may find a voice in you,
    Expressing all she holds most dear and true.

                                        Elaine Catley,
                                        CALGARY-Alberta

Sonnet to Norma Piper written by Elaine Catley, Calgary, 1934. GA M6340-214-v1-p60

In addition to enjoying Italian social and cultural life, she was getting a political education and had to face the realities of living in a fascist police state. When she first arrived at the Continental Hotel, the clerk had taken her passport and filled in a paper for the police. When they learned she was staying longer than three days, she had to go to the police barracks in Milan and fill in "a great paper like an income tax ... with all your past history etc."[24] Then, in mid-March, the police visited the boarding house to check on her. Luckily, the Amodeis' daughter warned her to say that she was a student who had never worked professionally—otherwise, the girl cautioned, she might have been taxed or even told to leave the country, as there was an increasing prejudice against foreigners taking "Italian" jobs and earning money. This was shocking to Norma, who told her father, "[We have] no idea of the way the Italian people live—at the small amount of freedom they have. Coming from a free country it is hard to appreciate the idea of the police knowing everything about you."[25] Although she had to update her information with the police every two years while she remained in Italy, she soon grew accustomed to the political system, occasionally adopted the Fascist style of dating with Roman numerals in her letters[26] and came to admire the decisive action with which dictator Benito Mussolini's government could act when it deemed it necessary. In fact, after only a few months' residence, she was so impressed that she told her father, "The longer I am here in Italy the more certain I am that the Italians have the right ideas about things."[27]

Her brother Lawrence had sent with her letters of introduction to two socially prominent Milanese families connected with some of his Italian coworkers in Trail, British Columbia. Norma was treated very kindly by the Kraftals and the Consolos, reporting to her father that the latter were "strong fascists" who had known fellow Calgarian Wilda Blow, a lyric soprano who had "moved in the highest social circles" while she studied singing in Milan from 1927 to 1931.[28] Norma's new acquaintances included her in a number of social gatherings and allowed her to sing for their musical friends, who advised her that until her Italian improved, there could be no chance of singing engagements. (Norma later recalled that during one of these early private recitals, a listener inquired of her companion, "What language is she singing in?"[29]) With their advice, she started taking Italian lessons with Maria Borchetta and soon reported that her Italian was improving daily. "Now that I am 'getting the ear' it is becoming very interesting. At first it was just like going to the market and hearing the Chinamen talk. Even words I knew if I saw them written I couldn't understand and of course my vocabulary was very limited."[30]

Her new friends also introduced Norma to Signor Bavastro, a "famous Russian teacher" who taught scena (acting lessons). Norma was pleased to discover that Wilda Blow had also studied with Signor Bavastro, who had a picture of her on his wall and remembered her fondly as a "beautiful girl with a beautiful voice."[31] Although her singing teachers saw no need for acting lessons, simply assuming that good acting would be an unconscious by-product of singing from the heart, Norma took the lessons very seriously and made detailed notes. The old criticism of her "cold" singing style by "RJ" of the *Vancouver Daily Province* still rankled, and she confided to her father, "I fancy that a few lessons would help enormously, especially a Canadian who comes from a country where people are not emotional."[32] She justified the additional expense, saying she had heard that Signor Bavastro had taken a "tall stiff girl even more unbending than I am" and made her into a "wonderful actress."[33]

Norma admired the flamboyant scena teacher, but soon after she started lessons she was warned off Bavastro by Brandli, who wrote disparagingly of the "no good Russian bluff" who likely would ruin her voice. He counselled her to "study patiently and hard the old Italian way. Become first of all an Italian operatic singer with no frills. I want you to be the equal of an Italian artist, and not one of these products of 'put it over' and 'showmanship.' Learn the different operas musically and with interpretation of heart and beware of any facial or bodily tricks. These types like Bavastro are only for Americans and other fools who will never amount to anything. Look around a little and you will see that not one Italian ever studies with them."[34] At the same time, she was becoming increasingly frustrated with her lack of musical progress. She had tried four different singing teachers and been dissatisfied with each one. She told her father that music in Milan was "a hotbed of jealousy ... [with] 5000 teachers," each with his admirers and detractors. "I have been advised by everyone I have met to study with someone different. It is terribly hard to know what to do."[35]

By mid-March she was "absolutely discouraged." Before leaving Calgary, she had talked with Elgar Higgin, a young basso cantante who had studied singing in Milan in the mid-1920s and was able to give practical advice. However, Elgar had lived in Italy when the lire was relatively weak in comparison with the Canadian dollar and had encountered a very favourable exchange rate of nearly 30 lire per dollar.[36] By the time Norma arrived in Italy a decade later, North America had suffered through four years of financial depression and the dollar was worth only 11 lire. As a result, everything was nearly three times more expensive than the Pipers had anticipated, and Norma could see her money disappearing quickly but with no clear benefit to her career. In desperation, she decided it was futile to continue in Milan and wrote to her brother's friend, Donald Baker, who was "high up" at the British Broadcasting Corporation in England, and "begged for a job."[37] Luckily, before Mr Baker could reply, George Pocaterra stepped into Norma's life.

~

After he had left Calgary the previous December, George had enjoyed a leisurely return to Italy. He had spent a wonderful 10 days as the guest of Frazier Hunt in New York before boarding the *Vulcania*. A week later, his sister Marta met the ship in Trieste and took him straightaway to Milan to visit his mother and the rest of the family whom he had not seen for nearly 25 years, since his visit of 1909. The next few months passed quickly and happily as George juggled business with pleasure, attending to the details of his father's will and estate while reacquainting himself with a style of life and level of culture unthinkable in the foothills of western Canada. His return even attracted media attention, with the publication of a long and detailed account of his Canadian adventures in the newspaper *Vedetta Fascista*.[38] Having left North America during the cold, grey days of winter, he especially enjoyed the heat and colour of his homeland. The realization that he had inherited the equivalent of 17,000 Canadian dollars (about 365,000 dollars today) only added to his satisfaction,[39] and he started to make serious plans to leave Italy in early May for his much-anticipated visit to the South Seas.[40]

In Milan, George stayed with his mother or his sister Emilia Pozza (known in the family as Ilia), but he loved to escape to the hilly country to the east where Marta lived. She and her husband, the wealthy industrialist Filippo Larizza, had a beautiful villa at Bassano del Grappa in Veneto, very near the area where George grew up. It was while visiting Marta in February 1934 that George received an important letter from a Calgary friend, the well-known photographer William S. Park. Bill Park had been the recipient of a Christmas card from George, mailed from the Azores in mid-December while he was in transit on the *Vulcania*, and Park was replying with Calgary news he thought might interest his old friend.

Among the tidbits was the information that another friend had recently sent his daughter to Milan to study singing. Bill told George that he thought the doctor's daughter had been "very plucky" heading to Milan all alone but was lonely and would appreciate a visit from home.[41] In case George felt shy, Bill included a letter of introduction for him to present to Norma Piper.

On March 3, George wrote to Norma from Bassano del Grappa, saying, "If you will allow me to call on you, I can't tell you how grateful I would be to meet somebody from our own dear Alberta."[42] Norma replied that she was "delighted with the prospect . . . of seeing someone from home,"[43] and so George called her when next he travelled to Milan, and he arranged a dinner meeting at the Restaurant Toscano for March 20. Slightly apprehensive, he arrived with Bill's letter, Norma's reply and a "whole armload" of copies of the *Calgary Herald* to prove his identity and good intentions.

Norma had never met George Pocaterra, but in the small society of Calgary she had certainly heard of the colourful rancher. In fact, during his hospitalization with appendicitis in May 1932 the daily newspaper updates on his health had convinced her that he was someone of importance. However, his appearance surprised her: "He didn't look a bit like an Italian" but rather like "a Scotchman."[44] They liked each other right away, and George, touched by Norma's tale of frustration, determined to help her if he could. Norma told her father that she had made a good impression on George by her "naturalness" and that "Canada and Canadians have been so kind and friendly to him that he wants to pay it back in some measure by helping a Canadian into the right paths in Italy."[45] George's approach was practical: he reminded her of the Depression in Canada and told her bluntly, "I don't care how much money your father has, if you have not a voice worth cultivating, there is no use in you staying here. The first thing to do is to see if you have a voice."[46]

Norma was to appreciate the effect of George's social position. Even though he had been gone from Italy for more than 30 years, his mother and older sister lived in Milan, were comfortably well-to-do and enjoyed social prominence as early and valued supporters of "Il Duce" and his Fascist government.[47] This connection likely opened many doors, leading Norma to assume at first an even higher social position for George and his family. Very impressed with all she saw, she wrote to her father, "One of the greatest strokes that ever came my way was when Mr Park wrote to Mr Pocaterra . . . [he] belongs to one of the old aristocratic families even though he doesn't look a particle Italian. (He looks like a Canadian rancher). Being in that position he is connected with the people who count and whom it is absolutely impossible for a foreigner to meet."[48]

One such person was Signor Camerino. Although she discovered he was "a Jew," Norma was impressed to learn that "he knows personally all the important musical people and belongs to the highest social level. And *social level is social level in Europe*. Not that these people put on airs, far from it—they are just like ourselves, but the gates cannot be crashed in a thousand years."[49]

Norma herself assisted in breaking down social barriers. When George introduced her to Camerino, who was a Venetian, she told him that her Italian teacher in Vancouver, Evelina Usigli Montalban also came from Venice, and he revealed in turn that his sister was married to an Usigli. Pleased with the family connection, Camerino persuaded his sister and her husband, who was president of the Italian branch of the Edison Company, to host an audition party for Norma. Twenty-five guests attended the elegant soiree at the Usigli home. In the "enormous drawing-room, with huge crystal chandeliers," Norma sang several songs and the aria "Una voce poco fa" from *The Barber of Seville*, which she had sung so successfully with the Calgary Symphony in 1932. Then, uniformed maids passed cakes and tea on silver platters while the assembled party discussed Norma's voice and prospects. Everyone was very kind and warm in their praise, and the conclusion was that she had a voice but that it needed training.[50]

Several days later, Camerino invited Norma to meet Signor Cenzato and Attilio Pavoni, two influential newspapermen who were "very very very high up." Typically gracious to a pretty young foreigner, they expressed great interest in Norma's career and she wrote to her father, "Can you imagine what that will mean when the time comes to put me before the public?" George was pleased that she had made such a favourable impression even though she was still unable to speak much Italian, and he told her, "I'm proud of you as a Canadian. You are making these people like you . . . and the reason is because you are natural. You don't pretend anything. That is what we Italians like." Camerino promised to find her a good teacher, and Norma exulted: "With the Usiglis, Cenzatos and Pavonis back of me, I have successfully crashed the gates of Milanese society, thanks to Bill Park . . . I feel very well satisfied that I have at last got into the right track."[51]

Meanwhile, Cenzato, who was the musical critic at the *Corriere della Sera*—an important musical newspaper at the time—invited Norma to sing at a party at his home. There she met Dr. Rizzardo Trebbi, who had been a singer at La Scala and secretary of the Department of Music in the government in 1933 and was therefore "high up in Fascist musical circles."[52] Trebbi enthusiastically declared that he was "thrilled with [her] voice" and arranged an audition for Norma with a former conductor at La Scala, teacher Riccardo Pettinella, and two of his students, Signor Morelli (a baritone) and Carlo Merino (a tenor from Chile). Norma reported to her father: "Dr. Trebbi had evidently raved about my voice to these people . . . [but] I came off well. They all liked my voice immensely and didn't hesitate to tell me that I should show more emotion in my singing. The very fact that they said bad about me shows they thought I had something worth while. I liked them. Their criticism was sincere and also their praise."[53] Norma started lessons with Maestro Pettinella the next day and soon located another scena teacher, Signora Lauro. She wrote to her father with relief, "At last my days of wandering in the wilderness are over, and my climb is all in one direction . . . upward! . . . Thank you so much, dear for giving me this chance. I will prove to you that it was worthwhile."[54]

True to his word, George guided Norma through this whirlwind period of musical assessment, working his influential contacts on her behalf, attending auditions and supporting her socially. Norma was grateful for his interest: "It is wonderful that Mr Pocaterra happened to come to Italy. He has been able to put me into a musical world I didn't know existed before."[55] After two weeks of lessons with her new maestro, Norma wrote: "Things are going marvellously for me. For the first time I feel secure."[56] Although she found him a "hard taskmaster," she considered Pettinella a "perfect follower-up" to Brandli, and he, in turn, complimented Brandli on having done a good job of Norma's early training and giving him a "good foundation" with which to work.[57] He told George that he was pleased with her quick progress and that "it was a treat to get a pupil from across the water who had the intelligence to grasp what he was trying to teach, and the ability to put it into practice."[58]

With a little prompting from George, Pettinella talked of a debut in the fall "to try her wings," but advised a year or more of serious, concentrated study before Norma would be ready for the operatic stage. Understanding that her family and friends had expected quicker results, Norma wrote, "I cannot be a great singer without it. It takes months to learn an opera, to have every note properly placed and one cannot immediately jump into a career." In spite of the longer time frame, she painted a rosy picture of the future: "Pettinella says it will take two years at least before I'll be able to command a big salary. I'll have to sing for nothing at first, then gradually get a little more money as I gain experience and finally when I sing at the Met and Covent Garden I'll make real money."[59]

In the interim, money was to become a real problem for all concerned. Dr. Piper's original plan was for Norma to put the finishing touches on her voice in Milan for six months or so, make an impressive European debut and then return to a North American career. However, he had not counted on the first few months in Milan being a false start musically and, of course, had not realized that everything would cost nearly three times more than expected. His own financial situation had not been a factor in making the decision to send Norma to Europe. Instead, he had simply assumed that her Canadian earnings plus the money inherited from Aunt Susie (1,200 dollars in 1934, with many hundreds of dollars still to come) would more than cover her expenses for the anticipated year away from home. As a bonus, he had sent about 60 dollars toward trip expenses, but he had never considered that Norma might stay longer than a year in Italy and need ongoing financial help.

By the time she had settled in with Maestro Pettinella in early April, her funds had decreased alarmingly, but she was far too happy musically (and personally, with George now in the picture) to do more than hint at the looming problem. Glad to be on the right track at last, she confidently assumed her father would be able to support her as long as was necessary. However, George soon realized that the long period of study recommended by Maestro Pettinella would require significant funds, and that Dr. Piper might want to share the burden. In late April he wrote to Dr. Piper and Bill Park, suggesting that they co-ordinate local service clubs and wealthy industrialists such as Pat Burns to contribute to Norma's support. He calculated that Norma needed a two-year commitment of 175 dollars per month to fulfill all their expectations. He told Bill that although he still intended to use his own inheritance money to fulfill his dream of a visit to the South Seas, he had postponed the trip to extend his stay in Milan because he was reluctant to leave his new young friend until he felt assured that she had adequate funds for proper career development.

While he tarried in Milan, George was Norma's constant companion. He enjoyed his new mentoring role, shepherding her to and from her lessons, which he attended, sharing little meals at cafes on the piazza and showing her the lovely lakes and countryside around Milan. Two weeks after their

Lake Como, Italy, April 29, 1934. GA PD-184-6-193

first meeting, Norma told her father: "It is very nice having Mr Pocaterra here. He seems like a friend of long standing. He is a very fine man."[60] The next week, George moved from his sister Emilia's house and into the Amodei *pensione*, and their friendship quickly blossomed into love. A year later, Norma documented the quick progress of their affection through April and May 1934: long walks home, "steal[ing] kisses in the dark street," intimate breakfasts in Norma's room at the *pensione* and innumerable little outings together. After a wonderful trip to Lake Como, George remarked "I think you are in love with Love," and to his delight Norma replied "no, I'm in love with you."[61] On May 1 they became engaged in a little ceremony in which they "plighted their troth" by repeating the words of the wedding vows[62] and exchanged specially commissioned rings whose arrangement of synthetic "jewels" spelled out the word DEAREST.[63] On May 21 they shared their joy with their Italian family and friends at a champagne engagement party, but fearing that Norma's family might think them unduly hasty, they did not inform Dr. Piper of their engagement for another four months.

George adored Norma's "marvellous smile, frank, open and sweet,"[64] her charming naturalness of manner, and her beauty and simplicity of youth.

119

This last perception she probably reinforced by leading him to believe, at least at first, that she was a decade younger than her actual age. In the 1930s, much of the advertising aimed at women implied that middle age (starting in a woman's 30s) spelled doom for women in every way unless they worked hard to keep themselves looking youthful and attractive.[65] Worried that her age (35) might impede her progress in Europe, on leaving Canada Norma had deducted 10 years from the birthdate shown on her passport. Her youthful appearance and girlish manner were in her favour, and she reinforced the perception whenever she could, once telling George disparagingly about a "foolish woman" she knew who was still trying to become a singer at age 38 (only a year older than herself at the time) and ending the story with the statement, "My but I am fortunate to be so young."[66] Even once he knew the truth, George loyally maintained the fiction: he told her father in 1936 "she looks positively sixteen," and he warned him in 1938 not to reveal her true age to the newspapers since "a woman is as young as she looks, and Norma looks under twenty-five."[67]

Norma and George breakfasting at the Amodei pensione, Milan, Italy, May 11, 1934.
GA PD-184-7-28

Conscious that her appearance attracted him, Norma worked hard to keep looking young and beautiful. She even tried to avoid wrinkling her forehead, because George so admired its smoothness. "I'm glad that you think I am so pretty," she once told him coquettishly, "Your thinking so makes me prettier."[68] He approved of her natural look, so she avoided lipstick and other makeup offstage, but she still relied on the regular use of face creams to work their magic. When she realized that he admired her hair, she determined to "wash it every three weeks and brush it every day" so that he would think it "the most beautiful hair in the world."[69] Aware that stress and fatigue aged her face (after one stressful period, she said "I actually looked a hundred years old"[70]), she was careful to get adequate rest and exercise, and she loved to take long walks in addition to the floor exercises she performed daily. She promised George, "I'll keep myself healthy and beautiful for you Darling. Your approval is music to my ears."[71]

At 5 feet 4 inches Norma was petite and well proportioned, but occasionally she struggled to achieve the thinner silhouette dictated by women's magazines of the time. Her father was well aware of her fondness for sweets and earlier in her career had cautioned, "Slim and healthy is what you must remain—this can be maintained by balanced diet, exercise, good judgment."[72] For a while, she followed Dr. Jackson's *How to Keep Well*, a book recommended by Dr. Piper, who was also a disciple. But Norma was not always able to follow this sensible advice and occasionally tried dieting. After a particularly arduous period of living off a "grass diet," which made her slimmer than George had ever seen her and even eliminated her perceived *pancia* (paunch), she finally decided that dieting was ruining her health and announced defiantly: "I am looking well . . . I'm fatter than I was in the summer and I've reduced for the last time—No more starving—I eat everything and look ever so much better by so doing."[73]

To assist in Norma's language training, the couple often spoke in Italian and frequently used it in their letters to discuss business and to express their love. Once, when he was away, George complimented Norma on her "wonderful progress" but playfully threatened to "come home to you, if for nothing else to spank you every time you use the past imperfect tense of a verb, in Italian."[74] This playfulness was one of George's attractions for Norma, though she was also impressed by his intelligence and "extraordinary culture." They both appeared to enjoy their respective roles of worldly sophisticate and youthful ingenue. Although he was 16 years older than she, and age 51 when they met, he was very fit after his years in the mountains and age was no barrier for them. She was proud of his distinguished appearance, which he seems to have given a more youthful look during this period through the use of hair dye.[75] Norma complimented him on the change, telling him that he looked "15 years younger" than when they had first met.[76] Certainly, his old friends were surprised when they received photographs from Italy. Dr. Morlan teased him, saying, "No joking, George, you really appear twenty years younger than when I last saw you—and that was not yesterday. How do you do it?"[77] Far from worrying about their age difference, Norma celebrated it and often referred to tenderly kissing his "darling eye wrinkles."

Although they worried about how the Pipers would receive news of their engagement, they were in no doubt that George's family accepted their relationship and welcomed Norma with love. His mother, several elderly aunts and uncles, his sister Emilia and her sons, Franco and Sergio, saw the couple frequently and seemed pleased that love had detained George in Italy indefinitely. In June, when the heat of Milan had become stifling, George concluded they should visit Marta at her villa in Bassano del Grappa.

However, first the couple decided to leave the Amodei *pensione* and take a "honeymoon trip," an extended motor tour of central Italy. In addition to Rome, they visited Perugia, Assisi, Siena and Florence. They arrived at Bassano in late July and spent several weeks in their "lovely villa" with Marta and her husband, who also joined them for a side trip to Venice. It was during this first trip together that George really began to amass what eventually became a huge collection of photographs and slides detailing their life together in Milan, their travels and his lovely Norma posed in costume for publicity purposes.

Blithely unconcerned about "appearances," Norma only worried that her father would not understand her long absence from Milan; she assured him that at Bassano she was put to "no expense" and managed to practise daily, often with Marta's accompaniment on the piano. Apparently, the locals also enjoyed these sessions: Norma reported a "burst of applause from the street" on one occasion.[78] It was a wonderful summer of traveling, and Norma reported details of the scenery and interesting sights in long letters to her father. He sent copies of her letters to the interested Calgarians on his mailing list, carefully omitting any reference in the typed transcripts to Norma travelling alone with Mr. Pocaterra.

When they returned to Milan, Norma and George decided it was time to inform her family of their engagement. Dr. Piper had already remarked on Norma's increasing dependence on Mr. Pocaterra, and in September she finally told him:

> He has been, Father, more than just a mere friend to me . . . He is the finest man it has ever been my good fortune to meet, has the highest ideals, the deepest reverence, the strongest sense of fair play and of defending those who cannot help themselves, and withal a spirit of fun and boyishness that is contagious. He has the great gift of being able to make friends and what is better to keep them, is always thinking of some kind deed to do for someone . . . and best of all a power to give people confidence in themselves and a desire to develop their natures to the highest capacity."[79]

In turn, George told his prospective father-in-law:

> At first it was a sense of pleasant duty towards the land of my adoption which prompted my activity on behalf of Norma's career . . . As I came to be thrown more and more together with Norma, I could not help but admire her wonderfully sweet, gentle nature and rare intelligence, her strength of character and clear sense of the truth, and very naturally, and, at first, unconsciously, I learned to do things for her for no other reason than that it gave me pleasure to do them for her, until one day we both realized that we loved each other.[80]

Dr. Piper quibbled slightly with George's religion, but Norma replied that the Pocaterra family had expressed no reservations in that regard. She assured

Top: Norma in St. Mark's Square, Venice, June 1934.
GA PA-2393-12-1-7

Bottom: George in St. Mark's Square, Venice, June 1934.
GA PA-2393-14-2-1

her father that although George had been born a Roman Catholic, he had left the church at age 12 and had switched to the Church of England in Canada, often attending the little Anglican church at Pekisko. Rather than adhering to any one faith, he now considered his religion to be "that of doing his best to make the world a better and a happier place."[81] Accepting the inevitable, Dr. Piper told his daughter, "I could see there was a love brewing between you two . . . I will be glad to welcome George into our family. I am sure he will make you happy—and be a loving husband." But he was honestly disappointed and worried about the future: "I had hoped that you would not enter the double harness hook up until after you had made your debut, and still trust that it will be thus." He gave his approval, but said, "This must not interfere with your Career and I hope you will be in no hurry to marry. You have a long time to enjoy each other's love so be patient . . . I advise no great speed."[82]

While Dr. Piper trusted to George's gentlemanly instincts, he also exerted a little pressure in his letter of welcome:

> You have won Norma's virgin love, for she has never loved a man until she met you. Norma will be a loving and dutiful wife and a charming companion . . . She is deeply in love with you for what you are—grateful for what you have done . . . I am sure that your love for her and your desire for her success will be your guide as to when the marriage will take place. My desire is to see her successfully launched in her career before you get married . . . nothing should be permitted to transpire that would prevent her achieving the success she so justly merits; with this I am convinced you are in perfect accord.[83]

George reassured Dr. Piper, and Norma told him proudly, "He is just as determined as anyone else that I must continue, make a try—even though we don't need the career to make us happy. On the contrary, we would be happier to live a simple life without it. However, he feels it would be unfair to me, my family and my country to give it up."[84]

In September 1934 George and Norma moved into a *pensione* run by the Casetti family. The Pocaterras looked forward to a very congenial atmosphere at via Ampere 40, as the landlady, Signora Casetti, was a "bosom friend" of Carmen Melis. Here they had "two beautiful rooms, exquisitely furnished" in a much quieter neighbourhood than Bianca Maria and at a savings of 20 dollars per month each. The savings were important to Norma, who could no longer ignore her dwindling finances. In early June, Dr. Piper had responded to George's frank "money" letter of late April by promising Norma guaranteed support from home of 75 dollars per month plus a lump sum deposit of 1,000 dollars on September 1. But times were still difficult in Alberta, and a hint from Jack finally made Norma realize that her financial support might be something of a burden to her father. She wrote, "I know things must be very slack in the office and with this dreadful drought we read about things will doubtless be worse . . . If we could just get somebody to advance a few thousand dollars it would relieve the strain on you dear."[85] However, she never seriously doubted that somehow he would find a way to keep her in Italy, and he was reluctant to dash her hopes by revealing the true extent of his financial difficulties.

So, as he had done during Norma's Vancouver days, Dr. Piper turned to Lawrence and Jack to help out with monthly contributions they were to regard as an investment in Norma's career. As before, Dr. Piper reminded them of Norma's past self-sacrifices in favour of themselves and assured them that Norma's career was sure to "pay off big" in the long run.[86] Each brother agreed to send 20 to 25 dollars monthly, which was a significant amount of their Depression-era paycheques, particularly for Lawrence, who had been forced to take a pay cut. Over the next few months Jack was able to send his monthly 25 dollars but Lawrence managed only 40 dollars in four months, and during the same period Dr. Piper was able to send only 60 dollars earned from selling some gold.

Although he was happy to fund little trips and some of the extras in their life together as an affianced couple, George was not a wealthy man in spite of his recent inheritance, and he was not prepared to take over the cost of Norma's career development. He saw this as her family's dream and responsibility, not his, and was confirmed in this supposition by Dr. Piper's conditional response to their engagement. In effect, it relieved George of the main responsibility for her financially, at least until they were married.

Knowing that Dr. Piper was a well-known Calgary dentist who had contrived to send his daughter for European musical training, George naturally assumed he was at the very least financially comfortable, and so he could not understand the doctor's seeming inability to make generous, consistent contributions to Norma's upkeep. He thought the money problem might be one of distance and logistics and suggested a solution that would benefit them both: instead of sending money directly to Norma, he suggested, Dr. Piper could deposit whatever he wished to give her to George's credit in a bank account George still held in Calgary; in turn, George would advance to Norma the equivalent in lire at the current rate of exchange.

This scheme would also let George bypass a new Italian law by enabling him to get a significant portion of his inheritance money out of Italy.[87] In addition to this plan, George devised a scheme to move money from Italy by sending a 500-lire note in each of Norma's letters to her father for a number of weeks. Suddenly concerned that the "secret service" might be monitoring George's activities, Norma checked with her father to see if he had received the "5 books of 500 leaves each?" After several additional letters to clear up Dr. Piper's confusion about the unexpected use of code words, he reassured them that he had indeed changed several thousand lire into dollars and had dutifully deposited the money into George's Calgary bank account.[88]

Increasingly uneasy about the erratic nature of the family's contributions, George pushed Norma to get a stable, long-term financial commitment from her family. At first she only hinted delicately about money, but finally, in early July, she spoke frankly, revealing that she had only 4,000 lire left (about 333 dollars) and that her current expenses of 2,100 lire a month (175 dollars) would allow for less than two months more in Italy.[89] On a note of panic, she wrote:

> As all my time is taken up in studying, I can see no way in which I can decently earn some money. As it is now I haven't even got enough money ahead to pay my ticket back should I have occasion to need it. This has been worrying me terribly for some time ... Now, Father, though I am just as keen as ever on my work, ... I am beginning to ask myself whether I have attempted the impossible, and whether it wouldn't be advisable that I come back. You can just imagine how hard it is for me to say that, but I can't face the near possibility of being stranded here without funds, which would be just terrible for a girl in a foreign land.[90]

She told him that George had offered to lead her a few thousand lire, but she felt it was unfair to take it when "I have no guarantee that my own people will be able to carry me later on." She ended with, "Now Father I hope I haven't spoken too plainly. I owe you all more than I can ever possibly repay, and it is for this reason that I am worrying myself sick. I shan't feel better until I feel my position safe and clear, either to remain here or to come back."[91]

Dr. Piper's return letter contained deposit slips and the reassurance, "Don't worry about finances, leave that to us, think only of your art and of developing yourself."[92] But because his own financial situation had not eased, Norma's relief was short-lived. In early October, he finally admitted that he was unable to raise sufficient funds in Calgary for the lump sum payment, even when he reduced it from 1,000 to 500 dollars and extended the promised deposit date from week to week. Norma sent several frantic letters in which she told her father that "it puts me in a nasty predicament" and "sweet words and talk of 'don't worry' are all right, but they don't buy food, and you can just imagine the position of any girl in any country without funds." She had "put [her] pride in her pocket" and asked George for a third time since September to advance her some cash, and without that she would have been "absolutely without funds."[93]

Now panicking, she raged: "It isn't fair that I should be so humiliated."[94] She begged her father to see the embarrassment of her position: "I can't possibly go on being dependent on a man who is not my husband. If this were known I would never be forgiven, would never be allowed to take my place in decent society."[95] Finally she gave her father an ultimatum: "I *can not* and *will not* remain if I have to have all this worry about expenses. I cannot study calmly with this insecurity in my mind constantly ... If my family or my country cannot possibly raise the money that is necessary for my keep here, we will have to bid good-bye to our dreams. This is the *last* time I shall write to you dear in this manner. When the necessity comes for another letter similar, I shall be already on my way to Canada." Her plan was to throw herself on the mercy of the British consul, who would be obliged to provide her with a third-class ticket home because she could prove that she had no means of support.[96]

Norma's hysterical letters brought results, as George had predicted. "Those dreadful letters didn't make them angry ... they [had] the effect ... of making the whole family jump into harness."[97] Shocked by Norma's vulnerable position abroad, Lawrence borrowed money against his insurance policy and sent 100 dollars, Jack promised to continue his monthly payments in spite of reservations about her engagement and Dr. Piper promised to place 500 dollars to George's credit and to provide 50 dollars monthly if only George could "take care of [Norma's] expenses a little longer."[98] Reluctant to cash his shares while they still were so devalued but desperate to obtain more ready cash for Norma's benefit, Dr. Piper decided to take in boarders. This income-generating tactic was not unusual among the owners of large homes during the Depression, even in Calgary's finer residential areas, and eventually Dr. Piper had two families living with him. His kind treatment of them during hard times was repaid as his health declined over the next few years.

The following spring, Dr. Piper acquired some additional cash by finally selling the Youngstown farm, which was a relief, as it had produced poorly for years and was considered "an awful drain on the funds and an awful strain on the nerves."[99] Humbled, he told George he was considering taking a second mortgage on his house or using his Royalite stock to compensate him for his generosity in making cash advances available to his daughter. He wrote, "Oh boy I wish I had controle [sic] of the money I had a few years ago" and apologized, saying, "I am sorry I have not the means to keep her abundantly supplied with cash."[100] In October Norma was relieved when her father wrote to say that he had sorted everything out and that he and "the lads" would keep her "supplied from now on ... so there will be no more such trying spells for you."[101]

However, brother Jack now precipitated a different funding crisis. He had received the news of his sister's engagement with joy at her happiness but with a question for his father: he wondered if continuing to support Norma was not now "a bit futile." The convention

Top: George at Lake Como,
April 29, 1934. GA PD-184-6-60

Bottom: Norma at Lake Como,
April 29, 1934. GA PD-184-6-61

of the 1930s was for women to give up work when they married, so that they could spend their time raising children and managing their husband's household; Jack's concern was a valid one for the times. "Why potter about . . . for two years more studying singing, and then throw it all up and get married?" he asked his father. "It will do no one any particular good and deprives yourself, Tass and myself of some benefits which might accrue from having a bit more cash." He worried that Norma's career might not develop as planned and reminded his father that "although of a very youthful appearance," Norma would be at a disadvantage competing with younger singers, as agents surely would realize that her career would be much shorter. He continued:

> Boiled down, what I mean is this. If Norma is going to study one year more, sing in small Italian cities for a year after (when her earnings will not be large) then do a couple of years work, even at 3 or 4 thousand a year salary, I don't think the sacrifices we are making are warranted. If she is going to sing 5 to 10 years after, whole time, and if her voice would carry through that length of time, OK. Further to my first if, I also do not believe Norma's sacrifice of 2 or 3 years of happy marriage would be made up for, by any small triumph or financial success she might have . . . my point is that, Norma must, or rather should, choose between marriage and a career, as if she tries to carry through with both, one of them is going to be neglected.[102]

Predictably, Dr. Piper told Jack that the family should follow through to the end their original commitment, especially since it had already taken seven or eight years and 5,000 to 7,000 dollars to get Norma that far. Norma argued that George was not typical, that he would always allow her career to come first, even after their eventual marriage. In response to a friend who advised her to give up singing, marry and settle down, she said, "You don't know Mr Pocaterra very well. He doesn't want to be considered a meal ticket and hotel for his wife, an excuse for her to get fat and lazy. One of the things he likes best about me is my ambition to be a personality on my own as well as his wife."[103] Although she agreed that "most husbands are naturally selfish and want their wives to themselves for one thing, and for another don't want to feel that the wife is admired perhaps more than they are," she would later tell her father, "George is the exact opposite of the husband who is jealous of his famous wife. On the contrary he is doing everything in his power to make her famous."[104]

Outnumbered, Jack submitted gracefully to the family decision and renewed his commitment to support his sister. This crisis resolved, Dr. Piper assured Norma, "We are all back of you . . . we want you to succeed and will support you . . . Don't worry about the money I spent on you. Nor what will be spent."[105] And, one way or another, the Piper family honoured this promise, and their combined support eventually totalled between 15,000 and 20,000 dollars.[106]

With Norma's maintenance secure, at least for the time being, the couple could concentrate on a money-making scheme that George had been drawn into some months before. In June, Attilio Pavoni had introduced them to a "celebrated Venetian artist," Pericle Menin, and George, always naive in business deals, had been convinced by Pavoni that Menin's *aquaforti* (engravings of local scenes) would be big sellers outside Italy. Impulsively, he spent 18,000 lire of his inheritance (approximately 1,500 dollars—23,000 dollars today) to purchase Menin's original steel engraving plates, plus 500 prints showing close to 100 different subjects. George was to have the exclusive right to sell the prints in Britain and North America, and he planned to hire agents in several major cities who would take care of business locally and receive 50 percent of the profits. At a projected selling price of "$30-75 or even $100," George and Norma anticipated a large income from the etchings business. Pavoni, glad to have found such a gullible investor, grandly promised that in return he would look for opportunities for Norma to sing and provide a good review of her first concert.

MOSTRA PERSONALE

DEL PITTORE **PERICLE MENIN**

con le sue ACQUEFORTI - DISEGNI - MONOTIPIE

Brochure commissioned by George to promote etchings by Pericle Menin, Milan, Italy, ca 1934. GA M6340-171-1

This scheme was to be yet another way for George to move money out of Italy, its intent not to fund Norma's career but rather to provide for the couple once they were married. George still longed for a boat and life in the South Seas or, failing that, a quiet life on an island off Canada's west coast, or as a last resort a return to ranching in the Canadian West. Norma had come to share his vision as their ultimate goal as a couple. Although she had assured her family that she was committed to the long-term development of her career, in private she counted on that career being short, though financially lucrative, planning only to "make enough money to more than cover what has been spent on my voice."[107] She anticipated that any earnings from singing or the etchings business would simply be a means to the end of buying their boat or settling down somewhere together, and both of them assumed that any profits from George's coal concerns would be a bonus, "a wonderful heritage for Junior."[108]

In the interim, the etchings had to be sold to turn the anticipated profit, and George planned a major sales tour through England and Canada during the winter and spring of 1934–35. However, before leaving Italy, he wanted to see Norma settled into an apartment where she would have the freedom to practise without fear of comment or criticism. The Casettis had proved noisy and quarrelsome, and several of their boarders had expressed violent prejudice against Maestro Pettinella, which George had always managed to quell, but he feared they would harass Norma when she was left on her own. Privacy was another consideration in leaving the *pensione* for an apartment, as their relationship had evolved to the point where the couple now considered themselves "married." In quick succession that fall, George had altered his will to benefit Norma, had taken out a life insurance policy in her favour and had opened a joint bank account from which they both could draw.

Before George left Italy, his sister Ilia helped them locate a modest three-room apartment on the fourth floor of a small building at via Eduardo Bassini 46, an area of "small clerks" near the railway tracks on the outskirts of Milan. George felt strongly that Norma should concentrate on her lessons and her practising while he was away, so he arranged to hire their favourite maid, Ena, from the Amodei *pensione* and agreed to pay her salary. Norma, quickly overcoming her scruples about having a servant, exulted, "I feel like a fairy princess . . . I have never been so free from work in my life. I have literally nothing to do—except study and write letters."[109] She came to rely on the young maid's loyalty and friendship during the lonely months of George's absence, and when George returned, Ena stayed on, remaining with the couple until they left Italy in 1939.

Several weeks after George's departure, Norma moved into the apartment and spent many happy hours decorating their "dear wee nest" with the help of "her best friend in Milan," Signora Lenzi (sister of George's Calgary friend, Mrs. Mamini). The friendship between the two women blossomed because Signora Lenzi was one of the few Milanese with whom Norma could speak English and because the older woman reminded her of her Vancouver friend Mrs. Middlemass and her dear Aunt Susie. Norma's housewifely instincts came to the fore with a home of her own, and she regretted not learning more from Aunt Susie when she had had the chance. Although Ena did most of the cooking and cleaning, Norma occasionally did some baking. She bought a small oven and sent for Aunt Susie's old recipe books so that she could make comfort food that she missed from home: "real roast meat," toast and "American light cakes that melt in one's mouth." [110] Before he left, George had given her a present of 500 lire (42 dollars) with which she bought various small indulgences and several lengths of fabric. She tried to rent a sewing machine, but when that scheme fell through, she and Ena spent many hours hand sewing new blouses and other items of clothing for Norma.

By the autumn of 1934, Norma was well settled in Milan, and her musical education seemed to be proceeding smoothly. With daily lessons and practices totalling six hours a day, six days a week, it was an intense period of concentrated effort. In June Dr. Trebbi had scored a coup when he arranged a private audition for Norma and Carlo Merino with Giulio Gatti-Casazza, the recently retired manager of the Metropolitan Opera Company in New York. Accompanied by Pettinella, Merino and Norma each sang two songs in the impromptu audition staged in Gatti-Casazza's hotel room. Norma's selections were from *Rigoletto*, and although the great man "sat like an image . . . listened and made no remark whatever," he shook hands afterwards and said "va bene, signorina" (it went well). Norma was excited and told her father "the audition will bear fruit later. When I am ready for the Met he will remember me."[111] In July Trebbi had her sing for the "great Italian director" Baron del Campo and for Tullio Serafin, one-time orchestra director of the Met, who was head of the Royal Opera at Rome and also Carmen Melis's husband. Norma was thrilled with the opportunities and said, "It is certainly marvellous that I have such men to direct my affairs. Alone I would have no chance in a hundred years."[112]

Impressed with Trebbi's "most dynamic" personality, George decided to leave him in charge of Norma's career while he was overseas selling etchings and paid him 10,000 lire (833 dollars) to take on the job. With typical enthusiasm, Trebbi had told the family what they wished to hear: Norma would debut late in the fall of 1934, have a season of three or four programs in the spring, make steady progress from smaller to larger theatres to La Scala over the course of 1935 and, within two years of arriving in Italy, be ready for "big contracts in America," with "of course" a European reputation.[113]

But Maestro Pettinella distrusted what he perceived as Trebbi's overconfidence and insisted that Norma would not be ready for a public debut before the spring or even the fall of 1935. She was progressing well but still had a lot to learn. When Dr. Piper pressed for an earlier debut, she reminded him: "Italy is not America . . . here there are a hundred good singers to one in America and . . . if I sing only well I am one of a great crowd."[114] Pettinella's approach was prosaic, and over the next months and years Norma learned the soprano roles of the grand operas slowly and thoroughly, one by one: *Rigoletto, L'Elisir d'Amore, Don Pasquale, Lucia di Lammermoor, The Barber of Seville, Semiramide, La Traviata, La Sonnambula, La Boheme* and others. Each new opera took many weeks to perfect, and she needed to have many in her repertoire to follow up a successful debut with operatic engagements.

Previously she had learned only concert songs or selected arias; now Norma found it an exciting and sometimes frustrating challenge to learn entire operas. After learning a new one, sometimes she was disconcerted to realize she had forgotten material she had learned previously, but she worked diligently to correct her accent and to add emotion and colour to her voice. At first Trebbi encouraged her, saying she had a double difficulty in learning the language as well as the spirit of each opera, but later he admitted that her voice needed much work to take it from the drawing room to the theatre.[115] She had never studied agility, and she needed to work hard to overcome her tendency to produce an uneven sound and to go either flat or sharp. To her great mortification, she now learned that she had always done runs "abominably . . . with 'scoops' up and down."[116] Discouraged by the unaccustomed criticism, her confidence ebbed, and she wrote to George: "I haven't the pearl-like brilliance necessary for leggero operas. I know my piccitato is not anything to compare with that of Galli-Curci, nor my scales to compare with those of [Italian Soprano] Toti dal Monte."[117]

Although Norma liked and respected Pettinella, and knew he was fond of her, too, she sometimes found his "wet blanketing" approach hard to bear.[118] In contrast to Brandli, Pettinella rarely offered praise and even discouraged her by commenting on every failing and discoursing on the effort involved in training "one of the common garden varieties of soprano."[119] Frustrated, she complained to her diary about the maestro's "cold water douches," suspecting that he was so accustomed to "great artists" that "this country hay seed doesn't impress him a bit."[120] She worried about disappointing her family with failure; that maybe "in their hearts they thought it was a wild goose chase."[121] Sometimes she was overcome with self-doubt: "I have so little faith in myself."[122] Early in their relationship, she admitted to George that she was her "own worst critic" and told him, "One of the biggest fights I have had has been against an inferiority complex."[123]

But Norma's "blue fits" always resulted in a new determination to show the maestro that she could overcome her deficiencies and to justify her father's faith in her and now, more than ever, to justify George's. She wrote to her father, "George despises a quitter,"[124] and she confided to her diary, "I wish I didn't have to bother with my singing but I must. Giorgio is insistent that I make good. He has great faith in me. Poor dear I'll do my best. But oh it is so hard . . . now my biggest spur is . . . Giorgio. He wouldn't love me if I lay down on the job. He wants a wife that can take her place in the world and also in the entertaining of his friends. No, being the wife of George Pocaterra is no snap."[125] She worried that "to be a successful wife to Giorgio Pocaterra I have to excel in at least one thing. I'll never be a brilliant conversationalist, nor a sportswoman, so the only thing that remains for me is to try to be a reasonably successful artist."[126] Dr. Piper sensed this shift in his daughter's source of inspiration and plaintively reminded her, "Now my dear little girl you know how I love you—the very centre of my affection."[127]

When George left for England in early November, Norma worried at first in case she had misread their relationship. She was reassured by the passionate tone of his letters, and in spite of her more restrained personality did her best to respond in kind. She wrote, "Dear Heart, how I miss you! The world seems horribly dark and dull since you went away . . . Oh Giorgio, darling Rainbow Eyes, I want to see you, to feel your kisses on my lips, on my forehead, to hear your voice whispering into my ear 'I love you,' and I miss your encouragement, your love. I feel horribly lost and alone. I had got to depend on you, dear, for so much, that now when I do not have you life is hopelessly blank. You are entirely, absolutely necessary to me."[128]

Love letters came more naturally to George, who wrote, "My heart is forever crying out to yours, dear Two Suns in the Sky, and will never be stilled until we are permanently together," "I never realized how your life had woven itself so tightly around mine," and "I live only for the time when we shall always be forever together as one . . . Dear, Dearest, my own Sweet Norma! I love you, I long for you, I live for you!" But George also admonished Norma to conquer her often expressed self-doubt and black thoughts and said, "Let us both work our best towards the successful completion of our common goal; our future life . . . together."[129] After reading a particularly dreary letter, he wrote, "If you don't write a decent letter soon I'll come back to give you a real 'panking,'" and she teasingly replied, "I almost decided to write another horrid [letter] just so you would come and spank me."[130]

In England George stayed at Holtsmere End, Hampshire, with his old neighbour and friend from the Highwood, Josephine Bedingfeld. Frank Bedingfeld had died in 1921, but Josephine and her daughter, Jo, were delighted to welcome George, who stayed with them for a month. The trip was only moderately successful. Although he took advantage of the opportunity to exchange "a good many" of his inherited lire into English pounds,[131] George was unable to sell more than a few etchings in England and Scotland and only for the relatively modest price of 45 dollars each. Discovering that promotion of the etchings was hard and mostly unrewarding work, he decided to postpone the Canadian portion of the trip until the new year, when ocean travel would be easier.

George at South Queen's Ferry, Scotland, November 24, 1934. GA PA-2393-14-1-5

After a month apart, he and Norma were desperately lonely for each other and she wrote excitedly, "Home dear! will be a real home with you in it. Oh how gloriously, marvellously wonderful the next month will be."[132] In fact, George ended up lingering in their "consecrated little nest" for nearly four months, finally leaving for England again in mid-March. During the intervening time, the couple enjoyed socializing with artists introduced by

Pavoni, although Norma later bitterly characterized them as a "blood sucking tribe" and "a lot of lazy loafers."[133] Foolishly, George allowed Pavoni to talk him into buying more etchings and eventually he had works representing seven artists, although Menin's were still considered the finest. Pavoni also introduced them to his "great friend," Mario Castagneri, described as "the most artistic photographer in Milan."[134] Impressed to discover that Castagneri had been photographer at La Scala for many years, George commissioned him to create a lovely photograph of Norma, using a special printing process that made the final product resemble a pencil portrait. Charging an exorbitant five lire each, the photographer later printed an additional 25 postcard-sized copies for Norma to use for publicity purposes.

Meanwhile, George and Norma used the time together over the winter of 1934–35 to solidify their relationship. Later she reminded him that in sorting out their differences and sometimes "hurt[ing] each other cruelly and unthinkingly," they had survived the traditionally difficult "first year which makes or breaks a marriage."[135] As a result, George departed Britain for Canada on April 12, 1935, on the SS *Duchess of York* with much more confidence in their stability as a couple.

Norma, Milan, 1935. Studio portrait with pencil effects by Mario Castagneri.
GA PA-2393-12-3-3

During this second, much longer time away from each other, they were more focussed on their two main goals: Norma's successful debut and a series of operatic engagements to appease her family, and the successful establishment by George of the etchings business in Canada, which would lay the financial foundation for their future life together. Although they really did not foresee Norma's career having a big or long-term impact on their future, they realized that they might have to tarry in North America for several years while Norma earned enough to pay back her family; they decided that an island off the west coast, such as Portman Island, would provide an ideal base while they investigated their final destination in the South Seas. Their plan was to save George's remaining capital for these big purchases, and they counted on the etchings business to supplement their resources in the meantime. Once Norma's family had been reimbursed, any profits from her singing would be an additional bonus. As she once reminded George when the effusive admiration of a male friend provoked a hint of jealousy, "The more that voice is admired, Dearest Love, the quicker we can buy that boat."[136]

Unfortunately, George was utterly unable to establish the etchings business successfully in Canada. He spent several weeks in Montreal with Jack, who enjoyed the visit and wrote to Norma, "I think your choice of a husband is wonderful. I have seldom talked to a more interesting personage in my life."[137] Leaving some etchings for Jack to sell among his acquaintances, George moved on to Toronto in late April. There he spent a discouraging few months searching for a suitable agent for that end of the business and trying without success to interest stores such as Eaton's in carrying the etchings. Norma sent letters of introduction for George to family and friends in Ontario, but although they were glad to meet her fiance, few were interested in making a purchase. Eventually George made an arrangement with J. O. ("Piper, William John (Jack)" or "Frase") Fraser, who was an inspector with the agricultural board of the Ontario government and the brother-in-law of an Italian friend living in Toronto. The next year, George authorized an American acquaintance, Leonard C. Jackson, to take stock from Fraser's supply and act as his agent in the United States. Fraser and Jackson tried to promote the etchings for several years, but the business never made any money, and Norma still found many etchings in stock when she visited the Frasers in 1941.

While in Montreal and Toronto, George met various influential people he thought should hear a recording of Norma's voice, brought along specifically for that purpose. This recording, made in the period between George's trips abroad, had delighted Norma's father and brothers. Dr. Piper had written, "I want to thank you George for your kindness and thoughtfulness in having this record made that we may hear the dear girl's voice—as I write she is singing to me and I can plainly see her dear face and loving heart as her voice rings through the rooms."[138] George often played Norma's record right after one by the great Italian coloratura soprano Toti dal Monte and was gratified when friends agreed that Norma's voice compared favourably.

Most listeners were family and friends and, quite naturally, complimentary. One old family friend, Reverend Dr. Andrew J. Vining, told Dr. Piper, "I was thrilled and thrilled!"[139] Other listeners, those involved in the music industry, were asked by George for critical advice. In Montreal George saw the *Star* music critic, Morgan Powell, and in Toronto he played Norma's recording for Carlo Peroni, conductor of the travelling San Carlo Opera Company. Peroni admired the record but found fault with Norma's inability to sing high E-flat. George also played the record for Raymond Mullens, former editor of *Maclean's*. Mullens had several constructive criticisms, particularly with regard to her "nasal American pronunciation," but was impressed with the "marvelous freshness and clearness" of Norma's voice and pronounced that she was "already much superior" to American sopranos Marion Talley and Grace Moore.[140] Excitedly, George wrote to Norma, "that record of yours is our best selling agent!"[141]

Dr. Piper's Rotarian friend in Montreal, John Nelson, was utterly charmed with Norma's voice and, at George's urging, immediately wrote to Edward Johnson, now manager of the Metropolitan Opera Company in New York. Admitting that he was "absolutely untutored in musical matters," Nelson reminded Johnson of his previous letter on Norma's behalf and requested that he arrange to hear Norma's record as a personal favour to himself, predicting that Johnson would be "sufficiently impressed" to take a "personal interest" in her career.[142] Johnson replied courteously that he would be happy to hear Norma in audition in New York whenever it could be arranged. Nelson was pleased with the result of his efforts and wrote to Dr. Piper, "Let us hope that everything will turn out in keeping with our fondest desires."[143]

In addition to promoting Norma, George used his time in Toronto to reconnect with several of his former dudes, including businessman Irving Hollinrake, who advised him regarding the North American investment of his inheritance money. George also attended several meetings of the Canadian Youth Council, an organization comprising "representatives of all religious sects and social and political opinions." At one of the meetings, Italy was roundly "stigmatized" for its proposed military action in Abyssinia (Ethiopia), and George wrathfully concluded that the majority of the audience had been "influenced by the most pernicious propaganda imaginable" against his homeland. Although he did not speak out publicly, he was glad when two representatives of the Canadian Fascists defended Italy, and afterwards he congratulated them for their "courageous stand in the face of a very hostile audience."[144]

George's business disappointments left him bitter about his Toronto experience, and he complained to Norma of the "complacent smug goodness" and "utter mediocrity" of Torontonians:[145] "I soon found out about these Easterners that they are very quick to make promises, but D...d poor at keeping them. On the whole I don't exactly care for them, like I do for the Westerners." He decided that a visit to the West would be a tonic for his disappointments in the East: "I am longing to breathe the peppy western air again; and to meet open-hearted people, to have a look at the dear Rockies and to talk to my Indians again. I KNOW WHERE I STAND with them!"[146] He headed to Calgary at the end of July and spent his last six weeks in Canada in a much more congenial manner: riding horses, renewing friendships on the Highwood and getting to know Norma's family and friends.

George and Dr. Piper hit it off very well and spent many happy hours discussing "the lassie we both love."[147] George reported to Norma, "He is one in a million. What a good, good man he is," and "your Father is a dear. I love him."[148] Norma was glad to have George see her home and meet her friends, and she sent him lists of things to bring back to Italy, including Vantine's Japanese incense, good white glue for compiling her scrapbooks, rolls of "soft, soft toilet paper," and various favourite beauty products including Ambrosia cleanser and Vita-Ray face cream. Eventually she realized that her growing list might be unmanageable and told him just to use his own judgment, but he managed to bring her almost everything she requested.

While George was in Calgary, their engagement was announced in the *Calgary Herald*, and the news was so enthusiastically received that Norma was prompted to write, "You are a dear to say that everyone congratulates you on your engagement to me. Father, on the other hand, says that everyone congratulates him on his prospective son-in-law. It seems this is a romance which appeals to the imagination of Calgarians."[149] She instructed George to give her regards to Bill Park ("the fatal Cupid") and was delighted with Paul Amos's reaction to their news and his name for her, Mountain Blue Bird. Painter Roland Gissing promised them a "magnificent picture" as a wedding gift, and George's old friends the Browns, from the 7U Ranch, gave them a gift of 20 dollars that George promised Norma could be used to buy a wedding present "when we do get married in a properly legal manner."[150]

He was less satisfied by his reception from Raymond Patterson. Previously George had told Norma he was not looking forward to their first meeting, "as I can't work up any of the old friendship again."[151] Since both men were equally opinionated and stubborn, perhaps misunderstandings, political or otherwise, had arisen during the course of their regular correspondence (no letters between them have survived from this period). On the other hand, perhaps Patterson was becoming impatient with George, who still refused to transfer ownership of the buffalo-head brand and had not made permanent arrangements for his horses and possessions left in Patterson's care in 1933. In any case, after their first visit George was "so fed-up with [Patterson's] tactics" that he impulsively put his furniture into storage with Dr. Piper at 227 Scarboro Avenue, moved his horses from the Buffalo Head to his friend Harper Sibley's Round T Ranch and decided to "be completely through with the man."[152] Predictably, the old friends soon made up their differences, and during a visit to the Buffalo Head, George was surprised to discover that he felt no regret at seeing his old ranch again. He was relieved that "it caused not one extra heart beat, nothing at all," and concluded that with Norma in his life, "the rest is chapter now closed."[153]

After a year back in Italy, George found the extremes of the Alberta climate less than ideal and said, "This trip here has pretty well decided me that we will have to make our home at the coast, or rather at the South Sea Islands!"[154] He actually made inquiries with estate agents in British Columbia regarding the purchase of land in the Gulf Islands there, but was shocked by the high prices (little Moresby Island, only 1,600 acres, was going for 50,000 dollars). He also took Dr. Piper to inspect the Ghost River property he had received in his earlier transaction with Patterson and decided that with the addition of a road and certain other improvements, it would prove valuable and saleable some day for summer cottages.

In spite of a good visit to the West, George was disappointed by the ultimate failure of his trip to Canada. By early June he had already spent 450 dollars "for nothing much in way of sales" but felt he had invested too much "to just give it all up."[155] Norma sympathized from afar, railing against Pavoni for having "taken [them] in." George delayed the inevitable, reminding Norma that "any new business takes time to get it started, and we still are in the midst of a depression!"[156] but finally had to admit the futility of staying on. He worried that their financial resources were "very sadly depleted" and told Norma he would have nothing to live on but his capital, "which is getting continually smaller."[157] Nevertheless, he still hoped to see a small profit from the etchings and was relieved when Aileen Holland (later Nilsson), of "the Little Gallery on 7th Ave in Calgary" (probably The Art Shop) agreed to be his agent in the West. In spite of her best efforts, however, she was unable to sell the etchings in Calgary, or later,in Vancouver, even when the price was reduced in 1936 to five dollars—just enough to cover George's "out of pocket expenses."

George's despondency about money made Norma fear that he might decide to stay on in the West or, worse, head to the South Seas without her. Desperate for his return, she proposed little economies that would enable them to live together in spite of their reduced prospects. With his help as her manager, she argued, they could develop her career sufficiently to supplement her family's ongoing maintenance, thereby reducing the call on his capital. George allowed himself to be convinced by Norma's rather optimistic figures, mainly because he missed her and was wondering just how well she was progressing without his support. In his letters, he offered constant direction and advice, but he could tell that without his strong presence, Norma was at a clear disadvantage in dealing with Pettinella, Trebbi and others in the musical world, who he suspected were taking advantage of her. Her passive nature and natural avoidance of stressful situations, along with her need for approval, meant Norma found it difficult to express anger or to stand up for her rights. ("How lovely it is to be liked," she once said. "I'll never win fame by being brilliant, but if I can have people love me, that is enough."[158])

Norma was well aware of her weakness and, after a series of disappointments, wrote despairingly, "Everything is a terrible mess and it needs your magic touch to straighten it out—though I don't believe even you dear, will be able to do much to get me going in a career."[159] By August, George was sufficiently roused by the increasingly frustrated tone of Norma's letters that he booked his return passage to Italy for late September. He disliked leaving the etchings business unsettled but told her, "I have got to take that risk, which I feel is much less than leaving you there to fight your battles out alone. We both need each other, and we are better together. SO I AM COMING."[160] She was happy and relieved, and, predicting "what a reunion that will be," she planned a little holiday—she would surprise him by meeting his boat in Nice and sailing with him to Genoa. This plan never materialized. Because of the Ethiopian crisis, George's ship changed its destination port from Genoa to Naples, and George travelled home alone from there to Milan by train in early October.

During the long months of George's absence, Norma had continued her daily lessons and struggled to achieve vocal perfection. Often, she found the whole process tedious and rather pointless, and once she confessed to George, "Gee I'll be glad either when (or if) I become great enough to be of some importance, or else when I give it all up and sell etchings."[161] She was working on consistency and yearned for a time when she could count on her voice to perform on command. "When I get my voice the way I want it, it will be a permanent thing," she told George optimistically. "How marvellous it will be when I can open my mouth knowing beforehand that the sound will be beautiful, not having any fears of incorrect placing."[162] In March she wrote to tell her father she was trying to learn three big operas, *Rigoletto*, *The Barber of Seville* and *Lucia di Lammermoor*, "so well that I can sing them in my sleep with pearl like runs and bird-like staccato notes. The coloratura voice is the most difficult in the world to train. Not only must it be warm, and express the meaning of the words, but it must also have the technical perfection of a great violinist. It is that, that is so difficult to achieve, and unless the cadenzas are perfect, and flawless, a singer does not have a great success."[163]

With the exception of Toti dal Monte, there were few first-class coloratura sopranos in Italy during the 1930s, a condition mirrored internationally. Only Lily Pons in North America seemed able to fill the gap left by the retirement of coloratura superstars from the previous generation such as Dame Nellie Melba and Amelita Galli-Curci.[164] Norma hoped that with hard work and good luck she might succeed these great singers; with the maestro's encouragement, she decided to emulate Toti dal Monte by specializing in one area and determined her specialty to be singing cadenzas *granito* (well articulated). "It is in that line that the Toti shines—and in that line that I shall try to win my spurs. In that there is absolutely no competition outside of Toti and Lily Pons. Surely there is room for La Norma."[165] Confidently she wrote to her father, "My fame will be made as Galli-Curci's, by my bird notes . . . In the field of coloratura I have very few rivals—In America only Lily Pons, and America is large—there is room for us both."[166] She told George she believed she was "going to be the greatest soprano Canada has ever produced."[167]

In her letters, Norma projected a confidence she knew George and her father expected but which she often did not feel herself. Generally, she confined her "black thoughts" to her diary, though self-doubt occasionally surfaced when she wrote to George. In April 1935 she told him that she had had a "shock" looking back over the old scrapbooks from her Canadian singing days, and she accused herself of being "a first class Gold Digger" when she realized that her family already had spent an estimated 10,000 dollars on the "possibly futile" endeavour to make her a singer.[168] In her diary, she was far harsher:

> It's too bad I didn't realize that five years ago. We would have saved such a nice lot of money and heart-ache . . . How stupid of me to ever get the notion that I could be a great singer some day. I shouldn't have come here. I've had my fun. I've had my career in Canada and have a whole book of clippings . . . I should have been satisfied with that. I should have stayed home and kept house for Father . . . How stupid we are. All looking forward to me earning fantastic sums with my voice. Bah! I'll never earn more than I have in the past, a maximum of $50 for a concert and $5 for radio. Fine chance I have to pay back the family and live up to their faith in me.[169]

She agonized over her seeming inability to sing well consistently, particularly under fire, and was bitterly amused at her own "pretensions" in the early years when the "flowery criticisms" and fuss of the local press blinded her to the valid criticisms of competent critics like "RJ" of the *Vancouver Daily Province*, who had "pulled her to pieces."[170]

In Italy she encountered a different problem: not enough encouragement. At one point she told George that, aside from himself, the only person in Italy she enjoyed singing for was his sister, Ilia, who was never critical and listened with a face "beam[ing] with pride."[171] In frustration she wrote:

> It isn't that I'm lazy. I like to work, I like to overcome difficulties, but I'm sick and tired of being considered a nonentity . . . when it comes to music, because of the tradition of the country, everyone, no matter how incompetent he is, considers himself an absolute judge . . . *Everybody* says [my voice] is nice, then goes and spoils any glow of pleasure I may have by making a reservation . . . the pronunciation, or its shrill, or its too weak, or too strong, or it lacks sentiment, or it lacks sweetness, or it needs to be warmed up . . . if only people knew what harm they did by their critical attitude they might (?) stop it.[172]

She found this venting therapeutic, and her spirits usually lifted soon after, but George found it very upsetting; she often begged his pardon for causing him such worry at long distance.

She was more circumspect in letters to her father, and he was able to take Norma's cheerful confidence at face value and naively bragged about her prospects to friends. She was pleased when he arranged a party to play her record for Calgarians interested in her progress (friends like the Browers and the Carlyles and musical supporters like Jascha Galperin and Frank Hemming) but was upset when she learned that he was trying to arrange for it to be broadcast on a local radio station. Morbidly conscious that her voice still lacked perfection, she told him:

> My heart sank because I knew how tremendously it would be criticized. Our dear friends will love to hear it but my many enemies will delight in picking flaws and saying "There you are. That's Italian training for you. Now if she had gone to the Royal Academy in London, her voice would be much better. And anyway, her voice is nothing exceptional, and never will be." So would say the great powers that be in Calgary. No sir! Not until I have really won my spurs will Calgarians (not the ordinary simple ones, but rather those who pose to be superior) give me credit. Of course you can hardly blame the poor dears because of the dozens of students who go abroad to study only a few ever amount to anything.[173]

She was especially nervous of Mrs. Sharples, who Dr. Piper reported as having passed him on the street with "a very broad, bland smile almost as much as to say Norma made a big mistake in not going to England."[174] He had given her "a real sweet smile" in return, but both father and daughter were well aware of her disapproval. In fact, Norma was wary of the Women's Musical Club as a group and told her father, "They are all in league for the Royal Academy and even if I sang as well as Toti dal Monte they would find fault."[175] She was relieved when the broadcast scheme fell through.

The Pocaterras were very kind to Norma while George was away. She saw Milan-based family members regularly and was included by Emilia in many family parties, meals and outings with her friends. While Norma was still learning Italian, Ilia tried to make her feel more at home by sometimes including other English-speaking guests. Marta's visits to Milan were rare, but she was friendly and generous with Norma whenever they occurred, sometimes treating her to feminine luxuries such as a new lipstick or silk stockings.

But Norma's main consolation through her periods of gloom was the love between herself and George. Their letters were full of endearments: she was his Normuccia, his Dear, Dear Mummy, Beloved Blue Bird, Twin Pools of Delight, Two Suns in the Sky; he was her Beloved Giorgio, Dear Little Sonny Boy, Dearest Rainbow Eyes, Darling Mountain Child. Norma thrilled to read his loving letters: "I am longing continually for our little home with my wife," "I long for you so much, that it almost hurts," and "Dearest Love, you have set fire within me to a flame that is ever growing and will follow me into eternity."[176] In turn, Norma told George, "You are my Love, my eternal Mate, my dearest wonderful Husband," "you are the sun and the moon and the stars to me. You are my whole life. I am only half alive now—waiting for your return,"and "I adore you . . . I worship you . . . my whole life is yours . . . you are my life, my joy, my peace, my light . . . I love you in every way in which it is possible for a woman to love a man . . . you are in short everything."[177] She missed him dreadfully at times, and was very touched when he marked the anniversary of their engagement on May 1, 1935, by having Ilia deliver nine white and nine red roses along with a very loving note.

When George departed in March 1935 he had left Dr. Trebbi and Maestro Pettinella jointly in charge of Norma's musical management. With very different approaches, there was bound to be friction between the two men, but they achieved a truce in the timing of Norma's debut. Pettinella still insisted that her official debut in an opera be delayed until the fall of 1935, but he agreed that Trebbi could try her voice with the public at a concert some months earlier. In May Norma was happy to report that Trebbi had placed her on the program of a benefit concert at the end of June at the Donizetti Theatre in the small city of Bergamo.

When the concert date arrived, however, Norma was dismayed to learn that there was another coloratura soprano on the program, the student of a rival teacher who was a good friend of Trebbi's. Deserted by Pettinella, who interpreted the arrangement as an insult to himself through his student, and feeling betrayed by Trebbi's "mighty dirty trick," Norma decided to swallow her pride and sing anyway. She feared that another chance to sing in public might be a long time coming, and with the etchings business clearly

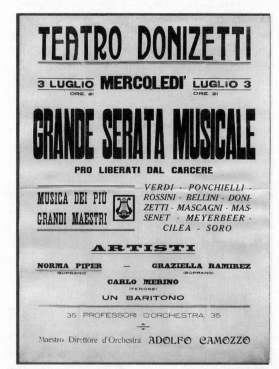

Advertising bill for Norma's singing debut at Donizetti Theatre, Bergamo, Italy, July 3, 1935. GA M6340-214-v1-p3

failing, she was desperate to start earning money. Anticipating that George might feel insulted and write angrily to Trebbi on her behalf, she reminded her fiance, "I hope we can get married this fall. But of course we cannot if I don't get engagements."[178] To give herself good luck for the important event, she planned her debut costume carefully, ensuring that every item from underwear to purse had been given to her by someone she loved.

The concert occurred on July 3, 1935, and a friend of George's, Mr. Veronese, assured him that "everything went very beautifully indeed" for Norma, who he felt had had "a real success."[179] With the Chilean tenor Carlo Merino also on the program, there had been "a few murmurs" about foreigners, so Norma had dropped "Annie Laurie" from her program and instead sang four Italian pieces, including arias from *Rigoletto* and *Lucia di Lammermoor*. George sent flowers, Dr. Piper cabled his good wishes and several Milanese friends were in attendance, although George was disappointed that no members of his family made the effort to attend in his stead. Relieved when it was over, Norma was pleased to note that her Canadian experiences had given her confidence: "I felt absolutely at ease on the stage, not for a quarter of a second did I suffer with nerves."[180] She told her father that it was a "decided success," "your daughter has had her Italian baptism and she pleased very much."[181]

Initially she told George "we have every reason to be pleased," but later she admitted she had suffered by comparison with the other soprano,

Gabriella Ramirez, who, as she said, had "a magnificent voice, and is very young, 19, and a pretty little thing."[182] With George away and no other real support available to her, there were several unfortunate mix-ups: her name went on the program as the very foreign-sounding Norma Mill Piper, and her encore music was not ready, so she confused the audience by appearing to refuse an encore. Miserably she wrote in her diary, "As for me, I played an excellent second fiddle to the Rammirez, in fact, because of me she made a greater success than she would otherwise have had . . . The whole thing makes me regret as I do 99% of the time that I ever started to sing for anything except my own modest satisfaction . . . Oh dear! how hopeless it all is!"[183]

The next day she recorded that she had felt so "let down and all alone in the world that I went on a spree. I went to the movies and ate two chocolate bars" and also ate most of a *torta* (cake) that sympathetic Ena had made for her. That finished, she went back on her "grass diet," saying:

> I surely need a strong person like Giorgio to take care of me. Alone I'll never amount to anything . . . I keep quiet when I should talk. I blab when I should keep quiet. In fact I'm a bit of a fool . . . How I wish I could give it up and do something really worth while. But I dare not. I'd break Father's heart. It is for me and my success that he lives, dear man . . . So for his sake I have to keep on with this stupid drudgery that I dislike . . . when I think of all the years I have studied and the thousands of dollars that have been spent on me to no effect, I lower my head in shame. I never did have the voice to merit such an expenditure . . . What an impossible fool I am and always shall be. How Giorgio ever can love me I'm sure I don't know. I certainly don't deserve his love.[184]

But Norma was not a quitter, and once she had released these bitter thoughts, she was calmly fatalistic. "Oh well! we learn by mistakes," she told George. She decided that, "considering my state of mind" during the concert, the write-up was a "very good criticism" and showed that she had a fair chance of making a "reasonable success."[185] Pettinella was pleased with her and promised that after a quick review of all her operas, he would start contacting agents to give her a proper operatic debut in the early fall. In the meantime, another important opportunity came her way.

Edward Johnson, recently appointed general manager of the Metropolitan Opera Company in New York, came to Italy in July 1935 to visit his daughter, and Norma was able to capitalize on the goodwill letters written on her behalf by their mutual friend John Nelson, of Montreal, to arrange a private audition at Pettinella's studio. Johnson was courteous and kind, congratulated her on her beautiful voice and the excellent way she used it, encouraged her to keep studying but promised her nothing. She cabled George, "Pleased Johnson," told her father "I am sure he was surprised—I was better than he expected," and naively concluded that his kind attention indicated a real interest in using her at the Met at a later date.[186]

To relax after the stress of her first Italian public performance, Norma allowed herself a holiday. Accepting the invitation of Milanese friends, the Farisatos, she joined them for a two-week vacation in Cadore in the Dolomite mountains. After the heat of Milan, Norma found the mountain air exhilarating and wrote to George, "How I love the mountains. I can easily imagine I am in our own dear Rockies."[187] Even more significant for their future life together, she told him: "Now I understand your great love for the mountains and I long for the day when we can go together with horses and tents way off into the virgin forest."[188]

After the Johnson audition, Norma's last musical hurdle for 1935 was her operatic debut. Early in their relationship, Trebbi had cautioned that "unfortunately [she] was being launched in the worst period of depression the theatre has ever known."[189] He told her that prior to the FirstWorld War, there had been more than 300 theatres operating six months of the year and plenty of work for singers of all kinds. In the intervening years, radio and cinema had become widely available and had profoundly influenced popular entertainment in Italy. Now, in the mid-1930s, 40 theatres operated for only a few months of the year and competition among artists was fierce.[190] Norma, well aware of the difficulties she faced in Italy, told George, "The musical world here gets worse and worse ... I am sure it must be better in America." Chastened by her experience in Bergamo, her goals had become more modest, and she told him, "I'll be glad when I can be ready, with the necessary experience, for, say, the San Carlo Company."[191]

Italian tradition dictated that singers, especially debutantes, pay fees and "gifts" to agents called impresarios, but with fewer theatres operating and with shorter seasons, and with new government regulations dictating artists' salaries, it was much more difficult for inexperienced singers to attract the attention and loyalty of these agents. As Norma matter-of-factly told George, "Impresarios do more for anyone who can pay more."[192] Wealthier students, particularly foreigners, sometimes paid substantial sums to orchestrate successful debuts.[193] They "purchased" the theatre, orchestra, conductor and other singers and gave handsome "gifts" to the impresario, the press and especially to the "claque" — professional clappers who, if unpaid, could ruin a performance by their booing and hissing. Having made a "successful debut" with favourable press notices, these fortunate performers could return to their own countries and boast of a "European reputation."

Norma realized she would have to pay something for each debut in a new opera, but she was philosophical, saying, "I don't blame the impresarios. They have to live too," although she also complained, "They are all wolves in sheep's clothing."[194] However, she could not afford to pay much and had to be content with a slower road to recognition, particularly now that relations with a few of her earlier supporters had cooled. Specifically, Trebbi had faded from view after the unhappy arrangements at the Donizetti Theatre in Bergamo, and Pavoni, who had promised to provide a good review of her first concert, reneged when she declined on George's behalf to purchase additional etchings from him. "What a nuisance it all is," she told George. "What I need is a publicity manager who has a million lire and who will spend the whole million to put me over."[195]

If her voice had been a "revelation" at Bergamo, she might have attracted the interest of more important impresarios, but unfortunately she had displayed only an assured stage presence and a lovely, well-schooled voice. She could sing various arias beautifully but was utterly untried in the performance of a full opera, and impresarios with important seasons were reluctant to take a chance. Hers would be a more pedestrian route to a European reputation: she would have to start with second- or even third-rate impresarios and theatres until she gained the experience and reputation to move up. With this realization, Norma's career expectations became much more realistic. She was amused to read an old diary entry in which she confidently expected to debut at La Scala: "It made me laugh and it made me ashamed of myself for being so stupid as to think I could sing there for my first appearance."[196] She wondered what the reaction would be among her friends at Brandli's studio: "When they learn that I have debuted in a place as important as Ogden [a small town near Calgary] and paid to do so, they will get somewhat of a shock."[197] Ruefully reminding him of her early expectation of earning 20,000 dollars a year, she told George, "How innocent and ignorant I was. Now I'd feel I was doing well if I made $2,000 a year."[198]

Her chance finally came in mid-August, when one of the smaller impresarios, who had worked with another of Pettinella's students, invited her to sing at a Sunday afternoon concert in the outdoor theatre at Loreto Arena in Corsico, just outside Milan. Pettinella was reluctant to have her sing outdoors, because he feared her voice would be lost, but Norma disagreed. The experience would cost her nothing, and she was anxious to impress the impresario, Signor Palminteri, so he would consider her for one of his future opera seasons. She was ready to try her wings and had come to realize that she needed to establish a good reputation with only a few impresarios to attract them all, for she had learned that the impresarios, great and small, congregated daily at the cafes in the Galleria Vittorio Emanuele II in Milan to share notes and gossip about artists and musical conditions. "This music game is the worst racket in the world" she told her father.[199]

But the concert was a success, and Palminteri invited her to debut in a production of *Lucia di Lammermoor* at a theatre in nearby Monza in the middle of September. With the Monza theatre similar in size and importance to the Grand Theatre at home, Norma excitedly told her father that this opportunity was akin to her 1932 performance there with the Calgary Symphony. However, Palminteri's backers objected to featuring an inexperienced singer at Monza and, even though she had signed a first contract, they insisted that Norma debut in *Lucia* one week earlier at the much less important Loreto Arena, as a trial run for Monza.

Norma found her operatic debut surprisingly nerve-wracking; she told George that by the time they opened, she was "worn to a rag" with nervous tension.[200] She discovered that Pettinella had been right to hold her back until she knew her operas thoroughly. Rehearsals were minimal: as Wilda Blow had told her years before, "One goes before a strange Maestro, and a strange orchestra and with unknown companions and one sings."[201] Luckily, Norma's Canadian touring had long since relieved her of stage fright, and she had gained additional confidence on the stage with her successful portrayal of Sally Hook in *Miss Hook of Holland* three years earlier. Her natural composure held, although she found it a challenge to watch the maestro, other artists and prompter while at the same time keeping track of the words, music, scene changes and acting. Many friends attended to lend their support—she had distributed free tickets—and one told her that "for a debutante I was marvelous."[202] She was relieved to have the debut over, although she cautioned her father not to brag, saying, "This is nothing to crow over. It is about like singing at Ogden."[203]

She told George, "I really enjoyed myself. I love being on the stage and I know that I shall constantly improve so that one day I should be a first-class singer," but she confessed to her diary that she had sung "without life or colour, and try as I would I couldn't get my voice to work."[204] Significantly, half the audience had left after she sang the Mad Scene. Her friend, Signora Lenzi was frank and told her she had "moved her to pity. There was my voice—that rich, lovely voice she knew I had. What had happened to it [?]"[205] Another friend told her years later that his impression at Loreto was that she was "just another singer with a pretty good voice but nothing special and as for acting not up to much."[206]

Palminteri's backers were not impressed. In particular, they criticized a bad high note, her acting ability and her poor-quality costumes, which she had borrowed from the company to save money. They decided to go with a more experienced singer, one with a "name," and approached the American-born Italian soprano Lina Pagliughi, who had been studying and singing in Italy for a decade. Despite her "unimpressive stage presence," Pagliughi was considered by many at the time to be "the leading Italian light soprano after Toti dal Monte" (but, of course, much less expensive to hire).[207] For Norma, all of a sudden Monza was "off," and she discovered two important lessons Pettinella had tried to teach: "A singer, especially a beginner, must wear a 'coat of mail,'" and one must never advertise upcoming plans as "one was never sure of an engagement until the engagement was finished."[208]

Pettinella consoled her that the bad high note "was no scandal," but she cried, "How terribly exacting this profession is" and told her father, "The trouble is that so much is expected of an opera singer. She must sing like a Melba and act like a Bernhardt—even in a fifth rate show."[209] But at least she had survived her debut and had proved herself capable of singing an entire opera before an audience.

With characteristic determination, she prepared to move forward. She realized now that Brandli's advice had been mistaken; she could not rely on the emotion of the songs to guide her onstage but needed intensive acting lessons to supplement Pettinella's work. She later told her father that although she had always felt "very much at home on the stage, and not at all nervous,"she had to work hard to "overcome my restraint . . . my stiff woodness of acting and of being afraid to show emotion in my voice, and in my portrayal of personality."[210]

Had she had unlimited backing, Norma could have followed up her debut by hiring an impresario, orchestra and press and toured Italy, putting on operas and learning how to perform them properly by practising in front of live audiences. But with her limited resources, she just had to make sure that she was better prepared the next time an opportunity to sing arose. She started studying the acting for *Lucia* with Maestro Galli the following week and planned to use him to perfect the scena for all of her operas in quick succession. In mid-September, she told George: "I am not anxious to sing for a month or so. I want to get the scena done well so that I am better prepared in every way."[211] Once she felt more confident, they could capitalize on the fact that she now had stage experience in opera and could start promoting her with impresarios.

In the meantime, George left the West and travelled to Toronto and then to New York, where he boarded the vessel *Conte di Savoia* on October 5, only two days after Italian troops crossed the border into Ethiopia. His ship stopped at Gibraltar, picking up Italian expatriates from Morocco who were heading to Naples; there George saw "thousands of volunteers" ready to sail to North Africa, "very happy and keen as could be . . . to do their bit for their Fatherland,"[212] but he headed straight home to Norma, arriving in Milan on October 12. Happy to be reunited at last, the couple now turned to the serious development of Norma's career.

Chapter 6

Norma & George: Waiting and Hoping
1935–1939

In New York and on the ship, George had been very anxious for Norma, a British subject caught in Italy during a time of intense patriotism there. In England, before his trip to Canada, Josephine Bedingfeld had offered her house as a refuge if things got "hot" in Italy, and he now feared that Norma might need to adopt this plan. However, when he reached Italy, he was relieved to discover that reports in North American newspapers had been exaggerated; aside from the troop ships leaving Naples, there was little evidence of war in the country itself. He assured concerned friends in North America that he had found an "absolute absence of war hysteria" in Milan and reassured Dr. Piper that "so far Norma . . . is very welcome everywhere. Everybody loves her, as she deserves."[1]

When the League of Nations introduced sanctions against Italy in November 1935, George was "disgusted with the hypocrisy of England"—which also had a stake in East Africa—and told friends that this action had served only to make the Italian people rally more firmly around their leaders.[2] Caught up in the general excitement, he could not resist the government's call for tangible evidence of patriotic fervour, and he joined 250,000 Italians in donating his and Norma's "wedding" rings to be melted down to help with war expenses. In exchange, they were given steel rings engraved with the words "ORO PER LA PATRIA—18 Nov. XIV" (Gold for the Fatherland—18 Nov. 1935).[3] But in spite of George's reassurances to Dr. Piper, he decided to take no chances and outside their apartment the couple spoke only Italian. With her operatic debut over and George back in Italy, they now settled down to seriously developing Norma's career. The etchings scheme had been a failure, and consequently Norma's progress assumed a new financial importance for their future life together. This was opposite to the conventional thinking of the time, which dictated that the man be the main breadwinner for the family and the wife play a secondary, support role. George and Norma both easily accepted this role reversal, though Norma acknowledged the irony, saying, "Isn't it rather odd, our relationship, and the fact that whether or not we see many places and do many things, depends on how successful is my career."[4]

Although she was delighted to have George home as her manager, Norma realized the importance of establishing a few ground rules now that they were together again. Even before he had returned, she had told him,

Last year we were wrapped up in the other and we knew that we would be together only a short time, so we let everything else slide, just to live our lovely romance. This year it will be different. We will love each other even more, but our love will not be hectic. It will be deep and smooth like a broad river that is very sure of itself, not a young tumbling mountain brook that is hurrying, rushing to get the most out of every minute of its life. So that we will adjust our lives around my career, the same as the lives of the family of the average businessman are adjusted to his work. That career will be our source of income and we *dare* not interfere with it . . . I must have time to practice and perhaps even more important enough rest, and enough exercise.[5]

George agreed with her sensible edict and contented himself with far fewer late-night smoking parties and other entertainments. Instead, he exercised his considerable social skills during soirees with some of the American music students and in intimate dinner parties with family and close friends such as the Farisatos and his old companions from the Highwood, the Fedelis.[6] He joined the Touring Club Italiano and the Comitati D'Azione per la Universalita di Roma, a social club for foreigners living in Italy. He also started writing a thinly veiled autobiography entitled "The European," but the story never progressed beyond a description of his early years.

For exercise, the couple took advantage of their location on the outskirts of the city to enjoy long walks into the countryside in the evening and on weekends. George introduced Norma to running in the early morning hours before breakfast; this was considered quite eccentric by their family and friends, as was their roller skating and ice skating. In fact, the family's amused tolerance of the couple's antics so impressed one of their great-nephews, Guido Pozza (a very young child at the time), that one of his few memories of Uncle George and Aunt Norma was of them skating hand in hand along the river on their way into the city.[7] Even their possessions were eccentric, as was their manner of dress on occasion. George, who still corresponded with

Top: George, Milan, 1935.
GA PD-184-7-37

Bottom: Norma, Milan, 1935.
GA PA-2393-12-1-5

149

his Stoney friends, enjoyed receiving their Christmas gifts of riding gauntlets and moccasins and especially enjoyed the startled reaction of guests when he donned Native regalia in suburban Milan.

By the fall of 1935, when Norma had been in Italy a year and a half and had debuted in only one opera performance in an obscure location, Dr. Piper finally understood that the process would take much longer than expected and would need a firm guiding hand while she was in Italy. Unable to offer any real practical help or advice from Canada, he was quite relieved to have George become a substitute for himself as Norma's manager and told him, "I will never be able to thank you dear boy for the part you have played."[8] George's Calgary visit had convinced him that Norma was in good hands. With relief, he had realized that George, much like himself, had an enthusiastic outlook and the drive to push Norma's career as far as it could go. Norma foresaw a wonderful partnership, particularly once her North American career was launched. She told her father, "George has splendid connections in America, in the U.S., so that with his connections and yours dear, we will likely be able to do quite well."[9] Brandli also expressed his approval of George as manager, telling him, "It is very gratifying to know that the . . . destiny of one's pupil is so faithfully taken care, as it is in your hands, and I . . . wish to thank you and again reiterate my humble gratitude for the interest you so generously show in Norma's success."[10]

Although he acknowledged George as Norma's manager, the project was too dear to his heart for Dr. Piper to abandon it entirely, and he continued his local promotional activities on her behalf. For the first nine months or so, he was assiduous in passing along Norma's letters to friends on his mailing list, who enjoyed the tales of sightseeing and the plucky singer's stories of trying to find a good maestro. They also appreciated hearing about George Pocaterra's role in the drama. Eventually the letters became repetitive, and then Dr. Piper produced the news bulletins only sporadically, when Norma had something really significant to report. Similarly, he advised the Calgary newspapers whenever Norma had important news, and his old friend Reverend R. J. Bowen did the same for him in London, Ontario. Norma sometimes worried that her father might be too optimistic in his reports, but she was grateful and reminded him only occasionally about the danger of creating false expectations about the speed of her progress. Her letters were full of fond endearments for her tireless promoter: "You surely do work for me . . . Bless your heart! You have done a tremendous amount for me for which I am very very grateful."[11]

Reverting to his former tactics, Dr. Piper wrote to many old friends in influential positions in Canada and Britain, seeking support for Norma's career. In particular he seemed to rely on R. B. Bennett's interest in the family to benefit Norma ("he has a warm spot in his heart for us," he told Norma[12]) and wrote to him in great hope and confidence many times over the years. Although Dr. Piper received kind replies expressing admiration for his talented daughter, the former prime minister was unwilling to do anything constructive for Norma beyond his original letter of introduction when she travelled to Italy. He made his position very clear to Dr. Piper, telling him on one occasion in 1933 when still prime minister, that he made it a rule never to interfere in that way because otherwise he would be inundated with similar requests.[13] In fact, none of Dr. Piper's influential contacts yielded any actual aid for Norma, although Bennett did help to resolve a few other family crises for his friend.[14]

Occasionally Dr. Piper's promotional ideas were vetoed by George, who complained to Norma about her father's use of "counterproductive" and "amateurish" tactics.[15] One of his schemes was a plan to send Norma's recording for endorsement to the Countess of Bessborough, who had complimented Norma when she heard her sing in Calgary in 1932. Although her husband was no longer Governor General of Canada by the time Dr. Piper contacted her in 1935, the countess was an active supporter of the Women's Canadian Club in London, England, an organization known to take an interest in music students studying abroad.[16] Used to her father's "boosting" approach, Norma saw nothing amiss in the plan and was pleased to think that with the countess and Mrs. Bedingfeld both behind her in England, "we might be able to do something."[17]

Dr. Piper did not send the record—he was afraid it would not be returned— but the countess's secretary arranged for a letter of support for Norma, and that duly impressed Maestro Pettinella, who observed, "It is not often that music students receive letters from royalty."[18] However, George felt this approach cheapened Norma, thought the tone of the letter condescending and considered the use of the secretary to be a deliberate snub on the countess's part. Determined on this occasion to assert his role as Norma's manager, George wrote, "I simply won't stand for it."[19] Chastised, Dr. Piper submitted meekly, saying, "No George, you are master of her career. I am confident that you are capable to guide this lass in her progress as a singer."[20] From that time on, whenever Dr. Piper made a suggestion regarding the direction of Norma's career, he always finished by saying diffidently, for George's benefit, "however, you know best."

After the Loreto debut in *Lucia* in September 1935, there was a brief hiatus while Norma reviewed her scena with Maestro Galli. To reinforce the role and to gain some publicity, in November she sang *Lucia* again at a *dopolavoro* in a nearby town. (A *dopolavoro* was a popular government-sponsored workingman's recreational club, something like the YMCA.) After she debuted in *The Barber of Seville* at Soncino in January 1936, she used the same strategy again and sang it three more times for local *dopolavoro* clubs. She was well received by these clubs, which promoted her to each other, and she viewed them as filling much the same role in building a fan base for her in Italy as Dr. Piper's service clubs had done in Canada. With increasing stage experience, she developed self-confidence and a reputation for dependability among the smaller impresarios with whom George was dealing.

Norma and the cast of the opera "Don Pasquale," Lonato, Italy, June 1936.
GA PD-183-5-37

She was still playing to less-sophisticated audiences in smaller centres, yet Norma often enjoyed a "real triumph," with numerous ovations and cries of "Brava, Bis" (good, encore). The first time he saw her perform in an opera, George was transfixed and enormously impressed. He told a friend, "Norma absolutely changes when on the stage. From the moment she steps on it she is a changed person, she dominates everybody and everything and by sheer IT always manages to get the audience on her side and to pay her a tribute of applause even before she begins singing."[21] In June 1936 she debuted in *Don Pasquale* at the Lonato *Dopolavoro*, where she also sang *Lucia* to much acclaim. After the performance, she proudly told her father that her acting had improved so much that "I was greeted by an ovation which crescended [*sic*] with each time I sang until I had the audience rejoicing and suffering with *Lucia* . . . so well did I live the part that all over the theatre I could hear sobs among the audience, and the thunder of applause at the end of the cadenza lasted a good ten minutes."[22] Sad that her father could not share these triumphs, she wrote detailed descriptions so that he could experience them vicariously.

With Pettinella's guidance, Norma's voice had continued to improve, but she credited George's love with giving her the capacity to express emotion in her singing. "My heart had to be touched by Love before my brain could properly direct my voice," she told George. "I've learned to 'feel,' and to interpret the meaning of the words, and my high notes are beautiful, so sweet and clear and not one bit shrill and I have learned to hold them for a long, long time. I please the public." She told her father, "You won't know me, dear when you see me on the stage. I am a different person and it has taken George two years of never-ending, continuous work, moulding me, developing my personality and my powers of interpretation."[23]

These changes in her outward manner were celebrated by Norma but sometimes questioned by her family. When George visited her relatives in London, Ontario, during his trip to Canada in 1935, her older cousin, Bertha Reid, was troubled by the changes in Norma's appearance and personality that George claimed to have engineered. In consternation, she wrote: "Mr Pocaterra spoke of you as being 'a very different girl' to the Norma I know. I hope this is not so, Norma dear. Please do not try to mold yourself into his or anyone else's form. Just be yourself and you couldn't be any sweeter and more charming. Your own little quiet dignity of manner and bearing, your own sweet natural and secure poise, are just the thing to be desired."[24] Bertha must have worried aloud, because Violet Johnston, a close Piper friend also from London, wrote to say how much Norma reminded her of her "unassuming and gracious" mother, Maud, and told her hopefully, "You are not the type which can be spoiled, nor will you become conceited—only with all your success will you be, our own darling Norma."[25] When Dr. Piper expressed surprise at the spirited opinions sometimes offered in her letters, she credited George with teaching her to hold her own in an argument and told her father proudly, "I have changed. I am not the quiet little mouse I used to be who always gave way to other person's opinions. I now have ideas and a personality of my own."[26]

George took his work as Norma's manager very seriously and quickly made it his full-time occupation. After he had filled the role for several years, he confessed to a friend that "it was rather difficult at first, not knowing any of the ropes (life on a ranch not being exactly conducive to fitting one for the job of manager of a lyric star in the lyric environment of Milan, Italy!!!), but now I find it very interesting, and at times even exciting, especially when something important turns up."[27] He attended all of Norma's lessons, and at home worked constantly on her main weakness, pronunciation. With his help, Norma's command of the language had improved dramatically, and she looked back on her early efforts with amusement. While reviewing *Rigoletto* in 1935, she confessed: "I am amazed that I was able to sing it at all last year. I had absolutely no idea of the meaning of 90% of the words."[28] But stage appearances required perfect pronunciation and no trace of foreign accent, and this was where George's help was invaluable. She told her father, "He sits by me and makes me repeat phrase for phrase my music, singing each one again and again until it satisfies him. Years and years of mispronunciation require patience to overcome."[29]

She also credited George with several musical breakthroughs that helped her to achieve astonishingly high notes with ease, eventually including E-flat, E and F, and these advances gradually brought more consistency to her singing. With his support, her self-doubt was kept in check, and she delighted in boasting to her father of her vocal improvements: "The voice is as sweet as a bell, never forced. I have learned to sing softly and put in lovely shadings of tone," "I am taking pleasure in something that I never used to do—that is painting and embroidering everything I sing," and "[I] have really perfected the agility, the staccati, the high notes so that everybody absolutely marveled ... and one orchestra conductor said to me 'you just toss them up in the air and there they are ... the ease with which you sing is astounding.'"[30] She was very pleased when Signora Consolo, who had not heard her sing for some time, impulsively kissed her after a private performance and said, "My dear, I am pleased."[31] Remembering former criticisms, she told her father that "RJ" of the *Daily Province* and Leonard Brockington of the CBC would be pleased with her improvement in expression, and, mindful that a smaller American company might be interested in her even if she was not yet ready for the Met, she asked Dr. Piper to tell conductor Carlo Peroni about her newly acquired high notes the next time the San Carlo Opera Company toured Calgary.

After her first operatic debut in Loreto, Norma had learned the value of having her own, good-quality costumes; that "a lovely costume ... [had] the audience favourably disposed" right from the beginning of a performance.[32] And so, as finances allowed, she gradually acquired an operatic wardrobe. George gave her several wigs, shawls and other items as gifts. Through Maestro Galli, she was able to purchase several lovely fans to use in *The Barber of Seville*; these were acquired "at a great bargain" from a retired artist, possibly the famous Italian soprano Rosina Storchio who had sung the role at La Scala.[33] But the bulk of Norma's costumes were funded by the last of her inheritance from Aunt Susie, which she finally received in June, 1936. To save money, the costumes were designed and made by Rosa Brigatti, who had retired from one of the big theatrical-costume companies that served La Scala. Much to Norma's delight, Signora Brigatti's skill and experience enabled her to substitute cheaper materials to create beautiful, hand-crafted costumes with exquisite trimmings.[34] But even with these economies, the costumes for seven operas plus accessories, concert dresses and a black velvet evening cloak eventually totalled about 7,500 lire (565 dollars—8,500 dollars today).

An impressive wardrobe was not the only expense for the couple. Friends in the business advised them that in order to impress audiences and impresarios with Norma's worth, she had to maintain a glamorous image, and they would need to travel and live in style while fulfilling engagements. George took the advice seriously, but it was all very expensive, especially the debut performances, which were all "out of pocket" with no actual pay. Norma told her brother Lawrence that as a beginner, she was expected to pay up to 50 percent of her earnings to impresarios for their help in procuring and arranging engagements, but once she was established, the rate would drop to 10 percent.[35] Her account books show that "presents" to impresarios for debuts in various roles ranged from 200 lire to 500 lire (16 to 26 dollars), and her tips to the "claque" varied widely as well, from 15 lire to 100 lire (1 to 5 dollars) depending on the relative importance of the theatre. With the addition of hotels, meals, train and taxi fares, and assorted other tips and gifts, Norma's debuts ranged in cost from a low of 378 lire (31 dollars—roughly 500 dollars today) for *Barber* at Soncino to a high of 906

Top: Norma in costume for the opera "La Sonnambula," Milan, ca 1936.
GA PA-2393-15-1-1

Bottom: Norma in costume for the opera "L'Elisir d'Amore," Milan, ca 1936.
GA PD-184-5-51

*Top: Norma in costume for the opera "Barber of Seville," Milan, ca 1936.
GA PA-2393-15-3-2*

*Bottom: Card enclosure from George, Milan, ca 1936.
GA M6340-194-2*

lire (48 dollars—about 700 dollars today) for *Rigoletto* in Turin. Once a debut had occurred, Norma received a negotiated rate of pay to perform that role again, but the few hundred lire thus earned in the smaller theatres where she worked often barely covered expenses, especially if the couple had to travel out of town for an engagement.

Even before they married, Norma felt that George's presence helped to raise her own status in the eyes of impresarios and other artists. At her debut for *Barber*, she noted that the company treated her very respectfully: "I guess they know they had better not try any superiority business when Giorgio's around."[36] He worked hard on her behalf, capitalizing on her experience to negotiate better and better terms from impresarios. In 1936 she was glad when an engagement cost her "nothing out of pocket" (though George still had to pay his own expenses). By 1937 she was making a little money on most contracts and could afford to stay in a good hotel, and by1938 George was able to insist that expenses for both of them be covered and that their train travel be as second- rather than third-class passengers. He revelled in his role as manager to a prima donna but sometimes took his position far too seriously, with ludicrous results. For example, at a performance of *Lucia* in Saluzzo in January 1937, George threatened that his wife would not sing if the impresario could not find him a good seat in the crowded opera house. Desperate to have the show proceed, the impresario had the stagehands move "the red velvet and gold throne that had been used the night before . . . in 'Rigoletto'. . . and put it right at the front of the centre aisle of the theatre. And there sat George, like a king, during the entire performance."[37]

Once she had sung numerous times in smaller theatres, proved herself to be competent in her scena and singing, and shown by her wardrobe and lifestyle that she intended to be first-rank, Norma, George and Maestro Pettinella anticipated that she would move ahead quickly. But although they held themselves ready by increasingly declining lesser offers, it seemed impossible to take that next step forward.

Early on they decided that Norma's nationality was at fault, the trade sanctions having created a feeling of animosity toward British citizens in Italy. At the time of her initial debut in the fall of 1935, "feeling was very hot [in Italy] against England and everything English, and there was a great campaign for 'All-Italian Art' and Italian born artists."[38] Consequently, soon after George's return to Italy, they decided to make Norma's stage name sound more Italian. This was sensible: not only did the name Piper look British, inevitably it was mispronounced by Italians as "peepeere," which sounded like a type of champagne. With apologies to her father, she became Norma San Giorgio, chosen because it honoured the patron saint of England as well as George himself and his birthplace. Although this strategy did not fool impresarios, who still knew her in private as Miss Piper, it did make her name relatively inoffensive on advertising material.

Norma had another small advantage because it was known that she was engaged to marry an Italian and that George's family was connected by marriage to an important government official, the *prefetto* who oversaw local government in Milan.[39] But George soon realized that his position of authority with the impresarios was compromised because he did not have the legal right to protect Norma and to negotiate as her husband. By June 1936 George was convinced that only through legal marriage to an Italian would Norma have a chance to break into the higher levels of the musical world, now tightly controlled by the Fascist government.

Government control had reduced the role of impresarios, thereby making it more difficult for unknown singers to rise into prestigious theatres. In cleaning up "that business" (i.e., the traditional system of buying the help and loyalty of impresarios through "presents"), the government had saved singers money but made the process of career building slower and more cumbersome. As early as August 1935 Norma had reported a new fee schedule for singers that had been imposed by the government; its fees were very low, even for well-established artists.[40]

To counteract the insidious effect of cinema and radio on popular culture, the government in 1930 had introduced the Carro di Tespi theatrical company, a sort of lyric chautauqua. Travelling to centres throughout the country, playing to huge crowds in outdoor facilities and priced to be within reach of all income levels, this initiative proved an effective means of exposing the population to high-class entertainment and reviving traditional Italian culture.[41] The drawback, from a beginner's point of view, was that the government hired only major theatrical and operatic stars for these productions. Even before her first debut, Norma had communicated to George the sense of unease she felt around her in the musical world of Milan. Telling him that music "is all run by the state now," she observed, "when the government starts controlling art it makes it hard for beginners."[42]

The government continued to tighten its grip on music with further regulations introduced early in 1936. It created the Centro Lirico Italiano (Italian Lyric Centre), an agency that co-ordinated opera seasons nationwide and controlled state funding of productions, which more and more often were required to be modern operas by Italian composers. Although impresarios were still involved, their traditional role was diminished when theatre managers were required to hire singers through a placement bureau called the Ufficio di Collocamento. This, in turn, was under the direction of the Ministry of Press and Propaganda (called the Ministry of Popular Culture after 1937), which had complete control over the granting of official registration to singers. Without this registration it was almost impossible for a beginner, particularly a foreigner, to develop a professional reputation because they were effectively barred from all productions that received government funding or sponsorship. This left only the smallest private seasons in regional theatres in which unregistered singers like Norma could gain experience.[43]

Acknowledging the importance of getting Norma registered, the couple worried that registration might be denied because of local chit-chat about the nature of their relationship. This gossip also bothered George's family, particularly his sister Emilia and several elderly aunts and uncles who were fond of Norma and wanted to see the couple legally married. They told George that Norma's professional reputation was suffering under the scrutiny of the Fascist regime, which was well known for its strict moralistic dictates regarding the private lives of public people.[44] Although she was unconventional for the times, even entertaining a male friend alone in her apartment in 1935 while George was overseas, Norma could be sensitive to public opinion. When George had planned to visit her relatives during his trip to Canada, she warned him not to mention their trip together the preceding summer as "old Ontario people are very conventional … They would probably be horrified if they knew I went alone with you."[45]

When they first became engaged, Norma had been anxious for an early marriage, telling George "Our Love is such a beautiful thing, such a lovely flower, that I hate to think it is spoken of with a sneer, as I know it is by our Canadian friends."[46] She often referred to the horoscope prepared by "Darius" several years before and now saw the significance of the words "I see a hidden warmth that is at present unsuspected." More importantly, Darius had predicted that marriage "would undoubtedly bring out the heights she is endeavouring to reach a little sooner than otherwise will be the case."[47] She often fantasized about her wedding to George, even describing to him the "very simple but very beautiful" cream-coloured wool suit she told him she planned to wear "since I cannot have a regular bridal outfit."[48]

However, while George was away, her father had again cautioned her against an early marriage, saying, "I don't suppose you will think of getting married in Italy or before you have got well started on your career—you must remember that once you are married—your [sic] married—so keep single until you are well on your way to success. George will likely desire to be married as early as possible but you have your say when the wedding shall take place and where."[49] Anxious to please her father, she also realized that she and George could not afford to lose the Pipers' financial support, telling her diary, "I cannot expect my family to continue keeping me supplied with funds after I am married."[50] Assuring themselves that "really we are wedded and mated already!"[51] the couple had chosen to live together rather than to marry once George returned from Canada. Now, however, the Pocaterra family pressured them to regularize their relationship. As a final argument, they pointed out to George that without legal marriage, Norma had few rights under Italian law should anything happen to him.

Norma and George were married by the mayor of Milan in a quiet civil ceremony at the Palazzo Marino on June 18, 1936, and afterwards hosted a celebration with relatives and friends at their own small apartment. They received some lovely gifts from the Pocaterra family, including a full silver service for 12 from the generous Marta. Norma was thrilled with her gift from George, a "magnificent" heirloom brooch that had been his mother's and was "as big as a walnut, a perfect Indian garnet surrounded by 24 large

George and Norma on the steps of city hall after their marriage in Milan, June 18, 1936.
GA NA-695-70

Indian pearls."[52] Before her death some months earlier, Ubaldina Pocaterra had told her son the brooch was for his bride, Norma, of whom she had grown fond.

The couple postponed their honeymoon trip until the late summer, when most affluent Milanese escaped the "breathless suffocating heat" of the city for holidays at the seashore or in the mountains. They headed to Sardinia in mid-August, and there they enjoyed swimming, sailing and horseback riding, a skill Norma remembered from "the old Acme days." During their long rides into the Sardinian countryside, which Norma described as "beautiful, just like our Alberta foothills,"[53] they visited local shrines and sanctuaries. This experience gave Norma a new appreciation for the beautiful trappings of the Catholic faith, and some time after the couple returned to Milan, they acquired a painting of a "Blue Madonna" at an art store in the Galleria Vittorio Emanuelle II. This became a treasured possession that hung at the head of their bed everywhere they lived until the end of their lives.

George and Norma neglected to tell Dr. Piper their happy news, and he discovered it only accidentally some weeks later through Mrs. Mamini, Signora Lenzi's sister in Calgary. Naturally he was hurt, but Norma and George defended their behaviour by saying the marriage had occurred only for convenience, and they had not broadcast the news because they did not want anyone thinking things had changed with regard to her career development. She told her father that as a married woman she had more respect and status in Italian society, adding, "Everyone knows that if a singer does not have a husband, she has in all probability a lover."[54] Anticipating one of his main concerns, Norma reassured him, "We have determined not to have any children until my career is quite established and we can really afford to have them, so have no worry on that score."[55] Although they did not say it outright, they were very worried that Norma's family would feel she was now George's complete responsibility and their support payments would cease. Fond of them both, and sympathizing with their situation, Dr. Piper granted his blessing and consented to support Norma for another year. But, worried about his sons' reaction, he delayed informing them; they continued in ignorance of the marriage for another year and a half until Lawrence accidentally learned the news from a friend in Vancouver.

The decision to marry was politically astute. Almost immediately, their connection with the *prefetto* yielded papers from the minister of press and propaganda giving Norma the coveted "permission to sing" at government-sponsored musical events. At last she was acknowledged as a registered lyric artist and her name appeared on the official government list, Cantanti Lirici Iscritti. As a result, Norma was included on the program of a big benefit concert in Milan in early July 1936. More importantly, she was one of a select number of singers invited to perform at the Grand Concert of the Royal Conservatory of Music Giuseppe Verdi in Milan on November 2, 1936. The concert was the culmination of a spring and summer of auditions of promising young singers sponsored by the Italian Lyric Centre.

In her audition on October 16, 1936, Norma had impressed the jury with her rendition of her old favourite, the Mad Scene from *Lucia di Lammermoor*. Of the 460 singers who auditioned, Norma was one of only 23 who were featured at the Grand Concert at which "Authorities, Directors of Orchestras, Impresari and the Press" were invited to attend. Norma sang exceptionally well. One review claimed, "Her difficult aria 'Bel raggio lusinghier' from G. Rossini's *Semiramide* carried her audience to such a pitch of enthusiasm that it could not wait for the orchestra to finish the number, but broke into a thunderous applause, which lasted for long, with shouts of 'Brava, Brava!' Her rendering was perfect in every way, impostation, time, sweetness and limpidity of tone, and extraordinary carrying power, so that even her pianissimos were perfectly and clearly audible all over the vast hall. Her graceful stage presence added an extra charm to her faultless lyric performance."[56]

Norma's success at the Grand Concert gave her career a much-needed boost. When his soprano fell ill, an impresario who had heard her at the concert hired her for the lead in *Rigoletto* at the Victor Emmanuelle Theatre in Turin in late December 1936. Since this was her debut in the opera, and the theatre was a more important one, she had to give bigger "presents" to the impresario and the claque and naturally had to fund travel and many other costs herself, but she considered the expense worthwhile as it was "by far the biggest thing I have done yet in opera."[57] As was usual, the opera was performed with very little in the way of rehearsal, but she was thoroughly trained and sang so well she received 7 curtain calls after one aria and 14 curtain calls after the first act. Backstage, George was gratified by compliments from the other artists and at the end of the performance astonished them by revealing that this had been his wife's debut in the role. Her success enabled her to debut without cost in *L'Elisir d'Amore* in March 1937. Again she received no pay, but she was not required to give a "gift" to the impresario, who actually then "paid real money" for her to sing *Lucia* as well. With this first real pay she bought a "lasting souvenir," a theatrical makeup box that was a replica of the ones used by artists at La Scala. [58]

An even bigger honour followed in April, when she was chosen to perform *Rigoletto* with Sir Riccardo Stracciari, a well-known baritone from an earlier period who had ended 15 years' retirement to attempt the revival of his career. Norma was thrilled and wrote to her father, "A month ago he was singing 'Traviata' with Toti dal Monte. This month he is singing 'Barber of Seville' with Norma San Giorgio. How do you like that?"[59] Initially hired for one or two performances, Norma pleased Stracciari so much with her "very rich" voice that she was asked to complete the "whole tournee" of 10 performances over several weeks through many small cities in northern Italy. The baritone and his wife liked the younger couple, and Norma was grateful when Stracciari took pains to help her with the scena for the role, in which she consequently became "well-nigh perfect." Norma was very pleased when Marta paid her the compliment of journeying from Bergamo to Rovereto to see her perform.

Although they were playing to less-important theatres in smaller centres, the company was given a good reception and received complimentary reviews everywhere it travelled. As a result, Norma had her first real taste of the kind of stardom for which she had been striving for so many years. She was particularly pleased with her reception in the Pocaterra family's city of origin, Ferrara: "I had the most magnificent ovation I had had up to then, in that very difficult city . . . [the audience] applauded and shouted 'Brava, Bis' for at least 5 minutes after Una voce poco fa . . . they went completely wild. It was a great satisfaction."[60] Another triumph was a review of the tour in the music journal *Giornale degli Artisti*. Entitled "A Great Promise," the reviewer observed that "the proximity of the great artist did not hurt the young singer, who through her brilliant vocal qualities and her intelligent scenic action, was capable of, and actually did successfully sustain the difficult comparison."[61] After the tour ended, Stracciari continued his friendly interest in Norma's career, and it was at his request that she was included with him in a big benefit concert held in Milan early the next year.

Dazzled by his former reputation, the Pocaterras naively assumed that Stracciari's recommendation counted for more than it really did, and, with the help of Maria Pia Pozza (George's nephew, Sergio's wife and the *prefetto's* niece), they arranged an audition for Norma in July 1937. with Maestro Marinuzzi, the "foremost" director of La Scala After the audition she told her father Marinuzzi was "very nice and paid me several compliments saying the voice was beautiful, absolutely in tune, that I was well prepared and sang correctly." However, to her great disappointment he also told her there was "absolutely no use in me even thinking of going to the Scala this year, that even with the finest recommendations in the world the most I'd ever get would be the understudy for [a very minor role]."[62] However, he encouraged her to continue studying and gaining experience in larger theatres so that once she was ready, La Scala could offer her better roles right from the start.

Top: Interior view of the Comunale Theatre, Rovereto, where Norma performed
"The Barber of Seville" with Richard Stracciari in April 1937.
GA M6340-214-v1-p29b

Bottom: George and Norma with Sir Riccardo Stracciari and his wife during a
tour of northern Italy, Spring 1937.
GA PA-2393-16-1-2

But operatic experience in larger theatres simply did not come, though she was invited to sing in a number of charity concerts in Milan and elsewhere during 1937 and 1938. Although she was not paid for these performances, the Pocaterras hoped that singing in such government-sponsored events would give Norma much-needed publicity. As time wore on, the Piper family at home became impatient, and the Pocaterras wrote many letters trying to convince them that Norma needed more time to develop a solid European reputation so that she could arrive in America with a "name." This was important, they argued, because of America's infatuation with young, attractive film stars such as the wildly popular teenager Deanna Durbin. "Anyone over 25 who does not go there with a name that already means something would have a terrible time to get people interested."[63] On the other hand, she said, "with an Italian reputation I would have a chance in the States to step immediately into something worthwhile,"[64] and she gave the example of Marian Clarke an American who had sung in Italy for some years as Franca Somigli but eventually sang at La Scala, Covent Garden in London and the Met. While the Pocaterras acknowledged that the time spent building Norma's career had been much longer than expected, they scoffed at the impression given by a popular Hollywood film, American soprano-actress Grace Moore's *One Night of Love*. "When it comes down to the real thing," they told Norma's family, "progress is always slow."[65]

In response to her father's worry that she would stay overseas forever, Norma reassured him, "My field is America. There is no chance to make a living here—here I shall get training and experience."[66] To keep her family interested and supportive, she glossed over many little disappointments and stressed instead her triumphs, no matter how small. George carefully translated her reviews, which were uniformly complimentary: "Endowed with a beautiful voice, of great ease and of an extended register, which she knows how to use with intelligence and sureness," "marvelous vocal and interpretative qualities," "another great success."[67] These reviews, and others that appeared in local newspapers wherever Norma sang, were reminiscent of the kind of enthusiastic, gushing promotional articles that had so delighted her in her early touring days in rural Alberta.

In private, however, George and Norma were becoming impatient with the length of time it was taking to achieve their goal even though Norma had earned a solid reputation among the smaller impresarios and had sung in public 26 times since her debut two years earlier. She consoled herself by saying, "Even the great Caruso sang as I have done in small theatres for years."[68] When her old friends from Brandli de Bevec's studio, Isabelle Logie and Margaret Lattimore, wrote asking for advice about studying overseas, Norma drew on her own experience to warn them about the years of patient, hard work and financial sacrifice required to develop an operatic career abroad, and she advised them not to come unless they had guaranteed incomes of 1,300 dollars per year each.[69]

George worked hard to attract more important impresarios, and Norma had many auditions, including one with a radio station in January 1937, but very few auditions resulted in offers, and few of the proposals resulted in actual engagements. Having at last sung with a "Great Artist," Norma now refused most of the many offers for engagements with "inferior companies." In fact, she told her brother Lawrence that she and George would have lost money accepting these lesser engagements: she would have been paid about 60 dollars per month, but it would have cost them 100 dollars per month in expenses.[70] George insisted they were "after bigger game," saying she "must now rise up another step and sing with better artists . . . all more the height of Stracciari."[71] To help Dr. Piper understand their strategy, they illustrated with examples from home; she had started in towns the importance of High River, Leamington and Kingsville, had gradually risen to cities the importance of Calgary, Hamilton and London, Ontario, and must now take another step up to cities equivalent in importance to Toronto, Detroit and Philiadelphia.[72]

In retrospect, this strategy may have been misguided. As Norma herself told her father in 1937, experience in singing a role was the main factor determining even a lesser artist's desirability for an agent. "After one has sung 20 or 30 performances one begins to have a certain value for impresarios but before no."[73] But Norma was never allowed to sing her roles this often, and this may have hampered her success. Overly impressed by her reception in second- and third-rate theatres, George seemed to believe that he was, in fact, the manager of a diva. He grew determined to propel Norma to the top, to fulfill his own early predictions and her family's expectations. In pursuing this strategy, he ignored his own concerns about Norma's voice. It is possible that a resume showing more experience might have attracted more important agents unwilling to take a chance on a relatively inexperienced singer. Norma's diaries and letters indicate she refused many, many offers from lesser impresarios from 1937 to 1939 while she awaited more important contracts, but these were slow in coming or non-existent, and her portfolio remained unimpressive. As a result, when she tried to compete for positions at La Scala, Covent Garden and the Met, her dossier showed remarkably few performances of the major operatic roles in her repertoire.[74]

In the summer of 1937, Norma ended her long relationship with Maestro Pettinella and started taking lessons from Giacomo Marino, who impressed George and her with his important connections (he was "a great personal friend of Caruso"). He also had a reputation for having "great success with coloratura sopranos, having had Galli-Curci for quite some time."[75] They felt he was a "go-getter" who would be more assertive than Pettinella in promoting Norma to government officials in charge of organizing and directing musical events and seasons. One of Marino's first promotional efforts was to write to Edward Johnson detailing Norma's North American plans and requesting another audition for her whenever Johnson next visited Italy. Although Norma also wrote to Johnson, saying that she would appreciate his opinion of her progress in the two years since he had last heard her sing, a second audition in Italy never occurred; possibly he was far too preoccupied coping with the negative impact on the Met of the Depression to arrange a special meeting with Norma when he visited his daughter in Italy. Marino's wife, an American opera singer named Gertrude Fleming, also gave her assistance on Norma's behalf. She wrote to an influential musical friend in San Francisco requesting that he use his "good offices" with American impresarios to suggest that they listen to her husband's talented student during their scouting trips to Italy.

The Pocaterras had assumed that once Norma was registered as a lyric artist, her career would develop more smoothly, but in reality her progress often suffered from the vagaries of government control. Traditionally, first contracts meant little more than an expression of interest and were signed and cancelled at will.[76] Norma experienced several occasions when the government did not give final approval for her participation in a performance, or where well-advanced plans were cancelled due to government interference. A number of times, local performances simply were cancelled because they might interfere with government-sponsored productions or tours (the Carro di Tespi) in nearby locations. With the government's nationalistic policy of promoting modern Italian composers and operas, there was an official move away from the old "grand operas," which were Norma's specialty, and she was hard-pressed to find roles for her voice among the modern efforts. She began studying a few modern Italian operas with Maestro Marino in 1937, but she was never hired to sing any of these new roles.

In 1937 George and Norma became convinced she was also losing precious contracts to other foreign singers because of pressure brought to bear by their governments on Italian authorities. To this end they urged Dr. Piper to ask friends in the Canadian government to pressure Italian authorities on her behalf, saying that "in the final count merit alone survives but if we wait for that alone the years will pass, we'll use up more of everybody's money and the return to America will be delayed that much longer."[77] In spite of frequent representations to the Canadian trade commissioner in Milan and persuasive letters from Dr. Piper and Norma to former prime minister R. B. Bennett, to the Canadian high commissioner in Britain Vincent Massey and even a letter from Dr. Piper to King George VI, support from Canadian authorities was never forthcoming. The Pocaterras were disappointed with the lack of interest shown by their government in Norma, who, they claimed, was "the only Canadian since Mme Albani and Edward Johnson to be considered here as being first-class!"[78]

By pursuing a strategy of rejecting offers to sing from lesser impresarios, George may have severely limited Norma's earning potential during this period. Determined to limit his investment in her career (which was mounting, nevertheless), the couple were quite dependent on the continuing financial support of the Piper family. However, by the end of 1937 this support once again became an issue. Dr. Piper's declining health prevented him from maintaining a very active dental practice, and he had become dependent on his Royalite shares and other stocks as his main source of income. In the late 1930s he reported, "My Royalite is slipping from me fast. I may have enough to last me the rest of my days, if I don't live too long."[79] When prices failed to recover, he blamed the economic policies of the Alberta government under Social Credit party leader William Aberhart. He told Norma, "Old Abie has ruined things for the next few years, I fear. The old Rascal is seated firmly. I do not know how we will get him out until his term is up."[80] She commiserated, saying, "What a mess Aberhart is making. George told some of our friends here about Social Credit and the stamps [one-cent stamps that had to be affixed weekly to the back of money-like "prosperity certificates" to keep them valid and circulating with the value of one dollar]. How they laughed. Some day the people of Alberta will wake up and kick the whole bunch out and get some sort of sane government."[81]

Trying to explain his irregular and reduced payments, Dr. Piper told her, "I find there are so many things I have to get and money is scarce. It does cost a lot to keep going. Mrs Fallis, upstairs, said today it takes all we can get hold of to buy food to keep us alive and when we have company it's that much worse . . . We don't have much company, it costs plenty without!"[82] Norma frequently acknowledged the financial strain on her father, but rather than releasing him from his commitment, she simply expressed gratitude for his sacrifices and continued to press for more, even chastising him on one occasion when a money order, which had been mailed instead of the usual bank draft, resulted in her losing 20 percent of the value when it was cashed.

Norma's brothers, learning at last of her marriage and feeling justifiably hurt and annoyed, felt their commitment to her was over and the responsibility for her maintenance now was George's. Norma pointed out that George had contributed about 10,000 dollars toward her maintenance in the three years since they had met.[83] She insisted that he could not be expected to take on all the expenses of career building, when the Pipers had initiated the project and would benefit from the expected profits. This raised another sore point: Ever since they had started receiving reports of Norma's singing successes, the brothers had desired a firmer understanding with their sister, something that would commit George and Norma to make good on Pipers' investment. Jack told her bluntly, "We are not going to have some Italian reaping the benefits of your work and our financial contributions."[84] And so, at the end of 1937, Jack and Lawrence requested that Norma come to some kind of formal agreement guaranteeing them a certain percentage of her salary.

In parrying these requests from her family, Norma pointed out that "opera stars, unfortunately, cannot live in 2 rooms and a kitchenette . . . I will have to live up to the position I hold . . . my expenses are bound to be high."[85] In the meantime, she pointed out, she and George were trying to live as frugally as possible in their small apartment on the outskirts of Milan and frequently bought their food in downtown markets where prices were cheaper, then carried the parcels home with them on the bus, "a thing that people in Europe in our social position never do."[86] She reminded them that "a singer is not like a business man or a doctor or a scientist who can keep on working until 70 or 80 years of age. The years of great earning capacity are limited and in that time the artist must think to put aside something for the time when his singing days will be over."[87] But she assured her family that although she was not yet making enough money to pay them back and, in fact, still needed their financial help, she had every intention of repaying them with interest just as soon as she was earning "really big money."

These vague promises did not satisfy Jack, who was also becoming increasingly disgusted with what he perceived to be pro-Mussolini statements in both George's and Norma's letters. He finally told his father, "I wrote Norma a letter today about her pro-Italianism and told her that she'd better snap out of it and realize just where her real interests lie. I am fed up on hearing her extoll the virtues of Mussolini, who, some day in the maybe not distant future, will be engaged in a war against the British Empire. I hope you concur."[88] Dr. Piper genuinely liked and respected George, but eventually even he protested against the strong bias evident in the Pocaterras' letters, and they tried to limit political references in their future correspondence. Unfortunately the damage had been done, and the brothers revised their earlier impression of George. Now they suspected that not only was he trying to shirk his duty to look after his wife, he might be influencing her against the best interests of her family.

Although he was reluctant to interfere directly in Piper family affairs, and usually directed from behind the scenes by helping Norma to frame her thoughts and compose her letters, George felt compelled to defend himself from what he considered unjust accusations. Attempting to elicit Dr. Piper's sympathy, he wrote that he regretted that so much of his money was tied up in the etchings that were sitting unsold with Mrs. Nilsson in Vancouver: "So many thousands of dollars frozen, when I really need them."[89] He reminded the family that he, too, was considered a foreigner in Italy and was not able to work there unless he renounced his Canadian citizenship. Though this tactic might have helped to promote Norma's career, he had refused to do it, because both he and Norma intended to return to North America once her career was launched. To the implied criticism that he should seek employment elsewhere, he told them that he could not leave Norma alone in Italy, as she needed his support as her manager. He told Dr. Piper, "As long as practically all my time is taken up with Norma's work and looking after her career, I can't earn anything and am using up my little capital."[90]

Clearly the Pocaterras felt this was a significant sacrifice, and when her father pointed out that George was not the only one to have made a sacrifice, Norma told him that the difference for her brothers was that they were making an investment out of earnings whereas George was using up his savings. Saying that she needed only "a few decent breaks" to get properly launched in a wonderful career, she begged for her family's continuing support: "Now that I can see and know that I am really good I can hardly bear the thought of having to give it up Father . . . I am going to go over and go over big . . . I am born for the stage, and . . . it would be a crime against nature if I should not be permitted to continue."[91]

Always reluctant to disappoint her, and convinced that by staying on just a little longer Norma would achieve the elusive European reputation needed to guarantee an American success, Dr. Piper asked his sons to continue supporting their sister even though she refused to make any kind of formal agreement regarding their investment. Grudgingly, they complied by continuing to send sporadic payments, but it must have been very galling for them to hear about some of the little luxuries that the Pocaterras considered essential even while they begged for financial support from Canada. After describing a new suit, ordered from a "most wonderful tailor," Norma told her father, "The expense of lessons is the smallest item in a lyric career. Clothes and travelling are what cost the most."[92] In her letters home she also tactlessly described innumerable small excursions around northern Italy and lovely boat trips on the lakes of Lombardy, Piedmont and Veneto. And she delighted in describing a new leisure activity introduced by George, sailing their convertible "orange and silver sailing canoe."

In February of 1937 George had written to Raymond Patterson in great excitement:

You remember the plans we used to make about a canoe trip through the heart of Europe? Well something like that is being done now often. There are in Germany seven hundred thousand Faltboats, which cruise all over the streams of Central Europe ... These Faltboats are all collapsible, they can be taken apart and put together in a few minutes, and as a boat capable of carrying 700 pounds, and unsinkable, will weigh only about sixty pounds divided in two bags of about thirty lbs. each, you can easily see how handy they can be ... The two-seater, cruising Faltboats are also equipped with a sailing arrangement, with Jib and Mainsail, with rudder and side-boards, like the Dutch sailing boats, to act as keep against side slipping, and in Germany there are many contests for these crafts ... They cost here, that is a cruising boat for two, of the best firms, around $125, with all equipment included, that is sailing arrangement, life-saving cushions, waterproof clothes bags, watertight compartments, and everything else needed. Also a collapsible bicycle wheeled (2) carriage, on which one can take the boat from place to place without having to take it apart when travelling on a cruise. Some of these boats are a bit too narrow for my taste, but others seem alright. In Germany they shoot almost any rapids with them. I have seen some marvellous films [photographs] of them.[93]

Soon afterwards, George acquired a kit for a faltboat and spent a happy spring building the craft, which he christened *Vellita II*. Almost as much as George, Norma loved to spend "a whole day in the out-of-doors" sailing on Lake Como north of Milan or down the rapids of the Adda and other rivers.

George and Norma sailing the "Vellita II"
at Lake Como, Italy, ca 1937.
GA PA-2393-1-2-1

Top: Norma on the shores of the Adriatic, 1937.
GA PA-2393-12-1-2

Bottom: George on the shores of the Adriatic, 1937.
GA PA- 2393-14-2-2

Dressed in matching "little blue shorts and sandals," they attracted attention whenever they pushed the boat to the water on its special two-wheeled cart. Even when the weather turned stormy and they were forced to paddle rather than sail, Norma told her father, she found the experience exhilarating.

The sailing provided many hours of evening and weekend recreation, but even more important to the couple, and more difficult for the brothers to understand financially, were their two annual summer vacations. To rest for the coming year, and to escape the stifling heat of Milan, they vacationed every summer for several weeks at the seashore and several more in the mountains. Norma's habit of continuing her daily singing practice while on holiday often attracted attention, and she related to her father an incident that she found particularly amusing and occurred during a holiday to the Adriatic in 1937. One day she was practising the *The Barber of Seville*, when George glanced out the window to see "a great crowd of people gathering from all directions and standing there listening with rapt expressions all the time I was singing. It was very nice, the sort of thing one sees in the movies. It was comical, I was just in the middle of a long high note at the end of one song, when a motor cycle went by and the whole crowd were so mad that they started to shout to him to get away with his noise, and leave them in peace to enjoy the music."[94]

Eventually, the dwindling and erratic nature of her brothers' financial contributions led Norma to suspect that some of their money was being diverted from herself to help her brother Dick and his family, who had been badly affected by the Depression. She accused her sister-in-law of turning the family against her. Her letter to Dr. Piper on the subject was perceptive and revealed more than a little guilt on Norma's side when she imagined Isabel saying to the others, "You have been sending money to Norma for years. What are you going to get out of it? She's living in luxury, seeing the world, and you and poor Dick are working yourselves to death. Poor Dick is the one who should be helped."[95] In fact, Norma's surmise was correct, but Jack rose to Norma's defence with the same family argument that had been used for years. Resenting Isabel's interference, he informed her:

> I will only say two things about your bitter, common and vulgar comments on my sister. In the first place, it is no business of yours if I take my monthly cheque and burn it in front of the Windsor Hotel at high noon on Saturday. I have always spent my money on whom I choose and I shall continue to do so in spite of any raving of yours. It is absolutely none of your concern—and in the second place, in case you don't know, my sister denied herself pleasures, clothes, boy friends, even girl friends, for many years in order that 'the boys' could have all the money and time spent on them . . . The boys each had a university education but Norma stayed home and did the housework.[96]

By 1938 George and Norma were thinking of leaving Italy. Although the Pocaterras publicly justified their extended stay, privately they admitted that Norma had achieved all she could there and that it was time to make a start in North America. Norma had been away from home for four years, and although she and her father had been faithful correspondents, she was saddened by his declining health and missed her family and friends. She wrote to her father, "Our hearts are longing to see you and our other dear ones."[97] She pressed him to visit Italy, but he told her that because of his health, his travelling days were over. He confessed, rather alarmingly, that even climbing a few stairs "makes my heart go pitty pat."[98] Often bedridden through illness, he had come to rely for companionship on his boarder-cum-housekeeper, Olive Parnell and her teenaged daughter, Glenna. The Parnells had moved in with Dr. Piper in June 1935, had nursed him through seven months of serious illness in the spring and fall of 1936 and had generally seemed to fill the void in his life created by the loss of his sister and daughter. When he was well enough to drive the car, he took them on little outings downtown or into the countryside and even included them in a road trip with a friend to Coeur d'Alene and Spokane one summer. But still he yearned for his daughter, saying, "I am longing for the day when you are on this side of the water" and telling her fondly "I think of you folk most of the time."[99]

With Norma's family so far away, the arrival in Milan of a few travellers from "home" was greeted with great excitement. Over the years, visitors included Percy Page (coach of the famous women's basketball team, the Edmonton Grads[100]), Norma's cousin Gertie and husband, Will Ferguson, from Ontario, and George's old foreman, Adolf Baumgart. This last visitor was particularly welcome. No doubt George had told Norma many stories of his hired man, raising his own expectations as well as hers for when they met Adolf's ship at Genoa in February 1938. They were not disappointed. As George reported to Raymond Patterson, "He looked exactly the same as when I last saw him in 1935, only better groomed." As with all their guests, the Pocaterras treated Adolf well, showing off their adopted city with pride. "We took him to see some of the most famous places in the city. Most important the Camp Santo, the wonderful city of the dead, celebrated in the whole world as the most magnificent for natural position, high up amongst the hills, and for the thousands upon thousands of the most gorgeously artistic monuments imaginable ... We took him there in an open carriage, horse-drawn, as something different and more attractive than the usual taxi." With amusement, George also noted his old foreman's keen eye for beauty: "We have a very attractive-looking maid, a typical Italian beauty, large dark eyes, with long lashes, lots of wavy brown hair, and poor Adolf could not keep his eyes away from her. It was funny to hear them trying to make conversation together ... It was rather sweet. Of course Ena has a fiancé, and it was all so guileless."[101]

Norma's old friends from Brandli's studio, Margaret Lattimore and Isabelle Logie, also visited the Pocaterras briefly on their way to investigate musical conditions in Germany. In 1937 Brandli had warned Norma to expect the "headstrong" women, who were determined to study in Germany despite his advice to the contrary. Taking seriously Norma's blunt letter written in response to their inquiries, in which she had outlined the high cost of European career development, the friends had delayed leaving until their financing was assured and then had prudently decided to investigate conditions before committing to a move overseas. Unfortunately, that meant their tour of Germany finally occurred just as the international situation was disintegrating, and this circumstance effectively ended the dreams of European study for both women. The Pocaterras went to some trouble to show her old studio friends that Norma's years away had been productive and successful; she was gratified when both professed themselves "frankly astonished at the way I sang . . . because, as Isabelle said, people used to say of me 'Norma Piper has a nice sweet voice but it is absolutely cold.'"[102]

There were practical as well as sentimental reasons to leave Italy in the late 1930s. With the devaluation of the lire in October 1936 from 12 to19 lire per American (and Canadian) dollar, it seemed at first that Norma's money from home would go further, but George's fear that prices would rise in consequence was soon realized and the cost of living increased dramatically. For example, Norma told her father in 1938 that they were paying 7 lire per kilo for oranges that had cost only 1 lira per kilo before devaluation.[103] As a result, George found himself having to cash in some of the Canadian dollars he had hoped to retain for their return to North America. He was also forced to draw on his capital by selling stocks more and more often to supplement Norma's occasional earnings and whatever money they still received from the Piper family. But even more importantly, the Pocaterras were finally becoming concerned about the changing political situation in Italy

George had been outraged by the "criminal sanctions" against Italy during the Ethiopian crisis in 1935–36, and this experience coloured his opinions for several years thereafter. Although he had been away from Italy for 30 years and considered himself a Canadian, he initially supported Mussolini, seeing himself as "a good Italian" and a good Pocaterra. The memorial card distributed at his father's funeral had described Giuseppe Pocaterra as a "patriot" and an "enthusiastic supporter of Fascism and the Duce," and George's mother and sisters continued the family tradition by showing their active support for Mussolini. In fact, Norma told her father proudly that "in the early years, George's mother was 1 of the first 35 supporters of the Duce."[104] During the 1920s Marta helped to organize a fascist youth organization aimed at young girls ("like the Girl Guides," Norma told her father[105]). When she saw the "Daughters of Italy" or "Little Italians" marching at rallies and

Il Duce (Benito Mussolini) at a rally in Milan, October 1934. GA PD-184-6-223

parades, Norma was proud to note that her sister-in-law had designed their uniforms. During the Ethiopian crisis, Emilia had been "very much agitated politically," and Norma had explained her interest by saying, "of course she is a Pocaterra, or perhaps better, her mother's daughter."[106]

The Pocaterras were typical of most Italians during the 1920s and 1930s. The government's cultural and social policies were popular, and the new feeling of national pride was welcomed after the bitter disappointments of the First World War. Until the late 1930s, the government soft-pedalled its totalitarian policies and expansionist plans and focussed instead on patriotism and the "cult of the leader." As a result, before 1936 "most people swallowed most of the propaganda most of the time, at a fairly superficial level. Italy was stable, the Duce was popular, open dissenters were rare. It made sense to go along with the regime . . . It took years for most people to see through Fascism."[107]

Like most of his family and friends, George admired Mussolini's "leadership" in promoting government efficiency, social welfare and cultural renewal in Italy. In a letter to Dr. Piper, he wrote proudly, "IN NO COUNTRY IN THE WORLD is the worker so well taken care of as in Italy. We are years and years ahead of all countries in social welfare work."[108] He was disgusted with the bias he perceived in the British and North American press and considered writing a series of articles explaining the "real" situation in Italy and Europe from an insider's point of view. However, he dropped this plan when he realized that such articles were certain to be rejected by Canadian newspapers as challenging well-accepted "truths." In frustration, he wrote to Raymond Patterson, "I have been able to check many of the deliberate lies in no uncertain manner myself, and have come to the conclusion that if one sees something in the Press, it is a wise policy to wonder at once how far from the truth any statement actually is."[109] Patterson agreed, going even further: "My only suggestion for peace perfect peace in Western Europe would be to muzzle absolutely all the press & radio for six months ... the incessant nagging of these damned newspapers should be made to cease. The Canadian ones are, as they have always been, sensational & absurd."[110]

It was a relief for George to exchange these opinions with Patterson, who was one of his most congenial correspondents during a time when many other friends found his views provocative. As always, the two old friends enjoyed engaging in a battle of wits, words and their own interpretation of reality. Although they often disagreed about particulars, they shared a more cosmopolitan approach to world affairs than did many of their Canadian friends and were quite tolerant of each other's frequently inflammatory viewpoints. With his British background and Great War experience, Patterson considered himself a "confirmed European" with a unique understanding of recent history and the "current problem." Perhaps this perspective enabled him to read George's pro-Italian statements without rancour, once even writing from England to reassure his friend, "There are many good friends of Italy in this country."[111] Similarly, George accepted Patterson's opinions, even one that must have proved controversial among other Canadian friends:

I suggested—& made a strong case for it—that Canada should be presented to Hitler, Mussolini or anybody else with a territorial grievance. My reasons ... were that it was a thinly ... populated country & that consequently only a few wd. be affected by the transfer—that its present inmates had made a frightful mess of it and ... had proved themselves unfit to run it, & finally that any connection between it & my own country was, as far as I could see, only a source of expense & weakness to the latter ... from which I should be glad to see England disembarrassed.[112]

In letters to other North American friends, however, George's pro-Italian bias was often unwelcome. Aware that some of his statements were annoying or even offending his Canadian family and friends, he tried for a more moderate tone but sometimes found this difficult. Eventually Raymond Patterson advised George of the "unfavourable" local reception to some of the ideas expressed in his letters, warning him that there was "a growing hostility towards Italians which has recently found open expression in this Highwood country & from people who used to be among your best friends."[113] In a letter to Dr. Piper, George once so vehemently praised Italy and defended Mussolini that he added the postscript "Please destroy this after reading."[114] Incensed, his father-in-law replied, "As you requested, committed to the flames. It may be a great country but I prefer the British Commonwealth and you are wasting time my boy in writing such letters as the last one."[115]

Initially Norma had been shocked by evidence of military preparedness in Italy. Even in October 1934, she was predicating her own success only "if no such catastrophe as a European war comes within the next year."[116] During the Ethiopian crisis, the piercing siren and public outpouring accompanying an *adunata* (call to arms) both impressed and frightened her: "I felt fear, a terrible fear ... It all seemed so dreadful ... I who have always lived in a land of peace had before no notion of just what a "call to arms" could be. Oh! The spirit of patriotism, the rallying to the colours is a wonderful thing — if I could just forget the terrible suffering which will ensue."[117] However, Fascist parades and rallies soon became an ordinary experience, causing much excitement among the Pocaterra family members who took part.

In letters home Norma praised the "magnificent spirit" in Italy and opined, "If dear old Alberta could only have the peace, security, the organization that holds sway here in Italy things would be much better there," and "what Canada needs is a Mussolini."[118] She adopted the prevailing attitude, one of admiration for Mussolini, and was very excited when she and George were able to hear the Duce speak in person at big rallies in Milan in 1934 and 1936. Caught up in the nationalism surrounding them, the Pocaterras bought a flag to display and, in March 1937, Norma cryptically recorded in her diary, "George bought a Black Shirt."[119]

However, by 1938 the Pocaterras were disillusioned with Mussolini's Italy. Revealingly, Norma told her father, "I don't mean to say that everything that is here is perfect"[120] and told him that they did not agree with Mussolini in everything. "George is very far from taking sides," she assured him, "he considers himself all the time the very best kind of Canadian."[121] In fact, George was finding the aggressive tone of Mussolini's foreign policy hard to defend, and he may have begun to worry about the direction of social policy as well, particularly when stronger ties with Hitler's Germany resulted in a "reform of customs" in 1938. Within a short period, military uniforms were everywhere in evidence, the goose-step march was adopted, citizens were forbidden to shake hands but had to perform the so-called Roman salute instead, and, most troubling, laws persecuting Jews were introduced. Like many of his countrymen, by the late 1930s George discovered that although he was a nationalist, he had little enthusiasm for fascism.[122]

At the end of 1937, the Italian government had forced George to prove his Canadian exemption from Italian military service during the First World War, which he did with the help of Dr. Piper, who turned to various friends in government, including R. B. Bennett. This sobering incident, and increasing evidence that a European war might be on the horizon, worried George sufficiently that in the fall of 1938 he asked Dr. Piper to verify his Canadian assets and informed him of their plans for a safe escape from Milan "if the thing that we all don't want to see should happen."[123]

For some time, George had been writing to various influential American friends from his dude-ranching days, requesting their help in promoting Norma in the United States. Even if a friend had no direct musical influence he wrote, hoping to create interest in Norma and her career. Casting a wide net, he even included his former fiancee, Amelie de Vauclain (by then Mrs. Francis G. Tatnall), in his campaign. Norma assisted by requesting that her father and brothers write to all their friends about her progress and prospects. Most of George's old friends were willing to assist and some had influential contacts in the musical world even if they themselves had no expertise. Guy Weadick provided a letter of introduction for Norma to a friend at an important musical agency in New York City. Frazier Hunt agreed to do some promotional work with regard to radio contracts in New York. Dr. Morlan not only had important connections with the Chicago Civic Opera Company but was also a personal friend of the great opera star Amelita Galli-Curci (Mrs. Homer Samuels), who had studied under Norma's current maestro, Giacomo Marino; responding to requests from both Morlan and Marino, the diva gave Norma the benefit of her experience and advice regarding opera in North America.

With these letters, George felt he was preparing the field for Norma's American debut. They still hoped that a British or American opera company might engage her from Italy, thus paying their expenses for the trip, but they told Dr. Piper they planned to return "home" in 1939 in any case, "to see you dear, and start our American career."[124] En route they planned to investigate musical opportunities in England, which they judged to be good because of Norma's British citizenship and the assumption that she might well be the "new Melba" the British were seeking. In anticipation, Norma added a number of English songs to her repertoire, although her father was disappointed to learn that most of the sentimental "Heart Songs" he favoured were pitched too low for her voice. In particular, he wished Norma to sing "When You and I Were Young, Maggie," which he told her was "[her] own song." (The words to "one of the most popular ballads of the early 20th century" were written in about 1864 by Norma's maternal great-uncle, George W. Johnson, for his young wife, Maggie Clarke, while they were living in Hamilton, Ontario.[125])

With the newspapers filled with reports of the growing international tension, Dr. Piper was very concerned for the Pocaterras' safety. Although he longed to see them, he thought Norma would do well in England and was relieved to think they would soon be in British territory. He wrote to several influential friends, asking for their help in promoting Norma to the BBC radio network: Leonard Brockington (former Calgary city solicitor, by now chairman of the CBC), Graham Spry (son and grandson of Dr. Piper's Masonic friends, now a prominent businessman in England but formerly chairman of the Canadian Radio League) and R. B. Bennett (now retired from Canadian politics and in the midst of a permanent move to England). As usual, Dr. Piper relied confidently on Bennett's interest in the family and hoped he might offer financial as well as promotional assistance, a hope fuelled by an interesting rumour circulating in Calgary in 1938: that when approached directly for funding, Bennett had provided some financial support to Jessie Cadman, a young lyric soprano from Calgary studying at the Royal Academy in London.[126] Excitedly, Dr. Piper suggested that Norma should likewise try the direct approach with their old friend.

Norma, Milan, Italy, ca March 1938.
GA PD-184-5-77

Norma had taken pains with her letter of condolence when Bennett's sister, Mildred, had died in the spring of 1938, and now she framed a very appealing letter seeking his interest and support. But when pressed for something concrete by way of help, the "good friend of the Piper family in high position" claimed that he could do nothing for Norma because he had no influence in English circles.[127] Norma interpreted this correctly as a very apparent unwillingness to become involved in her career, and she stormed at her father, "RB's letter proved one thing very strongly, and that is that Canadians in England are merely *Colonials*. It's no use to illude [*sic*] oneself."[128] However, Brockington promised to arrange an audition for her at the BBC whenever she was ready to move to England. With this in mind, she begged the family to continue their support, reminding them, "Even in England I have to . . . be a real revelation and jump right into the high pay class to make it worthwhile. And I have to pose as a real prima donna."[129]

The Pocaterras took the initiative and wrote to Covent Garden in London themselves, but they were assisted in contacting the British Glyndbourne Festival Opera Company by Brandli. One of his students, a Mr. Hogg, had a good friend, Aubrey St. John-Mildmay, of Vancouver, whose daughter Audrey was an opera singer married to John Christie, head of the Glyndbourne Festival Opera Company. When Mrs. Christie heard from her father, she graciously wrote to Norma, who happily reported to her father, "Apparently I have a kindly friend in Mrs Christie."[130] This was naive of Norma, because the singer never promised to do anything more than suggest an audition with maestro Albert Erede, the Glyndbourne's director of Italian seasons, who planned to be in Milan in December 1938. Norma felt she made a "very good impression" at the audition, but she was disappointed to learn that any roles in the Glyndbourne opera season for which she was suited were being sung by Mrs. Christie herself. When the Pocaterras heard that the Glyndbourne company was planning an American tour in conjunction with the upcoming New York World's Fair, their hopes soared again, but nothing came of it.[131]

Meanwhile, their letters to the Covent Garden Opera Company had resulted in a telegram in February 1938: "If willing to pay own expenses you probably could arrange for audition in Berlin between Thursday and Sunday next. Communicate Walter Legge."[132] They had "a hard time gathering together enough money for the trip," but Norma told her father, "We felt we had to make this sacrifice. Otherwise Covent Garden would wash their hands of us."[133] They travelled to Berlin by train, and characteristically George reported, "We were very much impressed by Germany. And by its spirit. That's a country THAT IS DOING THINGS."[134] Norma, who called herself Norma St. George for the benefit of the British, worried that she would be considered a "dark horse" but felt the audition went well, and she wrote a pretty note thanking Legge for his "kindly reception."[135]

After being prompted by the Pocaterras in several follow-up letters and a telegram, Covent Garden finally informed them in June that Norma's talents would not be required. They had chosen instead Italian coloratura Lina Pagliughi—"because she has a *name* which I, so far, have not."[136] Although Norma realized that her lack of experience might have been part of the problem ("it was expecting rather too much that they would take me this year with only 5 performances of *Rigoletto* to my credit"[137]), she was upset by the rejection and told her father it was "hardly fair after their having asked me to go to Berlin."[138] Forgetting how the audition actually came about, she complained, "That which we object to most is the way they asked us to get to Berlin and pay our own expenses which looked as if they were considering us seriously. That trip cost us a good many thousand lires and we are still feeling the financial pinch on account of it."[139] In fact, the unforeseen trip to Berlin had been such a drain on their resources that afterwards George was forced to borrow money from a good friend to help meet expenses.

In April 1938 plans to leave were put on hold when Norma finally had the satisfaction of being called "a revelation" by a Milanese impresario, who arranged an invitation for her to open an official season in the city of Campobasso by singing three performances of *Rigoletto*. As she explained later to her father (who dutifully notified the Calgary press), "This engagement marks a very definite step forward for me. Up to now I have always sung for impresarios who arranged and managed performances in privately arranged seasons or single performances. But this Campobasso affair [is] an OFFICIAL season. A season arranged for by the Ministry of Culture at Rome and by the City of Campobasso. And I was honoured especially by being given the coveted opportunity of opening the season with a gala performance. Can you see what THAT means? Recognition at last in high quarters and a chance to really prove myself."[140] Her notices were good, and she received many offers from lesser impresarios—which were "diplomatically refuse[d]" in the expectation of better offers from more important agents.[141]

These better offers seemed to take a frustratingly long time to materialize and negotiate, so, in the meantime, George arranged for Norma to audition a second time at La Scala. The first reaction from the officials at La Scala was "nothing doing," but once they had been advised of the Pocaterra family's "patriotism," they changed their minds and approved the audition in July 1938.[142] Norma's turn came after a dozen other singers, but when she stood before the impressive group of examiners and the audience of 200, she lost her nerve and sang only two concert songs instead of the aria from *La Sonnambula* that she had specially rehearsed for the audition. Although George told her afterwards that "the voice carried marvellously, was pure and clear" and the examiners were complimentary, once again she was rejected.[143]

Bitterly disappointed, she reproached herself for letting down George and Maestro Marino: "Everybody works for me. I have all the qualities and then I put on the brakes. What a fool."[144] Although the examiners might have been interested had she sung the aria, they simply were not impressed enough with Norma's voice to make her an offer. The main problem seems to have been the inconsistency of her singing, an early fault she had never totally overcome. Even after all the years of lessons, she sometimes had a tendency to shout, and she still needed the "the bull dog watching of both George and the Maestro to see that [she] produce[d] each tone right."[145] George was disappointed on several occasions by the unpredictability of her voice when she sang for family or friends, telling her that he "couldn't understand why [she] sometimes sang marvelously and other times nothing special."[146] Although his family was supportive publicly, privately many of them feared Norma would never rise to the level of George's expectation simply because of her vocal inconsistency.[147] Depressed by a sense of failure, Norma did not seek the usual solace of her father's sympathy following her second rejection at La Scala but confined her unhappy thoughts to her diary.

After Campobasso, her next two engagements were cancelled due to government interference, so she did not perform again until December 1938, when she did a brief "tournee" in Sicily; there she helped to inaugurate a new theatre at Catonia with performances of *Rigoletto*, *Lucia di Lammermoor* and

Top: Impero Theatre, Messina, Italy, 1938.
GA PA-2393-15-4-2

Bottom: Norma with advertising poster for
her performance of "La Sonnambula" at
Impero Theatre, Messina, December 1938.
GA NA-695-88

La Sonnambula. At times she was tempted to accept lesser offers just to help ease their finances (as she told her father, "It takes courage to refuse offers that bring good money"[148]). But George insisted they stay the course with their career-development strategy and, as usual, she turned to her family for help. With her slim figure, the Pocaterras felt Norma compared very favourably with the two top Italian coloraturas, Toti dal Monte (whose "sun is setting. . .[and who] has lost some of her top notes") and Lina Pagliughi (who "has a lovely voice but is far too fat. She makes audiences here laugh when she walks on the stage"[149]).

Norma told her father that given a chance she knew she could compete with them, but "what I most need now is to get known. I have done far more than most foreigners but I have really sung in only one official season and I shall have to sing a good deal before I get well enough known to command the large sums of money that will make all the sacrifices financially worthwhile." She pleaded with him to make her brothers understand and to continue their support: "We have all stuck together and pulled together in the past for this career. This is the crucial year, the year I need help as never before, the year when, if I cannot have it, all the years before will have been wasted and I shall finish my career by singing at the rate of five or ten dollars a night as there is no middle way—either among the great or one of the millions."[150]

As usual, Dr. Piper was sympathetic: "You must be weary my dears. So many disappointments."[151] Although his failing health had put a big strain on his resources, he continued to send the Pocaterras what he could and even offered to "help to the utmost" by once again offering to take a second mortgage. This generous offer was gratefully declined by Norma, who wrote, "Dearest it is too much. Don't do it yet. We will try to get along and hope that . . . things will begin to come our way."[152] But her brothers were increasingly antagonistic toward George and reluctant to help him at all. In fact, her letters only became effective again when they realized Norma was trying to leave Italy. Jack told her frankly that was the "only basis on which I would concur in continuing financial assistance . . . [as] I am not desirous of having Italians or Italy spending any more of my nice American dollars."[153]

By May 1939, when Mussolini signed a military alliance with Hitler known as the Pact of Steel, the Pocaterras were making serious plans to leave Italy. Although Norma had been informed of Dr. Piper's serious illness, hospitalization and long recovery in 1936, and she was well aware of the resulting ill health that had plagued him ever since, she seemed oblivious of the fact that her father had aged greatly during her five years of absence. She assumed that he was his vigorous old self and plied him with instructions to make inquiries and arrangements on her behalf. She asked him to investigate everything from the amount of duty that would be charged on her costumes to the possibility of arranging a Canadian concert tour so that she could earn some money while waiting for things to develop in New York or Chicago. Recalling that Olga Nickle was the Calgary representative of several organizations that toured professional musicians across western Canada (the Celebrity Concert

Series and the Frederick Shipman Famous Artist Series), Norma suggested that her old friend and supporter might help facilitate such a tour. But she told her father not to bother contacting the San Carlo Opera Company, "as we feel, and it is everybody's opinion, that I have reached far higher than that degree now and we must really try for big things." However, she conceded that a guest appearance with the company would be acceptable.[154]

Earlier in the year, Dr. Piper had warned that there was a lot of prejudice against Italy and things Italian in North America. When he attended a concert by Calgary-area soprano Odette de Foras in February 1939, he witnessed a cool audience reception toward her Italian songs.[155] Anxious about the heavily Italian focus in Norma's repertoire, he wrote to some friends in Detroit, who sent him programs from the Ford Hour, a popular American radio show that featured operatic selections. He passed these programs along to Norma so that she could see which English songs were being sung successfully by other coloratura sopranos and could add them to her syllabus for North America. In response to his advice, new recordings were made of Norma's voice that included a few English songs ("Lo, Hear the Gentle Lark" and "Oh My Laddie"). When these were sent to Calgary, Norma warned her father, "The voice does not sound as sweet as it is in reality, but they give an excellent idea of the techniques and agility."[156]

A promotional photo of Noma, Milan, ca 1939.
GA PA-2393-12-1-4

After much discussion, the Pocaterras decided to let their apartment go, reasoning that if Norma's career became international and they decided to make Milan their home base, they could always find another. They planned to leave Italy at the end of June. Although their hopes were pinned on the United States, they still felt that "it would be foolish to leave this side of the pond without trying our luck in England first,"[157] and therefore they requested another audition with Walter Legge at Covent Garden. Covent Garden made no reply.

Even while they made plans to leave, they still hoped for the elusive "big break," and George continued to negotiate with impresarios for engagements. Norma told her father, "We are working hard dear, with not one but 20 irons in the fire, 20 roads before us, and working on them all ... [because] we have learned to our bitter experience that if one puts all one's money on one horse it doesn't pay as he often runs off the track."[158] As summer began and still they lingered in Italy, Norma revealed that she had auditioned for

182

a number of important opportunities and they were waiting to see if any of them resulted in a contract: a short season of three to six operas at the end of October in the new Italian city of Tripoli in North Africa, a performance during the same period at the Royal Opera of Rome, and two weeks in early September singing four operas in the big season in the city of Montecatini. In early July she hinted to her father about an additional opportunity, "a very big deal" which, "if it materializes . . . will give you great pleasure."[159]

Finally Norma reported that she been given a "marvellous opportunity," chosen to lead a company inaugurating a new opera house and singing for a three-month season in Manila in the Philippines.[160] She was engaged to sing nine operas in her repertoire, and in seven of them she was to be the prima donna. George had negotiated well and won her a "50% rise on the original terms offered," plus round-trip passage for them both. Although she had signed only an initial contract, the Pocaterras had taken the unprecedented step of informing her father and a few close friends but cautioned Dr. Piper not to tell the Calgary newspapers until they had given him permission. A rumour that the organizing group was an "American concern" with interests in many theatres around the world, including the United States, led them to believe that a contract with them "would be a passport into the USA."[161] Further, they were "given to understand" that a successful season in Manila might lead to a three-month extension of the tour to Australia and California.

After so many years of patient manoeuvring and negotiating, the Pocaterras were delighted with the prospect of Manila and incautiously began to view the business as a "done deal," even though they waited week after week to sign the final contracts (which, they were always assured, were "on the way"). Realizing that this might be Norma's big opportunity to break into the North American market, they drew on their connections to ensure an enthusiastic reception for Norma in the Philippines. Frazier Hunt, who had spent time in that part of the world, promised them letters of introduction to his contacts among the press and dignitaries in Manila. George also wrote to E. R. (Dick) Wright, who ranched near Cochrane, Alberta, and who had lived for many years in the Philippines and was presumed to have useful contacts and suggestions. Remembering her father's successful strategy during her early days of touring, Norma asked Dr. Piper to check with his old lodge friends to see if any had connections in the Philippines that might prove helpful. Happily, George and Norma made plans to supplement their wardrobes with cooler clothing and decided to buy some new costumes, reasoning, "One cannot have the ladies in the audience saying 'my goodness! she wears the same clothes in both operas'."[162] Of course, they anticipated all this costing "big money" so expressed the hope that the Pipers would see them through financially—and then headed away to the mountains in early August for a two-week vacation to rest for the exciting time ahead.

During their holiday in the Dolomites, which Norma found to be "exactly the same as our Rockies," the couple took several strenuous hikes that she described in allegorical detail to her father. Although George found these walks "fairly easy" because he was a "mountain man," the experience was new for Norma and she found them "rather heavy weather."[163] After the first hike, she told Dr. Piper that she was "astonished to think that we had had the courage and the strength to climb so steeply. It is true that I had often got tired on the way up but George had encouraged me and led me on." When they reached their destination, "George preached a nice little sermon" to her: "That is life. It is only when we work and go forward in spite of terrible hardship that we reach the heights and gain the reward."[164] Norma felt great satisfaction at her physical achievement, and at the top of a pass she sang the cadenza of *Lucia* and enjoyed the resulting mountain echo.

Top: George in the Dolomites, ca 1937-39. GA PA-2393-14-2-3
Bottom; Norma in the Dolomites, at the top of a pass, ca 1937-39. GA PD-184-7-133

All of a sudden, at the end of the summer, international tensions increased with the signing of a non-aggression pact between Germany and Russia, and the Pocaterras were forced to make some tough decisions. Norma's final contracts for Manila still had not arrived, and they began to fear yet another disappointment, though she assured her father optimistically that "[they] are on the way and should arrive in a few days. If all goes well, we should leave as soon as possible after the present tension is cleared up."[165] In the meantime, they were uncertain what to do. They had waited so long for an opportunity such as Manila offered that they were loath to leave Italy if there was any chance the political situation would be resolved in time for the tour to proceed.

Worried that the Pipers would criticize them for staying in Italy when it was obvious the circumstances were disintegrating, they explained that they had consulted the British consul and "at the present moment there is nothing we can do. This thing came up unexpectedly and suddenly. And now there are no ships running."[166] If Milan was evacuated, they planned to go to Marta's villa in Bassano del Grappa, and if the situation disintegrated to the point that the Americans sent ships to remove their nationals, they hoped to be allowed to evacuate with their American friends.[167] They told Dr. Piper to remain calm, that "people here feel that no real conflagration will come, that there will be conferences and that the different problems will be settled once for all . . . there is unlimited faith here in the Duce, everybody feels that his great desire is for peace and that he will leave nothing unturned to bring it about . . . At any rate no matter what the papers say *'Don't worry about us.'* Please dear, don't worry. We will be *absolutely safe*. The one thing that worries us is the fact that you are apt to be worried."[168]

They were concerned about Dr. Piper's reaction mainly because of his current state of ill health. In early August Norma had learned that her father had been hospitalized for a week in late July. Home again, and under the care of Mrs. Parnell (in lieu of an expensive trained nurse), he was bedridden and very feeble and had to have Glenna Parnell scribe his letters for him. Both Norma and George misunderstood the serious nature of his illness: George admonished his father-in-law for overdoing things, saying, "We all need to know that you are always first class. Norma was quite upset about it and it took quite a while to cheer her up"[169]; Norma wrote, "We think of you so much dear and trust that your little disturbance is all cleared up and that you are feeling fine again."[170] Reluctant to worry them, Dr. Piper downplayed his condition, simply informing them, "I am not gaining as fast as I hoped but I am making progress."[171]

Dr. William Piper with Glenna and Olive Parnell, Calgary, July 1, 1939.
GA PA-2393-9-3-1

They, in turn, downplayed their own worries, but privately they were concerned about the conditions in Italy. Everyone predicted that Mussolini would not sign the non-aggression pact, but in the last days of August George and Norma grew anxious watching trainloads of soldiers passing their house. City streets were darkened at night, and citizens were asked to keep their blinds drawn. With the situation in Milan looking tense, on September 1 they again consulted the British consul, who must have had advance warning of the British declaration of war against Germany set to occur the next day, because this time he advised them to leave for Canada as soon as possible via Switzerland, France and England. George's passport would expire in October, at the same time his Canadian naturalization papers were due for renewal, and neither could be renewed before their due date. They were afraid to remain in Italy in case a war with England should cause the British consulate to be given up, with the result that George, without valid documents, might never be able to leave Italy to return to Canada. Afraid to gamble on Italy remaining neutral, they panicked and left for Switzerland that very afternoon without even informing their maid, Ena, that they might not return. Once in Lugano, they sent a telegram to Jack, "Both safe here. Address American Express Lugano Switzerland. Tell Father relatives. Love N G."[172]

But once they reached Switzerland, their escape plans fell apart. Norma later remembered that they found themselves "lost in a panic-stricken sea of humanity battling to be first out of the war-zone. But options were few. The French border was already closed, and the Nazis were threatening on both sides. Italian money was suddenly worthless, and within two days we were left without any means of escape except back through Italy."[173] After a very expensive week, in which they often wished they had saved their diminishing funds by fleeing to Marta's villa instead of to Switzerland, they learned that the Italian government had declared non-belligerency, and so they returned to Milan.

After the panic and "crush of refugees" in Switzerland, they were relieved to discover that all was calm in Italy; the blackout had been lifted and ships were sailing again. They packed their trunks, paid off Ena and determined to leave Italy no matter what happened with the Manila tour. When they learned that they could not take money or valuables out of the country, they put their sterling silver wedding gifts into a bank safety deposit box and, glad that they had not surrounded themselves with "a lot of expensive objects that we can neither sell nor take with us," gave everything else in the apartment to Ena.[174] Grateful for Norma's calm acceptance of the situation, George wrote to his father-in-law, "You Pipers are good stuff! Norma is a wonderful trump!"[175]

During the next two weeks—in which they "lived in hell," worrying that their escape from Europe might be prevented by Italy entering the war[176]— the Pocaterras tried to book passage on two different ships leaving Genoa but were forced to wait for the *Vulcania*, sailing from Trieste on September 18.

Norma told her father that sailing from Trieste not only was inconvenient, it also would cost four times what they would have paid to ship their trunks and make the rail journey to Genoa. They became frantic about money when they learned that the cheapest tickets would cost 540 dollars and could be paid only in American dollars.[177] Norma told Dr. Piper, "I really don't know where we will find the money," but George cabled a Canadian friend who responded with an immediate loan of 300 American dollars.[178] He borrowed additional American funds from a friend in Milan, and Norma warned her father that they would be very short of money upon their arrival in New York City and "we pray that the boys may continue to help us."[179]

Although she told her father it "breaks our hearts" to leave the little home where they had been "so wonderfully happy," Norma readily confessed, "We will surely be glad when we reach New York."[180] The *Vulcania*, which was comfortably equipped for 600 passengers, was overflowing with 1,500, and the deck was filled with automobiles.[181] Third class was fully booked by the time the couple arranged passage, so they had to be content with tourist-class tickets, although George arranged "at tremendous expense" for them to occupy a small stateroom, formerly a petty officer's cabin.[182] Worried about the high price of the tickets, Norma feared at first that they would have to forgo small on-board luxuries, such as cups of coffee and deck chairs, but upon arrival they were glad to report "a pleasant peaceful trip with no alarming incidents."[183]

Program for evening entertainment for first class passengers on the SS Vulcania, October 1, 1939. GA M6340-202-3b

The ship was crowded, but the company tried to maintain its usual standards, serving elaborate multi-course meals even in tourist class and providing evening entertainment throughout the two-week crossing. Glad to have escaped the European war, the Pocaterras enjoyed the voyage, and Norma was featured in one evening's entertainment. Crew members had overheard her daily singing practice, and so she was invited to sing four selections in the Grand Concert held in the Music Hall for first-class passengers on Sunday, October 1. As the *Vulcania* came in to New York Harbour the next day, the Pocaterras looked forward with some trepidation to the long-awaited launch of Norma's North American career.

Chapter 7

Norma & George: On the Highwood
1939–1941

When the *Vulcania* docked in New York on October 2, 1939, the Pocaterras were relieved to find a telegram from Jack inviting them to draw on his account at the New York office of Ames and Company for ready cash up to 100 dollars and suggesting that they visit him in Montreal. However, a second telegram arrived soon after and shocked Norma terribly: it reported that Dr. Piper was gravely ill, and it advised Norma to travel to Calgary immediately. Arranging for their trunks to be stored with the Frazier Hunts in New York, since George and Norma intended to return as soon as possible, the couple left at once for Montreal. George carried on to Toronto to check the etchings business with Jack Fraser, to make financial arrangements for their return to New York and to visit Irving Hollinrake.[1]

On October 7, Norma and Jack boarded a Trans-Canada Air flight for Calgary. These were early days for transcontinental flights, so the long trip was broken into five shorter legs: Montreal to Ottawa, Ottawa to North Bay, North Bay to Winnipeg, Winnipeg to Regina and Regina to Calgary. In spite of her anxiety, Norma was thrilled with the experience and impressed to learn that the first officer was Herbert Hollick-Kenyon, who had been with the American explorer Richard E. Byrd in the Antarctic and was one of Canada's first pilots to carry airmail. She reported all the details to George, telling him that the sensation of traveling in a plane was like being in a boat or on a train and that "flying is lovely and I hope that we will do lots of it."[2] (However, she was not impressed with the cold and snow she saw on her return journey a week later and told George, "Some country! I'd give it back to the Indians. Just remember dear Italy in October."[3])

Jack and Norma arrived in Calgary to sombre news. Dr. Piper had been very ill for three weeks. He had been in hospital for a week in early September, but since then had rested at home with nursing care and the attentions of Mrs. Parnell, her daughter, Glenna, and his good neighbours the Campbells, the Browers and the Moodies. He was considered too sick to receive the news that both his sister-in-law Min and his former partner, Dr. Roy Thorpe, had died in September. Although he had rallied slightly from the "terrible spell" that had precipitated the telegram calling Norma home, she was shocked to find that he "suffer[ed] terribly," spoke "very badly" and had "great difficulty expressing his thoughts." "He is very sick," she told George. "It breaks my heart to see him in this condition, he who was always so full of fun and good spirits." However, he still delighted in having her sing to him, and she found that in some ways Dr. Piper was "still his old self despite pain and weakness." He reprimanded her for speaking in "the sweet voice" she used with George, saying, "Talk in your natural voice. I'm afraid people will laugh at you," and, just as he had been wont to do in the past, reminded her sharply, "Don't grin so much."[4]

Norma felt guilty for having been away from her father for so long and for having put him to more than five years of worry and expense on her behalf. She told George, "I feel I was too slow or too careless or too stupid or too something," and she was relieved that family and friends did not reproach her: "Everybody is kind to me. Nobody has criticized me."[5] But she worried that it was more important than ever to justify her family's financial sacrifice, just at a time when her career had suffered major dislocation. Saddened by her father's approaching death, she longed for their "beautiful life in Italy" and privately brooded over the injustice of recent events. In public, however, she bravely maintained the persona of a European opera star, giving the *Calgary Herald* the benefit of her observations on the European situation and confidently reporting that her engagement in the Philippines might still occur and that she was looking forward to starting her North American career in New York. She also arranged to have the rest of the etchings, which had been stored in Dr. Piper's care, sent to Vancouver to Mrs. Nilsson, though George advised her to keep back one as a wedding gift for Bob Hunt, the son of his old Highwood friend, Frazier Hunt.

The family acknowledged that Dr. Piper might be dying, but after a week they judged that he was stable enough to leave in Mrs. Parnell's care and that it was time for them to return to jobs and other commitments. On October 14, Jack and Norma flew back to Montreal, and the next day Lawrence returned to Trail in British Columbia. Dick had remained in England, where he was training with the Royal Air Force to be a bomber inspector.

Dr. Piper passed away the very next day, and only Lawrence was able to return to Calgary on such short notice. In lieu of family, various old friends assisted Lawrence with funeral arrangements. Among the pallbearers were Frank Moodie, Bill Park and the Pipers' early boarder, George Bell.

As executor of his father's will, Lawrence had the unwelcome task of overseeing division of the estate, a job that lasted several years because much of Dr. Piper's estate of 25,000 dollars was in the form of stocks, which took some time to liquidate. There were many headaches, and at times Lawrence was hard-pressed to make his siblings understand his interpretation of his father's wishes. Although Jack and Dick, and even Lawrence himself, all felt they could justify a bigger share for themselves for various reasons, Norma's attitude proved especially difficult.

Having left Italy in a panicked rush and been forced to leave their Italian money behind, the Pocaterras arrived in North America saddled with a debt for their passage to New York. Thirty years later, Norma described their money problems in 1939 as "desperate," claiming they had "exactly 50c to [their] name" by the Christmas of that year.[6] Although they probably did have very little cash on hand when the *Vulcania* docked, her statement was an exaggeration; George later told friends "we only had $700—" when they started over again in Alberta nearly a year later.[7] Jack's generosity had given them some immediate relief, and George still had investments in Canada on which he could draw; with Dr. Piper's help in 1934, and during his own trip to Canada in 1935, he had been able to move many thousands of dollars out of Italy into bank accounts and investments in Canada. However, the devaluation of the lire had affected George's Italian investments badly, and he could foresee big expenses ahead while Norma attempted to establish herself in the United States.

Norma loved her father dearly, and her grief was deep and genuine, but she was a pragmatist, and all of these pressures dictated that she should try to get as much as possible from his estate. When they received the initial valuation of the estate in January 1940 the Pocaterras happily concluded that Norma would receive a one-quarter share of 25,000 dollars, or approximately 6,000 dollars. More than a year later, when the will finally went to probate, Norma was dismayed to learn that her share would be about one-third that amount. The Pocaterras had not taken into account the various debts and bequests that had to be paid before the remainder could be divided, but the long wait for probate also resulted in a reduced estate because stock values had declined significantly in the intervening year and a half.

Disappointed, the Pocaterras resorted to many of the same old arguments in trying to persuade her brothers to allow Norma a greater share, but the long, haranguing letters she composed with George's transparent help only served to annoy the Pipers and to harden their antagonism toward George. Once, Jack became so irate that he reopened old sores by referring to "George's obvious pro-Nazi leanings, and his lack of desire for work," and he told his sister, "I feel perfectly convinced that George has put you up to this, and that he has some strange power over you."[8] Responding furiously, Norma said George's "strange power" was love and that she resented the aspersions cast on him as "both unjust and most unfair." She then accused her family of leaving them "high and dry" just when they most needed their help.[9]

To a certain extent, Norma's accusation was true: the Piper brothers did use their father's death as an excuse to relieve themselves at long last of the financial burden represented by the Pocaterras. Although Jack and Lawrence never attempted to recover the considerable amount of money they had invested in Norma's career over the years (up to 5,000 dollars each), they steadfastly refused to give their sister any more money or to accede to her pleas for more than they considered her fair share of their father's estate. In fact, in one of his first decisions as executor, Lawrence instructed the family lawyer, Percy R. Bryenton, to veto Norma's claim against the estate for the cost of her air ticket (225 dollars), justifying his decision by saying that he and Jack had made no such claim. Closer to his sister, and hearing about her money worries first-hand during their visit together in Montreal, Jack told Norma privately, "It was a good try, anyway."[10]

Norma's response to her brothers' withdrawal of financial support was shrill. With little regard for their feelings, she discounted their financial support over the years, saying, "My family spent far less on me than the family or supporter of any other singer I know," adding "Burnada cost Pat Burns . . . considerably over $100,000 [and] they say that Wilda Blow cost her family $50,000."[11] She also claimed, falsely, that her own family had agreed to send 200 dollars per month to Italy, and then upbraided them for having failed to honour that agreement. Dick, who had never been involved financially with his sister but had been hurt by his father's obsession with supporting Norma during the Depression years, when Dick would have welcomed financial help for his own young family, wrote bitterly, "The fact that $15000-$20000 was spent on your music seems to mean nothing."[12] Norma countered with the inflated estimate that George, who had never intended to help fund her career, had spent 14,000 dollars on it because of the shortfall in her family's commitment.[13] But still the brothers would not back down.

After nearly two years of petty accusations on both sides, Dick became so exasperated that he wrote to Norma, "The thing is a muddle—you can't understand my arguments and I certainly can't see yours."[14] He took his sister to task, saying, "Considering the probable $15,000 spent on your singing I believe you have done very well indeed. That results are disheartening is indeed unfortunate, but the whole affair was carried on contrary to the advice of people who had had similar experiences. The fact that all that money was spent in enemy country makes it worse again."[15] When this reasoned approach failed to convince Norma, Dick was goaded into revealing the brothers' true feelings about her Italian venture:

Is it not clear that the whole career was undertaken . . . only on the advice of a teacher who apparently gave no thought to possible difficulties . . . Your trip to Italy was a mistake from end to end and the blame is Father's. This family would have been much happier had Jack and Lawrence refused to have anything to do with such a scheme but perhaps they had no idea of the probable cost. It was a worry to Father as I know, though he wouldn't write that to you, while at the same time it was a source of pleasure. He would have been happier if you had never gone except for year or two, we all would have been better off financially and this wrangling . . . would never have occurred. Father was good to all of us but he shone chiefly in his profession. He had no business head but once embarked on a course was likely to stick to it good or bad . . . the Italian incident might have turned out very profitably but it didn't.[16]

Once the Pocaterras had finally accepted that Norma would not receive a greater portion than her brothers, their next concern was to maximize as much as possible the value of the estate, the bulk of which consisted of 540 shares of Royalite Oil Company Limited valued initially at nearly 22,000 dollars. During the delay in settling the estate, the siblings watched in disbelief as Royalite prices dropped from nearly 40 dollars in January 1940 to less than 20 dollars per share when they were finally available for liquidation in July 1940. At George's urging, Norma tried to persuade Lawrence to delay cashing the Royalite stock until prices had increased substantially. She told him, "We can't afford that kind of loss . . . it would mean practically bedrock for us . . . our future seems to depend a great deal on it."[17]

Although they told her they were sympathetic to her financial situation ("it's tough on you my dear," acknowledged Lawrence[18]), the brothers had financial plans of their own and were anxious to get some cash from the estate. Unlike the Pocaterras, they had reckoned their inheritance would be relatively modest, in the hundreds rather than the thousands of dollars, and they were pleasantly surprised by the total value of the estate. They decided to start selling the Royalite stock 50 or a 100 shares at a time, hoping the price would gradually improve; unfortunately, it did not. Their one concession to Norma's plea was the assignment of 20 shares of Royalite to each sibling to be disposed of according to their own best judgment. Dick and Lawrence cashed their shares immediately; Jack and Norma held on for some time, but prices never really recovered. George was disgusted with his in-laws' apparent indifference to their sister's precarious financial situation and wrote angrily to Norma, "On both sides our dear nearest relations have HELPED THEMSELVES to our own detriment."[19]

After the Royalite shares, the house proved to be the biggest problem in settling Dr. Piper's estate. While visiting their dying father, the siblings had agreed to keep the house, rent it out furnished and split the income. The house was in Norma's name, an arrangement made by Dr. Piper in 1932 before her marriage and career as an attempt to reward her for past sacrifices and to guarantee her future security, while at the same time safeguarding the family home should he ever be sued for an error in his dental practice.[20] When their father died, his will gave clear directions for disposing of the house at 227 Scarboro Avenue.

Accordingly, Lawrence asked Norma to decide between keeping the house as her share of the estate or relinquishing entitlement in favour of a four-way split of all assets. In either case, she had to take into account that Dr. Piper had raised a mortgage of 3,500 dollars on the house for her benefit in 1935; Jack and Lawrence had helped him to repay this mortgage by contributing from their share of Aunt Susie's estate when it was settled in 1936, and now this debt needed to be repaid. With the house initially valued at 5,500 dollars, at first Norma decided to give it up. However, once she had realized that her home was likely to be in Calgary and that her cash share would be considerably smaller than expected, she tried to persuade the others to let her keep the house in addition to a cash share. Dick wrote in disbelief, "It would appear then that you are asking us to pay the mortgage and then give you the house."[21]

With a great deal of passionate language, Norma accused her brothers of denying Dr. Piper's wishes and cheating her out of her inheritance (i.e., her home). With a great deal of patience and some exasperation, they finally made Norma understand that they would not back down about the house or the division of the estate, though they were willing to overlook the thousands of dollars their father had spent on Norma's career. Probably this was because each brother had inherited money from other family members and Norma had not; Dick and Jack from namesake uncles and Lawrence from Dr. Piper himself to compensate for this inequity.[22]

Each brother reacted differently to Norma's attempts to sway their opinion. Dick was unhappy and urged her to "give it a good straight look" and said, "Do not think you are being treated badly by your family."[23] Jack was angry: "You seem to believe you have some right to ask me to forego [sic] my share of the cash value of the house. This I refuse to do."[24] And Lawrence, final arbiter as executor, was firm and blunt: he told Norma, "It is very clear what Father intended and I do not propose giving away any more money than I've done in the past. I cannot expect you to be pleased about it but that is my stand."[25] They were tired of supporting the Pocaterras, and each wanted the money for some immediate use (Jack and Lawrence both planned to marry in 1940, and Dick had been struggling financially for years). Lawrence even rejected Norma's request to take a larger share of the furnishings, pointing out that a stripped house would not be attractive to renters.

Mrs. Parnell, who had been very fond of Dr. Piper, was given a cash gift of 200 dollars for her faithful service while Dr. Piper was sick and was allowed to stay on in the house with her daughter, rent-free, until the end of the year, and then for a token rent of 10 dollars a month until new tenants were found for the upper and lower suites in the spring of 1940. She then became the manager of a local boarding house, The Wigwam. Although the new renters requested its removal to make more space for their own things, George's old Buffalo Head furniture and the items inherited by Norma were stored in the basement of the Scarboro Avenue house until it was sold in May 1942. Ultimately, Norma's share of the rental income amounted to only 50 dollars, but she did receive a quarter share when the house sold for 4,600 dollars. In total, she inherited about 2,000 dollars from her father's estate (approximately 25,000 dollars today), a very comfortable sum in the early 1940s, but many thousands less than she and George had originally anticipated.

Throughout most of the long period of estate settlement, Norma and George were trying to re-establish her singing career. As her father had always done in periods of family crisis, Norma wrote to R. B. Bennett requesting his assistance in some undefined way, but because he was now out of politics and living rather obscurely in England, he was perplexed by her petition. He regretted the death of his old friend, "for whom I had a very warm place in my heart," but dealt firmly with the daughter, writing coolly, "Frankly I do not know a way I could assist you in the realization of your wishes ... Do you not know persons who are connected with music and singing in Canada?"[26]

Back in Montreal after Dr. Piper's death, Jack, who was an opera lover, determined to help his sister re-establish her career by making use of his own musical contacts. He arranged for Norma to sing for various influential media friends who then provided letters of introduction to people of consequence in New York at the NBC radio studios and at the Metropolitan Opera Company, where the weekly concert broadcasts were directed by Montrealer Wilfrid Pelletier. Before the Pocaterras left for the United States, they decided to improve Norma's chances by artificially reducing her age; they acquired a copy of Norma's Ontario birth certificate and altered it to show a birth date of 1908 instead of 1898, thus making it agree with the date on her Canadian passport of 1933 and her police registration papers from Italy. No doubt they

Norma in concert attire, New York, ca 1939-40. GA PA-2393-15-5-1

justified this deceit by reasoning that if Norma's real age (now 41) were known, it might hinder her in the highly competitive musical world of New York.

As a result of their networking in Montreal, Norma auditioned in New York for radio work with the Met on December 18 and at the NBC studios on December 20, 1939. Although she felt she did well and directors at both institutions expressed a willingness to hear her again, neither offered her a job. In fact, the circumspect report from NBC was that her voice had "great carrying power" and was "ideal for the theatre" but was "too 'divine'" for radio.[27] Obviously, during her years of singing for the stage, Norma had forgotten the good advice about radio singing given by a friend of her father's in 1930: "the best results are obtained by singing very softly and with the mouth almost touching the instrument ... if you stand back and sing as you would in a concert it will not be nearly as effective."[28]

Early radio microphones were very sensitive, and many singers discovered through trial and error that a "crooning" style of singing was much better adapted to radio than was Norma's powerful, operatic voice production.[29]

194

They often felt homesick for "beautiful Italy" in New York over the winter of 1939–40, but the Pocaterras were determined to pick up the threads of Norma's career and decided to persist. They knew that as a last resort they could retreat to George's Ghost River property in Alberta, yet were reluctant to do so before making an effort in the big eastern cities. As Norma told Lawrence, they worried that going to what amounted to a cultural backwater "would be tantamount to los[ing] everything I have spent and work[ed] for up to now."[30] Still under the impression at this time that Norma would be inheriting many thousands of dollars, and anxious to project a "diva" image for her in New York, they rented a lovely apartment at a very fashionable address, 14 Washington Place. Their costs there for the next seven months were very high, about 200 dollars per month; in addition to monthly rent of 75 dollars, they had many business costs such as a telephone line, piano rental, singing lessons and entertaining.

Several years earlier, Norma had been given some advice by opera star Amelita Galli-Curci regarding the different expectations in America for opera singers. Whereas Italians "demand and love 'noise' and a different tone quality than is enjoyed here," she told Norma, in America "a smoother tone" was expected, "fuller and more rounded and finished with grace of handling and acting ... combined with [an] elegance of style not used in Italy or elsewhere in Europe."[31] With this advice in mind, the Pocaterras realized Norma needed some training to meet American expectations. They were fortunate to locate maestro Paolo Giaquinto, a former conductor at the Metropolitan Opera who had worked with many coloraturas, including Galli-Curci herself. After the long disruption in her training, Norma was eager to start lessons again but found that Giaquinto's style differed significantly from her previous maestros', and she spent many frustrating weeks trying to learn new methods of singing.

However, once she felt she had mastered Giaquinto's techniques and regained her confidence, she sang whenever and wherever she could. "How we tried," she later told her brother Lawrence.[32] She sang at formal auditions, at the Steinway Hall and for various people in the music world, and informally for groups of new acquaintances, who always were "enthused" and "greatly surprised" by her voice. After one of these private recitals, she was very pleased by a review that appeared in the American Italian-language newspaper *Corriere d'America*; music critic "Kim" (Pasquale De Biasi) gushed, "She feels music exquisitely ... she abolishes, with the warmth and richness of her tones and feeling, the legends of the colorless frigidity that marks almost all coloratura sopranos ... a coloratura of this calibre is destined, without doubt, for the great international theatres ... Norma San Giorgio cannot fail to achieve in New York the full success she has obtained in Italy."[33] This review, along with selected translations from reviews of her Italian performances, information on the roles she could sing and a list of the Italian theatres she had sung them in, formed the basis for a promotional package used over the next few years while the Pocaterras attempted to establish Norma in North America.

In late May she was finally able to arrange another audition with the Metropolitan Opera Company, this time with manager Edward Johnson in attendance. Once again, Norma thought she sang well and received kind and friendly compliments from Johnson, Pelletier and others at the audition. But once again they did not offer her a job, despite the fact that she "begged [Johnson] to give [her] a chance."[34] This bad news may not have been totally unforeseen: after seeing Johnson several days earlier, Norma had written in her diary "abbattuto" (I feel defeated/ despondent), so it seems likely he had tried to prepare her for disappointment.[35] She told Lawrence that Johnson had warned her that "unfortunately for me, Lily Pons has tremendous power and . . . she has enough 'pull' to keep out any possible rival" (though later she told a friend that George had overheard this supposition at the Met as gossip).[36]

Although Lily Pons was married to the well-known conductor Andre Kostelanetz, it seems unlikely that she was in a position to dictate hiring at the Met or was responsible for destroying the chances of an unknown singer such as Norma. More likely, Johnson felt that Norma's experience was insufficient to warrant her being offered a position at the Met, especially when he expected to be able to pick and choose among a flood of talented European refugees and Americans returning because of the onset of war. And this is exactly what he was able to do. In October 1939 he had hired several refugee artists, including a singer who had been "driven out of Prague" and was to share coloratura roles with Lily Pons.[37] When the Met announced in October 1940 that it had hired 10 new artists, 3 out of the 4 sopranos were Europeans.[38] To soften the blow and to ease Norma's pride, Johnson may have led her to believe that Lily Pons would not sanction her hiring.

Alternatively, it is possible that Johnson said nothing about Lily Pons and the Pocaterras simply made the gossip the basis of an explanation for why Norma failed in her approach to the Met. In any case, it was a bitter disappointment to learn that "the music world in New York [was] a closed circle."[39] Agents and radio producers told the Pocaterras quite frankly that without the Met's stamp of approval, Norma did not have a chance of being hired in New York. This experience coloured the Pocaterras' attitude toward Lily Pons, whom formerly they had admired and now actively disliked. Seven years later, when Norma saw the star in a movie, she reported happily to George that Pons "sang badly and . . . looked so thin and scrawny and ugly."[40] In turn, after hearing her on a radio broadcast from the Met in 1951, George noted with satisfaction "Pons very poor, flat and sharp."[41]

To promote Norma effectively to people of influence, George had exaggerated the success of her "European career" to supporters such as his old newspaper friend, Frazier Hunt, who unwittingly perpetuated the myth in a testimonial circulated on her behalf. As George was well aware, the reality of Norma's overseas career was a total of four dozen performances of five different operas and about a dozen general concerts, mainly in the smallest theatres in the smallest towns of Italy. But this was now described in Norma's promotional material as an interrupted "international" career. The

Pocaterras told family and friends that impresarios had been writing to them all winter, regretting their departure and "begging" for their return because there were now no coloratura sopranos in Italy as good as Norma.[42] The couple also exaggerated the loss incurred through their hasty retreat from Europe by telling family and friends that if Norma had not been forced to flee, she would have filled contracts in the 1939-40 season earning her a total 40,000 dollars for "the big govt. season at Montecatini, . . . the reopening of the Lyric theatre at Milan, . . . the Royal Opera season at Tripoli, [and] the Royal Opera of Rome," as well as the three-month opera season in Manila followed by a three-month tour of Australia and Calfornia.[43]

It is true that before they left Milan George had been investigating every one of these possibilities with various impresarios, and some of them would have paid very well indeed if Norma had managed to secure them. (For example, Norma had told her father after her audition that the four operas in the Montecatini season were worth 1,000 lire each[44]). However, few inquiries and auditions resulted in firm offers, and based on past experience there was not even the likelihood that more than one of these prestigious engagements would have come Norma's way. As she herself had told her father, the only one with even an initial contract had been the season in Manila, and if that had come through she could not have fulfilled any of the others.[45] But the story of her lost contracts was used as a publicity tool and was perpetuated so well and for so long that Norma herself eventually seemed to believe it; by the end of her life, she included the story every time she wrote a biographical sketch and or gave an interview.

Frustrated with their lack of progress in New York, George and Norma decided to return to Montreal at the end of May 1940. This decision was partly financial; the seven months in New York had cost them more than 1,500 dollars. With Norma's share of her father's estate looking much smaller than expected and financial support from her brothers definitely at an end, the Pocaterras could not afford to continue living there while Norma searched for work. In retrospect, they began to regret their hasty departure from Europe. Italy had delayed its entrance into the war, and now they wondered if some of the lucrative singing offers of which they had bragged really might have materialized. Maestro Giaquinto was "very much moved" to see them leave New York and attempted for a short time to offer vocal advice by mail.

Aware that financially "our only hope is my voice,"[46] Norma, with the help of Jack's musical friends, attempted to generate interest at CBC Radio in Montreal and Toronto. At the same time, she was arranging for an audition with the Chicago Opera Company. In this she was aided by George's old friend Dr. H. J. Morlan and by Nelyon Dewson, the wealthy daughter of Dr. Piper's old mentor, Dr. C. N. Johnson, of Chicago. Mr. and Mrs. Dewson were heavily involved with the Chicago Opera Guild and felt certain that their influence would benefit Norma. She travelled to Chicago in early July and auditioned with 30 other singers for the 1940 season. Although she felt that she sang well and that most of the other singers were unimpressive

("I myself would hire myself," she told George), she was upset by a rumour that the decision had already been made and that the audition was "all a fake."[47] Whether the rumour was true or not, she was not offered a job in spite of being assured "I have everything. Marvellous range, agility, presence."[48] "Very much upset," she recorded in her diary. "Another dream smashed!"[49]

Back in Montreal, George, and Norma, were faced with a key decision. In spite of their best efforts, it seemed impossible for Norma to gain entry into the big opera companies in the United States. As they had always supposed, it would have been easier is she had been hired from Italy by an American opera company than it was to compete in America with Americans. Unfortunately for Norma, her timing coincided with a particularly rich period of musical development in the United States, and the big companies were overwhelmed trying to accommodate talented American singers during the late 1930s and 1940s.[50] Without the top-notch European reputation for which she had been striving all her years away, she found it impossible to compete with this strong local talent plus the flood of musical refugees arriving from Europe.

By now George was more worried than ever about their financial situation. In the 10 months since leaving Italy, he had spent about 3,000 dollars bringing them to North America and trying unsuccessfully to re-establish Norma's career. Although he had been willing to fund the extravagant months in New York on the assumption that Norma would inherit several thousand dollars to compensate, now that it was clear that this would not occur, he was loath to see more of his own limited resources drain away with no apparent gain in sight. He confessed to Harper Sibley, his old friend from Rochester and fellow rancher in the Highwood, that his stocks had "depreciated to a terrible extent" that left them with "a very, very small lee-way" unless Norma found something soon or they headed to"somewhere where we can live very cheaply, hoping that soon this terrible war . . . may end." Humbly, George petitioned his wealthy friend:

> There is no place I know and love as well as the foothills of Alberta, and the Highwood. Would you consider renting to me the Fedeli quarter and the use of the cabins, when you do not need them? My wife and I would keep everything in good order, and could look after you, whenever you came out there. I hope that you will see your way to do this. I would not have bothered you, were it not that we find ourselves suddenly in a really tight fix. Rents in the cities are far too expensive for us in our present conditions, there doesn't seem any possibility of a job for me here, and Norma will not hear of being separated. On the Highwood I know my way, and we'd live very cheaply there, until the storm will have passed.[51]

Some years earlier, Sibley had built a rustic holiday retreat known as Twin Falls Cabins on land right across the Highwood River from the Buffalo Head Ranch. Now he agreed by return post that the Pocaterras could rent one of three guest cabins on the property for 1 dollar a month. George gratefully replied, "It has taken off quite a weight and worry for our immediate future ... It is in times such as these, when one finds out one's true friends."[52] Apparently, Sibley never collected his rent.

Twin Falls (Sibley) Cabin on Highwood River, ca 1941. GA PD-184-8-54

After one more audition with the CBC in Montreal, where she was told the network would be happy to give her a radio spot but not for at least six months, Norma wrote a last, desperate round of letters seeking support from people whom she judged to have some influence with the CBC in Toronto. Mentioning old friendships with her father when she could, she wrote letters to Leonard Brockington, Hector Charlesworth, Gladstone Murray, Reginald Stewart and Sir Ernest MacMillan. Their responses promised nothing but were sympathetic, and most said they would be happy to hear her audition when next she came to Toronto. Brockington, who was now a wartime government adviser on Commonwealth affairs and living in England, told her he was no longer involved with the CBC but said she could use his name with the new general manager, Gladstone Murray, and with Toronto conductors Stewart and Sir Ernest. Charlesworth, still bitter about being ousted four years earlier from his position as chairman of the Canadian Radio Broadcasting Commission (CRBC), informed her that he no longer had influence with the broadcaster. However, he was sympathetic, writing, "It is tragic that you in company with other gifted Canadians should have had their careers frustrated by this deplorable war."[53]

The Pocaterras finally left Montreal by train on August 14, 1940. Their arrival in Calgary three days later was reported in the *Calgary Herald*, which noted that after a short stay at The Wigwam (the boarding house now managed by Mrs. Parnell), they would leave for a "holiday at Sibley's Cabins, up the Highwood."[54] During their short time in Calgary, they reconnected with old friends and acquired supplies for the rigorous months ahead at the cabin. A week later, Norma's former neighbours, the Campbells, drove them out to the Buffalo Head Ranch, the nearest access point to the old Fedeli quarter. After borrowing a democrat wagon and horses to ferry their possessions and supplies across the river, they settled down to pioneer life in their rustic home.

The next few months at Twin Falls Cabins were filled with hard work, but Norma thoroughly enjoyed the new experience and the respite from years of relentless career development. As she recalled years later, "Pioneering was not new to George but it was to me. So George made bread and snared fool hens [spruce grouse] and rabbits for our food and we went fishing." No matter how well George set her up, Norma never caught a fish, but George was a "wonderful fisherman" who always returned "loaded down" with his catch. After being cleaned and smoked on racks built by George, the fish were stored for use all winter. Kind neighbours supplemented the Pocaterras' meagre diet that winter with "sacks of potatoes and things of that sort."[55]

George and Norma spent many hours cleaning the cabins and chinking their main one with sphagnum moss from the "Fedeli swamp." Well aware that they had much work ahead to get ready for winter, George made a sleigh to haul logs and hay. Norma assisted in all these tasks, as well as making the old family recipe for San Giorgio wine and chokecherry jelly. When the weather grew colder, they hauled the old Buffalo Head stove in from Calgary, where it had been stored in the attic of Dr. Piper's garage, and George made a bed warmer for "the cozy big bed by the fireplace with the Madonna guarding" from the wall above.[56] Experienced with surviving foothills winters, George insulated the little cabin using natural materials at hand. He and Norma gathered 26 sacks of leaf mould to bank around the outside walls. While George dug out the cellar, Norma carried 80 pails of dirt outside and banked it over the leaf mould. They gathered sacks and sacks of cones to burn, and when George chopped wood, Norma piled it. By the end of November, George was finally satisfied that they were prepared to survive the winter.

After weeks of back-breaking work, Norma wrote in her diary, "Life here consists of fighting the elements, working to keep warm. No time for anything else."[57] However, that was not strictly true, and she enjoyed meeting and socializing with George's friends up and down the Highwood: the Joe Bews, the Verdun Hunts, the 7U Brown sisters, Jean and Sarah, and Marigold Patterson at the Buffalo Head (husband Raymond seems to have been away adventuring in British Columbia that fall and did not reconnect with his old friend until January 1941). The Guy Weadicks at the Stampede Ranch were especially welcoming and, in addition to frequent social calls, the Pocaterras used their place as a post office and stopping house on many occasions. Interested in Norma's career since George's visit in 1935, they encouraged her to use their piano for singing practice, as did the Bob Hunts of the Eden Valley Ranch. A promoter after George's own heart, Guy Weadick suggested they pitch a concert tour for Norma to the Canadian Pacific Railway for its nationwide chain of grand hotels.

George was happy to report to Dr. Morlan: "All the Indians were extremely pleased to see me back." Paul Amos made many visits to Twin Falls Cabins to see his pal and blood brother. Norma liked him at once, recording in her diary after his first visit in early September, "My! but he is

Top: Norma on Grey Cloud, Highwood River valley, ca 1940. GA PD-184-8-48

Bottom: George cutting wood at Twin Falls Cabin, Highwood, ca 1941. GA PD-184-8-55

a nice chap."[58] She confirmed her friendship later that fall by knitting him a pair of mittens for Christmas. The Pocaterras' Calgary friends, the Browers, Campbells Underwoods and Carlyles, all made regular visits, taking turns travelling out to the Highwood to bring them into Calgary for errands or appointments. Lachie Campbell drove them up to the Ghost River one day in October so that George could show the property to Norma, who reported, "Good prospects. Beautiful spot."[59]

As soon as they arrived in the Highwood George retrieved the six horses remaining from his Buffalo Head days, which had been boarded at the Runciman ranch for several years. His own favourite was Darkie. He gave Grey Cloud to Norma to ride. Although she had ridden years before when Dr. Piper kept a horse at their home in Scarboro, on farm visits around Alberta and more recently during their holiday in Sardinia, Norma was a petite woman and it took her some weeks to ride Grey Cloud confidently. With her first encounter, she noted, "Very tall horse. Had difficulty getting on him." But five weeks later she was able to say, "I got on my horse 7 times alone—Hurrah! Giorgio will be proud of me."[60]

During the fall of 1940 Norma's singing career was on hold, though she managed a few local singing engagements with the help of friends. Soon after moving to the Highwood, she received an invitation from Canon Samuel H. Middleton (whom she had met at a dinner at the Verdun Hunts) to sing at St. Paul's Indian Residential School in Cardston, Alberta. Canon Middleton, who was principal, invited her to sing at the school's diamond jubilee celebrations in mid-October, and she enjoyed the chance for a public performance, even in such a small setting.

Concert at St. Paul's Indian Residential School, Cardston, Alberta, October 1940. Canon Samuel H. Middleton is to the left of Norma. GA PA-2393-8-1

More important for Norma's career was an opportunity that came her way later that fall. Anxious to help her reconnect with the local musical community, Mrs. T. M. (Stella) Carlyle had ensured that Norma's name was included in a program organized by Mrs. Ernest (Dorothy) Mather to entertain the airmen training at the No. 2 Wireless School at the Provincial Technical College (today the Southern Alberta Institute of Technology). In the usual circuitous manner of rural postal delivery, Norma received Mrs. Mather's invitation via the Pattersons' governess, Cecily Baldwin, who rode over from the Buffalo Head Ranch one evening in mid-September to deliver the letter and await its reply. Norma was delighted to sing again in Calgary but told Mrs. Mather that she could do so only if "it didn't cost any money, because we had none." Mrs. Mather's reply assured her it was "all arranged. Your accompanist will be Helen Boese, your hostess Mrs TM Carlyle, and I reserve the pleasure of coming to get you."[61]

To give additional exposure to her friend, Mrs. Carlyle invited many musical guests to sit in the balcony of the auditorium while Norma sang to the airmen. Luckily for Norma's later career, one of the listeners was her old friend Jascha Galperin, now director of the Conservatory of Music at Mount Royal College. Norma's return to the Calgary stage after a seven-year absence was a gratifying success. According to the *Calgary Herald*, her program "delighted" the airmen, "who applauded her songs strenuously and kept calling for more."[62] Eager to re-establish her name locally, her friends arranged for various follow-up engagements, and over the next few days Norma sang many times privately and for her old supporters at the Rotary, Kiwanis and Canadian clubs. She enjoyed reconnecting with various musical friends, including Helen Boese and Isabelle Logie, the latter returned from her adventures abroad. Most gratifying to Norma, Mrs. Sharples and other leaders of the Women's Musical Club decided to forget their old prejudices against Italian training and welcomed her back into the Calgary fold most cordially.

While Norma and George were in New York City they had arranged, with the help of Dr. Piper's friend Reverend R. J. Bowen, for Norma to sing for the Women's Musical Club of London, Ontario, the next winter. And so, at the end of January 1941, Norma left home to fulfill that engagement and to try to get her career going in "the east." In an incredibly busy two months away, she tried everything she could think of to generate interest in her career. As soon as she arrived in Toronto—she was staying with George's old etchings partner, Jack Fraser, and his wife, Elsie, in relatively nearby Oakville—she started making good use of personal contacts. First she visited Dick Claringbull of CBC Radio, who had worked with her in Vancouver and assured her gladly that he would give her a "couple of [radio] spots," no audition required.[63]

Next Norma contacted Hector Charlesworth, former chairman of the CRBC, who had been introduced to the Pipers by Leonard Brockington in Calgary in 1933. Charlesworth had heard and admired Norma's voice on that occasion and heard her Italian records during a subsequent visit to

Dr. Piper. For several decades he had been music critic of *Saturday Night* magazine and used his chatty weekly column several times over the years to include news of Norma's singing activities at home and abroad. Now, he and his wife invited Norma to tea, and Charlesworth said he would give her some publicity in his column, which he did. He also said she could use his name with Reginald Stewart of the Toronto Philharmonic Orchestra and with Sir Ernest MacMillan, principal of the Toronto Conservatory of Music and conductor of the Toronto Symphony Orchestra.

Finally, Norma contacted Bill Park's niece, Mrs. Guy (Irene) Hume, who had studied singing in Vienna and, according to her uncle, knew "everybody worth knowing in [Toronto] music circles."[64] Mrs. Hume took her to a Royal Conservatory alumni luncheon at the fashionable Granite Club, where the well-known violinist (and former Calgarian) Kathleen Parlow was guest speaker and where Norma was introduced to Sir Ernest. In an audition with the great man the next day, he was "perfectly charming," and when she asked if he thought she "had a chance," he replied, "I don't see why not." However, he was not able to commit himself for the 1941–42 season, so she had to be satisfied with begging him "not to forget me, to remember that I was a war refugee, a real Canadian, and also that I need the work."[65]

After a week in Toronto, Norma headed to London, Ontario, where her reception was most gratifying. She was guest of honour at a luncheon of the executive of the Women's Music Club, entertained at tea by her old Marian Keith Club friends and honoured by two big receptions hosted by the Pipers' old friends the Nelson Georges (with whom she was staying) and by Mr. and Mrs. George Copeland (she was president of the Music Club, he was president of the local Community Concert Series).

London Free Press article promoting Norma's London concert, London, Ontario, January 31, 1941. GA M6340-v1-p4

The big concert for the Women's Music Club was a major social event; as Norma informed George, "Everybody was thrilled. Lots told me that London had never had such a concert."[66] The *London Free Press* welcomed back its "distinguished graduate" and praised the "melodious tone" and "accustomed ease" with which she sang the major arias from *The Barber of Seville*, *The Magic Flute* and *La Traviata*.[67] It was at this first big concert since her return from Italy that Norma started the tradition of introducing each operatic selection with a brief synopsis of the opera's plot and an introduction to the scene about to be sung. Her London audience appreciated this novel approach, as did all her audiences in years to come.

In an otherwise positive review, the music critic took exception to Norma's "over emphasized" expression in several numbers. This criticism annoyed Norma, who felt she had toned down her expression considerably on the advice of Mrs. Carlyle, who had overheard complaints in Calgary after the No. 2 Wireless School concert about her overdramatization of English songs. Noting to George the irony, since she had been criticized years before for *lack* of expression, Norma responded with characteristic fatalism: "I'll have to tone down still more . . . Oh! well! Guess that's what they like"[68] The next day she sang in a concert broadcast from her old high school, London Collegiate Institute, and thoroughly enjoyed touring the school with the principal and Reverend Bowen and signing autographs afterwards. Her cousin, Mary Belle Edmonds invited her to nearby St. Thomas, where she entertained the Business and Professional Women's Club with tales from her student days in Italy.

During her two weeks in London, Norma was entertained constantly by friends and family in the surrounding area. They were so pressing in their invitations that she found it a burden and complained to George: "I was run off my feet with teas and luncheons and entertainment in general where I was Exhibit A . . . till [I was] worn to a rag . . . I am so tired, so weary, and people have kept me so terribly on the move that I don't know where I am." Although she enjoyed talking to Mary Belle, the Georges and others who had travelled abroad, she confessed to George, "These dear country souls that are tremendously good hearted and love me to death, really bore me to tears. I have to do all the talking."[69]

As always when separated, Norma was lonely for George, and she became very nostalgic for the life they had left behind in Italy. At one point, she told him of "a perfectly dreadful longing for our dear home over there" and worried him by saying that she had experienced a "crisis" and that they "must, must, must return" to Milan.[70] Concerned and upset, he wrote back: "What in the world is the matter with my Darling? With all these crises, Sonny Boy will have to 'pank Mummy! Whatever has got into you, Norma? I don't like you having these lows."[71] Norma apologized and made light of her "crisis," saying it had been "just nostalgia for the city we love, dear, nothing else. I know we will see it again."[72] Away from him for so many weeks, she missed George's steadying influence and the calm, "sane" life in the "free spaces of Alberta."[73] Her letters were full of longing: "I want to get home and into your arms"; "My! darling, how homesick your letters make me. How I long for you and that gorgeous country life"; and "Oh! if only I too could gather pine cones and ride Grey Cloud."[74]

George's letters to Norma during her absence were full of love and reassurance and the small details of pioneering on the Highwood: cooking, coning, cutting firewood, melting snow for water and mending clothes. But he was often lonely, too, and wrote to her saying, "I am STARVING FOR YOU, Darling Norma Mine! You can't simply imagine how I have missed you all these long, long weeks,"[75] and "I can't for the life of me understand how I ever could last sane for so many years of lonely living as I have done in the past."[76] Part of the problem, as far as George was concerned, was that Norma was away from him during "the worst time of the year," when it was difficult for him to amuse himself in the mountains because trails were often icy or covered in deep snow, or too muddy and slippery for the horses to negotiate easily.[77] However, he was a sociable man and often relieved the boredom by visiting his neighbours.

Of particular importance to him during this period was a renewed cordiality with Raymond Patterson. With the onset of war, their correspondence had become somewhat strained, and in 1940 George had written to his old friend with concern: "[Your letters] show ... me, who know you so well in most of your changeful moods, that you are far from being a happy man ... pleasant memories rush to my mind, when I knew you as a very different man, gloriously happy in a very simple way during our mountain trips and first times together."[78] Perhaps George had antagonized his correspondent by expressing his pro-Italian sentiments too forcefully. When Patterson learned that the Pocaterras were planning a return to the Highwood, he had issued a warning:

> I found it hard to answer one of your earlier letters of this year as I didn't want to start a pointless controversy ... If it was some sort of propaganda I'm afraid I'm a bad subject ... I tried your stuff on various other local commentators, old friends of yours, and the reception was unfavourable. Of course, the disturbed political conditions in Europe today are apt to affect people's feelings even up the Highwood ... The outlook is not very encouraging. But if you come up here take my tip and lay right off all politics—by word or letter—with the Anglo Canadian community. It will help to avoid unpleasantness.[79]

Patterson's advice was apt; during the war years many Italian Canadians suffered from prejudice and discrimination, and those who had not become naturalized citizens prior to 1929 were declared enemy aliens.[80]

Patterson seems to have been away from the Buffalo Head when the Pocaterras arrived in the Highwood in late August 1940. Although it is possible that cool relations between the men had prompted this apparent neglect, in a letter to George dated a few months before their arrival, Patterson had offered to have a team ready to assist them across the river and had finished the note by saying, "I shall be glad to see you when you come."[81] In fact, Patterson was going through a difficult period personally (much to his disappointment, he had been turned down for active wartime service), so perhaps his extended trip to British Columbia in the fall of 1940 had more to do with working through these feelings of frustration than avoidance of George Pocaterra. In any case, their first meeting at Twin Falls Cabins in late January 1941 appears to have been very cordial.[82]

A few days later, George was Patterson's guest at the Buffalo Head Ranch. His last visit had been six years earlier during his 1935 etchings sales tour, and he noticed many changes that he reported to Norma.

> This morning after the usual things that have to be done, I caught Darkie again, and went over to Patterson arriving a little after 11 a.m. Patterson being the cook, pro tem, Janet [Patterson's daughter] and I went and made a round of all the new and old cabins. P. did make quite a few improvements, some of them I like, others not quite so much, but taken all in all he has done well by the place. Everything is kept up, outside of the kitchen linoleum, which is holy (not sacred!) in several places. The best thing he has done, is the arrangement of the water supply. They also have a practical shower-bath cabin, by itself, where also the hot and tired men, in the summer, can cool themselves off with a fresh shower. After a pleasant lunch, P. J. and I, we went for a ride all over the place. There are also some improvements, but not so many as I half expected. All though, are good ones. One can see that P. really loves country, as such, and hates to do anything which might spoil it. We finally rode part way up Bellavista and down Vallombrosa. There is now a much plainer trail down it, than when I left, and it looks lovely. One of the things I did not care for, was the living room, which has had all the walls and everything possible, stained dark, sort of dark oak stain, and it makes the room, which was once too bright and cheerful, rather gloomy. It is positively extraordinary, how English people always go for dark coloring, and love their places of abode sad and gloomy. It's the same in their country, overseas. I saw one of my easy chairs. Before leaving I told P. and asked also for the saddles. He was quite decent about it, and hope he won't change his mind. Altogether we had a really pleasant time together, and naturally talked mostly about the mountains.[83]

In spite of her longing to be home again with George, Norma was well aware that their financial future required her best effort, and she told him, "I want to succeed for your sake" and "I've got to earn money if I can. *I've got to.*"[84] At George's urging, she had taken a suitcase full of etchings with her from Oakville to London, but she was unable (perhaps unwilling) to make any sales among her family and friends. Searching for a way to make money that would not entail long separations from each other, she suggested that Harper Sibley might hire them to manage his property as a guest ranch. Admitting that she knew nothing of the business, nevertheless she was enthusiastic:

"It would be nice to run a tourist ranch in the summer together, and then go singing in the winter *together*." A little dismayed when he learned that Norma had written to Sibley herself, George told her, "I am NOT angry at your having tried. And one NEVER knows! Here's hoping!" But he cautioned that her figures were overly optimistic and said, "I believe that if we can get that Ghost place started we can make more easily all the living expenses there, with ponies."[85]

In fact, the more George thought about the old Patterson place on the Ghost, the more he became convinced of its prime location and potential for commercial development. After nearly a month camping in the old log cabin on the property, he wrote enthusiastically to a friend and outlined his plans for the property he had acquired as part of the sale price of the Buffalo Head.

> It is a jewel! Almost two miles of river front, very beautiful; only a few hundred yards from the head of a lake, the Ghost arm ... which is most attractive[,] and almost greatest advantage of all, on the best hard surfaced auto road in Alberta ... We are going to build quite near the river, on a nice grass flat, surrounded by groves of poplars, spruce, firs, and black birches, with high banks near, and magnificent spruce woods opposite. On the top benches there is good grass, and some hay; all we will need for our horses ... About half way to Banff, on good swimming, sailing, motor boating water, in winter ice-yachting, marvellous riding country, with a back-ground of mountains, even more rugged and varied than on the Highwood[;] near the Rocky Mountain Park, and lots of game around, there is some quite eager interest on the part of Calgary residents to buy lots for purchase [for] building summer cottages on them. There are quite a number of such country places built already on the banks of the Ghost river, but much further up, on worse roads, and most of the banks near the auto road are very high cutbanks, ours being almost the only really suitable and available site. There are two level flats near the river. One, we are going to keep to ourselves, the other, about three quarters of a mile long, I am thinking of surveying into building lots, and selling some now and then to willing purchasers. This should provide some of the necessary sinews of finance.[86]

Meanwhile, back in Toronto after her busy London schedule, Norma boarded for several weeks with Jo Tearney and her husband on Balmoral Avenue (having declined this time the Frasers' offer of accommodation, as she had found the long commute from Oakville both time-consuming and expensive). To her delight, Norma discovered that Mrs. Tearney, who was the sister of her Calgary friends the Thomas Underwoods, had gone to Dr. Piper for dentistry while living in London and knew "everyone" Norma knew from that part of Ontario. In Toronto, Norma took advantage of her more relaxed schedule to connect with her cousin, dentist Ross Thomas, whom she asked to repair a tooth with a broken crown. She was relieved when he accepted only a token fee, "in memory of Father."

With socializing at a minimum, Norma resumed her habit of daily walking and enjoyed exploring the surrounding area. One day, she visited St. Paul's Anglican Church on nearby Bloor Street East, and when she discovered a copy of Donatello's statue of Saint George at the back of the church, on a whim she signed the guest book "Norma St George—Milan, Italy."[87] When relatives of the Tearneys arrived at the beginning of March, Norma moved to a house on Avenue Road, next door to the Brown School, and rented a "nice front room" for one dollar a night. Her hostess, Mrs. Tilley, had known Dr. Piper when she lived in Calgary 40 years before and still had a sister living there (Mrs. Alex Hornibrook). Norma ran into several other people in Toronto who had known Dr. Piper either in London or Calgary, and finally she said to George "Can you beat that! I run into friends wherever I go."[88]

While in London, George Copeland had introduced her to Ward French, head of Community Concerts Incorporated, which was a branch of NewYork–based Columbia Concerts Corporation. French admired Norma's voice but told her quite frankly that Columbia would consider her only if she had good New York notices. These were obtainable only if she could get some publicity by appearing in an important music festival, by paying approximately 800 dollars for a town hall recital or by singing with an important orchestra such as the Toronto Symphony. This was discouraging news, but French suggested that she get an agent who could help her to investigate other, cheaper publicity options as well as working with the rival Celebrity Concert Series, which toured in western Canada.

Norma in Toronto, 1941. Studio portrait by D'Angelo, Toronto, 1941. GA PA-2393-12-1

Accordingly, when Norma returned to Toronto in mid-February she contacted George H. K. Mitford, who had been recommended both by Ward French and Hector Charlesworth and ran a musical management company in Toronto under his own name; he was also director of the Canadian Concert Association, which promoted the Celebrity Concert Series in Canada. Norma was pleased to learn that he "used to live in Lethbridge, loves a ranch, and wants to help Canadians." He seemed impressed with her talent, and she told George, "[He] fell for me like a pound of bricks and I believe feels he can make something out of me."[89]

Mitford confessed to Norma that it was very difficult "selling Canadian artists to Canada," but he said her European training might make her more saleable.[90] They discussed town hall recitals, and when he understood that she could not afford to pay anything to promote herself, he encouraged her to pursue Claringbull's offer of a spot on CBC Radio, saying that although the recital fee was only 25 dollars the publicity value was very great. He also arranged an audition with his friend William Hearst, of NBC radio, who verified Ward French's advice: before any big company would hire her, it was essential that she have a "name" and New York notices. When he suggested that singing with the Toronto Philharmonic Orchestra might attract sufficient notice, Norma contacted its conductor, Reginald Stewart, and arranged for an immediate audition. Stewart, who was also director of the Promenade Symphony Concerts (a summer series in Toronto) and therefore doubly powerful, was uncharacteristically charming and complimentary to Norma. But although he told her, "That was really splendid. You certainly *should* be singing," he would not commit to using her as a soloist in either of his next musical seasons.[91]

Norma's 15-minute spot on CBY (CBC) radio finally occurred on the evening of February 22, 1941, and was broadcast in southern Ontario, much to the satisfaction of various family and friends. She had been disappointed to learn that because of the war "they don't want much Italian on the air," which meant some of her most impressive selections could not be sung.[92] She refused a 15-minute spot offered by the Montreal office of the CBC, as the time and cost involved in getting there did not seem worthwhile, but did inquire about additional airtime in Toronto. Disappointingly, she was informed that there were many more singers available than time slots to accommodate them. This time constraint may have resulted from a deliberate wartime policy by the broadcast networks to restrict serious musical and dramatic programs in favour of "light" entertainment.[93] Possibly, local managers at CBC Toronto also considered that they had more than honoured Claringbull's promise to the unknown singer.

Mitford, who loved Norma's voice on the air, was agog with plans for a tour the next winter of small towns in southwestern Ontario. He proposed a set fee of 100 to 200 dollars for smaller places and a 50-50 split for the bigger towns. With the prospect before her of 600 dollars in earnings, Norma's spirits lifted and she told George, "I feel fine and optimistic."[94] With all her expenses, she had made no money on this trip, but the future looked bright, especially when George told her that if they developed the Ghost River property as a guest ranch, "the singing would be mostly velvet."[95]

Another piece of luck came her way when Dr. Piper's old friend Reverend Dr. Andrew J. Vining suggested to his son, who had worked at the *Toronto Daily Star*, that Norma would be a good addition to the newspaper's upcoming charity concert. Vining put her in touch with the *Star's* music critic and concert organizer, Augustus Bridle, who told her, "We pay nothing but do give excellent publicity."[96] Contrary to his earlier advice to "never, never sing for nothing," Mitford was enthusiastic because of the publicity potential and the fact that this concert might lead to a bigger concert at the Eaton Auditorium the next year, or at least give Norma more leverage with the Promenade Concerts committee. However, he still advised her against singing at a luncheon meeting of the Hamilton Rotary Club, saying, "I've never known anybody who sang for service clubs, to ever get an engagement out of it. Never."[97]

Charlesworth's was the lone voice discouraging the plan to sing at the *Star* concert, but Mitford counselled her to ignore his advice, saying Charlesworth was getting old and out of touch and was possibly biased, since he worked occasionally for a rival newspaper (the *Globe*). Heeding everyone else's good advice about the *Daily Star* concert, Norma decided to stay on in Toronto for another few weeks, although she was desperately lonely for George's support and companionship. "Sweetheart, if you only knew how I want to come home! I'm sick and tired of this striving to put myself over," she told him. "I don't ever want to go away again alone. There is no real pleasure if I can't have my Sonny Boy in my arms to talk things over with."[98]

She filled the time waiting for the concert date with more visits to relatives but found the days long and tedious: "Life is such a bore away from you . . . I am just living for the time when we will be together again."[99] At last, the *Toronto Daily Star's* Free Concert "Melodies Past and Present" occurred on March 17 at Parkdale United Church, and Norma was received very warmly. Brandli de Bevec wrote a complimentary letter, saying "an accomplished artist of your calibre should be out on the battlefields" and that he was glad to be hearing "something more . . . tangible, after so long a time."[100] Naturally, Bridle wrote the *Star's* review, and he raved about the "coloratura skylark from Alberta, Vancouver, London, Ont. and Milan" who had sung "with such piquant dramatic realism and sheer vocal beauty."[101] With this most satisfying review to add to her promotional material, Norma finally returned to her "cozy Western Home" on the Highwood.

Pioneering again with George in the grand open space of the foothills seemed like heaven after months of city confinement. Always game, and determined to join George in everything their new life had to offer, during the summer of 1941 Norma accompanied him on several pack trips into the mountains. Sharing his old haunts in the Kananaskis with her had long been George's dream. In 1937 he had written to Raymond Patterson, "Oh, I am longing for some of my old camping places, and to show Norma that kind of a life too. Curious isn't it, that I, an Italian born, should be wanting to show Norma, a Canadian, a feature of purely Canadian life!"[102]

Their first trip was a practice run for several that George had been hired to guide for Harper Sibley's son and his young friends and for a wealthy young American couple of Sibley's acquaintance, the Edmund H. Kelloggs of New York City. Outlining his plans to Mr. Kellogg, George had said, "I'll take an Indian helper, who has worked for me in the mountains for over twenty-five years [King Bearspaw], and my wife, who will superintend the cooking."[103] Norma reported on their practice trip to her brother Dick: "George wanted to try me out and see if I could stand the long hard rides and living in the ways of the wilderness. I loved it. We had all kinds of weather, from bright sunny days to rain and even two snow storms and a terrible blizzard while negotiating some of the high passes."[104] Years later, her strongest memory of the Highwood days was "the lovely rides over the beautiful country side," and she enthused, "To me it was all such a new experience . . . I loved it."[105]

George and Norma in the Highwood, ca 1941.
GA PA-2393-18-1-1

When Norma had left for the East, it was with the confident expectation that her friends and admirers in Calgary would organize a concert upon her return. However, she was disappointed to learn while still in London that Calgary Women's Musical Club president Madge Anderson had had no success in creating a "citizen's committee" to organize a concert. Apparently all likely candidates, including the various service clubs, claimed to be far too busy with war work to take on another project. This poor showing by her adopted "cowpatch of a town" so upset Dorothy Mather that she wrote to George, "I wish I had let no one but the Press and the airmen hear her."[106] After her warm welcome in Calgary the preceding December, this apparent snub threw Norma "in the depths."[107] Anxious to do something for Norma, her friends had suggested to the Women's Musical Club that it sponsor her in one of its monthly programs, but they were distressed when the club said it could afford to give her only a token fee. George was irate; writing wrathfully of their "effrontery," he said to Norma, "To me it seems that those W M Clubs are the essence of selfishness," and "you know what kind of pikers that W M Club bunch is."[108] Hurt and disappointed, Norma decided that any offers from the Women's Music Club would be met with a "sweet refusal" and that she would never sing in Calgary again, except privately for good friends like the Browers and Carlyles.[109]

However, once she was back in the West, Norma realized that she and George needed whatever income she could generate if they were to realize their dream of building a home on the Ghost River property, and so she swallowed her pride and offered her services at a reduced rate to various Women's Musical Clubs for the 1941–42 season. The Edmonton club turned her down, saying it still could not afford her fee, but the Vancouver club offered her an engagement for October 22, 1941, and the Calgary club offered her January 14, 1942; both offered an agreed fee of 100 dollars. These were important engagements, because the Women's Musical Club recitals always attracted large audiences of music lovers (sometimes up to 500 in Calgary for performances at the Palliser Hotel.[110]) The credit for both engagements was due to her longtime accompanist, Helen Boese, who was an active member and past president of the Calgary Women's Musical Club and had "pulled hard" for Norma because "of the happy time we would have working

212

together."[111] She had also sent a recommendation on Norma's behalf to the Vancouver Club, mentioning both the artistry and charm of her old friend. Another booster in Vancouver was Mrs. Gammie, who joined the music club when she moved there from Calgary and also had attended and enjoyed Norma's No. 2 Wireless School performance the previous year.

Another of Norma's staunch supporters was Vancouver friend and her CBC Vancouver accompanist Magdalene Moore, a talented pianist who had studied at the Chicago Musical College. She told Norma she was "thrilled over [the] prospect of seeing and hearing you soon"[112] and suggested other potential singing venues to extend Norma's earnings while in Vancouver. In a series of enthusiastic follow-up letters, Mag Moore proposed "another of my bright (maybe) ideas": a joint tour of western Canadian cities, sponsored by service or music clubs, over the winter and spring of 1941–1942.[113] This plan never materialized, likely because Norma was loath to be away from George for another extended period—her plans with Mitford for a tour of southern Ontario cities had included much higher fees and presupposed George's accompaniment. Also, by the time Mag Moore's plans started to really evolve, Norma was considering another attractive option closer to home.

After a summer of pioneering, Norma realized in early October that she needed a few days of intensive musical preparation for her upcoming engagement with the Vancouver Women's Musical Club. She was staying in Calgary with the Browers, who did not have a piano, so she contacted Jascha Galperin at Mount Royal College to inquire about using a piano at the conservatory for a few days prior to leaving for the coast. Much to her surprise, Galperin claimed that he had been searching for her ever since the No. 2 Wireless School concert because he wanted to offer her a job teaching singing at the college, to start January 2, 1942. Although this offer might have originated from simple friendship, Galperin may also have calculated that with her European singing background, Norma would be a significant draw for students. In addition, he may have been prompted by one of his staff members; one of Norma's former accompanists, Phyllis Chapman Clarke, was head of Theoretical Work at the college at the time and could very well have encouraged Galperin to offer her old friend a much-needed job.

George and Norma in the Highwood, ca 1940-41.
GA NA-4390-237

Galperin's offer was flattering but required careful thought. Norma's focus for a decade had been the stage, but in the two years since her return to North America this dream had faded, and she was more open to a different career path by the fall of 1941. A radio announcer in Toronto had told her that Canadian musicians could never make a decent living without supplementing their income by teaching,[114] and she had often felt that she would have been a good teacher if she had followed Aunt Susie's advice of long ago. In fact, she had already arranged to earn a small fee by helping the daughter of a Calgary friend to prepare for the Alberta Musical Festival in the spring of 1942. Although she and George still assumed that the war years spent in Alberta were simply a hiatus in developing her European opera career, they could see the benefit of a regular income during this period of enforced inaction. Teaching in Calgary instead of touring across Canada would allow her to stay settled with George while they waited out the war. At the same time, she could solidify her local reputation and earn a small but steady income, which would enable them to develop the Ghost River property. Norma went off to Vancouver by bus in mid-October with much to think over.

She enjoyed her two weeks in Vancouver as the centre of attention for her many friends in the city. Calling herself Norma St. George, her recital for the Women's Musical Club was successful, and one member of the club told Mrs. Middlemass that the applause was "wonderful [for Vancouver]."[115] The event was attended by visiting Calgarians, including Odette de Foras, Eleanor Carlyle and the Mathers' daughter, Alice, who said, "Oh! Darling! It was marvellous! I'd forgotten just how marvellous you would be."[116] Norma was less enthusiastic about her own performance, but to her relief, "RJ" of the *Daily Province* was impressed with her improvement and gave her a very nice review. She was pleased, and wrote to George "wonder of wonders, I have succeeded in making him like me." In marked contrast to his criticisms of 1933, "RJ" now praised her "dramatic intensity" and noted her "genuine skill in the art of fioriture and her ability to invest her music with penetrating emotional warmth and clarity of diction."[117]

Norma was touched to see Brandli, who had aged greatly due to illness during her absence. His occasional letters had informed her that Mrs. Brandli now lived in an institution, though she was "quite rational" much of the time,[118] and that he himself had been hospitalized several times with heart problems. A student who had scribed a letter for him during one of his periods of illness had told her that Brandli was "so very easily upset by things and his business has not been going so well the last year," but that he continued to teach and hold studios when he could.[119] After Norma saw him in Vancouver, she told George "he looks pretty sick, poor man" (in fact, he died the next year at age 60). However, Brandli was energized by Norma's visit, brought his students to her performance and was so thrilled that he "let out a few 'Bravos'" while Norma was singing.[120] She gratified him further and impressed his students by singing for them privately at their Studio Club.

In addition to the many social events in her honour and a visit to Aileen Nilsson about the etchings still in her care, Norma fulfilled the other purpose of her visit, to investigate the career potential of Vancouver. She had meetings with influential people in the Vancouver music world including "RJ"; the manager of the Capitol Theatre, Maynard Joiner; local music agent and composer Arthur Benjamin; and the managers of several radio stations, including her old employer, the CBC affiliate CBR. All were impressed with her voice but quite frank about the difficulties of career building in Vancouver. Because of wartime policies, local radio stations had very few time slots available; "practically all programs originate[d] in the East." Ernest Morgan of the CBR was particularly discouraging; as manager of a government station, he was required to transmit "a great deal of overseas broadcasting" that cut into local program time, and he told Norma, "As long as the war is on there is no chance here." Mr. Benjamin was equally gloomy: "No concert artist . . . could hope to make a living out of his profession here, that is, by performing." According to him, the only musicians doing well were very versatile and could conduct, teach or lecture as well as perform. This echoed the advice given to Norma in Toronto that "no-one could make money in Canada with music alone." She concluded, "I might do fairly well as a teacher here, but then, as Mr Joiner . . . said, 'if you are going to teach it would be much better to do so in Calgary where everyone knows you. You might not make quite as much but your expenses would be less'."[121]

Norma also realized that she no longer wanted to live in Vancouver. "I'm getting to hate this dullness . . . I'd rather have brown Alberta, but with sunshine, to all this gloom even though the grass is green."[122] The decision to accept Mount Royal College's offer now seemed obvious, and she wrote to George, "As we figured, we'd be much better off developing the Ghost and teaching in Calgary . . . I'll be happy to get into the Music World of Calgary . . . as we had already planned before, work always on the voice, ready for the great day in which we will be able to return to that other glorious life, and build up the Ghost so that we get the where-withal to return . . . that is to be our program for the future."[123]

Chapter 8

Norma & George: Valnorma
1941–1955

Now that the decision was made, George was anxious to move to the Ghost River property before winter set in. Even though they could not start building until spring, he had been planning the house for nearly a year and wanted to move to the site to start preparations. He also wanted to be closer to Calgary for when Norma started teaching in January, and he felt they could be quite snug over the winter in the old Patterson cabin. "Quite sufficient for our present needs," he wrote to a friend, "only about 45 minutes from Calgary."[1]

Kind friends took many of their bulkier possessions into Calgary for temporary storage, but George and Norma still had to move six horses and their immediately needed belongings the 50 miles cross-country from the Highwood. With George mounted on Darkie, Norma on Grey Cloud and leading four pack horses, they started out for their new home on a beautiful day in early November 1941. Getting to the Ghost River was quite an experience, which Norma described in great detail in her unpublished 1972 biography of George, entitled "Son of the Mountains":

> Our first overnight stop was to be at the Basilici place on the north fork of Sheep Creek ... We had a lovely trip but the old original trail had been crossed by fences in many places and George had to leave me frequently with the horses and go seeking a gate through which we could pass ...
>
> We spent our second night out at the Muncaster ranch on Fish Creek ... During the night the wind started to blow ... [and] in the morning ... the ground was covered by two feet of snow.
>
> That day was a nightmare. The snow was very wet and the horses found the going heavy.
>
> We ploughed through the snow until we crossed "The Jumping Pound Creek" about three o'clock in the afternoon and got into the Valley of Bow River. Here there was no snow but we had to ride into a strong wind. Far to the west of us we saw the Copithorne Ranch house and we headed for it. By the time we got there, the early fall twilight

was not far away, and we wanted to get over the Ghost Lake Dam before darkness set in. We got instructions from the Copithornes how to reach the dam, and fortified by a warm cup of tea, we set out.

When we reached the dam we found to our horror, that the strong wind of the night before had whipped the water from the lake up over the dam where it had frozen, and the whole dam was a solid sheet of ice. George got off Darkie and tried out the footing. He told me to dismount, then he said, "We'll have to walk across, and lead our horses and go very carefully. Our horses are not shod, and they could quite easily slip and fall and perhaps slide under the railing. I'll go first with Darkie, and then we'll put in two of the pack horses, then you come with Grey Cloud and the other two pack horses will follow. If they see that we are not afraid, it will give them courage."

And so we did it. George and I were wearing rubber soled overshoes that gripped the ice, and though the horses skidded around a bit, still they each had four feet, and we finally all got safely across. By this time it was nearly dark and we still had four miles to go to reach our cabin on the Ghost River.

The horses were dead tired . . . About a mile above the dam we saw the lights of Miss Agnes [sic] Hammond's ranch. This gave the horses new energy. Those lights to them meant a warm barn, and a good feed of hay, and relief from their burden.

But when we came close to the ranch buildings, we kept on going up over the hill for another three miles. It was hard work to keep urging them on. Finally we came to our gate, opened it and entered into our own property. We were high up above the river and we had to zig-zag down a narrow grassy coulee to reach the river flats and the tiny cabin. It was by now pitch dark.

George unlocked the door, and lit the coal-oil lamp, and by its feeble rays we unpacked the horses and piled all their loads in the middle of the floor . . .

On a previous trip . . . we had brought out a roll of blankets, and a couple of pillows. These had been hung from the ceiling. George now got them down. We took off our shoes and our buck skin coats and keeping on the rest of our clothes, we lay down on the plank bed with our heads gratefully resting on the pillows and covered with the Hudson Bay blankets. We were so dead tired that in a few minutes we were sound asleep.[2]

After Norma had returned from Vancouver, her friends Lachie Campbell and T. M. Carlyle had helped her raise money on the strength of her Royalite shares to fund building the house on the Ghost.[3] However, in spite of George's optimistic description to friends, the Ghost River property was an awkward one—in Norma's words, "like a piece of pie." It consisted of a narrow strip of flat land in a bend of the river, "a natural meadow that was fringed along the water's edge with spruce and poplar. The site was in a deep glen that was flanked by steep bunch-grass slopes to the north-east, and by cliffs and thickly wooded slopes on the south-west."[4] The property included pasture located across the river, above the cliff. The house was to be built down near the river but on a slight rise a short distance back from the old cabin, which was right at the water edge and vulnerable to flooding. Adding to the challenge of reaching their home, there was no track to river level until George carved a steep zigzag pathway down the northeast hillside.

Not surprisingly, George was unable to locate a builder for the money he had available and ended up building most of the house himself, with Norma's help. While this was accomplished, they continued to live in the primitive, 15-square-foot Patterson cabin with only the bare minimum of furnishings and comforts. But they made a few improvements. The plank bed in the cabin proved so uncomfortable their first night that one of George's jobs the next morning was to make a mattress out of green spruce boughs. He also

cut a trap door in the floor and dug out a root cellar for food storage. The cabin was heated by an old tin stove, but they patched the gaps in the log walls with gunny sacks full of moss to make it warmer for the coming winter.

The Pocaterras ended up pioneering in this cabin for two years. George started digging out the foundation for their new home in the summer of 1942 but did not start building the actual house until April 10, 1943. He had contracted Paul Amos and other Stoney friends to cut logs for the walls during the

The old Patterson cabin on the Ghost River, ca 1942.
GA PD-184-8-62

winters of 1941 and 1942, and the logs were floated down the river or dragged to the top of the cliff and pushed over, as were many of the other building supplies. Other items of immediate use were dragged down the steep path on a "stone boat," a low sled with wooden runners.

George had built many houses, barns and other buildings during his Buffalo Head days, but never before had he planned and executed with "so much care and thought."[5] Norma was extremely impressed with his handyman skills and worked hard assisting wherever she could. Rocks were removed from the zigzag pathway to be used for the foundation, and at the same time the soil removed from the new cellar was hauled to the top of the path, where it was dumped and smoothed by Norma. In this way, they were able to fashion "quite a respectable road" down the hillside by the time the cellar was excavated.

The next spring George prepared the 120 logs needed to build the cabin, removing the bark and notching the ends ready for construction. It took him many weeks to build up the exterior and interior walls 12 logs high, and Norma was an appreciative audience, writing later, "It was fascinating to watch that house go up."[6] After the fact, she described her main job in house building as keeping George supplied with cement while he built the foundation and cellar, but she also helped him to trim the ends of the logs, and once the walls were up she helped to cut the eight windows and five doors (three external and two internal) with a two-handled crosscut saw. She also assisted with roofing and flooring and with all finishing details. The house was finally furnished and ready for occupation on November 3, 1943, almost two years to the day after their big trek from the Highwood to the Ghost.

The house, which George christened Valnorma (Norma's Valley), was much larger than originally intended because friends had convinced them that if their ultimate intention was to develop the property as a resort area, they should make their own house an attractive example of what was possible in a summer cottage.[7] When finished, the house was a 1,600-square-foot bungalow with a spacious living area, small kitchen and bedroom, a fireplace and lots of windows. Since Norma had admired the steep roofline and front veranda of the Sibley cabin, George incorporated these features into the design. He was proud that the sharply peaked roofline over the living area allowed for good acoustics when Norma practised, though guests later remembered finding her voice too powerful for comfort in the enclosed space.[8]

Soon after the house was completed, Norma's furniture, the bulk of George's old ranch possessions—in storage at Dr. Piper's since 1935—and other items temporarily stored with friends were transported to Valnorma by a friend who owned a small moving company. George had built an extra-strong, extra-wide sleigh to move everything down the steep hill to the house. Items were cushioned with hay, and the sleigh was pulled by one of the horses while George held on to ropes at the back to provide a brake. Down at the house, heavier items were rolled up a ramp to the front door. Over the course of several weeks, George and Norma used this method to move everything into the house, including Norma's old family piano and the cast iron cookstove from the Buffalo Head Ranch, which they had been using at the Sibley cabin and apparently weighed 600 pounds.[9]

Although the house was isolated and had no running water or electricity, the Pocaterras considered Valnorma "heaven on earth," and it remained their main residence for the next 13 years. They were fortunate to have nearby a few good neighbours who helped them out on many occasions and provided opportunities for socializing: the Roland Gissings, the Hamish Beggs, the John Motherwells and Jean and Laurie Johnson. As their nearest neighbour, Agness Hammond had to be particularly kind and forbearing because the only way for the Pocaterras and their visitors to reach Valnorma was to cross a corner of her property, the Ghost River Ranch. Since she did not get along very well with George, this caused a certain amount of friction at first, but that was resolved when he hinted at legal action to enforce right of access along the old wagon trail.[10]

Top: George building Valnorma, 1943.
GA PD-184-8-93

Bottom: Valnorma under construction, 1943. Note the steep
access road. GA PD-184-8-167

Living in the country provided many opportunities for neighbours to provide assistance to each other. They collaborated during haying time, moving mowers and rakes from ranch to ranch to help each other out. Since George did not have machinery to contribute, he usually got his hay cut on shares by Laurie Johnson. In March 1942 the Pocaterras spotted a grass fire when they were out riding. It was at the head of the lake near the Motherwells' cabin and seemed to be moving quickly. George was concerned for a lovely stand of spruce trees in nearby Gun Sight Coulee. They rushed home to get gunny sacks to soak in the river, and then, while George started back-firing to protect the trees, Norma raced to Agness Hammond's place to warn her that her hayfields were in danger. In the dry, windy conditions the fire spread quickly, but it was finally extinguished with the help of firefighters from Cochrane.[11] Later that spring, Norma stayed overnight with the Gissings when George feared that she might miss her appearance on a radio program in Calgary the next day because the old Patterson cabin was in danger of being flooded by the rising Ghost River. However, in spite of these friendly interactions, Norma's teaching career soon dictated that the Pocaterras spend more time in Calgary than in the country, with the result that they never fully integrated into the local community as they might have done as permanent residents.

Miss Hammond was not alone in her dislike of George. Although he and Norma patronized shops in Cochrane and occasionally hired local men and boys to help with building or clearing projects, many local people found George's foreign manner argumentative and overbearing, and they whispered among themselves about the rude and impatient way in which he sometimes treated his wife.[12] On the other hand, near neighbours such as the Johnsons became friendly with the couple and even enjoyed socializing with the irascible George over Italian meals, which were considered rather exotic in rural Alberta. One guest remembered George's pride in the spaghetti dinners served with plain salad (he insisted on no dressing) and "very strong coffee in little demitasse cups with six spoons of sugar and cream."[13] For a while, in the early 1940s, the Johnsons sent their daughters every Saturday during the winter to Norma for piano lessons and to George for Spanish lessons. The girls rode their horses the 10 miles to Valnorma for the joint lessons, and while they enjoyed a snack afterwards, they heard stories of Norma's Italian career and sometimes heard her sing. In this way Donna Johnson grew to be very fond of Norma, and the women remained firm friends after Donna married local rancher Richard Butters. In 1953 the Pocaterras became godparents to the Butters' first son, Eric.

Once she started teaching at Mount Royal College, Norma received a warmer welcome into the local music scene. Traditionally, the Calgary musical community supported and showed its approved for successful artists who returned to give impetus to musical progress in their home city,[14] so Norma's engagement with the Women's Musical Club in January 1942 was a decided success. The *Calgary Herald* voiced its approval, saying,

"Those who heard Norma Piper before she went abroad report that her development from a shy, gifted but musically unformed young woman, to the poised, dramatic artist of today is outstanding." The reviewer, who was impressed with Norma's demonstration of "vocal gymnastics," noted "the higher the note the sweeter the tone in this singer's case." Saying that her delivery of Italian songs far outshone her English ones, the critic concluded, "Calgary is, however, fortunate to be able to keep Miss Piper here for the time being, and the announcement that she has been appointed to the staff of the Mount Royal College Conservatory should be welcome news to young operatic aspirants."[15]

Shortly after this success, the Canukeena Club sponsored a concert for her at the Grand Theatre, and in June she was invited to sing a solo at the Citizens' Complimentary Dinner at the Palliser Hotel honouring the retiring principal of Mount Royal College, Reverend George W. Kerby. The Calgary Women's Musical Club invited her back in October for a program arranged by Mrs. A. I. Schumiatcher, and in November Norma was the soloist at Scarboro United Church's anniversary services.

However, Norma's biggest coup in solidifying a local reputation was a grand concert organized for her at Central United Church in May 1943 by Calgary violinist and friend Olga Nickle. Advertising herself once more as Norma San Giorgio, she was accompanied by her old friends Helen Boese, pianist, and Phyllis Chapman Clarke, organist. When the Pocaterras had returned to Calgary in 1940, they left Norma's costumes stored in Montreal because at the time they assumed she would be resuming her career in the East, or even overseas, and they were reluctant to pay heavy shipping costs back and forth across the country. Now, Norma sent for her costumes and wore them to perform four of her big arias from *La Sonnambula*, *The Barber of Seville*, *La Traviata* and *Lucia di Lammermoor*. She thoroughly captivated her audience with her lively introductions to each piece and "her strong, splendid voice, her charming manner, her flawless acting, and her beautiful gowns and jewels." The Calgary *Albertan* reported her triumph: "Receiving an ovation from her audience, Miss San Giorgio further endeared herself to it by saying quite simply how happy she was to be back among her own people. 'Calgary is my home and my heart will always be here,' said Calgary's own Norma Piper . . . Miss Piper, her arms filled with flowers, then sang, 'Home Sweet Home,' after which she was called back time and again by her cheering audience."[16]

With this wonderful reception, Norma's acceptance into the local musical scene was complete. Along with violinist Olga Nickle and pianist Jean Farquharson, she toured armed forces bases in southern Alberta in the fall of 1943, helping to entertain the soldiers stationed there. She also performed at a concert for prisoners of war at Kananaskis-Seebe Camp 130 (now the Kananaskis Field Station operated by the University of Calgary).[17] Her friends Phyllis Chapman Clarke and Helen Boese included her whenever they could in programs they arranged for the Calgary Women's Musical

Club, and probably they were instrumental in drawing her into the Calgary branch of the Alberta Music Teachers Association, with which they and many of Norma's other musical friends were very involved.

It is a measure both of Norma's acceptance into the tightly knit musical community and her friends' powerful influence within it that she was even allowed to join this association, which became the Alberta Registered Music Teachers Association (ARMTA) after 1947. An advertisement for local music teachers placed in the *Calgary Herald* in 1942 by the Calgary Music Teacher's Federation informed the public that "the association is composed of teachers who have graduated from recognized colleges and universities and have had a minimum two years' teaching experience, assuring the best in musical education."[18] Although she had gained some prestige as one of Mount Royal's singing teachers, there is no evidence that Norma ever received a teaching certificate, and she certainly did not have any prior teaching experience when she joined the conservatory. In order to admit her to the association, her friends must have persuaded the executive to waive the usual requirements and to recognize instead her background, training and current teaching position in lieu of paper credentials.[19]

However it occurred, Norma appears to have joined the Calgary Music Teacher's Association soon after she started at Mount Royal College, and she was included in both organizations' annual advertising campaigns aimed at students in the fall of 1942. In October 1945 she was the featured entertainment at the association's Calgary branch general meeting. She spoke on her student days in Italy "in a very entertaining and humorous manner," and entertained afterwards with a "beautiful solo from 'La Sonnambula' [that] was greatly enjoyed."[20] She was unable to play a very active role in the group until later in the 1940s, when she and George spent a greater portion of each week living in their city apartment, but Norma appreciated the professional and social contact provided by ARMTA. By 1951 she had a seat on the local executive as "singing teachers' representative," and from then on she continued her active participation in the club for 30 years.

A very different venture in the mid-1940s helped to consolidate Norma's reputation in the musical community. In January 1945 she and George helped form a group called the Alberta Operetta Company, whose other founding members were Dr. and Mme de Molnar and Baron Endre Csavossy. It was formed with the express intention of producing the operetta *Countess Maritza*, with all proceeds going to the Kerby Memorial Building Fund of Mount Royal College. As general manager, George raised the necessary capital through an appeal to eight businessmen in the community, including the Pipers' old friend, T. M. Carlyle. Norma was singing director for the production, and several conservatory colleagues lent their support: Jascha Galperin was musical director and Cyril Mossop was choral director. Norma's students took part in the operetta, and one of her advanced students, Cleone Duncan, played the lead. Radio station CFAC gave free publicity to the production, which played for three nights to packed houses at the Western Canada High

School Auditorium. *Countess Maritza* was well received and earned a profit of 445 dollars, which was duly donated to the college for its building fund. However, in spite of its success and pressure from friends to mount another operetta the next year, the Alberta Operetta Company was not revived.[21]

When Norma first started teaching at Mount Royal College in January 1942, she had only a small number of students and so taught on only one day a week, Saturday. For many months the kind-hearted Mathers went out to Cochrane each Friday afternoon, picked up George and Norma (who had ridden their horses into town, or come by sleigh or snowshoe) and took them back into the city. After Norma finished teaching, the couple often stayed overnight with the Mathers or other friends, who returned them to Cochrane either Saturday evening or on Sunday. Eventually this complicated arrangement broke down, and in the fall of 1942 the Pocaterras bought a car of their own. It was a "beautiful big grey Graham Paige for the princely sum of $375," which George whimsically named "Pegasine" after the mythical winged horse Pegasus.[22]

Even with a car, it was not always easy for Norma to get to Calgary for lessons with her students or for her own occasional recitals and radio programs. George built a garage at the top of the property to house Pegasine, but sometimes the car refused to start in cold weather, even though George conscientiously removed the battery after each excursion to store it in the warm house. When it would not start, a horse was hitched to the car and it was dragged down the hill until it did. If it still refused to start, the Pocaterras were forced to hike the four miles down the arm of the reservoir to the highway to flag down the bus to Calgary. This exercise was accomplished on snowshoes in wintertime, Norma later recalling that "very often it was so cold that our eyelashes froze almost shut."[23]

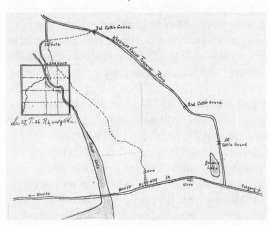

Handrawn map by George locating Ghost River properties, Valnorma and Chio-abba-tinda, ca 1960s.
GA M6340-189-2

Once, when Norma had to get to Calgary for an important concert and the buses were not running because of a heavy snowstorm, she called the superintendent of the Calgary division of the Canadian Pacific Railway, who was an old friend of her father's. He arranged for the six o'clock transcontinental train from Banff to make an unscheduled stop at the Ghost Lake flag station, two miles from the Hammond ranch. The passengers were amazed when the train stopped to pick up the nearly frozen couple patiently waiting in the snow. After they were helped onto the train and plied with hot coffee, the Pocaterras were amused to think of the speculation swirling about them: "Who were we anyway, who could get the Imperial Limited to stop in the middle of nowhere!"[24]

During the war George had been out of touch with his Italian friends and relatives. When communications resumed in late 1945, he was relieved to learn that all had survived the war and everyone was "okay" in spite of wartime privations. Proudly, he told North American friends about his family's wartime experiences. Unwilling to support the Germans, a number had gone underground with the "partisans," and one had even blown up his own metallurgy factory rather than see the Nazis make use of it.[25] Once he was back in touch, George maintained a steady correspondence with his sisters Emilia and Marta, nephews Franco and Sergio Pozza, and various Italian friends. He appreciated Marta's annual Christmas gift of panettone and also her many gifts of money over the years, whenever the Pocaterras expressed a need for financial assistance. She was very wealthy: when she visited the Pocaterras for several weeks in 1953, she bought four sable stoles at Holt Renfrew to take home as gifts. Her monetary gifts to George and Norma helped to heal a slight rift between the siblings; ever since their father's death, George had privately harboured a grudge against Marta, wondering if her close relationship and strong influence with their father had somehow caused him to inherit less than his rightful share of the estate.[26]

Between George's old furniture from the Buffalo Head and the pieces that Norma had inherited from her family home, Valnorma was fully furnished and very cozy, with lots of books and pictures, including the precious Italian Madonna that hung, as always, over their bed. The living room was very impressive with its high east wall featuring a big black bear skin between the windows, flanked by Native snowshoes, skis and beaded accessories. Other walls sported animal heads and antlers. As soon as communications with Italy reopened after the war, George began negotiations with his bank in Milan to recover the sterling silver cutlery, plate and tea service stored there since the Pocaterras fled Italy in 1939. Finally, in 1948, after "a fight that lasted over two years and cost … hundreds of dollars," all 97 pieces were delivered safely to the log cabin on the Ghost River.[27] As George wrote ironically to a friend, "You can imagine Norma's and my joy at having them again. They brought back the memories of another, and very much more gracious way of living."[28] However, in spite of the appearance of comfort, even luxury, George and Norma were very aware that at Valnorma they still were pioneering, "living in idyllic seclusion—and genteel poverty."[29]

With no amenities and such a long and often complicated journey to reach the city, it was not surprising that Norma's personal appearance sometimes suffered. One early student at the college was astonished to discover that the woman she took to be a "charlady," so slipshod was her manner of dressing and disordered her hair, was the well-known opera star and singing teacher![30] Another young student from the early days marvelled at the transformation of her teacher when she left the college to catch the bus back to Cochrane.

With no concern for her appearance, and anticipating the long journey at the other end on snowshoes, in winter Norma dressed in a pair of old "breeks" (breeches), high boots, a big old jacket and a fur helmet. Like George, she also carried a big backpack full of food supplies for the cabin.[31]

The situation soon improved. As Norma's teaching load increased year by year, the Pocaterras found they were visiting longer and longer with friends and feared they were imposing. But eventually they realized they could afford to rent accommodation of their own in the city. By 1945 they were renting an apartment at 815 13th Avenue, but they relocated the next year to be closer to the college, which was located downtown on 7th Avenue at 11th Street. They kept this second apartment, at 1106 14th Street, for nine years, and there they eventually spent most weekdays, returning to their beloved Valnorma only for weekends and in the summer. Both apartments were small and sparsely furnished, viewed simply as a convenience necessitated by Norma's increased teaching load. Interestingly, there are no entries in the city directories for those years under "Pocaterra," only for "Norma Piper, teacher, Mount Royal College." As Norma later explained, "We lived in the country and camped in the city."[32]

With no previous experience as a singing teacher, Norma was very lucky to have been offered the post at Mount Royal College and was grateful to Jascha Galperin and others for the friendship and kindness that had prompted the offer. On his side, Galperin probably anticipated that Norma's international background would create public interest and raise the profile of Mount Royal's singing program. After all, his stated goal as director was to build the conservatory's reputation beyond the city of Calgary, to put it "on a par with some of the better Eastern musical institutions."[33] Certainly, publicity from the conservatory emphasized Norma's Italian studies with "outstanding teachers" and her success as "Prima Donna in Grand Operas." As well, advertisements piqued local interest with something unique in the city; the new addition to the faculty would be teaching "the art of coloratura singing." Luckily, Norma's first engagement with the Calgary Women's Musical Club in January 1942 coincided with the announcement of her appointment to Mount Royal College, and the press obligingly provided free publicity for both events.

This publicity was important to Norma, as she was not on salary with the college but instead was paid as a freelance teacher affiliated with the Conservatory of Music. The first month she earned only $7.52. However, she quickly established herself, because she was one of only a few music teachers in the city at the time who taught singing exclusively and could actually demonstrate with her own voice what she wanted her students to do. (In the early 1940s, fewer than a dozen teachers offered singing lessons in Calgary. Most of these taught another instrument as well, usually piano, and very few could boast any kind of professional singing training or background.) As a teacher, Norma had the additional credibility conferred by her affiliation with the college. By the end of her first term of teaching, in the spring of 1942,

*Top; Norma doing laundry in the
Ghost River at Valnorma, ca 1940s.
GA PD-184-8-82*

*Bottom; George haying at
Chio-abba-tinda, ca 1940s.
GA PD-184-8-84*

she was earning about 25 dollars per month, and this rose steadily over the year so that by the spring of 1943, only one year after she started teaching, she was earning close to 100 dollars per month. When enrolment stabilized after 1946 at 30 to 35 students, she was earning a comfortable income of close to 3,000 dollars per year, an amount that compared very favourably with salaries for women in other professions at the time.[34]

After years of negotiating for erratic concert fees and living on very limited resources, this was good, steady income for the Pocaterras, and it is not surprising that once Norma settled into teaching at Mount Royal College, there was no more serious talk of returning overseas to pick up the thread of her international career, even once the war ended. Unthinkable several years before, she was no longer interested in performing full-length operas and was content just to sing their famous arias as part of a popular concert program. Since she performed whenever asked, she was able to supplement her teaching income regularly with small broadcast and recital fees, which usually amounted to 15 to 20 dollars per performance. George, who was 60 when Norma started teaching in 1942, contributed a small monthly income by doing water-level readings on the Ghost River for the Alberta provincial government and by making occasional hay sales, but Norma's earnings as a teacher remained the mainstay of the family income, even after she left the college in 1955 to teach privately from her own studio.

Norma's income allowed for a few improvements at Valnorma. In 1945 George enclosed the porch as a sunroom, and in 1947 he installed pipes from the lowest of their five springs so that they could have water at the house and sprayers for their many flower and vegetable gardens. After several years of hauling water, this was an unaccustomed luxury, and George once shocked her teaching colleagues by referring to Norma's nude outdoor showers.[35] In addition to the horses, the couple began to keep hens and a rooster they called King Arthur that they won in a community Red Cross raffle organized in 1942 to help the war effort. In 1947 they also began to keep bees, and Valnorma honey became another small source of income as well as a staple gift for family and friends for as long as they had the Ghost River property.

As George outlined in letters to Mrs. Mather, they were quite self-sufficient at Valnorma. One fall, he detailed for her their preparations for winter:

I stayed home one week and hauled, and hauled fire-wood, and now we have a pile of fir and poplar wood about fifty feet long and higher than a man. Also some of the hard coal from my mountain land. The vegetables: 14 sacks of potatoes, two of carrots, one of beets, half of one of parsnips are already in the cellar. The honey is all put away, and all together we are not so badly off. We also had a marvelous crop of hay put up, and should be able to sell several hundred dollars worth of it next winter. We now have a much larger flock of pure-bred Leghorns, and have enough eggs ... for us and to sell, with which to buy our meat, now terribly expensive.[36]

A few years later, he marveled:

> People often wonder what we do there to keep us busy. Ye Gods and little Fishes! We wish that those good people could stand alongside of us while there and work at the same tasks, and at the same speed ... But Valnorma is doing us both a world of good. We are always in such good health and I don't think you would find either one of us changed in the least. In fact people stop us often in the streets and ask us how we manage to look always just the same. I claim it is Norma and she claims it's me.[37]

Finally, in 1947 they replaced their increasingly unreliable car, Pegasine, with a Jeep. Norma was delighted with the Jeep, which could descend the new road down the steep hill to Valnorma at a cautious 2 miles an hour but was "gunned" back up again at 20 mph. Now guests could be ferried in comfort to and from their cars, which they left parked by the garage at the top of the cliff. Prior to "Jeepy," visitors had been forced to trudge up and down the steep path, assisted if they wished by holding onto one of the horse's tails.[38] The steep slope and rigorous climb to and from their house did not bother the Pocaterras in the slightest; George was physically strong and accustomed to climbing, and Norma had developed a wonderful lung capacity and stamina from years of voice training and from hiking with George.[39] Although the Jeep was a very practical vehicle for country living, it looked somewhat out of place in the city and contributed to the Pocaterras' growing image as local eccentrics, particularly as they continued to drive it rather erratically into old age.

Among Norma's first students at the college were two young women, Eleanor Carlyle, daughter of her good friends the T. M. Carlyles, and Cleone Duncan, daughter of one of Dr. Piper's dental colleagues, Dr. Wilfred M. Duncan. Eleanor had shown early promise as a singer and competed at the Alberta Musical Festival annually from 1931 to 1935. While overseas, Norma had heard of her young friend's musical progress with interest, and in the late 1930s she applauded Eleanor's decision to follow Norma's example by moving to Vancouver to study with Brandli de Bevec. Several years Eleanor's junior, Cleone started competing at the Alberta Musical Festival only in 1936, but by the time Norma returned to Calgary, she had become a serious competitor in the young adult soprano category.

The Duncans were pleased to have a professional singer to advise their daughter, and even before she started teaching at Mount Royal College, Norma had been engaged to assist Cleone and her friends to prepare for the Alberta Musical Festival the following spring. Happily, Norma's first teaching venture was a success; Cleone received a first in the lyric soprano class at the festival in 1942. Cleone and her friends were some of Norma's first students at the conservatory, and when Brandli died in 1942, Eleanor returned to Calgary and began studies with Norma at Mount Royal College as well. Both young women continued with Norma for several years, were featured in a number of local recitals and then travelled to the United States to continue their studies and to attempt musical careers.

Eleanor headed to New York in 1945 and reported to Norma that her new teacher, who had been recommended by Edward Johnson (with whom she had auditioned), "really was most impressed with the teaching I had had in Calgary—in fact I really think he was quite amazed by it . . . He said you had really been first rate . . . So there's a feather in your cap, Norma."[40] Unfortunately, her father's death later that year interrupted Eleanor's studies; she returned to Calgary, moved to Vancouver and eventually settled in the United States. Much as Norma had done a decade earlier (and continued to do on occasion), Cleone gained much of her professional experience by singing for local groups willing to sponsor recitals or simply requiring entertainment at their meetings. After doing very well in radio work in Calgary, she was featured on the national voice competition "Singing Stars of Tomorrow" and also sang the lead very creditably in Norma's 1945 production of *Countess Maritza*. In 1945 Cleone headed to Los Angeles for further musical study, an experience that included singing with the American Opera Company. She had a long career in television and radio in the United States and Canada and also sang for many years with the Charlottetown Festival.

Another talented early student of Norma's was Shirley Flock. As a child during the Second World War, she had entertained troops stationed in Alberta by singing and dancing in the Flock Trio, a popular family act directed by the children's father, pianist Henry Flock. As a teenager Shirley studied with Norma from 1950 to 1952, also returning for a guest appearance at a studio recital in 1953. In addition to her other honours, she won two Galli-Curci awards sponsored by the Calgary Women's Musical Club at the Alberta Musical Festival; those enabled her to study at the Music Academy of the West in Santa Barbara, California, for several summers while continuing with Norma during the school year. She was guest soloist with the Calgary Symphony Orchestra in a debut performance at the Grand Theatre in 1952, but she returned to California to complete her studies and to sing with the Los Angeles Opera Conservatory.

Other early students of note from the Mount Royal days were Shirley Johnston (1943–1949), who sang in several local concerts and was on "Singing Stars of Tomorrow" in 1949, and Fiona Skakun (1946–1949), who sang on "Singing Stars of Tomorrow" in 1951 and was featured on the first Birks Singing Awards radio program on CFAC in 1947.

The musical success of these early students helped to establish Norma's reputation as a teacher. But it also was an open secret at the college and among the older students that in the early years her teaching inexperience meant she often taught "by the seat of her pants" and that George was just as involved as his wife in the actual teaching, particularly of more advanced students.[41] Although Norma had studied singing for 15 years, naturally she had never studied how to teach what she herself knew and could rely only on examples provided by her own teachers for her own type of voice.

Top: Valnorma, early 1950s. GA PD-184-8-227

Bottom: George and Norma at Valnorma, late 1940s. GA PD-184-8-160

George, on the other hand, felt quite confident about training voices. With a natural love of music and singing, he had sat in on most of Norma's lessons over the years and considered himself her mentor. When Norma first started teaching at the college, George sat in on student lessons simply to give her advice and confidence, but he enjoyed the role and had little else to fill his time while in the city, and so this arrangement quickly became a habit. One of Norma's colleagues, Leona Paterson, who joined the conservatory a year after Norma to establish the new Speech Arts department, recalled that George was extremely involved with Norma's students and lessons and that Norma deferred to him in all matters musical. He had an "elderly" rocking chair that sat alongside the baby grand piano in Norma's studio, and during lessons he would often beat time to the music while advising on technique, pronunciation and music selection.[42]

The degree of George's involvement (some thought interference) varied according to the level of the student. Often he skipped lessons with young children or beginners, or was simply a benign presence in the room, but Norma seemed to rely heavily on his advice for the more serious and advanced students. One of these, Shirley Flock, confided that she disliked George's presence at her lessons and was irritated by the continual interruptions that ensued. She felt especially uncomfortable because the long discussions about her between George and Norma were often in Italian.[43] Although the other teachers at the conservatory accepted this unusual arrangement, they also regretted the degree of George's involvement and felt that Norma's own "sweet" personality was overshadowed by George, whom they viewed as excessively domineering.[44]

However, the combined result of their teaching was effective: a number of Norma's students over the years earned high marks in Royal Conservatory and Western Board of Music exams, won prestigious awards at music festivals, sang for local radio and television stations and for programs such as the Birks Singing Awards in Calgary and the Toronto-based competition broadcast by the CBC, "Singing Stars of Tomorrow." A few even went on to musical careers on the stage and in television, and apparently one (unidentified) student sang with the Chicago Opera Company. With this successful track record, it is not surprising that during the 1940s and early 1950s Norma was considered by many to be "the" singing teacher in Calgary.[45]

By the late 1940s her career emphasis had changed. The advance publicity for her guest appearance with the Calgary Symphony Orchestra in 1950 implied that she was considering a request from Milan to return to the Italian operatic stage, and George's letters to friends during the late 1940s make similar claims. In explanation, George liked to tell friends that in Italy before the war Norma "had truly arrived and they still remember her there."[46] But it seems unlikely that there were serious offers or, indeed, anything other than flattering compliments from family and friends. If there were, the Pocaterras never pursued them in any way. In fact, the news they heard from Italy when mail started flowing again after the war served to discourage them rather than otherwise. George was worried about the post-war political situation in Europe, concerned that things would reignite and that there would be another war. He told American friends, "Matters in poor Europe do not look at all rosy, and the terrible mistakes made by ALL will have to be paid for, I fear."[47]

Although they continued to claim for some time that Norma was considering a return to Italy, this was simply a publicity gambit; in reality, quite soon after the war they decided against returning. As early as May 1946 George wrote to his old friend Dick Wright, "We have been getting quite a bit of mail from Europe, and I can tell you that it has taken away a desire we might have had to return there again,"[48] and he said more emphatically, some months later, "We have given up all ideas of Europe . . . we almost got caught once . . . and that's enough."[49] But this decision was actually motivated by contentment in Calgary as much as by fear of Europe. In 1946 George told a friend that in Europe "they . . . seem to be going through difficult times. Here we are quite satisfied."[50] And he was quite frank about the reason for their satisfaction, writing in 1947: "Norma has been exceedingly successful here. In fact she is on the way of creating a legend about herself . . . She has made a marvellous reputation for herself as an exceedingly capable teacher and also as a person, and as a singer. Any time she sings at a concert the place is packed so . . . I guessed right in coming here."[51]

Norma dropped all plans for future concert tours, including Magdalene Moore's proposed tour of western Canada and George Mitford's five-city Ontario tour. Although she had left Ontario in the spring of 1941 with the intention of pursuing Mitford's promotional ideas the following winter, there is no evidence that Norma made any effort to contact Mitford or any other musical agent ever again. And although she spent her days at the conservatory training others and continued herself to practise daily, she never again sought professional training for her own voice. She settled effortlessly into a new role as a busy and popular teacher active in the local musical community.

Her transition no doubt was eased by her treatment as something of a legend, a glamorous opera diva whose fading glory but still considerable talents made her a popular sentimental favourite in the community. Always happy to perform, she accepted all invitations and delighted in recounting her days in Italy and the international career that might have been. As time went on, some of the facts regarding her career were forgotten or exaggerated. Newspaper interviewers assured the public that she was "likely the very best coloratura soprano in Canada during the early 1930s," that the combination of her beauty and her voice in the early days had been "overwhelming" and that she had lived a life "as spectacular and as tragic as any of the great operatic heroines."[52]

It is difficult to determine how much of the embellishment came from Norma herself (or from George) and how much was assumption made by admiring listeners and interviewers eager to fill in the blanks. For example, many people came to believe that Norma had worn her beautiful costumes while singing at La Scala, and that she had sung in Italy and all over Europe with some of the greatest conductors and artists. Some people believed that George was a count, who had played some kind of Svengali role in Norma's career; that he had "discovered" her in Calgary as a young girl and swept her off to Italy to develop her talent. Many believed that the Pocaterras had escaped Europe absolutely destitute, "on the last boat out," or even "on a cattle boat."

The Pocaterras were proud of Norma's Italian operatic career and enjoyed bragging about it. They loved to recount richly detailed stories from their days in Italy for family and friends, and Norma included these anecdotes in many of her concerts and all of her talks and interviews. Generally the stories did not contain outright fabrications, but embroidery resulted when admiring listeners filled in the gaps in what was already a glamorous and exotic narrative far removed from the experience of most Calgarians. Sometimes the Pocaterras simply told part of a story and let listeners draw their own, somewhat erroneous conclusions. For example, many of the conductors and artists with whom Norma sang or auditioned really had enjoyed important careers. However, her singing with them did not indicate success on her part; invariably, they had retired from their position of power (Gatti-Casazza, Trebbi, Pettinella, Marino), or were past their prime (Stracciari) or had listened to an audition but had not hired her (Serafin, Del Campo, Erede, Marinuzzi, Legge, Johnson). Similarly, although Norma did indeed sing at La Scala—twice—her listeners no doubt were unaware that both times were for auditions that unfortunately were unsuccessful.

One story Norma liked to tell was that she was given the fan she used in *The Barber of Seville* by the great soprano Rosina Storchio as a compliment for her performance of the role. Although it is quite possible that Storchio, who lived in Milan, heard her sing, and that the fan indeed was Storchio's, when Norma acquired it in 1936 she made no mention of the anecdote in her diary or in letters to her father. She simply recorded that she had purchased the fan second-hand from a "retired artist" through the good offices of her scena teacher, Maestro Galli. This stretching of the truth became more noticeable as time went on, and Norma's Italian career attained a rosy glow with details forgotten even by the principals involved. It was relatively harmless and only added to the enjoyment local people felt in having a "star" in their midst. Ignorant that her Italian career had never risen above second- and third-class theatres, admirers provided Norma with a stage and the esteem she craved and, in George's opinion, deserved. Always proud of her voice and sensitive to criticism, he helped to foster the image with his own reminiscences and by treating her in public like the diva he insisted she had been. Their sweeping entrances into theatres and other public events became legendary.

Norma did have a few detractors in the musical community, one of the most vocal being Odette de Foras. The daughter of an aristocratic French rancher in the High River area, she became a protege of early local musical mavens Annie Glen Broder and Dorothy Ellis-Browne. At the Alberta Musical Festival in 1916, de Foras won an associated board scholarship to study singing at the Royal Academy of Music in London, England, which she did from 1919 to 1922. She sang many times at Covent Garden, and after her return to Calgary in 1936 she had a long teaching career. Her voice and technique were very different from Norma's; de Foras was an intense dramatic soprano and she had inherited the old Calgary bias in favour of English training and the Royal Academy. She also seems to have adopted her mentor Mrs. Broder's dislike of Italian training and Norma herself. Privately, de Foras was dismissive of Norma's singing. She was one of the few locals to divine the truth about the pedestrian nature of Norma's overseas career, and she delighted in pointing out that, unlike herself, Norma had never attained her dream of singing at a major international opera house such as Covent Garden or the Met. Luckily for Norma, Odette's opinions were not widely known, and many who did hear her views may have discounted them as arising from professional jealousy. On the advice of friends, including Wilda Blow, the Pocaterras chose to ignore her ill-natured comments and graciously attended Odette's Calgary concerts.

Teachers at the conservatory were a social group, sharing afternoon tea every day in a basement staff area, and many of Norma's colleagues became personal friends who supported her musically in the community. Organist and conductor Cyril Mossop, director of the conservatory from 1944 to 1951, included Norma in the first Mount Royal College Conservatory Chamber Music Concert in 1947; Norma sang four songs, including an aria from *La Sonnambula* by her "beloved Bellini." In 1949 she donated 70 percent of the proceeds from a special concert she organized and performed with former college staffer and organist Phyllis Chapman Clarke and pianist Jean Evely to aid the Kerby Memorial Building Fund at Mount Royal College. The event generated about 170 dollars for the building fund and much admiration from the social elite in attendance. Mrs. William (Alice) Toole wrote a note thanking Norma for the "rare treat," saying, "I haven't heard anything so beautiful since the good old Covent Garden days ... Mrs W. R. Hull who came with me said she had never heard a more lovely voice."[53] In 1950 violinist Clayton Hare, who had worked with Norma at Mount Royal College and now was conductor of the Calgary Symphony Orchestra, featured her as guest soloist for the orchestra's May program at the Grand Theatre. Pianist Leonard Leacock, violinist John Sebastian Bach and organist Harold Ramsay (director of the conservatory after 1951) were welcome visitors to Valnorma and occasional dinner guests in Calgary, and Bach even took some singing lessons from his old friend near the end of her career.

In November 1950 Norma gave a "delightful" reprise of her 1943 welcome-back concert at Central United Church under the auspices of the Women's Musical Club. "Well, Norma still sings beautifully," one admirer told the *Calgary Herald*, which also told its readers she was "long considered a favourite with local audiences." The *Herald* praised her sincerity and obvious enjoyment of her craft, but the assessment was honest and somewhat painful: "Her strong coloratura was at its best in the higher registers. Her high notes were clear, unwavering and at times quite thrilling. However, the lower tones were occasionally harsh and once or twice seemed rather off key."[54] The review of a recital the previous year had criticized "the rather piercing quality of a couple of high notes."[55] Not surprisingly, reviews like these were not saved among the Pocaterras' personal papers, and George, ever protective, was quick to take umbrage if anyone dared to suggest that Norma's voice or performance was less than perfect.[56] Norma continued to sing publicly into her early 60s and in private recitals for many years thereafter. As her voice aged, the danger of critical reviews grew, but luckily for the Pocaterras most of these later events went unreviewed or were handled sympathetically by tactful reviewers who no doubt were aware that the public no longer expected perfection from their favourite diva.

As opportunities for public concerts gradually declined, the Pocaterras discovered a new way for Norma to showcase her still-impressive voice. Soon after she started teaching at Mount Royal College, she introduced June recitals to give her students an opportunity to perform for parents and friends. There were regular recitals at the conservatory where advanced students of all the teachers could perform, but many teachers held their own independent recitals so that all students had a chance for public performance. This was especially important for Norma's studio, because she developed a reputation at the college for specializing in teaching younger, less-experienced students; without a separate recital, they would have had no other opportunity to demonstrate publicly what they had learned. By 1947 Norma's independent recitals were twice yearly, and in 1950 she not only added a third recital in the spring but started the tradition of closing each by herself singing an operatic number to inspire her students.

Usually dramatized and performed in full costume, Norma's arias at the end of the recitals were perennial crowd-pleasers, which impressed both students and parents. Admirers were astonished to watch her metamorphose onstage into a vivacious young coquette or a pretty and witty young widow or a bride driven mad to the point of murder. As one student observed, in costume and while acting a role, Norma "would somehow transform right in front of your eyes and be entirely believable as the young character she was playing."[57] Her domination of the stage surprised many an unbeliever who was ready to snicker and jeer at her first appearance in wig and costume but was silenced in appreciation for her art.[58] As long as she continued teaching, as she did into her early 80s, Norma performed arias at her student recitals and always relished the excitement and uncritical praise that ensued. George enthusiastically recorded her recital triumphs in diary entries: "Norma wonderful," "Norma marvellous," "Norma sang like a lark," "Norma's singing outstanding."

George's original intention in developing the Ghost River property was to give himself and Norma an inexpensive home where they could wait out the war, the subsequent sale of which would fund their return to Europe when Norma was ready to resume her operatic career. However, when a potential buyer made inquiries in 1946, George quibbled with the offer of eight dollars per acre and then stated firmly that the property was not for sale.[59] Of course, by this time they realized they would not be returning to Europe and had become attached to Valnorma as their Calgary base. But they still cherished their dream of moving somewhere with milder weather, and George told a friend that the only drawback in their otherwise complete satisfaction with Valnorma was the climate: "Both Norma and I are really children of the sun, and are longing now for some place in a warm country."[60]

As early as January 1946 George's interest in the South Seas revived, when his friend Dick Wright visited various islands in the Pacific with a view to settling. He peppered Dick with questions about Tahiti, asking, "Would it be feasible to buy a few acres in the outlying districts and leave the place for several months a year? To return each winter? . . . What we have in mind is a place where we could live simply (we are both fond [of] and able to do quite a bit of work) during the cold months of the year, believing that the cheaper life there would make up for the extra expense of the ... voyage."[61]

When the Pocaterras' friends the Mathers moved to Tahiti in 1947, George's longing for the sun reached fever pitch, and he determined to make a permanent move. The Mathers encouraged him, writing teasingly from their new beach home, "Strawberries and bees, tourists and singing lessons sound like an awful lot of work."[62] Norma was enthusiastic, and told them, "What we want in Tahiti is Peace and time to think, and a chance to build up a perfectly lovely home. Valnorma is glorious. I know of no lovelier place in Canada, but we have only 2 months of flowers! What we want is a chance to grow things 12 months in the year, a chance to go swimming, mountain-climbing, chatting with friends, and not be caught by the throat, because winter is on its way, and we haven't gathered enough firewood."[63]

Confidently, George outlined their plans:

> We believe now, that our best bet is to take a trip to Tahiti ... then after a little stay with you to get orientated, we would like to take a very leisurely trip around the island, even if we have to walk. By then I shall be able to talk Tahitian sufficiently to get by. And French is almost like my mother tongue to me. Norma also can get by, when pushed to it. We figure that after a few months looking around, we will be able to form a more or less correct opinion about the possibilities of the country as applied to us. Do not forget that I am an old colonial and that pioneering is second nature to me and a source of happiness. Also, since a child I have always been able to get natives to like me very much.[64]

Unfortunately, they lacked the necessary funds. Searching for some way to augment Norma's teaching income, George revived his original idea of running Valnorma as a guest ranch. He wrote to the Mathers, "There is a real boom in Dude Ranches now, and we think that if we can start one operating successfully, it will be that much easier to sell Valnorma at a good price . . . we may even be able to run the tourist business in the summer and go to Tahiti in the winter."[65]

In 1947 they decided to make a start. In April George wrote to a friend:

We intend to get what help is required to run it properly. For this year's beginning we will get a girl, but if necessary we know of a very efficient woman who is ready to come for the season. It will all depend on the amount of tourists we can get. Though our accommodation is going to be limited this year. We hope to get the motor road finished down to the house, a fire-place built, running water in the house, and showers, hot and cold built in an outhouse. Also more cabins and a barn. Norma is set on doing what we do really well; rather less, but better.[66]

Over the spring, George made good progress on all the improvements except for the cabins, for which he had logs hauled by Stoney friends but never had the time to construct. That summer they entertained only a few small parties of friends for a few days at a time but reported in the fall, "What little we did we liked."[67]

George and Norma sailing on the Ghost Arm. ca 1940s. GA PD-184-8-71

The next year they decided to expand, but George was still cautious, telling his friend Dan Campbell at the Alberta Travel Bureau that he planned to "start slowly, as I want to be sure that Norma will really like it before going into the venture more deeply." He said, "What we would like to do this summer, is to take in a party of two or three for as long as possible (NO week-enders) who want to stay in a place where they can forget the turmoil of the world, in a cultured environment, and enjoy the healthy great Outdoors, with riding, swimming, hiking an every day occurrence if desired. Our charges would be $40.00 per week, which would include, besides meals and lodging, a horse and equipment and guiding."[68]

Valnorma Guest Ranch was included in a listing of "Dude Ranches of Western Canada" produced by the Canadian Government Travel Bureau, and for several summers the Pocaterras had a "succession of guests, some for stays of weeks at a time."[69] But although they thoroughly enjoyed their visitors, the scheme never took off to the extent they had imagined and the guest cabins were never built; guests continued to be housed in the old Patterson cabin by the river.

As another means of funding a move to the South Seas, in the late 1940s George attempted to revive interest in some of his old coal-development schemes. In 1947 he wrote to Raymond Patterson, outlining recent developments and sounding him out (unsuccessfully) about getting his "cousins from the Old Country" to invest:

> As you may well believe I have done my best to keep in touch with whatever trends could be of use in the development of my old claims. Nothing much stirred until about two years ago, when quite a bit of talk was going the rounds about the Ribbon Creek coal being on the point of being developed ... As quietly as possible I tried to interest several people, I had a party in from B.C. rather hot, also some people from L.A. when one evening an old friend of the Piper family (a musician in the past, and a supposedly well-informed oil man now) approached me and mentioned having heard that I had done some prospecting in the past. To make a long story short we arranged to go into it together, 50/50, I to show the claim or claims, and he to provide all the finances. Fortunately, though, I did not confide in him altogether, and we finally staked and leased only the Pocaterra creek claim, and not the old Ings claim on the Porcupine. It would be too long to explain everything in a letter ... Anyway his son got the claim, he disclaimed having made anything out of it and I.... In the meantime I had gone up the Kananaskis and put in some hard work to locate a truck road from the mouth of Pocaterra to the mine, and I followed this by superintending the job of building seven fairly large bridges and three small ones (glorified culverts), and a little over seven miles of road. Also got my men to build three cabins. And for all that work (almost three months of it) and being during the months of October, November and December last year, it was far from a pic-nic. And I tell you, I got nothing at all, and , so far, I have not been able to collect anything! . . . In the meantime I was being warned by some of the best known men of the city to be on my guard. The outcome was that I even had a meeting with the minister of Lands and Mines about this matter, and made it clear, that I wished to disassociate myself completely from such shady characters. And THAT'S THAT!
>
> But ... I would not give up my struggle to get something out of a quest that has lasted since 1906. That is a longish time out of any man's life! So since last spring, together with some good, honest

friends we have staked two very good claims, one (the Ings one) on Porcupine, and the other in the Pocaterra creek valley, where I once found some very hard coal in a very large seam. And if things turn out at all favourable we hope to get into some production sometime next summer. I think the idea will be to strip mine the coal. The seams are large, as you remember, and many, and we believe that quite a lot of coal can be stripped on top of the middle ridge.[70]

Working in the bush, clearing trails and building bridges together reminded George how much he valued a close relationship with his Stoney friends. In 1947 he confessed to Harper Sibley, "I found them far more interesting than the whitemen. They seemed to be interested in far more, actually, serious matters than the whitemen, who did not seem to be able to talk of anything else, but movies, and the latest stars, radios, and the silliest programs, and DRINK or worse. At times I could not help but ask myself: 'Quo Vadis?' Oh, Civilization and Culture?"[71] In 1949 George took advantage of his renewed familiarity with the Stoney language to write an article for the *Calgary Herald* in which he explained to readers the proper pronunciation and frequent mistranslation of many local place names of Native origin.[72]

Bridge building in Pocaterra Creek, late 1940s. GA PD-184-8-247

George's friendly feeling toward the Stoneys was genuine, but in 1949 it was based in part on his relief at having resolved a slight rift with Paul Amos that had threatened their long friendship the year before. Learning that George intended to develop his old coal claims, someone goaded Paul into writing to George and demanding compensation for the coal deposits shown to him 40 years earlier by Paul's father, Three Buffalo Bulls. George was stung and reacted angrily; he wrote to Paul:

I read your letter over a few times and from it I understand again and again that which I have known for quite a long time, and that is: that you are all-right yourself, but that you let somebody (*and I know who it is*) bother you with some foolish and sour thoughts. I say foolish because if you only thought for one little moment you would know that if it had been possible to make something good out of that coal I and my partners would have done so long ago. If we did not yet, that is not our fault but the fault of two wars and the money hard times which we have had for so long ... Your Father showed me that coal, not because I promised anything first, but because I had done something good for him ... and he wanted to pay it back by doing something good to me ... It has cost us around $70,000 (seventy thousand dollars) and that is *A LOT OF MONEY*, over THIRTY YEARS of Worry and on my part also many years of work for *ABSOLUTELY NOTHING*. Do you get THAT Paul? You at least got paid always with the best wages of the times for everything you did, so what are you kicking about? If anybody has a right to kick it is me and my partners. You Stonies made at least something out of something that God made, not you ... Do you think, that if I could have made money out of that coal I would have been working as hard as I still do at my age? ... All the rest is just a lot of silly, stupid, foolish talk, and both I and you also, Paul, are now old enough to know better than to listen to foolish, jealous childish talk ... For the sake of the country I hope that all those coal mines get worked right, and I will be ready to watch and do my best, but that's all I can do, as I AM NOT God ...

I am NOT mad, Paul, I still feel like a good friend to you; we have been together for so many years and in so many dangerous and difficult places and times, that small talk does not make any difference.[73]

Bowing under this storm of righteous indignation, Paul withdrew his claim and renewed his friendship with George, who reciprocated by hiring Stoney workers whenever possible for coal-related projects over the next few years.

During his many trips into the mountains, George recaptured some of the excitement and hardship of his old way of life. In 1947 he wrote to the Mathers, "Some of these trips have been very exacting. Once in the early spring I traveled for days in snow and pouring rain, riding through the soaking wet bush all day long, and sleeping in my fur sleeping bag at night with all my clothes on, still wet from the day's soaking. But I kept well all along, and then the homecomings to my dear girl repaid me for all hardships passed. The season, last winter, was a truly terrible one, and even in June I was tramping at times in over TEN FEET of snow!"[74] The next year, he reported, "On May 24th I was behind the second range with two of my partners, and two Indians. I was driving our jeep. That night it rained and rained, it came very hot. The falling water started snow-slides all around us. It was a continual rumble all night long. Truly apocalyptic, and terrifying. Next morning all sixteen bridges between us and civilization were out! We made it all right, or I wouldn't be writing this."[75]

George crossing between the two Kananaskis lakes, ca early 1950s-.
GA PA-2393-3-1

His most truly dangerous experience had occurred some months earlier:

Last Fall, driving our Jeep down the Kananaskis road towards civilization again, I had a great gas truck side-swipe the rear end of the Jeep, on an especially dangerous bit of road; in consequence of which the light Jeep was turned around, and sent crashing down a very steep mountain side, which ended in a deep man-made lake (power). I managed to aim for a clump of jack-pines clinging to the side of the hill. Some were sheered off, and the others managed to break the speed of the Jeep, which turned over … gently, without damaging me in the least, and with only a few bumps on the vehicle. The truck winch pulled the Jeep back on the road, and within a few hours I was back in our home in Calgary [i.e., their apartment], nothing the worse.[76]

While George was away in the Kananaskis Valley, Norma continued teaching but spent every weekend keeping things going at Valnorma. Her routine consisted of heading from Calgary to Cochrane on the bus every Saturday afternoon, usually taking the Campbell's 11-year-old son, Neill, with her because George had made her promise never to go alone. By the time she and Neill hiked or snowshoed in from the highway, it was after dark, and so the main work of the excursion was accomplished on Sunday. This was a day of hard effort: they caught and saddled the horses so they could "ride the rod" to check water levels for George's government report; they checked fencelines and the other horses and made sure the chickens had enough feed for the coming week (George had made special feed hoppers to let down "just so much food at a time" while Valnorma was untenanted). Late Sunday afternoon, they headed back out to the highway for the three-hour bus ride back into the city. As this arrangement lasted from the early spring to the late fall, Norma was glad to report to a friend that young Neill "loves it."

George was diligent in his efforts to develop various coal sites throughout the late 1940s and 1950s. He regularly sent coal samples to be assayed and forwarded the resulting positive reports to potential investors and supporters such as his old friend Harry Monahan. Over the years George formed a number of small companies with various of his business associates as directors and himself as chairman. Cloudburst Coal Company Limited was the first, formed on October 22, 1949. Although it was not struck from the Alberta companies register until March 30, 1957, in reality it was only active for three years, becoming Mineral Resources Limited (MRL) as of February 1, 1952.

This new company, comprised of "three [investors] from Calgary, one from Vancouver and others from Saskatoon," incorporated George's coal interests along "with others', [and] with about 10,000 acres of proven oil lands" ("proven, by drilling, to have a reserve of around 30,000,000 barrels of heavy oil," with potential for light oil production at the lower horizons). He told Mrs. Mather in 1952 that he had a "fairly large amount of shares" in the company but that they were being held in escrow pending government approval. He was also excited about a recent discovery of "a good seam of industrial coal (coking and welding coal)" and told her, "With the proven smokeless and anthracitic varieties we already knew of, this new development should prove of some worth."[77] The next year, he informed her that MRL had gone public with "a $300,000 issue for development purposes,"[78] but ongoing financial difficulties plagued the company and in 1958 the investors would vote to "wind it up."

A very different project claimed George's attention in 1952–1953 and provided a much-needed diversion. Because of his long-standing friendships with the Stoneys, George was approached by a Hollywood film company in 1952 to find actors among his Native friends for a movie they planned to film in Banff National Park. Throughout the summer of 1953, director Raoul Walsh of the Universal International Film Company (Warner Brothers) used George's services and those of Banff photographer Bruno Engler to scout locations and wrangle Native actors for the movie *Saskatchewan* starring Alan Ladd and Shelley Winters. The plot was a straightforward adventure: a Canadian mounted police officer raised in a Cree village discovers that the Cree have been unfairly blamed for a massacre actually performed by the Sioux. When he receives orders to disarm the Cree, he must choose between the people who raised him and his commanding officer.[79]

Because the movie required several hundred Native actors, and there was deemed to be little appreciation of tribal differences in the movie-going audiences of the 1950s, George saw no difficulty in recruiting "his" Stoneys

Top: George (right) with director Raoul Walsh (centre) and Robert E. Mercer, (former officer commanding the Calgary subdivision of the R.C.M.P.) on the set of the movie "Saskatchewan," Banff, August 1953.
GA M6340-v3-p6

Bottom: Calgary Herald advertisement for "Saskatchewan" at the Grand Theatre in Calgary, March 15, 1954.
GA M6340-v3-p12

to play Cree and Sioux. In the end he needed more actors than the Stoneys could provide, so he also recruited from the local Sarcee and Hobbema Cree reserves. The director disliked the pillbox hats worn by the North-West Mounted Police of the 1870s, so he substituted the more distinctive wide-brimmed hats of the 1900s, but George successfully insisted that the Native costumes be as accurate as possible. Each morning, he headed to their camp to inform the actors "what kind of Indians they [would] be that day." Occasionally there were problems: according to the *Albertan*, "in chilly weather everyone wants to be a Cree because they get to wear warm leather clothes, whereas the Sioux must cavort half-naked before the cameras."[80] In addition to working with the Native actors, George also spent time teaching Alan Ladd a few elementary hand signals to use in the movie.[81]

For about seven weeks, George was in charge of the more than 200 actors and their families, all camped at Banff. Afterwards, he was relieved to report, "At times there was not much love shown between them, still old enmities cropping up, but I managed to keep them off any real trouble."[82] Since the production schedule conflicted with haying and harvesting time, he recommended competitive wages for the actors (between 7 and 12 dollars per day plus subsistence) to forestall problems.[83] The actors were taken by by each day to whatever scenic location was serving as that day's backdrop (including Bow Lake, Peyto Lake, Moraine Lake and Takkakaw Falls). George's voice was used on the soundtrack, when he said a short piece of Stoney dialogue in a scene at Moraine Lake showing an Indian scout tracking Mountie horses.[84]

George's good relationship with the Stoneys, and his knowledge of their language, proved invaluable and resulted in a smooth production schedule with no labour problems. Director Walsh complimented George, later writing, "Never in all my experience of making pictures have I met a finer bunch of boys, and I personally want to thank you for your great cooperation."[85] According to one report, when the shooting was finished, "the director was made a member of the [Stoney] tribe, and renamed Painter of the Mountains."[86] Norma managed to visit George several times over the summer, and while he truly enjoyed the excitement of movie making, he was glad when filming ended in mid-September. In relief, he told his diary, "Happy both to be back to our way of life."[87] However, he was delighted to share his experience of making "A Movie in the Mountains" in a presentation to the Knights of the Round Table several years later.[88]

Now in his 70s, George's active life at Valnorma and in the mountains had enabled him to remain physically much younger than his chronological age. Relating to Dr. Morlan an incident in the mountains, when three younger men had difficulty keeping up to him on snowshoes, George bragged, "I had a check-up, for car insurance ... and the doctor told Norma, that he could hardly believe what he saw; he said that my heart and blood pressure was like that of a twenty year old, the same with my lungs. I have always been very moderate in everything, no credit due me, because I apparently did not feel the temptations most other people have. Just plain born lucky ..."[89]

However, in June 1954 George had a very serious accident at Valnorma, which plagued him for the rest of his life. As he related to the Mathers some six months later:

I was riding alone, when the horse [Grey Cloud] stumbled, but I managed to lift him up twice, but the third time he rose high on his hind legs and flopped down on his right side. It was all so terribly quick, that I had no time to throw myself aside, and was caught under the horse. I thought for a moment that I had had it, but after some minutes I was able to get up, in fact quite a bit before the horse was able, with my assistance to stand up again. Some campers, who had seen, ran up to me with HALF a glass of brandy, I drank it all at once and it tasted just like water. After a while worrying about Norma, I rode home. Of course I was not quite up to my usual self all summer, and I took off the corset [sic] only about a month ago. Now I feel my usual self in every way. Norma has always been her wonderful self with me, and THAT helped a lot.[90]

In fact, he was left with permanent damage to his left knee and later told Dr. Morlan, "Norma had a cripple on her hands for almost a year."[91] Even surgery a decade later left him with a slight limp.

It was during this time that George's very conflicted feelings about development in the Kananaskis Valley became apparent. Hoping to make a fortune, he had worked for many decades trying to develop coal sites in the area, but he was upset when another equally disruptive development project came to fruition. In 1955 Calgary Power constructed two dams and hydro plants at Kananaskis Lakes. Writing to Raymond Patterson, George condemned the ugly new structures and their destructive impact: "Yes I did see the MESS the Power company made of both lakes, but especially of the upper lake, the most magnificent scenery in the whole world, I verily believe. I fought their ruining it for two years, and had all the Park protective associations of Canada helping."[92] And again, "One of the greatest disappointments in my life has been the desecration of the most beautiful lake and mountain scenery I have EVER seen, and that takes in Switzerland, where I went to college for six years, and Italy too … And it had been incorporated in the National Rocky Mountain park for a generation!"[93] He lamented the changes in a speech to the Historical Society of Alberta: "The drowning of the marvellously beautiful islands, and exquisitely curving beaches, and the cutting down of the centuries old trees, and the drying up of the twin-falls between the two lakes, and of the falls below the lower lake."[94]

Ironically, in view of George's public condemnation of the project, Calgary Power announced in 1955 that the lower dam would be called the Pocaterra Dam. George was incensed. Not only had the company failed to ask for permission to use his name, but now it also appeared that he had given his tacit approval to the project by allowing it to be named in his honour. He complained bitterly to Patterson, "I knew nothing about all this, until I read my name in large letters in the *Herald*, on the front page. Many of my friends thought that I must have made a pot of money. Nary a cent, as a cowboy would say."[95] Later that year the company arranged to have his portrait taken, and in February 1956 he was featured in Calgary Power's weekly radio tribute to local personalities, called "Here's Alberta—People and Places."

Somehow, George failed to see the irony of continuing his own development in the Kananaskis Valley while condemning other commercial ventures. Financial reality dictated that most mining in western Canada be surface or strip mining, where whole mountains would be torn down in order to harvest the coal, and that was the method George had always assumed would be used for his mines.[96] Undoubtedly, development of his coal claims would have left an ugly scar in his beautiful valley scenery.

Possibly he was able to compartmentalize his feelings so neatly because he did not really see the ruin of forested areas as equivalent to the destruction of the lakes, a place that had always been so special for him. For such a romantic man, he could be very pragmatic. After his initial anger and disappointment, he told Dr. Morlan, "I should cover my head with ashes in despair and regrets, but I simply don't feel that way; I long ago forsaw what the future was bound to bring, and discounted it, and so saved myself from lots of heart-aches ... I try to see the good 'as it is now ...' and not as a man centred in selfishness, who would keep all beauty solely to himself, keeping everybody else away, so that nothing could be changed from when he first enjoyed it. Nothing in life remains put. So we might just as well make the best of it."[97] Similarly, he later wrote, "One must learn to be wise and NOT be sad, harping on something beautiful lost, but instead be grateful that so much of BEAUTY surrounds us yet."[98]

The "logged off shoreline" of Upper Kananaskis Lake. Photo R. M. Patterson Collection.

With no money coming in from George's coal schemes, the Pocaterras were not able to retire to or even visit the South Seas as planned. But, aside from lacking the funds to make such a move, their ardour for the scheme cooled somewhat as they read the Mathers' detailed accounts of the problems they encountered while trying to live out their own fantasies in Tahiti. Just before they left Tahiti to relocate to Spain, Dorothy Mather wrote a frank letter in which she discouraged her friends from pursuing their long-cherished dream: "You would be I think very silly to leave Alberta just now when your financial prospects look so very bright . . . I don't believe that what you propose to do here (i.e. buy land, build a house and make a little money to live on) is possible anymore. Everybody who has come in lately has had to put down certain specified sums of money and to guarantee to spend them . . . Also it is very difficult to buy land."[99] Nevertheless, George never really abandoned the dream, and his letters to the Mathers in the 1950s still reflected his old longing: "I am a terribly determined person, very patient, but I simply MUST realize my dreams. Most I have already, there is still an important one and that is to go to the Islands. To me it will be a going home. How? Well it would be very hard, almost impossible for me to explain THAT!"[100]

When they realized they would be remaining in the Calgary area indefinitely, the Pocaterras decided that Norma's teaching reputation was such that she could leave Mount Royal College and start her own studio. For some time, in fact, George had felt the college "had nothing to offer [Norma] for the $1,000.00 and over she paid them a year"[101] and he was anxious to make a savings. The cost of renting studio space as well as maintaining their city apartment seemed prohibitive, so they decided it was time to purchase a house in Calgary. This would become their permanent residence as well as Norma's studio, while their beloved Valnorma would still be available for recreational use.

After nearly 13 years, Norma left Mount Royal College on excellent terms. In April 1955 she submitted her resignation to conservatory director Harold Ramsay, who replied that he "very much regret[ted]" her decision and hoped she would reconsider.[102] To her great satisfaction, she was told that the board of governors of Mount Royal College had expressed regret at her decision and had passed a "unanimous resolution of appreciation for your loyal and efficient service."[103] In late May, Norma was honoured by the staff at a farewell party, but it was not until they moved into their new home at the end of June that the couple allowed themselves the happy anticipation of the next phase of Norma's professional career.

Chapter 9

Norma & George: The Studio Years
1955–1972

With the purchase of a house in Calgary and the opening of a private studio for Norma, 1955 started a new phase of life for the Pocaterras. Although they had spent most of their time in Calgary over the past decade, their transient lifestyle of weekday apartment living and weekends out at Valnorma had prevented them from feeling really settled as part of the community. With a house in the city, they now had scope for entertaining and could become more involved in the musical and cultural life of Calgary.

Even after they moved into Calgary, they still visited Valnorma frequently, always expressing great joy to be "home" again. Their original plan had been to decamp there entirely each year when Norma ceased teaching for the summer. This occurred for several years after they bought their city home, but they found it difficult to get reliable tenants for only two months of the year and abandoned the plan after 1960. Since their visits to Valnorma were less predictable, George had to resign from his position as water-level reader on the Ghost River. The horses were pastured with kind neighbours, the Richard Butters (who also did their haying), but the Pocaterras took great pleasure in locating and riding them whenever they visited their "ranch" to do chores. George sadly noted in his diary the deaths of his two old friends, Darkie in 1951 and Grey Cloud in 1959.

To help fund the house purchase, which cost them 15,800 dollars, George revived the idea of subdividing the Ghost River property for summer cottages. They had one and a half miles of riverfront along their land, and George's plan was to develop lots on the opposite side of the river from Valnorma, on the 145-acre parcel known as Chio-abba-tinda ("the spruce meadows" in Stoney). George may have tried to interest his wealthy sister, Marta, and her husband in the idea, promising to repay them 9,000 dollars through a clause in his will, but nothing seems to have come of this scheme[1]

The only investors seem to have been Ken and Betty McIntosh, who advanced the Pocaterras 4,000 dollars in 1955 for the development of six lots.[2] George and Norma were glad to have the loan, the bulk of which became the down payment on their Calgary house, but unfortunately for the McIntoshes, the Pocaterras had a different understanding of the terms of the loan. Not only did they take 13 years instead of 10 to repay the money, but they had to be reminded several times to make annual payments and seemed surprised when the McIntoshes referred to the previously agreed interest due on the loan. After several slight reductions in the amount owing, the debt was finally repaid in 1968.

Family relationships were sometimes strained during this period. The money disagreements following Dr. Piper's death had caused some tension among the Piper siblings, but Norma had gradually re-established friendly relations with her family and they looked forward to receiving a jar of Valnorma honey each year at Christmastime. However, negative feelings that had formed during the couple's Italian years lingered, and the brothers still mistrusted and disliked their brother-in-law. On their infrequent visits, the Pipers were uncomfortable and annoyed by George's domineering manner with Norma. After a particularly boring visit, during which he felt frustrated because he was not allowed to play with any of George's interesting Native artifacts, young Michael Piper (Lawrence's son) concluded that Uncle George disliked children.[3]

This conclusion would have surprised George who viewed himself as tolerant and affectionate with Norma's young students and often commented in his diary quite favourably after visits from various children of their acquaintance. Possibly he (and Norma) viewed their close, almost daily association with children through her work as compensation for never having had children of their own. During their early years together, Norma's career had come first. As George had later explained to a distant cousin, "Norma is a coloratura soprano and we were warned that it was quite usual for such high voices to lose the top notes after giving birth." When they married, Norma had promised her father they would wait until her career was established before starting a family, but their future plans clearly assumed the eventual addition of "Junior." However, their subsequent experiences affected them deeply. As George had continued to his cousin, "We just managed to get back to America four weeks after [the war] started, but lost almost everything. And with such a slaughter going on we did not feel encouraged to bring children into such a world mess."[4] They might have modified this view over time, but when they moved to Calgary Norma was already in her 40s and once again busy career building. In any case, neither of them ever expressed regret publicly or privately with regard to their childlessness. They concentrated on enjoying the children they knew and on their own relationship as a devoted couple.

Always impatient and rather imperious, as he aged George seldom troubled to soften his manner and often appeared abrupt, dismissive and rude. Ghost River neighbours sometimes felt sorry for Norma, who patiently bore the brunt of his frustration and displeasure when things went wrong at Valnorma.[5] Even her young students were shocked by his loud outbursts and demanding behaviour, which sometimes interfered with their lessons.[6] But after all their years together Norma was used to George's moods, understood him thoroughly and still adored him. The feeling was mutual, and although he sometimes spoke roughly, George could be very charming and loving with his wife, whom he invariably called "my Norma." Acquaintances thought their loving ways were very sweet; they went everywhere together and often held hands. The relationship was old-fashioned and simple: Norma deferred to George in everything, even allowing him to choose her clothing,[7] and George, in turn, was loving and protective even while he domineered over his docile "little girl." Their bond appears to have been mutually satisfying; after one particularly trying visit with the Pocaterras, Jack asked angrily how Norma could put up with George's behaviour, and she replied simply, "I love him, Jack."[8]

The Pocaterras' new house was a nice, modern bungalow in a new part of Calgary known as Glengarry subdivision now known as Richmond Park. It was located at 3003 25th Street South West, right across from where the new high school to be named after Dr. Piper's old friend R. B. Bennett, since 1941 a viscount, was being built. They moved in at the end of June 1955. Norma loved the scope that the big corner lot gave for gardening and, with George's help, established large flower and vegetable beds and eventually a small greenhouse. George bragged to the Mathers that the house was located "on one of the highest parts of the city; the air is simply wonderful as it is 400 feet above the waters of the Bow river. We have a gorgeous view of the Rockies from our dining room windows, from the den … and from the kitchen. We have a drive-in garage, a comfort on a stormy day, and 150' on Richmond Road, and 110' on 25th St. S.W."[9]

Norma on the steps of the Pocaterra home at 3003-25th Ave. S.W., Calgary, ca 1955. GA PA-2393-9-5-1

With a house to maintain in the city, the pattern of their lives changed, and by the 1960s trips to Valnorma were made only occasionally—in nice weather— to check on the cabin and the "livestock" (at first, horses and chickens, but eventually just the bees). They still relied on "Jeepy" for visits to Valnorma and a continual round of errands in Calgary, which usually included stops at Italian grocery stores and bakeries in Bridgeland and at Rideau Music for student books and supplies. They attended any opera productions that came through Calgary and were well-known figures at most other musical, cultural and historical events in the city.

Top: Norma in her home studio, Calgary, ca late 1950s. GA PA-2393-12-2-1

Bottom: George on Darkie and Norma on Grey Cloud during a visit to Valnorma, August 1956. GA PA-2393-16-1-1

One of the Pocaterras' first purchases for their new city home was a beautiful old piano, acquired through a friend for only 550 dollars.[10] Norma's music studio was in the living room, which was dominated by the piano and a big easy chair where George sat during lessons. Students were impressed with ornate vases, pictures and mementoes of the Italian years and with large portraits of the couple on the living room wall. George's portrait had been painted at the Buffalo Head Ranch in the 1920s by Ted Schintz, a Dutch painter who spent a summer with George during the dude days and later made the Highwood his home. The portrait of Norma that hung by its side was painted by one of her mature male students, Michel Michoustine; commissioned by George in 1967, it was copied from a photograph of Norma in *Lucia* costume, taken by George in 1936 in Italy.[11]

Students from this period remember Norma as a kind and gentle teacher who concentrated more on developing a love of singing than on teaching technical skills. By and large, she allowed her students to set their own programs according to their individual musical interests. This approach partly reflected a change in the kind of student she had as a private teacher. Generally, her students after 1955 were taking lessons for recreational reasons rather than for career development. She enjoyed teaching beginners and had become known for her patience and success with young children. This is not to say that she did not develop or attract some serious students during her private-studio years, but even with these students her approach was much less structured than that of other teachers, and some of the more ambitious among them eventually "graduated" from Norma to other singing teachers with more technically demanding programs.

Despite this change in orientation, Norma happily prepared students to compete in the local musical festivals or to take Royal Conservatory exams. When she allowed less able students to compete, and even encouraged their less-than-stellar efforts, some teachers viewed her as less competent or lacking in judgment. But admirers chose to view these incidents as indicative of Norma's inherent generosity toward anyone interested in music. Calgary Kiwanis Music Festival secretary Florence Musselwhite observed, "Norma wasn't in it for the glory; she was in it because she loved the kids and she loved music."[12] This was echoed by both of Norma's long-time accompanists, who agreed, "Norma just loved to teach."[13] Noting the lack of competition among students at Norma's studio and her own lack of "ego" at the festival, one accompanist concluded, "Winning wasn't the main object for Norma."[14]

With every student, Norma taught basic skills such as scales and breathing techniques, never criticizing a student's effort or chiding lack of practice. Several former students thought they worked harder for Norma out of love than they did for other technically more demanding teachers, one recalling fondly, "Norma challenged but never pushed."[15] She never raised her voice but was firm in a calm, quiet way. Although she did not pressure children to earn certificates, she spent many hours helping to prepare those students who wished to try exams or compete at the music festival. She wrote out scales and music, recorded practice tapes, arranged choir numbers, prepared pronunciation guides and served as a role model by demonstrating techniques and singing along with the students during lessons. Advanced students studying operatic arias loved the accompanying acting lessons in which Norma taught them dramatic flourishes and useful techniques such as how to "faint" or "die." She encouraged a confident stage presence by relating examples from her own career, and rather than appearing to brag, she spoke unselfconsciously of her triumphs as matters of fact. A favoured few students were allowed to view her scrapbooks and costumes.

Sheet music for "Cavatine de Leila" from "The Pearl Fishers." Handwritten by Norma, ca 1950s. GA M6340-191a-1-p29

George was still very much a fixture in Norma's studio, but his presence in the living room of his own home seemed more natural and was better tolerated than it had been at the college. Because the studio now consisted of a high proportion of beginners, there was less for George to concern himself about technically in Norma's teaching. His involvement mostly consisted of sitting in his easy chair, switching his lamp off and on while ostensibly reading and interjecting the odd comment, criticism or piece of advice, usually in Italian. By this time Norma had been teaching successfully for many years and probably had little need of his advice or support, but because he was very knowledgable musically and his criticisms were constructive and to the point, older students usually understood the value of his contribution. Norma was grateful for his ongoing involvement, always sharing with him the credit for her teaching success. She told one interviewer, "George and I love our work and our students."[16]

This attitude was transmitted to her students and they accepted George's presence during their lessons as a given. However, their parents and Norma's accompanists privately considered him a "disruption," particularly near the end of his life when he was bedridden and often "cranky." They admired her devotion, but grew tired of George's continual demands for Norma's attention, even during lesson times; he would call peremptorily from the bedroom "NORMA!" and she would cheerfully excuse herself to attend to him. First-time and younger students often found George "scary," especially if their behaviour aroused his disapproval. Even older students were a little intimidated. In spite of his "big smiles and twinkly eyes," 17-year-old Eve Zacharias quickly realized that George was "a force to be reckoned with" and worried more about his reaction to her singing than pleasing mild and gentle Norma.[17] Still, most students eventually discovered that George's gruff exterior masked a kindly interior and a genuine interest in their lessons and success. In fact, he truly enjoyed interacting with Norma's students, and young singers who found favour were often asked for a hug and a kiss when they finished their lessons; "tanti baci" (lots of kisses) he would say as he pointed to his cheek. Often the young sons and daughters of Norma's mature students and accompanists spent lesson times waiting for their mothers while perched on George's knee.

He was delighted to assist the more advanced students with the pronunciation in their Italian songs and arias. In fact, although it was not credited, his main role in Norma's studio was clearly indicated in her publicity material of this period, which advertised "Instruction in English, Italian, French, German, Spanish and Latin diction," all clearly George's domain. Sandra Munn, a young pianist who had won a scholarship to study in Siena, Italy, went to George for Italian lessons for some months before her departure in the summer of 1961. She remembered the sessions fondly, not so much for the help with Italian vocabulary and pronunciation but for George's long discourses on various aspects of Italian culture, Norma's reminiscences about grand opera in Italy and the warm atmosphere created by the couple as they plied her with their homemade San Giorgio wine and Italian meals that included Norma's excellent zabaglione.

The promotional brochure for Norma's studio advertised that she was a registered music teacher of "Bel Canto Singing and Voice Production." Although she taught a variety of voices over the years, because of her own background and technique young girls with soprano voices tended to predominate. Since she herself had a somewhat girlish, even flirtatious personal style, some observers found it amusing that her students at the annual music festival typically were pretty little girls in party dresses and singing similar songs year after year. Talented mothers contributed to this illusion by creating beautiful costumes, some of which were remembered with envy by participants years later. One of the most distinctive was created by Lil Wilson, who made matching dresses decorated with a big musical staff and notes for her young daughters, Cheryl and Melody.

In reality, Norma tolerated a wide variety of voices and musical styles, and her students sang everything from popular tunes to classical opera at the thrice-yearly studio recitals. No matter what they sang, she never let them strain their voices or sing beyond their scope and "always got a beautiful tone from her students."[18] This ability was applauded publicly by Reverend Dr. Frank S. Morley of Grace Presbyterian Church. In a letter to the *Albertan* in 1963, he said, "Mrs Pocaterra has developed a large class of pupils to whom she has passed on her tremendous knowledge and training. Her pupils all possess the exquisite bell-like purity of tone and superb platform manner, so that even the weakest of voices is a delight. All their words, but especially their Italian, are beautifully enunciated, while their singing is easy and unlabored."[19]

To save money, but also to create rapport and a more intimate atmosphere, Norma usually accompanied her students on the piano during regular lessons and hired accompanists only for the practice period leading up to recitals. In her early years at Mount Royal College, she had used various accompanists shared with other teachers at the conservatory, but had eventually settled on Edith Scott, who assisted her from 1948 to 1954. During her private-studio years Norma again employed various accompanists, but she favoured four who served in succession and occasionally overlapped: Millicent Mauchline, an "amazing lady" who accompanied Norma's recitals from 1959 until her death in 1967,[20] Elsie Wiebe (1968–1972), Susan Milner (1972–80) and Sylvia Jones (1974–80).

Norma met Susan Milner through her father, Norman, who owned the nearby Texaco service station to which "Jeepy" frequently headed for maintenance and repair. In the early 1970s she asked the teenager to become her Saturday accompanist and noted in her diary that Susan was "thrilled" to be playing for the students.[21] After the children left, Susan often stayed on for a second hour to accompany Norma's own singing practice. The ritual at the end of the session was always the same: Norma would accompany Susan to the door, take the girl's hand in both of hers, and slip a folded and previously hidden five-dollar bill into her hand. Norma exuded great personal charm, and in spite of the big difference in their ages, their friendship lasted until Norma's death.

Sylvia Jones first met Norma in the late 1960s, when she was hired by one of Norma's advanced students to accompany for an important music exam. Recognizing a kindred spirit, Norma later wrote in her diary, "Going to enjoy her"[22] and invited Sylvia to become one of her regular accompanists, an arrangement that lasted as long as Norma continued to teach. The two women were very compatible and sometimes attended local musical functions together. Before or after lessons and rehearsals, they usually made time for a cup of tea, served impressively by Norma from her beautiful Italian silver tea service.

Norma's recitals maintained the same basic format she had developed at Mount Royal College: the younger students performed before the break, often in duets or threesomes, and the older students performed after the break. George took a lively interest in the placement of the students, and before each performance began he usually called Norma over to suggest some minor improvement that she patiently executed. With more than 50 students in her private studio, she was able to add a new dimension to the recitals with the introduction of the Norma Piper Pocaterra Singers, a massed choir with all students dressed alike in simple costumes of white "angel" gowns with coloured bows tied at the neck. The massed choir sang at the beginning and end of each recital, an experience that helped to give cohesion and build friendships in Norma's studio as well as preparing the students for group appearances at other community events. Occasionally Norma had her students perform a very ambitious number for the recital finale, something requiring exciting dramatic touches or simple costuming, which enhanced the confident stage presence of the students involved.

As always, the penultimate act of every recital was Norma singing one of her big operatic arias in full costume to the delight of the audience and to a great storm of applause. Very occasionally, in later years she performed a duet with a capable student: arias from *La Boheme* (1966) and *La Traviata* (1972) with Charles (Charley) Western and the duet from *Lucia* with Doreen Chinneck (1974). For the first few years after she started teaching privately, the recitals were held in the Richmond School auditorium. In 1959 she switched to the Golden Age Club auditorium on 11th Street Southwest, and when this was torn down in 1974, she moved to the Pleiades Theatre in the new planetarium, where she stayed until she ceased teaching in 1980.

In various combinations and groupings, the Norma Piper Pocaterra Singers appeared at many local musical events in the community. They sang on the Rocket 4 Club on CFCN television, at Flare Square during the Calgary Stampede and frequently at hospitals and seniors' homes. They were particularly busy around Christmastime and participated in the Calgary Junior Chamber of Commerce Christmas Carol Festival for a number of years, as well as the

The Norma Piper Pocaterra Singers in recital at the Golden Age Club, Calgary, ca early 1960s. GA PA-2393-5-1

Woodward's Department Store "Breakfast with Santa" events. The Norma Piper Pocaterra Singers also did very well at the Calgary Kiwanis Music Festival, usually achieving first or second place in every category they entered. On several occasions Norma was delighted with adjudicators' private comments, which she recorded in her diary; the two that brought her particular pleasure were "you [all] have good teachers but this girl [one of her students] is wonderfully trained,"[23] and "you're lucky kids having so wonderful a teacher."[24] She was so busy and musically fulfilled during her private-studio years that she declined an offer in 1962 to become director of the Golden Age Club Choir.

Norma's advanced students also usually did very well at competitions, often earning high marks and awards. Norma had been pleased when a few of these students had followed her from Mount Royal College to her private studio and was particularly proud of Dorothy White, Lois Callaway and June Forsey Rance. Dorothy started with Norma in 1946, studied with her until 1963 and was featured at a number of local musical events and on radio and television. June Forsey Rance started studying with Norma at age nine in 1947 and continued with her for 10 years. She won a number of awards, including the Birks trophy (for highest marks overall at the Alberta Musical Festival) and silver medals from the Toronto Conservatory of Music.

Lois Callaway had the distinction of being the first "very young student" ever taught by Norma. In an article entitled "On Teaching the Very Young Student," which Norma wrote in 1969 for submission to the Canadian Federation of Music Teachers' Associations News Bulletin, she recalled thinking that Lois was far too young for singing lessons when her mother had brought her to the Mount Royal College Conservatory in 1944.[25] Only six years old, Lois had "a tiny sweet voice" and was eager for lessons. Her mother, who was very musical, had been training her voice at home on their farm near Cochrane. After she heard Norma in concert, she was determined to have her help in developing Lois''s potential as a coloratura soprano. In spite of Norma's reservations and George's objections about attempting to teach such a young child, Mrs. Callaway persisted in her pleas and Norma finally agreed to become the little girl's teacher.

Lois Callaway with Birks Trophy, Calgary, 1948.
GA PB-589-9

Just a few years later, Lois fulfilled expectations, by earning the highest marks in Alberta in the Grade I singing examination and, in consequence, the Birks trophy and the first of many silver medals from the Royal Conservatory of Music in Toronto. Won over, George now called her "my little girl" and revealed to her "a heart of gold" beneath his "blustery" exterior.[26] Lois continued with Norma until 1956 and was featured in a number of local live and radio performances and on a local version of "Singing Stars of Tomorrow" on television station CFCN in 1954 and 1955. Although she impressed local scouts with her voice, at the time she was too young to compete at the Toronto competition, and "Singing Stars of Tomorrow" had ceased production by the time she reached the requisite age of 18 in 1956. Subsequently, Lois became a music teacher and music program adviser with the Calgary Board of Education.

In contrast to Norma's early years at Mount Royal College, there were many singing teachers offering programs in Calgary when she started her private studio. More than a dozen affiliated with the Alberta Registered Music Teachers Association (ARMTA) advertised themselves in the *Calgary Herald* at the beginning of the school year in September 1955, and undoubtedly there were a number of others who were unaffiliated. Although Norma still managed to attract a number of accomplished singers, some of the more serious students went on from her to study with other well-known teachers who were able to build on the musical foundation she provided. Among those talented students who started with her, studied with other teachers and eventually continued into musical careers were Carol Holder, Jamie MacKinnon and Molly Blanchfield Hamilton.

Carol Holder studied with Norma for several years in the early 1960s, then with Blaine Chapman. She won the highest vocal award, the Stutchbury Cup, at the Calgary Kiwanis Music Festival in 1966, performed locally in concerts and on television and sang in the Calgary Theatre Singers production of *The Sound of Music* in 1966 and with the Calgary Philharmonic Orchestra in 1965 and again in 1969. Jamie MacKinnon studied with Norma from 1966 to 1974 and later with Blaine Chapman. She won 50 firsts at the Calgary Kiwanis Music Festival and many other awards, including the Pocaterra Rose Bowl and the Norma Piper Pocaterra Scholarship, and she later pursued a singing career in opera. Molly Blanchfield Hamilton started with Norma in 1975 and moved on to other teachers only when Norma stopped teaching in 1980. In 1976 an agent for the Calgary Stampede discovered her and she started a long and successful concert and recording career as "Miss Molly." The Huget family, mother Angela and five children, also studied with Norma in the late 1970s, took many awards at the Calgary Kiwanis Music Festival and enjoyed wide popularity performing locally as a family act.

Norma was always very supportive of her students, recording their Royal Conservatory marks in her diary and always attending their performances at the music festival. While this support was appreciated by her own students, some pupils of rival teachers found the Pocaterras' presence in the audience unsettling.[27] As a form of encouragement, Norma had a habit of mouthing the words to every song for her own students and seems to have done the same thing sometimes while other competitors were singing. Probably because George was hard of hearing (he wore a hearing aid after 1957), the Pocaterras always sat at centre front during the festival and whispered back and forth throughout the performances; sometimes students suspected they were making critical comments or deliberately trying to unnerve them. More likely, they were just commenting on the pieces and performances and unaware of the stir they were causing.

Norma had a reputation for being very fair, always willing to compliment a good performance no matter whose student sang well. Florence Musselwhite, who was involved with the Calgary Kiwanis Music Festival as assistant secretary and executive secretary from 1960 to 1976, described her as "one of the least egotistical teachers" she had known during those years, never quibbling about marks or expressing any jealousy of other teachers or students.[28] However, there seems to have been an undeclared rivalry between Norma and another singing teacher during this period that fuelled George's antagonism.

Eileen Higgin had started teaching in 1943, about a year after Norma, but she employed a very different teaching style. Unlike the more operatic, bel canto approach favoured by Norma, Eileen prepared students to project their voices for the musical stage, and in 1960 she formed the popular Calgary Theatre Singers. Her husband, Elgar Higgin (also a singing teacher), was very involved in his wife's activities and was president of the Calgary branch of the Alberta Musical Festival Association from 1950 to 1953 and then remained active on the advisory committee until 1969. Although their approaches were so different, many observers remember a definite feeling of rivalry between the two women. In local musical circles, there was even a suspicion that Eileen's heavy involvement in the Banff School of Fine Arts summer programs from 1948 to 1960 as co-ordinator of singing and associate producer of operatic productions effectively precluded Norma's involvement at the school.[29]

Norma herself maintained a discreet silence throughout, never admitting to any jealousy or rivalry, and indeed may have felt none because of her non-competitive approach to lessons and the festival. She and Eileen were both active in ARMTA, and when they served together on the executive and various committees, as they sometimes did, it was essential for the sake of the group that they smooth over differences and get along. Generally George followed Norma's lead, refraining from comment in his diary when students occasionally decided to try lessons with the more dynamic Eileen and declining to gloat when they switched back to Norma. However, sometimes he thought he detected bias in the adjudicating at the music festival in favour of Eileen's students, and sometimes he suspected that her husband's position was the cause. He vented his frustration in his diaries, complaining at various times throughout the 1950s: "Adjudication most unfair, very unsatisfactory and smells to high heaven," "adjudication unfair. Seems like the old racket," and "adjudication again favouring the H's."[30]

It seems George was not alone in his dissatisfaction. In 1951 there was a flurry of letters to the editors of both Calgary daily newspapers. George's own letter provoked an angry response from Elgar Higgin on the *Calgary Herald*'s Letters page. In his capacity as president of the Calgary branch of the Alberta Musical Festival Association, Elgar demanded that the writer who signed himself "Also Interested" (whom he must have known was George by the Cochrane address) "submit proof of alleged dishonesty regarding contestants performing in the classes other than those for which they are eligible" (George's accusation).[31] Because George had no real proof, the controversy died down. However, 10 years later, George was so incensed with the adjudicator, who he felt "*again* showed unfairness, partiality and inconsistency in his judgements," that he sent letters of protest to both newspapers, although he was persuaded by the *Calgary Herald*'s city editor to omit Norma's name from the complaint.[32] George's diary entries during the 1965 festival were also pointed and bitter: "He knows better but to me it looks like [the adjudicator is] being influenced by the usual dishonorable people," and "[he is] continually influenced by favouritism. He knows but is not honest in placing the winners. Influenced by the usual racketeers. H—"[33]

Luckily for Norma's professional reputation, George usually confined his observations to herself and to his diary, and she earned admiration from others in the music business for rising above the petty squabbles entertained by some teachers on behalf of their students. As Sylvia Jones remarked, "She just ignored all the rivalries and backbiting" that occasionally infected the festival.[34] Tellingly, Florence Musselwhite observed Norma many times at the festival congratulating the students of "rival" teachers who she thought had performed well.[35] Norma proved herself magnanimous in other ways. If a student returned to her after trying other teachers, she was very gracious and, to their relief never held their temporary defection against them.

She also supported her students and former students by attending as many of their shows, concerts and public performances as she could, and she never saw this as an onerous duty or charged them for her professional time. Often she was specifically contracted to help a student get ready for a part in a musical production or for singing at some special occasion, such as a wedding, so the number of student performances to which she was invited was considerable. Similarly, she supported other teachers and musical colleagues by attending their events, even concerts by current and former rivals Odette de Foras and Isabelle Logie Herd. In fact, their generous attendance record eventually earned the Pocaterras a reputation for supporting anything musical, theatrical or cultural that occurred in the city.

While at Mount Royal College, the couple had started the tradition of sending a Christmas card to each student. These cards, which also went to family and friends, usually featured a photograph of Norma in opera

A Pocaterra Christmas card, Calgary, ca 1960s. The photograph shows Norma in costume for one of her favourite operas, "Lucia di Lammermoor," Milan, ca 1936. GA PD-184-8-22

Season's Greetings

Norma Piper Pocaterra
in
Lucia di Lammermoor

Mr. & Mrs. George W. Pocaterra
3003 - 25th Street S.W.
Calgary, Alberta, Canada

261

costume, a scene from the couple's Italian years or, later on, pictures of Valnorma and the Pocaterras themselves. Students often treasured these cards, which contained not only a brief description of the opera or scene depicted on the front but also a personal message from their teacher. Another treasured gift for older students getting married was Norma and George's standard wedding gift of an Italian etching. Of course, these were the same etchings that had given George so much grief over the years, but now they were framed and proving their worth as esteemed wedding gifts from the Pocaterras to family members and young friends. To make the gift more meaningful for the recipient, the couple often provided details about the artist and outlined the scene's significance for themselves. This tradition started when the financially struggling Pocaterras realized the gift potential of the etchings and gave them to Norma's brothers and other friends who married in the 1940s, and it survived into the late 1970s.

Now that the Pocaterras were living in Calgary, Norma found more time for professional activities and became very involved in the Calgary branch of ARMTA. She had started on the executive in 1951 as the singing teachers' representative and from 1953 to 1955 was treasurer. She was pleased to be included as a member of the executive in receptions for visiting musical dignitaries such as Edward Johnson in 1951 and Sir Ernest MacMillan in 1955. Also in that role she took part in the celebration parade during the province's jubilee year, 1955, George proudly noting in his diary, "Norma beautiful on the ARMTA float."[36]

Norma riding the Alberta Registered Music Teachers Association float in the Jubilee Parade, Calgary, 1955. GA PA-2393-9-1-1

In 1956 she became vice-president of the Calgary branch of ARMTA, and in 1957 was she elected president. In that year, the Calgary branch hosted the 20th annual ARMTA provincial convention, inaugurated a series of bimonthly recitals at the Calgary Allied Arts Centre's Coste House for advanced students of ARMTA members and sent students to perform on a weekly local radio program, "Music and the Lively Arts," hosted by the director of the Calgary Allied Arts Centre, Archie Key. Dorothy White was featured during this series, and Lois Callaway sang six songs in a second series later that year. For this

262

second series, 10 programs prerecorded in June 1957 and aired at a later date, Norma substituted as host for the vacationing Key, during the hour-long program, she delivered musical commentary punctuated by classical and operatic record selections, conducted interviews and featured talented students and their work. In this period Norma also served occasionally as a singing adjudicator at various music festivals, including the Indian School Festivals held on the nearby Sarcee and Stoney reserves during the late 1950s.

In 1959–60, Norma was the Allied Arts Centre representative on the executive of ARMTA and organized a fundraising benefit for the centre's building fund by co-ordinating (and performing in) a concert entitled "Springtime in Music," presented by ARMTA members at Central United Church. Her involvement at the Allied Arts Centre also led to membership with George in the Calgary branch of Jeunesses Musicales, a group dedicated to the musical development of young people. Social convener of the Calgary branch of ARMTA in 1961, Norma was vice-president again in 1962 and president for the second time in 1963. During this year, the Calgary branch again hosted the ARMTA annual convention in Banff at the School of Fine Arts, but Norma's proudest achievement was the research and printing of a little booklet

Top: George in Calgary, 1956.
Portrait taken for Calgary Power Ltd.
GA PA-2393-14-1-7

Bottom: Norma in Calgary, ca 1950s.
Studio portrait by Matthews.
GA PB-589-5

of "regulations." The booklet was designed to address the problem of missed lessons and dropouts before the end of term, and members eagerly purchased the booklets to hand out at lessons. After this busy year and the next, when she was past president, Norma's active participation in ARMTA declined, though she became more involved again in the mid-1970s after George died. Along with other past presidents, she was honoured by the Calgary branch in 1974 for her leadership and presented with a silver spoon.

Throughout this period Norma continued to sing when invited, but big public engagements were very few. She sang "O Canada" at the opening of Banff Indian Days in 1951, was the entertainment on the program of various club meetings and fundraisers over the years, entertained at several ARMTA annual conventions and sang "Ave Maria" and "The Lord's Prayer" at countless weddings and funerals. Bigger opportunities to sing presented themselves only occasionally. Accompanied by Phyllis

Chapman Clarke, she sang selections from *The Barber of Seville* and *La Traviata* during inauguration ceremonies for the new Southern Alberta Jubilee Auditorium in Calgary in May 1957. Later that year, and accompanied by Sandra Munn, she sang at the Jubilee Auditorium for a radio broadcast sponsored by Calgary Power Limited and part of a series called *Henry Plukker Presents the Story of Music*. Norma's segment consisted of doing vocal demonstrations and singing snatches of songs to illustrate commentary provided by Plukker, conductor of the recently formed Calgary Philharmonic Orchestra. Hopeful that this experience might lead to some work with CBC Radio, Norma made several audition tapes in December 1957 and sent them to her old friend Dick Claringbull, now manager of the Edmonton studio. He duly sent the recordings on to the Winnipeg office for adjudication, but no offer was forthcoming.

One of Norma's last public singing engagements was with the "Volunteer Vaudeville" presented in 1963 by the Calgary Volunteer Bureau on behalf

Program for Volunteer Vaudeville, Calgary, September 24, 1963. GA M6340-202-1

of the United Fund (the precursor to the United Way). In the program she was listed as "Calgary's beloved coloratura soprano," and she sang an aria from *The Barber of Seville* accompanied by Phyllis Chapman Clarke Ford. When Phyllis retired in 1968, Norma was asked to give the official speech at the ARMTA dinner in her honour. With characteristic grace, she gave an amusing tribute to her old friend, and it was "very well received."[37] Honouring another old friend, four years earlier she had made "a marvellous presentation speech" at Helen Boese's retirement celebration.[38] As opportunities to sing declined, invitations to speak and be interviewed became more frequent. In 1967 she was asked to speak about *Don Pasquale* on the CFCN television show *Calgary Today* before a production of the opera opened in the city, and in 1979 her interview with local broadcaster Mona Cozart was included in a CBC Television program entitled "Famous Opera Stars."

Initially the media were drawn to Norma because of her very visible role in the cultural life of the community, but George's early days in Alberta as an explorer and rancher became more interesting to interviewers as the city grew up and looked back to its pioneer roots. Encouraged to share his memories, George spoke about his adventures on the Highwood to various groups including the men's Canadian Club, the Kiwanis Club and the Cosmopolitan Club. These speaking engagements prompted him to reflect on his life, with the satisfying conclusion that he had no regrets. Writing to Raymond Patterson in 1961, he said, "Though I am quite happy and contented in my present way of life, I shall always look upon that period and the time of having been able to realize the dreams I had since my earliest childhood, a time of physical hardships and of wonderful exaltation and satisfaction, a time of something more than just material and intellectual enjoyment, but also of character building and spiritual development, and I would not hesitate an instant in choosing the whole again, had I the opportunity of re-incarnating again under the same circumstances, hardships, heartaches, disappointments and all."[39]

George had a great zest for living, enjoying each phase of life as it came to him. Sixty years earlier he had revelled in life on the range and in the mountains; now he found the stimulation of city living invigorating and was continuously busy. Without obvious regret, he confessed to Dr. Morlan: "For several years I have only taken trips in the car, not because I don't feel up to my old ability, but mostly because there is so much else to do now, and being adaptable I DO enjoy it all."[40] In addition to the many musical and cultural events that now claimed his attention, he was an active member of the Beekeepers Association and enjoyed attending literary and historical lectures.

In 1963 the Historical Society of Alberta taped George speaking to the group about his relationship with the Stoney First Nation and his early explorations with them in the mountains. Although his words and attitudes might be considered patronizing and politically incorrect by today's standards, he genuinely tried to enlighten his non-Native audience about traditional Native values, hoping thereby to increase their respect and understanding. His description of the Stoneys' nearly vanished way of life and plea for cultural understanding was eloquent, and that year the society published his talk as an illustrated article entitled "Among the Nomadic Stoneys." Several years later, the society again featured him on a panel discussing early ranching and the traditional Native way of life.

Increasingly, George worried about the declining lifestyle of "his Indians" on the new Stoney reserve at Eden Valley, created in 1948 on Frazier Hunt's old ranch property, and he was saddened that so much of value from their traditional life had been lost over the years. He wrote:

Then they had ability and COULD rely on themselves to solve any problem of life that could arise THEN ... Now they are continually told that they had better learn the whiteman's way, and forget the old ways. I feel sad when I talk to the young fellows ... they have NEVER known the real Indian way of Life, as I have. It also disturbs me when I hear or read statements by 'phony people making themselves up as Indian experts ... HOW can any whiteman know anything about such a different people as the North American Indian, when they do not know the language, when they have NEVER lived with them as one of them?[41]

However, George attended with interest meetings of the new Friends of Indians (later, Indian Friendship) Society. Although he was somewhat dubious about the efficacy of the group ("words, words" he said after the first meeting in 1959[42]), he admired the good intentions of some members, particularly Ruth Gorman, and often gave his own support to Native issues, particularly issues affecting the Stoneys. In 1954 he had written to H. M. Jones, director of the federal Department Indian Affairs, protesting the proposed route of the new Trans-Canada Highway south of the Bow River since the route would further divide the Stoney Reserve, already crossed several times by the existing Calgary-to-Banff highway and the river itself. George had patiently explained to the government official: "The Stony Indian Reserve would again be divided, leaving the Indians with FIVE LONG NARROW strips of land to their credit. When one takes account of the fact that the Stonies are mainly raisers of cattle and horses, you will easily understand at what a disadvantage they would be put to in grazing and watering their stock under such handicaps."[43]

Afterwards he was disgusted by the insensitive way in which the government handled the issue and wrote bitterly to Raymond Patterson:

> You probably heard all about the bitterness engendered amongst the Stonies on account of the uncouth and dictatorial way the ministry of highways went about surveying the Transcanada across their land, South of the Bow. The Indians stood their ground for over a year, but in the end they were offered more land. They thought that they were going to get it south of the reserve, perhaps on the Jumping Pound, where some of the land is fairly good grazing, but in the end they were granted land North West, on the North of the Bow; burnt-out land, some swamps and sloughs, poor, poor. The Americans may have been hard on their Indians, but at least they have mended their ways now, and are doing quite a bit for them now. We can't be self righteous. We may have tried to keep the letter, but oh! the spirit! How it has had to suffer.[44]

Old Stoney friends Paul Amos and Johnny Bearspaw and their families were regular guests at the Pocaterras' Calgary home and at Valnorma. George hired them and their friends for odd jobs at Valnorma whenever he could, and his account books show a steady record of small gifts of money and sometimes cigarettes. When he visited the reserve, he took gifts of clothing and household items; the Stoneys reciprocated with gifts of game. Ironically, several times he lent them his old Native outfits, with which they won prizes at Banff Indian Days and the Morley stampede. Saddened by Paul's death in 1958, George recorded in his diary, "Paul gone. My dearest Indian friend."[45] After Paul's death, some of the younger members also benefited from occasional gifts of money from George and later Norma. Paul's grandson, Donald Rider, visited the couple so often that one of Norma's students assumed he was an adopted son.

Top: George in the Pocaterra
Creek valley, ca 1960s.
GA PA-2393-14-1-6

Bottom: George and Norma in the
Kananaskis Valley, ca late 1960s
GA PA-2393-16-1-3

Social and gregarious, George loved to entertain and be entertained, and the Pocaterras' social life in Glengarry consisted of endless evenings of dinners, slide shows and lively conversation. Often Norma prepared an Italian meal that included zabaglione and "very strong coffee" (cappuccino), but occasionally they made another old favourite, "Buffalo Head Beans." And, of course, they always served their San Giorgio wine, which George now made from grapes crushed in a homemade press. His diaries show a loving, affectionate side that he demonstrated publicly, even before guests, who were charmed by the romantic old couple punctuating their conversation with endearments. One visitor to their home was amused by an incident that typified their relationship: Norma was hovering while George attempted to carve a roast. Eventually, sensing his frustration, she asked, "Darling, am I in the way of the light?" to which he replied, "You're very beautiful, darling, but hardly transparent." This rejoinder was so appreciated by the listener that it was incorporated into her own family's conversational shorthand.[46]

The Pocaterras' love of entertaining was facilitated in the 1960s when they found they could afford a weekly housekeeper. For several years they paid a woman named Ilse to help Norma with the heavy work, the cleaning and laundry; then, in 1966, they hired Brigitte Klouth, who cleaned for them for the next 15 years. During their years of employment the women became friends, brought their families to visit and even attended Norma's student recitals. With their usual personal charm, the Pocaterras reciprocated with invitations, gifts and even a few loans and gifts of money.

In addition to entertaining old friends like Ernest Mather, Jack Fraser, Harry Hutchcroft and Mrs. Harper Sibley when they came through Calgary on short visits, George maintained a regular correspondence with pals from his dude ranch days. His regular correspondent and occasional visitor Raymond Patterson had sold the Buffalo Head Ranch to P. Burns and Company in 1946 and moved to Victoria to concentrate on his writing career. When Patterson first informed him of his intention to sell the ranch, George wrote "You are absolutely right about the two of us having had the best there was to get out of the old place." He reassured his old friend, "Do not think for one moment that I entertain any feelings of regret. One thing LIFE has taught me is never to look back … And I am happy that you sold BHR in a way satisfactory to you. I know you have loved my old home well."[47]

George reconnected by letter in 1960 with Amelie de Vauclain Tatnall. Long since married and living in Philadelphia with a husband and four nearly grown children, Amelie corresponded with the Pocaterras for several years. In her first letter, after a gap of 35 years, she referred obliquely to her foolhardy adolescent infatuation for George by describing the growing pains faced by her own teenaged daughter: "If only I can remember that nothing at this age is permanent and slowly good sense and reliability will come."[48] The Pocaterras tried to interest Amelie in their spiritual study of the yoga philosophy, "trying to learn the answer to some of Life's Riddles."[49]

Her responses were polite but distant, and the correspondence gradually faltered, then ceased.

On March 5, 1963, George and Norma marked the 60th anniversary of his arrival in Canada with a quiet celebration. Always a healthy man, George stayed active even as he aged. An operation on his left knee in December 1963 slowed him down only for a few months, although it failed to correct his slight limp. Very involved and visible in the community, the Pocaterras were increasingly viewed as a pair of slightly exotic and charming eccentrics, a view reinforced by Norma's public persona, which somewhat incongruously combined glamorous diva with girlish charm, and by George's old-world manners, forceful personality and increasingly erratic driving style. During an extended visit to the Pocaterras, nephew John (Jack's son) soon discovered one reason for his uncle's lack of control while driving. Much to his consternation, he observed Uncle George looking away from the road whenever he talked to his passengers. This bad habit did not seem to worry Aunt Norma.[50] In 1962 the Pocaterras traded their original Jeep for a newer, green· one (also known as "Jeepy"); George actually rolled this vehicle in a ditch in 1965.

The Pocaterras loved to meet and entertain new acquaintances made through their many cultural activities, people such as local pianist Gladys McKelvie Egbert, theatre director Betty Mitchell, artists Jim and Marion Nicoll and *Albertan* social columnist Eva Reid. George was particularly

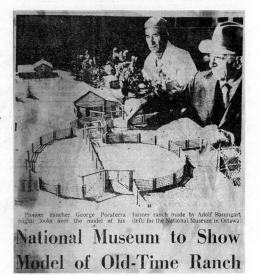

Pioneer rancher George Pocaterra former ranch made by Adolf Baumgart (right) looks over the model of his (left) for the National Museum in Ottawa.

National Museum to Show Model of Old-Time Ranch

Article in the Calgary Albertan on completion of the Buffalo Head Ranch model by Adolf Baumgart, August 5, 1964. GA M6340-v3-p21

pleased to reconnect with his old foreman, Adolf Baumgart, when he returned to Alberta with the help of Raymond Patterson and George himself after the war. Married and living in Calgary, Adolf occasionally did little building projects for the Pocaterras at their Glengarry home and sometimes accompanied them on visits to old friends from their Highwood days.

Adolf and George became involved in the early 1960s in a project for the National Museum of Canada. In 1961 Raymond Patterson had published his book *The Buffalo Head*, recounting early days on the ranch and in the Highwood. In 1962 assistant director Clive Wilson decided that the Buffalo Head would be the perfect ranch to represent western pioneer days at the museum and contacted George as the ranch's original owner. George recommended Adolf, whose trade was carpentry, to build the scale model and agreed to provide text for the accompanying labels.[51]

Some of George's pleasure in the project faded when he visited the Buffalo Head with media people after the model's completion in 1964. Confronted with the many changes to the house and property that had occurred since the last time he had seen the ranch, he complained to Raymond Patterson that the De Paolis, who had bought the ranch from P. Burns and Company in 1949, had "ruined the place."[52] On another occasion, after he toured the North American representatives of the Italian airline Alitalia through the Buffalo Head to show them "a real western ranch," he grieved to Patterson, "It hurt my heart to see what my old home had come down to ... Oh! jerum, jerum, jerum! oh! quae mutatio rerum! [roughly translated as "Oh dear, oh dear, oh dear! How things have changed!"] I was a fool to return to it at all. One should Never try to turn life's pages back again."[53]

George and Norma at Italian Bakery, Calgary, 1958. GA PA-2393-12-2-2

In addition to disappointment at seeing changes to his old ranch, George was critical of the De Paolis' lack of hospitality. Although they were Italian, George felt no bond: the De Paoli family had immigrated from the south of Italy; he was from the north and of a higher social class, and he made no effort to hide his contempt for people whom he described as "peasants." They, in turn, considered George's behaviour rude and were angered by his dismissive and overbearing manner.[54] Although it made for several awkward visits, their antipathy was not unusual at the time; complicated social relationships among Italian immigrants of differing regions and social backgrounds frequently caused friction in the Calgary Italian community during the post-war period.[55] However, George supported local Italian businesses whenever he could. He and Norma included the Italian Supermarket and the Italian Bakery in their weekly shopping excursions, called on the Shatto brothers for construction projects at Valnorma and relied on photographer Tony Attanyi to produce their annual Christmas cards. George was also active in the Calgary Italian Club, which acknowledged his role as an Italian pioneer by presenting him with a pen in 1961.[56]

One of George's Italian Canadian friends was Antonio Rebaudengo, who had been appointed Italian consul in Calgary by Mussolini in the late 1930s but continued in the role unofficially after the war. In addition to helping new Italian immigrants with settlement issues, Rebaudengo and his wife, Angelina, were often called on to meet and entertain officials and other dignitaries visiting from Italy.[57] Since the Rebaudengos admired and respected George, the Pocaterras met most of these visitors as well. In 1966 they were invited to attend a banquet for Senator Giorgio Oliva, undersecretary of state for foreign affairs and visiting from Rome. Seated across from them, the senator showed great interest in George's experiences in Canada and requested that he send a snapshot of himself to the Italian foreign office. George was delighted with the outcome: "Imagine our surprise when I received a very complimentary letter from him, and later on copies of two different Italian newspapers with full page articles telling about my life in Canada, and with my photo in the middle!"[58] Similarly, after entertaining two young professors from Rome, George received copies of articles about him they had published in Italy and also in the Toronto-based Canadian Italian newspaper, *Corriere Canadese*.[59]

In 1968 George felt honoured to be asked to submit entries for Norma and himself for inclusion in the publication *Who's Who in Alberta*. In his usual flamboyant style, he introduced Norma as a "noted Canadian coloratura soprano" and described her operatic career at home and abroad in great detail. Not surprisingly, he included the usual story of wonderful opportunities lost when the couple had been forced to flee Europe in 1939. Referring to himself as a "retired rancher," he detailed his involvement with the Buffalo Head Ranch and noted that he was probably the first white man to see Kananaskis Lakes from the south. His concluding remarks were revealing: "Mr Pocaterra has a great love and knowledge of music, a cultured patron of the arts. His list of friends includes many world-famous musicians, writers, businessmen as well as innumerable Alberta cowboys and Indians. He speaks many European languages fluently, is widely read, a student of history, a quiet and modest man. His proudest boast is that he is a Canadian and an Albertan, not by birth but by choice. The things he values most in life are ranching, friends, music, and a charming wife."[60]

In the late 1960s, when George was in his mid-80s, his health began to decline, and the Pocaterras decided that it was time to revisit Italy. They had considered an offer from Marta in 1965 to help them with their passage money, but George wanted his first trip away in 25 years to be to the west coast and the Pacific Ocean, and so they travelled to Vancouver that summer. They had tickets booked to visit Italy in 1967 but Marta's husband, Filippo Larizza, committed suicide that spring, and they cancelled those plans in consideration for his widow. Instead, they made their first trip east since the war to visit family and friends in Montreal (where they toured Expo 67 with Jack and his family), Toronto and New York State. The next year, George was sufficiently anxious to see his family and birthplace one last time that he started making definite plans. To earn a little extra income, in 1968–69 the Pocaterras appear to have boarded a former student of Norma's now studying at Mount Royal College.

In the fall of 1969 the Pocaterras decided to raise additional funds by selling some of the Ghost River property. In a long and detailed letter to Harry Strom, premier of Alberta, Norma requested that they be allowed to sell part of the property, explaining that they had always paid taxes separately on the two distinct parcels that constituted their land: the 20.8 acres where Valnorma was located and the 145 acres known as Chio-abba-tinda located above the cutbank on the south side of the river. The land was naturally divided by the river and was not even accessible as a parcel; the Valnorma section was accessed by a trail through Agness Hammond's property from Highway 1A northwest of Cochrane, and Chio-abba-tinda was serviced from the west by the Keystone Valley road.

For two decades, George had tried to promote river lots for summer cottages but—although he finally received approval for their development in 1962—the project never progressed. He told a friend in 1963, "If I had known what I was running into with the burocratic [sic] red tape, and all the expense it was going to entail before anything could be made out of it, I would never have gone into it."[61] The provincial planning board stipulated that a proper gravel access road be built before any lots could be sold, and when George realized that the cost of this plus a complete survey of the lots would amount to 14,000 dollars, he reconsidered. In checking with the government about income tax implications he also learned that if he sold the lots one at a time, he would be considered a developer and taxed accordingly, but if he sold Chio-abba-tinda as a single parcel of land there would be no income tax levied.

The choice was clear, and around 1960 George had started conducting friends and prospective buyers up onto Chio-abba-tinda on horseback, promoting this part of the property for its recreational use. There were many inquiries and even a few tentative offers, but it was not until 1969 that a good offer to purchase the parcel came from Walter Shatto, co-owner of Shatto Construction Company Limited in Calgary. It was Shatto's offer that precipitated the Pocaterras' request to have Chio-abba-tinda legally separated from the Valnorma part of the property. Without legal separation, they would not be able to sell, so Norma begged the government to give their request every consideration. As she explained in her letter to Strom, "For 66 years [George] has contributed to the development of this country … living through depressions and hard times, and this is the first opportunity he has had to realize something for his labours, and a chance to take a trip. We have never been back to Italy in 30 years to see his remaining relatives." [62] To their relief, the planning board approved the subdivision of the property in the fall of 1969 and the final papers for Chio-abba-tinda were signed in April 1970.

After the demise of Mineral Resources Limited in 1958, George had managed to reclaim the coal leases. The next year, on February 17, 1959, he and the Shatto brothers had formed a new company, Pocaterra Mines

Limited. Promoting the steam-generating potential of its coal, Pocaterra Mines had attracted the notice of Japanese and German electrical companies. Even the City of Calgary had expressed interest in using the coal for thermal power production. By 1970 several companies had taken out options on the property, and George was delighted to note in his diary: "Much interest in the coal. Six companies are after it."[63]

In good spirits, the Pocaterras finally took their long-awaited trip to Italy. In a nod to modern convenience, they flew from Calgary to New York on July 24, but the rest of their trip "home" was sentimental in every detail. The 10-day journey from New York to Genoa was on SS *Leonardo da Vinci*, and they stayed for three weeks at the Grand Hotel Duomo in Milan. While there, they revisited many of their old haunts and George had a grand reunion with his sister Marta (Emilia had died in the early 1960s) and with various nieces, nephews, relatives and friends. The return journey from Venice on SS *Cristoforo Columbus* ended in New York City on September 8, and they returned to Calgary by air the same day.

After their trip to Italy, George began to age quickly and experience several falls. Possibly aware that their time together was coming to an end, in June 1971 they commissioned Tony Attanyi to create a charming anniversary portrait of

George and Norma on their thirty-fifth wedding anniversary, Calgary, June 18, 1971. Photographer Tony Attanyi. GA PA-2393-9-4-1

themselves. Posed under a tree in their back garden, with frail-looking George seated and Norma standing lovingly at his side, the couple look fondly into each other's eyes. As George's health declined, this became Norma's favourite picture, hung in a place of honour over his chair in their living room. The first Christmas after his death, Norma used it for her greeting card, adding the caption, "Sweethearts for thirty-seven years—Love's radiant sunshine in your dear dear face."[64]

In mid-September 1971 George entered Sarcee Auxiliary Hospital, a nursing home located just a mile from their house. As Norma explained to one of his old friends, "he suffered no pain and his mind was constantly alert. He just was not able to walk and he gradually got weaker."[65] In fact, he was still so alert during most of his hospital stay that he helped

Norma to compose letters in Italian to his family and corrected her pronunciation when she read their replies. During the six months that George was in hospital, Norma continued their routine at home, giving as many lessons as ever, and visited the hospital at least once daily. There she assisted George with eating, bathing and shaving, held his hand, read to him and continued to work on the story of his life, which she had started writing with his help during their trip to Italy. The full title of the lengthy manuscript in Norma's handwriting is a fitting tribute all on its own: "Son of the Mountains: The Story of George W. Pocaterra, Pioneer Alberta Rancher, Explorer and Friend of the Stoney Indians." George lived for Norma's visits, and even when he was reduced to a liquid diet, he still loved the zabaglione she prepared at home and took to the hospital. Just a few weeks before he died, he told one of his nurses, "I have the finest wife in the world."[66]

George died quietly on March 13, 1972, with Norma by his side. He was 89 years old. The funeral service took place on the morning of March 16, and among the many floral tributes, Norma placed in George's hands three red roses: one for Marta, one for Emilia's sons, Franco and Sergio, and one for herself.[67] The morning funeral service took place at McInnis and Holloway's Park Memorial Chapel and Norma's student, Angela Huget, sang the solo "Ave Maria." Among the honorary pallbearers were Walter Shatto, Michel Michoustine and Charles Western. Interestingly in view of George's long absence from the Roman Catholic Church, while the Reverend Lucien Bianchini officiated at the funeral home, the bishop of Calgary said a mass for George at St. Mary's Cathedral. Through Father Bianchini, Norma later donated 100 dollars to the Sisters of the Precious Blood as a thank you for the church's services.[68] By his own wish, George was cremated, so after the funeral service Norma simply returned home with a few friends and had a quiet lunch with Sylvia Jones.

Grateful for the press coverage of George's death, Norma dutifully collected newspaper tributes and had them translated to send to George's family overseas. The tribute on CBC Radio that played on the afternoon of the funeral especially pleased her. It was prepared by local broadcaster Temple Sinclair, who was a personal friend. As a young man in the late 1940s, he had taken singing lessons from Norma at Mount Royal College, and she had sung at his wedding in 1951. She was overwhelmed by the public outpouring of sympathy and fond remembrance that followed George's passing, and it took her many weeks to answer the more than 100 letters of condolence. Recognition of his early contributions had continued to build from the 1960s, and at the time of George's death a documentary film on his life was being prepared by the Alberta Department of Education for use in the elementary school curriculum.[69] Unfortunately, many interviewers had not realized the importance of harvesting George's memories until it was too late, and after his death they had to be content with Norma's sometimes sketchy version of her husband's experiences.

Typically, as soon as George died Norma began to plan a Memorial Recital. It occurred at the Golden Age Club on March 25 and featured her students singing and herself performing an aria from *Madam Butterfly*. In tribute to his long support of the arts, on May 13 she presented the George W. Pocaterra Rose Bowl in his memory at the Calgary Kiwanis Music Festival, a prize that was to be awarded each year to the winner of the Italian Opera Solo class.[70] The first winner of the Pocaterra Rose Bowl was Norma's own student and George's friend, Michel Michoustine.

Portrait of George by Ted Schintz, ca 1920s. GA PA-2393-14-1-4

Norma was very touched when some of her mature students arranged to reframe the 1920s Buffalo Head portrait of George by Ted Schintz and presented it to her after their June recital. At about this time, she finally collected George's remains from the funeral home, but there is no indication of their ultimate disposal. Norma had continued to visit Burnsland Cemetery in Calgary every year in early September to leave flowers on the graves of her father and Aunt Susie, but she never mentioned George in this context. Possibly he had requested that his ashes be scattered at the Buffalo Head or on the Morley Reserve or in his beloved Kananaskis Valley. Although her diary maintains a discreet silence, she did revisit all these areas in a day-long excursion with a friend in August 1974 and may have performed a private ceremony on that occasion. But it is equally possible that Norma simply scattered George's ashes at Valnorma during her first sentimental visit in July of 1972 to the home they had built together and loved so well.

Chapter 10

Norma: Alone Again
1972–1983

After George's death, Norma's life continued in the same long-established groove for another decade. Naturally, she missed him and loved to reminisce in her diary and with friends about their wonderful life together, particularly on significant anniversaries such as his birthday, death date or their wedding anniversary. But Norma was a practical person and did not brood. In fact, she heartily enjoyed a friend's recounting of a dream about George, in which he had said, "Tell Norma that my limp is almost gone. I can almost walk normally now. I'm still working on my spiritual limp."[1] Forced to be more independent over several years as George's health had declined, she continued driving "Jeepy" and doing her own yardwork and snow shovelling until she was forced to give up the house in her early 80s.

Soon after George died Norma investigated selling Valnorma, but she did not find the right buyers until Kenzie and Faye Macleod approached her in 1975. Since they had moved into Calgary in 1955, the Pocaterras had spent less and less time at Valnorma, and as George had aged the cabin had fallen into disrepair. After George's death, Norma spent many strenuous weekends working at Valnorma, sometimes with the help of friends, getting the cabin ready for sale: oiling the log exterior, tarring the roof, laying a new floor, painting the floor and walls and improving the road. The property was quite isolated, and neighbours concerned about trespassers were anxious to see it occupied. By 1975, management of the property was too much for Norma. She was very happy when Royal Canadian Mounted Police officer Corporal Kenzie Macleod approached her after discovering while he was investigating a nearby break-in that the property was for sale. Undeterred by her asking price of 27,000 dollars, the Macleods completed the purchase of Valnorma in October 1975. A year later, Norma finally sold George's old Buffalo Head brand for 100 dollars to Louis De Paoli, who had coveted the brand during his 25-year ownership of the Buffalo Head Ranch but had never been able to persuade George to sell.

Although she cleared out some books and other personal possessions, Norma was surprisingly unsentimental about the contents of Valnorma and left it furnished even with her family piano and the old Buffalo Head Ranch cookstove. However, she was somewhat dismayed on her first visit after the sale to discover that the new owners had made some minor changes and improvements and were calling the property "Pocaterra" (they later reverted to the name Valnorma). But she was flexible in her thinking and voiced her approval of other little improvements on subsequent visits. Typically, she remained friendly with the Macleods, and they visited her, Faye even attending her student recitals. Some time after they purchased Valnorma, the Macleods discovered three trunks full of old papers—including diaries and letters—in the long-disused chicken house. Norma had forgotten about the trunks and was delighted with the find, and she spent many happy hours reliving old memories while sorting through the papers before eventually donating them to the Glenbow Archives. Over the years the Macleods honoured the original owners by minimizing changes to Valnorma, keeping and using most of the original furnishings and lovingly restoring the old cookstove and piano.

A year later, George's dream of developing his coal claims finally came to an end. Soon after his death, the Shattos had taken over the direction of Pocaterra Mines Limited and continued serious discussions with various electrical companies interested in the coal for steam generation. At one point their discussions apparently featured "figures in the millions of dollars," but all negotiations were suspended in 1976.[2] That year, the Alberta Department of Energy and Natural Resources adopted "A Coal Development Policy for Alberta," which provided guidelines for categorizing coal applications. Since the designation of Kananaskis Provincial Park occurred only two years later, it is likely that negotiations with Pocaterra Mines were suspended because the company's properties fitted within Category 1 of the regulations (no exploration or commercial development permitted in parks, protected, research or recreation areas).[3]

She no longer gave public performances, but Norma was often invited by friends to sing at weddings and funerals. Students and friends who were fond of her found her voice on these occasions as beautiful as ever, though less-biased observers now described it as starting to sound "old." At times she was brutally honest in her diary on this matter, on one occasion writing, "I taped my voice. Very bad. I didn't realize how badly I was singing."[4] She continued practising daily, telling an interviewer in 1978, "Singing has always been very important to me ... I keep on doing it because I love it and will keep on doing it until my voice gives out."[5] She was never disappointed with the audience reaction to her performances at student recitals and always recorded her impressions: "Tremendous applause," "got a standing ovation," and "everybody impressed with my singing."[6] Naively pleased by compliments, she also noted with pleasure such polite fictions as "the years haven't changed you much," "you get younger every day," and "someone said I didn't look a day over 19 at the recital."[7]

Right to the end of her teaching career, Norma maintained her interest in ARMTA, serving as "voice representative" on the executive in 1973, on the social committee in 1974 and as vice-president for a third time in 1979. Occasionally she was asked to adjudicate at music festivals in Red Deer and Edmonton, and once in Calgary in the music category of the Golden Age Club's "Olympic Games." Financially comfortable, she was one of the original supporters and subscribers to the Southern Alberta Opera Association when it formed in 1973, and in 1972 she endowed a Calgary Kiwanis Music Festival prize of 100 dollars, the Norma Piper Pocaterra Scholarship for Junior Folk Song.[8] Two years later she moved the scholarship from the folk category and asked that it be awarded annually to junior, intermediate and senior students in the Light Opera category. In 1975 she added another 50 dollars to the scholarship so that 50 dollars each could be awarded to the three winners of the Light Opera classes. In 1976 she added another scholarship of 100 dollars in George's name for the most outstanding performance in Italian Art Song.[9] During the 1970s these generous activities earned her a well-deserved reputation as a "fervent supporter of the arts in Calgary."[10]

With her long hair dyed light brown or blond and rolled up and pinned to frame her face, and wearing the youthful style of dress encouraged by George, Norma still looked much younger than her advancing years. She carefully omitted any reference to her age in sessions with interviewers, who gamely helped her to keep "her greatest secret."[11] In 1971 one reporter enthused, "She still retains that great beauty and poise that an opera singer must have … instant vivacity, enthusiasm, and warmth … Her unusual voice was a gift, of course, but her energy and how she persevered in training that voice and the courage required to be a solo performer, has never left her."[12] Another termed her "the happiest and most well adjusted person I know,"[13] and she confirmed this assessment herself by telling a third, "I have loved teaching singing. It's a wonderful life—I wouldn't change it for the world."[14]

George had absorbed most of Norma's attention and energy, particularly in later years, and consequently she had had neither the time nor motivation to develop new friendships of her own. Instead, she had continued to visit old friends and to enjoy casual friendships with musical colleagues. She looked forward to the weekly visit of her housekeeper, Brigitte, and usually cooked a roast that day for the two women to share at lunchtime. Norma was very loyal to old friends, and in addition to receiving gifts and loans of money over the years, Brigitte was remembered generously in Norma's will.

After he died, Norma continued to visit George's old friends from his ranching and dude days. It was after one of these long pilgrimages with Adolf, several years after George's death, when they went to visit Sam Smith in High River hospital, that Norma used George's old nickname, Pokey, for the first and only time in her diary.[15] She also kept in touch with George's family in Italy, their Italian friends in Calgary and some of his Stoney friends and their descendants. In 1973 she gave most of George's clothes and "Indian costumes" to Johnny Bearspaw, though she kept for herself several items, including his bathrobe and a favourite old outfit to wear while gardening. She gave financial help to Donald Rider several times over the years in fond memory of his grandfather, Paul Amos.

With widowhood, Norma expanded her social circle but came to rely on a select few friends, particularly her long-time next-door neighbour, Betty Goodman, and Dorothy Hawley, who quickly became her best friend. Miss Hawley, who lived quite near the Pocaterras, had introduced herself to them in the mid-1960s. At the time, she had been teaching French at Viscount Bennett High School directly across from the Pocaterra home, and she asked their help in identifying a piece of opera music she had heard and was still able to hum but could not place. George immediately recognized it as being from Verdi's opera *Nabucco*, and thus began their acquaintanceship. Miss Hawley was added to the Pocaterras' circle, but she found George a little too domineering and the friendship remained casual for several years.

In 1972, after she had returned from a big post-retirement trip overseas, Miss Hawley discovered that George was in hospital, so she reconnected with Norma, who was lonely on her own. But the friendship took off only after George was gone. At the first opera presented by the newly formed Southern Alberta Opera Association several months after George's passing, Miss Hawley met Norma in the parking lot and observed that the older woman had to clamber awkwardly out of her Jeep in evening attire. Impulsively, she offered to drive Norma to subsequent operas. Sharing a passion for music and opera, the bond between the women developed quickly, and soon they spent much of their free time together attending social as well as musical events or spending quiet evenings at each other's homes watching Miss Hawley's television set or simply doing little chores such as mending or taking turns reading out loud. Miss Hawley began attending Norma's student recitals, supporting her as George had done in the past by helping with ticket taking and attending to innumerable details. In spite of their intimacy and in the manner of the times, it was several years before Norma allowed herself to call her friend Dorothy, even in the privacy of her diary.

Norma also relied on her older students and colleagues for friendship. Her first Christmas alone, she was very pleased when Dorothy and Clayton Hare not only invited her to their annual party but also accompanied her singing of "Ave Maria" for the entertainment of other guests. Although she sometimes found her teaching schedule exhausting, she truly enjoyed her students and formed a close relationship with many of them. In 1976, at the age of 78, she still noted "terrible long" teaching days, sometimes 8 or 10 hours in length, but also said, "I'm enjoying my students and I know they are enjoying me."[16]

In many ways, after George died Norma's students became her substitute family. She often bought an extra ticket to a musical event and invited a friend or student along as her guest. Students and young friends honoured in this way had very fond memories of Norma, who always dressed up in long gowns and her black velvet cape or fur coat and projected a regal, diva-like quality while sweeping them along with her into an exciting, glamorous, grown-up world. Still vain about her appearance and now able to afford more luxuries, she convinced herself after some debate that George and her father would have approved and treated herself to a new mink hat in 1973, a mink stole in 1974 and a stylish leather hat and coat in 1975.

Norma encouraged her older students to attend several times when the Southern Alberta Opera Association performed, and she usually bought a block of seats for opening night so that they could all sit together and attend the reception afterwards. Dorothy Hawley usually attended along with the students, who knew her well from her presence at their recitals. She and Norma always went to at least one further performance of each opera, often accompanied by other students. Norma felt the experience of opera differed from location to location and made sure they sat at the very back of the auditorium (her favourite location) at least once for each opera.

Given her family's dislike of George, it was not surprising that Norma drew closer to the Pipers after his death. Relationships strained by George's sometimes obtuse treatment of his in-laws gradually healed. For the next eight years, while she was able to travel, Norma made a number of trips to visit her brothers and their families in Montreal, the Toronto area and Vancouver and was delighted by the fuss and attention accorded her. With no children of her own, she found her nieces and nephews charming. In turn, although they considered her something of a character, the younger Pipers were fascinated by her stories of grand opera and her diva-like transformation when she performed for them. One memorable Christmas, she entertained Lawrence, his wife, Nora, and their extended family in Vancouver with several operatic selections and was accompanied the entire time by the yowling of the resident cat, Sam. The family was both mortified and amused, but Norma's legendary calm remained intact; unruffled, she simply praised Sam's good taste in music and thanked him for the "kiss" on her cheek.[17]

Dick Piper stayed with his sister several times on his way from his home in Ontario to visit Vancouver, and in 1975 she was delighted when all of her brothers assembled in Calgary for a family reunion that included Jack's daughter, Julia. After several days of fond reminiscing, Norma reported, "They all had a real good get-to-gether and I'm so happy we had it."[18] Sharing a lifelong bond with his older sister, Jack made her several generous gifts near the end of her life: 100 shares of stock, in 1976 (which she sold through A. E. Ames and Company for about 1,000 dollars),[19] and a holiday to England in 1979 to visit the Piper and Mill family sites with himself, his wife, Betty, and their brother Dick. (Larry had had surgery several months before and could not join the party.) Norma had a wonderful time in England, and after their return she worked for several weeks creating trip diaries for her brothers.

In 1978 she attended the official opening of Kananaskis Provincial Park (later renamed Peter Lougheed Provincial Park) as a platform guest. Although she enjoyed meeting Premier Lougheed, backcountry lodge operator Lizzie

Rummel and other notables during the festivities, Norma knew that the honour bestowed upon her was actually in tribute to George. This was confirmed with the announcement that the ski hut in the park was to be named after him. In fact, the new park abounded with names honouring its early explorer: official ones like Pocaterra Creek, Pocaterra Trail, Pocaterra day-use area, Elpoca Creek, Elpoca Falls and Elpoca Mountain, and unofficial ones such as Mount Pocaterra, Pocaterra Tarn and Pocaterra Ridge (which George had called Pocaterra Peaks).[20] Norma was well satisfied and told a reporter, "I think George would be quite pleased with the area now that it's all grown up again," adding, with evident pride, "I'm also thrilled to death that they are recognizing George."[21] She regretted his absence at an occasion he would have loved and noted in her diary the sad irony of the dedication date: September 22, George's birthday.

Norma Pocaterra at the opening ceremony.

George Pocaterra honoured

Right; Norma at the opening of Kananaskis Provincial Park in 1978. Cutting from the Crag & Canyon, September 27, 1978.

Left; Norma at Pocaterra Creek, ca late 1960s. GA PD-184-8-221

Unlike George, Norma suffered from increasing ill health as she aged. She had frightened George in 1952 when severe pain led to an emergency appendectomy and again in 1962 when she underwent a hysterectomy and follow-up radium treatments. He was worried and lonely, and when she returned home he wrote in relief, "God Bless Her! Wonderful to have her back home!!! God be thanked."[22] Sometime during her 70s, Norma developed diabetes and then peripheral arterial disease. She complained in her diary for years about sore feet and legs, and there were many references to her trying various homeopathic cures and to having frequent blackouts and "bad spells" as a result of her circulation problems. Several times she scared young students by fainting during lessons, one "spell" in late December

1977 resulting in hospitalization for a few days. Accustomed to looking after the house and yard by herself since George's death, she was touched when her friends and students rallied to her aid by shovelling snow and running errands. "What lovely friends I have," she observed gratefully.[23]

By 1980 the circulation in one of her legs was so bad that gangrene set in, and Norma had to have it amputated below the knee. With this change in her life, she was forced to give up her house and her teaching and to enter Bethany Care Centre. Family and friends were impressed with her bravery during this period of crisis, her lack of complaint and her calm acceptance of this new direction in her life. Her naturally optimistic and determined nature rose to the occasion, and she learned to walk with a prosthesis, which she nicknamed "Abigail." [24] One of her proudest moments was the first time after surgery that she walked down the aisle of the Jubilee Auditorium. Using a cane and leaning on the arm of Charlie Chinneck, husband of student Doreen, she ascended the stage before the April 1980 production of

Norma, Calgary, 1979. Photograph by Paul Godin accompanied Calgary Herald article by Eric Dawson, July 23, 1979. GA PA-2393-12-2

La Boheme to accept a floral tribute honouring her professional and singing careers and her generous early support of the Southern Alberta Opera Association.[25]

Once it was clear that Norma would not be returning home from the Bethany, Jack arranged for the house to be sold to fireman Jeff Orton and the contents divided. But first he honoured Norma's wish that the Glenbow Museum be given the Ted Schintz portraits of George and Paul Amos, which had been admired by the museum's director of Collections, Hugh Dempsey, during social visits to the Pocaterra home. Learning from Jack that except for a few items gifted to family members, everything else belonging to the couple was to be included in an upcoming sale, Dempsey suggested donation to the museum and the Glenbow Archives of all important personal papers, photographs and artifacts relating to the Pocaterras. Norma acquiesced.

Only days later, Jack and Betty held the sale at which many former students, glad to acquire a memento of "Mrs. Pocaterra," eagerly paid a token price for everything from a beaded evening purse to the piano on which she had taught for so many years. Florence Musselwhite was asked to sort and dispose of several boxes of old sheet music that had been in the home, and she chose to give Norma's many friends and admirers first opportunity to acquire these items, many of which had been autographed by Norma Piper Pocaterra. For many months, favoured clients were allowed to go into an inner office at

Rideau Music to select a memento of Norma's long career, and eventually the hoard was dispersed. When Mrs. Musselwhite took the proceeds to the care facility, Norma was at a loss as to what to do with the money, but eventually she asked that it be donated for the residents' pleasure.

This decision was in keeping with Norma's positive attitude while at the Bethany. After her surgery and consequent relief from pain, friends noted that her old personality reasserted itself, almost as if she had "regained her life."[26] She was full of fun and loved to entertain the other residents of the nursing home with music and stories of her days singing in grand opera. Some of her friends and former students were faithful visitors to the end, gathering en masse with her each October to celebrate her birthday, even continuing the tradition of meeting together for several years after her death. One long-time student, Sophie Kok, helped Norma to make some progress in writing the story of George's life (and Norma's own) by typing the laboriously handwritten manuscript "Son of the Mountains".

By 1983 the circulation in Norma's other leg was so poor that it required amputation as well. Her brother Jack rushed to her side and called in for consultation their nephew Michael, Lawrence's son, who was an orthopaedic surgeon in Vancouver. Unfortunately, as Michael observed, the second amputation was "too little, too late,"[27] and this time Norma never recovered. She died at Calgary General Hospital on July 10, 1983, and was buried with her father and Aunt Susie at Burnsland Cemetery on July 13.[28]

Long-time friends from her teaching days provided the music at the funeral service held at McInnis and Holloway's Park Memorial Chapel on July 14. Sylvia Jones played the organ and accompanied Sophie Kok and Doreen Chinneck in the duet "Belle Nuit" from *The Tales of Hoffmann*. Norma's brothers Jack and Dick attended the service (Lawrence was too unwell to travel), as did Jack's children, John and Julia; Dick's daughter, Pamela; and Lawrence's son, Michael, and his wife, Shirley. Among the honorary pallbearers were Charles Chinneck, Dr. C. W. Kok, Kenzie Macleod, Michel Michoustine and Walter Shatto. After the service, the Chinnecks hosted a reception for family and friends at their home in Lakeview.

In tribute to good times together, Doreen Chinneck collected 1,000 dollars from Norma's last students and their families to subscribe for a seat plaque in Norma's honour at the new Calgary Performing Arts Centre, which opened in 1985. Doreen had conceived of the plan because, shortly before her death, Norma and a few close friends had subscribed for a similar plaque in George's name. Fittingly, their seats sit side by side in the Jack Singer Concert Hall.[29] Norma's substantial donation to the new Performing Arts Centre during its fundraising campaign prior to construction also resulted in plaques in the lobby honouring herself and George, alongside many other leading names from the Calgary arts community, as "Pioneers in the Arts."

In addition to serving as co-executor of the estate with Jack Piper, Dorothy Hawley was remembered generously in Norma's will, as were Norma's brothers, nieces and nephews. With no children of her own, Norma had arranged that in addition to financial bequests her family also inherited various possessions, including the old silver pieces brought from Italy, her jewellery and various treasured personal items.

Characteristically, Norma also remembered in her will a number of local cultural groups, including her three favourites: the Calgary Philharmonic Society, the Calgary Kiwanis Music Festival (for a scholarship honouring George) and the Southern Alberta Opera Association. In a fitting final tribute, in lieu of flowers at her funeral, mourners were requested to contribute to her memory by donating to the Norma Piper Pocaterra Memorial Scholarship Trust Fund, a prize to be awarded annually to an outstanding vocal student competing at the Calgary Kiwanis Music Festival. These bequests, and her years of serving as "an inspiration to opera enthusiasts and aspiring singers," led one of her many admirers to conclude that at the end of her life "ironically, the tragedy of Norma's career was Calgary's gain."[30]

Two of Norma's most enduring qualities, celebrated after her death by friends and family alike, were her determined persistence and her ability to enjoy the present moment, to make the best of every situation and to be positive and thankful no matter what life offered. Life on the Italian operatic stage, life in a crude cabin in the Alberta foothills—she never mourned what might have been but took each new experience in stride and appreciated it for all it was worth. Soon after she met him, Norma shared her philosophy with George: "Generally I don't long for the past to repeat itself because the future seems so much more interesting."[31] And she had thoroughly enjoyed discovering what the future held for her: a long and loving relationship with a husband she both respected and adored, an impressive talent which she had managed to parlay into a lifelong passion as well as a fulfilling career, and the fond admiration and respect of local arts lovers and generations of students.

Her own summary at age 81 was apt: "I've had a very interesting life, don't you think?"[32]

Epilogue

The Pocaterras continue to haunt their old stomping grounds in Kananaskis Country. While explaining place names in the area, guides and outfitters often relate stories to their dudes of George's early explorations, his friendship with the Stoneys and his futile attempts to get rich by mining coal. Listeners are fascinated with the romantic tale of the rancher who married an opera singer, and they love the local legend: that George called the beautiful valley below Elpoca Mountain after his wife so that "he could look down on his beloved Norma for all eternity."[1]

In the early 1980s, long before the legend grew up, Gillean Daffern submitted the name "Piper Creek" to the Geographical Names Division of Alberta Culture for the stream in the valley that runs out to the Elbow River between Elpoca and Tombstone mountains. The name was rejected at the time, but Gillean decided to include it anyway in her popular guidebooks to Kananaskis Country, reasoning that "if a name comes into general use it will most likely be officially recognized at some point."[2]

Her patience was rewarded. When Calgary concert pianist, music teacher and long-time Norma admirer Dale Jackson inquired about the status of the name more than a decade later, Gillean encouraged him to resubmit it to the government with the backing of the Kiwanis Music Festival committee. Their letter-writing campaign was successful; several years later, on April 22, 2003, the name "Piper Creek" was given official approval based on "demonstrated local usage."[3] With that, a fanciful local legend neatly became a romantic reality.

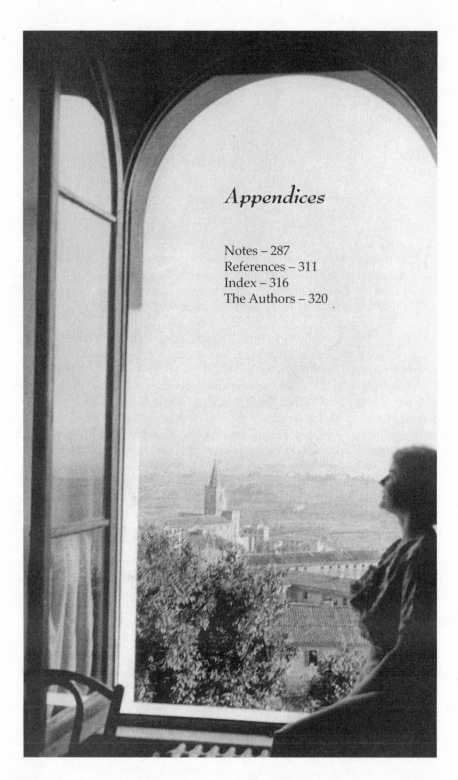

Appendices

Notes

Abbreviations

AHR—*Alberta Historical Review*
Albn—*Albertan*
BCA—British Columbia Archives
CDH—*Calgary Daily Herald*
CH—*Calgary Herald*
Ed J—*Edmonton Journal*
G—George Pocaterra
GA—Glenbow Archives
GW—*Golden West*
Int—Interview with
LAC—Library and Archives Canada
N—Norma Piper Pocaterra
RMP—Raymond M. Patterson
Sat Nt—*Saturday Night*

Chapter 1—George: The Buffalo Head, 1882–1910

1. GA M6340/181 Foreword to "Son of the Mountains," ca 1972. Manuscript biography of George and Norma Piper Pocaterra written by Norma between 1970 and 1972, probably to George's dictation. Much of the information on George's early life was taken from this invaluable source.
2. GA M6340/17 nd fr G to ----[fragment]
3. GA M6340/160 Jul 19/01 fr Lund, Delius
4. GA M6340/144 Nov 27/00 fr Spence to G
5. *Alberta in the 20th Century* pp 138–140
6. GA M6340/18 nd [Jan/69] fr G to Mrs Schwa----[illegible]
7. GA M6340/181 Son of Mtns pp 6–7
8. GA M6340/144 Mar 14/01 fr Spence to G
9. GA M6340/181 Son of Mtns pp 8–9
10. GA M6340/18 nd [Jan/69] fr G to Mrs Schwa----[illegible]
11. GA M6340/181 Son of Mtns p 12
12. GA M6340/18 nd [Jan/69] fr G to Mrs Schwa----[illegible]
13. BCA MS-2762/1/14 Feb 28/56 fr G to RMP
14. Ibid.
15. East Longview Historical Society p 158
16. Patterson, *Far Pastures* p 116
17. BCA MS-2762/1/14 Feb 28/56 fr G to RMP
18. Ibid.
19. GA M6340/181 Son of Mtns pp 18–20
20. BCA MS-2762/1/14 Feb 28/56 fr G to RMP
21. GA M6340/168
22. GA M6340/6 Sep 9/09 fr G to [Mercedes White]
23. GA M6340/181 Son of Mtns p 20
24. BCA MS-2762/1/14 Oct 29/61 fr G to RMP
25. GA M6340/18 nd [Jan/69] fr G to Mrs Schwa—[illegible]
26. According to Raymond Patterson, George's horse brand "started life as a bluebell in silhouette" but was modified when a local justice of the peace remarked that it looked more like an old buffalo skull. (*The Buffalo Head* p 4)
27. GA M6340/17 May 28/63 fr G to Doctor [Morlan]
28. AHR Summer/63 pp 12–13
29. GA M6340/15 Dec 1/55 fr G to Jack Danciger

30. GA M6340/178
31. GA M6340/180
32. GA M6340/14 nd [ca Jan/48] fr G to RMP
33. GA M6340/181 Son of Mtns pp 26–28
34. AHR Summer/63 p 14
35. Ibid.
36. Ibid.
37. BCA MS-93-6227 Dec 1/30 fr RMP to Fenwick
38. AHR Summer/63 pp 16–18
39. BCA MS-2762/1/14 Feb 28/56 G to RMP
40. AHR Summer/63 p 17
41. AHR Summer/63 pp 18–19
42. Patterson, *The Buffalo Head* p 88
43. GA M6340/16 Feb 28/56 fr G to RMP
44. Ibid.
45. GA M6340/17 May 31/62 fr G to Doctor [Morlan]
46. GA M6340/103 Nov 6/09 fr Moore to G
47. GA M6340/144 Oct 18/09 fr Smith to G
48. GA M6340/103 Jun 11 [1910] fr Moore to G
49. GA M6340/103 Apr 8/11 fr Moore to G
50. GA M6340/141 Nov 22/09 fr Mrs White to G
51. GA M6340/141 Oct 8/09 fr Mrs White to G
52. GA M6340/141 Feb 24/10 fr Mrs White to G
53. GA /6 nd [1909] fr G to [Mrs White]
54. GA M6340/6 Sep 9/09 fr G to [Mrs White]
55. GA M6340/6 nd [1909] fr G to [Mrs White]
56. Ibid.

Chapter 2—George: Dudes and Coal, 1910–1933

1. GA M6340/17 Sep 21/61 fr G to RMP
2. GA M6340/6 Mar 22/10 fr G to Mrs White
3. GA M6340/181 Son of Mtns pp 27–28
4. BCA MS-93-6227 Dec 6/30 fr RMP to Fenwick
5. Chiniki Research Team pp 36–37, 39
6. BCA MS-93-6227 Dec 6/30 fr RMP to Fenwick
7. GA M6340/14 Oct 17/47 fr G to Friends [Mathers]
8. GA M6340/6 nd [ca Oct/13] fr G to [Mrs White]
9. BCA MS-93-6227 Dec 6/30 fr RMP to Fenwick
10. GA M6340/144 Jan 12/18 fr Stansleigh to G
11. GA M6340/6 nd [ca Oct/14] fr G to [Mrs White]
12. GA M6340/14 nd [ca 1948] fr G to RMP
13. GA M6340/181 Son of Mtns p 28a
14. GA M6340/165
15. GA M6340/144 Jan 12/18 fr Stainsleigh to G
16. GA M6340/165
17. GA M6340/119 Letters fr Giuseppe Pocaterra to G, 1914–1917 (translated by Evelina DeZorzi)
18. GA M6340/168 Homesteading and ranching documents
19. Patterson, *The Buffalo Head* p 108
20. GA M6340/18 Sep 3/66 fr G to Ed and Marguerite ---- [surname unknown]
21. Colpitts p 40
22. Int Baumgart
23. Sheppard, *Just About Nothing* p 15; Patterson, *Far Pastures* p 139. According to Bert Sheppard, Walter Ings of the Rio Alto Ranch had rechristened Eden Valley "Looney Lane"

after a comic strip of that name. Patterson then elaborated on the theme by adding "Mad Valley" to the description.

24. BCA MS-2762/1/14 Apr 19/38 fr G to RMP
25. *High River Times* Nov 3/21
26. Ibid. Jul 6/22
27. Ibid. Jul 31/24
28. GA M6340/198
29. GA M6340/16 Feb 7/59 fr G to Doctor [Morlan]
30. GA M6340/7 Apr 6/33 fr G to Colin F. Heseltine
31. GA M6340/14 nd [ca Jan/48] fr G to RMP
32. GA M6340/111 Mar 7/63 fr RMP to G
33. Int Page
34. GA M6340/17 Sep 21/61 fr G to RMP. An approximate translation of George's gaucho song: "I have a little ranch—Covered with flowers—All is pretty and small—And there is my love— She is pretty like a star—Soft as honey—No other is as beautiful—This is the life!"
35. GA M6340/17 Jul 27/60 fr G to Morlan
36. Ibid.
37. GA M6340/139 Aug 27/26 fr Amelie to G
38. GA M6340/139 Sep 21/26 fr Amelie to G
39. GA M6340/6 Oct 14/26 fr G to Amelie
40. Ibid.
41. GA M6340/67 Nov 10/26 fr Dippie to G
42. GA M6340/6 nd [ca Oct/26] fr G [to Amelie]
43. GA M6340/6 Oct 14/26 fr G to Mrs Bedingfeld
44. GA M6340/6 Dec 16/26 fr G to Morlan
45. GA M6340/6 Oct 14/26 fr G to Mrs Bedingfeld
46. GA M6340/144 nd [ca Fall/27] fr Doane to G
47. GA M6340/83 Jun 7/32 fr Irving [Hollinrake] to G
48. GA M6340/12 Mar 25/38 fr G to Amelie
49. GA M6340/144 nd [ca Fall/27] fr Doane to G
50. GA M6340/12 Mar 25/38 fr G to Amelie
51. CH May 31/28
52. *High River Times* Dec 5/29
53. Int Baumgart
54. George later told Raymond Patterson that the word *vellita* meant "narcissus" in Serbian. (GA M6340/18 nd [Jan/69] fr G to RMP
55. Int Page
56. Jul 14/32
57. GA M6340/83 Jun 7/32 fr Irving [Hollinrake] to G
58. GA M6340/12 Mar 25/38 fr G to Amelie
59. GA M6340/144 May 10/29 fr McDaniel to G
60. GA M6340/144 Jul 29/30 fr Dept of Interior to G
61. GA M6340/12 Mar 25/38 fr G to Amelie
62. GA M6340/17 Feb 9/60 fr G to Julio Pocaterra Montel
63. Patterson, *Far Pastures* p 4
64. BCA MS-93-6227 Sep 20/30 fr RMP to Fenwick
65. BCA MS-93-6227 Dec 9/30 fr RMP to Fenwick
66. BCA MS-93-6227 Feb 1/31 fr RMP to Fenwick
67. CH Jan 23, Oct 22/32
68. Int Patterson
69. BCA MS-93-6227 Dec 1/30 fr RMP to Fenwick
70. Ibid.
71. BCA MS-93-6227 Nov 9/30 fr RMP to Fenwick
72. GA M6340/14 nd [ca Jan/48] fr G to RMP

73. BCA MS-93-6227 Dec 1/30 fr RMP to Fenwick
74. BCA MS-93-6227 Dec 6/30 fr RMP to Fenwick
75. BCA MS-93-6227 Mar 25/31 fr RMP to Fenwick
76. BCA MS-93-6227 Dec 1/30 fr RMP to Fenwick
77. BCA MS-93-6227 Dec 6/30 fr RMP to Fenwick
78. BCA MS-93-6227 Feb 1/31 fr RMP to Fenwick
79. BCA MS-93-6227 Dec 9/30 fr RMP to Fenwick
80. BCA MS-93-6227 Dec 1/30 fr RMP to Fenwick
81. BCA MS-93-6227 Jun 19/31 fr RMP to Fenwick
82. GA M6340/111 Apr 22/56 fr RMP to G
83. GA M6340/14 nd [ca Jan/48] fr G to RMP
84. BCA MS-93-6227 Sep 20/30 fr RMP to Fenwick
85. BCA MS-93-6227 Dec 9/30 fr RMP to Fenwick
86. GA M6340/17 Nov 11/61 G to Editor, Albn; Albn Feb 12/31; Ed J Feb 16/31; Primrose, Albn Nov 8/61
87. BCA MS-93-6227 Apr 1/31 fr RMP to Fenwick
88. BCA MS-93-6227 Sep 20/30 fr RMP to Fenwick
89. Patterson, *The Buffalo Head* pp 87–88
90. BCA MS-93-6227 Nov 1/31 fr RMP to Fenwick
91. Patterson, *The Buffalo Head* p 88
92. BCA MS-93-6227 Nov 1/31 fr RMP to Fenwick
93. George's name for the lake was never made official. It is now called Abruzzi Lake.
94. Pocaterra, Giorgio. "Nelle Montagne Rocciose della Colombia Britannica." Club Alpino Italiano, Sezzione de Milano, Mar/32. (GA M6340/o.s. Scrapbook, v. 3). Translation by David Finch with assistance from Antonella Fanella.
95. GA M6340/12 Mar 25/38 fr G to Amelie
96. Patterson, *The Buffalo Head* p 107
97. GA M6340/12 Mar 25/38 fr G to Amelie
98. Int Patterson
99. BCA MS-2762/1/14 Apr 25/56 fr G to RMP
100. GA M6340/12 Mar 25/38 fr G to Amelie

Chapter 3—Norma: Life at Home, 1898–1926

1. GA M6340/34 Jul 21/38 fr N to Dr P
2. GA M6340/220 Dec 10/38 fr Dr P to N and G. Although Dr Piper understood from his siblings that his parents had come to Canada with their respective families, there is some evidence to suggest that William Piper emigrated independently. He was recorded in August 1843 along with Richard Mill, his wife and eight children as an "indigent emigrant" requiring government financial assistance to travel from Kingston to Port Stanley. Since there is no mention of any other Pipers in the group, it is possible that William emigrated with the Mills, perhaps as Ann's fiance. (LAC, Dept of Finance records)
3. London City Directories, 1901–1908
4. GA M6340/219 Nov/34 fr Dr P to G ; GA M6340/86 May 23/38 fr Violet Johnston to N
5. *Who's Who in Chicago* p 508
6. CH Jun 24/43; Smith pp 2–9
7. GA M6340/219 May 12/35 fr Dr P to N
8. GA M6340/86 Jan 12/31 fr Violet to Dr P
9. Over the course of her 60-year writing career, "Marian Keith" (1876–1961) wrote 17 "memoir-style" books detailing life and social change in small-town southwestern Ontario, but she is mainly remembered today for *The Black-Bearded Barbarian* (1912), a short biography of Presbyterian missionary George Mackay. (Schuck, *London Free Press* Jan 1/00)
10. GA M6340/29 Aug 28/35 fr N to G
11. GA M6340/29 Aug 11/35 fr N to G
12. CH Oct 17/39

13. GA M6340/179

14. GA M6340/65 Oct 18/30 fr Aunt S to N

15. GA M6340/27 Jun 25/35 fr N to G

16. GA M6340/217 Apr 30/30 fr Dr P to Min

17. GA M6340/116 Nov 24/38 fr Jack toIsabel

18. GA M6340/216 May 4/28 fr Dr P to Jack

19. GA M6340/216 May 31/29 fr Dr P to Sons

20. Snow pp 39–40; Peach, CH Jan 12/85

21. Wetherell p 54

22. CH Dec 12/25; CH Apr 10/26

Chapter 4 — Norma: Calgary Songbird, 1926–1934

1. GA M6340/RCT-132 Int Gerry Dunsmore, 1973; GW Fall/71

2. Dawson, CH Jul 23/79; GA M6340/65 Oct 18/30 fr Aunt S to N

3. Snow p 38

4. CH Oct 18/26

5. *The Crazy Twenties* p 17

6. *Youngstown Memories* pp 236–7. The legal description of Dr Piper's land was SW-15-29-9-W4. It was located about four miles south of Youngstown, adjacent to several other properties farmed by the Knudsens.

7. GA M6340/228 Agreements. In July 1929 Piper and Bell dissolved their partnership, and the company name was transferred to R. R. Hagerman. (GA M6340/216 Jul 11/29 fr Dr P to Alta Govt)

8. GA M6340/115 Aug 8/41 fr Dick to N

9. GA M6340/3 N Diary Jul 4/35

10. Ed J Feb 19/31

11. GA M6340/23 Nov 29/34 fr N to G

12. Ed J Feb 19/31; CDH Feb 20/31

13. Albn Feb 14/31

14. GA M6340/216 May 31/29 fr Dr P to Sons

15. GA M6340/217 ca Feb /30 fr Dr P to Min; Feb 6/30 fr Dr P to Frank ---- [surname unknown]

16. GA M6340/217 Apr 30/30 fr Dr P to Min; ca Feb /30 fr Dr P to Min

17. Strong-Boag, *Janey Canuck* p 2

18. GA M6340/217 Jan 14/30 fr Dr P to principal, University of British Columbia

19. GA M6340/217 Jan 18/30 fr Dr P to Buchanan

20. GA M6340/217 Feb 30/30 fr Dr P to Brandli. The Brandlis might have resented this "economical" scheme; certainly they seem to have rejected it. Years later, Norma recollected that when she arrived in Italy in 1934, it was "with no Italian and only a little French at her disposal." (*London Free Press* Jan 31/41)

21. GA M6340/217 Apr 30/30 fr Dr P to Min

22. GA M6340/25 Apr 28/35 fr N to G

23. GA M6340/65 Feb 27, Apr 21/30 fr Aunt S to N

24. GA M6340/65 Apr 9, Oct 18/30 fr Aunt S to N

25. Strong-Boag, *The New Day* p 86. In 1932 the average Canadian woman spent approximately $3.39 annually on cosmetics; the average American woman spent $12.32. According to her account book, in 1930 Norma spent about $13.00 on beauty products.

26. Oliver p 123. In today's terms Norma cost her father about thirteen hundred dollars per month while in Vancouver.

27. GA M6340/216 May 31/29 fr Dr P to Sons

28. GA M6340/217 Apr 22/30 fr Dr P to Bertha

29. GA M6340/217 Aug 25/30 fr Dr P to Ag[nesse] ---- [surname unknown]

30. GA M6340/116 Aug 5/30 fr Jack to N

31. GA M6340/79 Dec 17/30 fr Hal J---- [surname unknown] to Dr P

32. MacLean p 51

33. GA M6340/218 Jun 28/32 fr Dr P to Elizabeth "Lizzie" Tackabury
34. GA M6340/217 Oct 3/30 fr Dr P to N
35. GA M6340/217 Oct 10/30 fr Dr P to N
36. *Vancouver Sun* Oct 25/30
37. *Daily Province* Dec 19/30; Van *Morning Star* Dec 19/30
38. GA M6340/217 Dec 27/30 fr Dr P to N
39. GA M6340/217 Oct 31/30 fr Dr P to N
40. GA M6340/218 Jan 20, Feb 2/31 to W K Porter fr I W Fitch (copies of Canadian Club executive correspondence in Dr P's possession)
41. GA M6340/29 Aug 8/35 fr N to G
42. GA M6340/47 Oct 17/38 fr RB to Dr P. Mildred Bennett lived at the Palliser Hotel in Calgary with her brother from 1929 to 1931. (Waite pp 70–72)
43. GA M640/RCT-132 Int Dunsmore
44. Dawson, CH Jul 23/79
45. GA M6340/117 Dec 11/30 fr Lawrence to N
46. Albn Feb 20/31; Albn Mar 6/31
47. GA M6340/218 Feb 3/31 fr Dr P to N
48. CH Feb 20/31
49. GA M6340/218 Jan 19/31 fr Dr P to N
50. Ed J Feb 26/31
51. GA M6340/218 May 1/31 fr Dr P to Bowen
52. CDH Apr 20/31
53. GA M6340/218 May 1/31 fr Dr P to Bowen
54. GA M6340/218 Sep 9/31 fr Dr P to Mrs E H Johnston
55. Ibid.
56. GA M6340/163 nd [1931] fr Hutchcroft to Dr P
57. GA M6340/218 Aug 15/31 fr Dr P to Bowen
58. GA M6340/218 Aug 24/31 fr Dr P to RB
59. GA M6340/218 Aug 11/31 fr Dr P to John Nelson
60. GA M6340/218Aug 24/31fr Dr P to RB
61. Brewer, *Music and Musicians* Oct/31
62. *Sunday Province* Sep 13/31
63. GA M6340/218 Dec 30/31 fr Dr P to Johnson
64. GA M6340/147 Jan 25/31 fr Evangeline Lehman to N
65. GA M1700/10 Rotary Club
66. GA M6340/218 Aug 11/31 fr Dr P to Nelson
67. GA M6340/218 Aug 24/31 fr Dr P to Bowen
68. GA M6340/218 Sep 21/31 fr Dr P to Bowen
69. Albn Sep 17/31
70. CH Sep 17/31
71. GA M6340/218 Feb 16/32 fr Dr P to Bowen
72. Albn Feb 10/32
73. CH Feb 10/32
74. Ibid.
75. GA M6340/218 Feb 16/32 fr Dr P to Bowen
76. CDH Feb 16/32
77. Ed J Mar 10/32; *Edmonton Bulletin* Mar 10/32
78. GA M6340/218 Oct 20/32 fr Dr P to Rev R W Dalgleisch
79. CDH Mar/33
80. GA M6340/192
81. Albn Nov 18/32; CDH Nov 18/32
82. GA M6340/218 Mar 22/33 fr Dr P to Dr G D Stanley
83. CDH Mar 9/33
84. Depending on the engagement, Norma was paid any amount from 3 to 50 dollars during

this period and sometimes sang for no fee, just for the publicity. Her account books reveal that, with expenses, she earned only about 260 dollars between 1931 and 1933. (GA M6340/154 Expense books)

85. GA M6340/218 Dec 20/32 fr Dr P to William Moffatt
86. Ford p 103
87. GA M6340/218 Sep 22/31 fr Dr P to Harold Stutsbury
88. GA M6340/3 N Diary Jul 4/35
89. GA M6340/25 Apr 6/35 fr N to G
90. *North Battleford Optimist* Oct 15/31
91. GA M6340/27 Jun 6/35 fr N to G
92. *Didsbury Pioneer* Mar 2/33
93. GA M6340/116 Mar 7/33 fr Jack to N
94. GA M6340/49 Jan 25/33 fr Brandli to N
95. GA M6340/25 Apr 8/35 fr N to G
96. GA M6340/218 Mar 22/33 fr Dr P to Stanley
97. GA M6340/218 May 8/33 fr Dr P to Stanley
98. GA M6340/27 Jun 23/35 fr N to G
99. GA M6340/218 Oct 6/33 fr Dr P to N
100. GA M6340/27 Jun 29/35 fr N to G
101. GA M6340/218 Nov 18/33 fr Dr P to N
102. *Province* Dec 19/33
103. CDH Dec 29/33; Albn Dec 29/33
104. Born in Guelph, Ontario, Edward Johnson studied in Italy and made his opera debut there in 1912 as Edoardo Di Giovanni. After a successful European career, he returned to North America in 1919 to sing with the Chicago Opera. In 1922 he joined the Metropolitan Opera, singing for 13 consecutive seasons and then serving as general manager from 1935 to 1950. (*Encyclopedia of Music* 1992 p 662)

Chapter 5—Norma and George: Milano, 1934–1935

1. GA M6340/219 Jan 5/34 fr Dr P to N. Dr Piper was referring to Mark Twain's book *Innocents Abroad* (1869).
2. GA M6340/219 Jan 6/34 fr Dr P to N
3. GA M6340/218 Nov 18/33 fr Dr P to N. In 1930 Dr Piper sent each of his children a letter on notepaper sporting the Piper family crest and told them the family motto, Feroci Fortier, had been translated by Uncle Jack as "Brave but not Fierce." (GA M6340/217 Aug 11/30 fr Dr P to N & Gaffers). This seems to have been a mistranslation, since both Latin words describe the characteristics strength, bravery and courage.
4. St. Thomas *Times-Journal* Feb 26/41; LAC R-500-P 1933-34 Dec 19/33 fr Bennett to Muddiman. During the 1930s Canada was represented in most foreign countries only by a trade commissioner. It was not until 1947 that a Canadian embassy was established in Italy.
5. GA M6340/179
6. Dawson, CH Jul 23/79
7. GA M6340/22 Apr 1/34 fr N to Dr P
8. GA M6340/22 Feb 17/34 fr N to Dr P
9. GA M6340/24 Mar 31/35 fr N to G
10. GA M6340/28 Jul 13/35, Jul 8/35 fr N to G
11. In 1938, closer ties with Nazi Germany prompted the Italian government to pass "racial laws ... [that shook] the operatic world as well as the rest of Italian society" because they prohibited Jews from participating in any way in any theatrical field. (Bianconi and Pestelli pp 202–03)
12. GA M6340/22 Feb 9/34 fr N to Dr P
13. GA M6340/22 Apr 1/34 fr N to Dr P
14. GA M6340/22 Mar 3, Jun 4/34 fr N to Dr P
15. GA M6340/33 Jun 10/38 fr N to Dr P

16. GA M6340/22 Feb 9/34 fr N to Dr P

17. GA M6340/22 Mar 18/34 fr N to Dr P

18. GA M6340/22 Mar 11/34 fr N to Dr P

19. GA M6340/22 Jul 5/34 fr N to Dr P

20. GA M6340/22 Mar 19/34 fr N to Dr P

21. Isabel Logie gave several concerts in Calgary during this period and sang with the Calgary Symphony. In the mid-1930s she headed to Vancouver to continue her studies with Brandli and developed a friendship with Norma's friend Margaret Lattimore. The two women planned to emulate Norma by studying overseas, but their plans took several years to mature, and Norma watched from afar with some amusement and cynicism as a result of her own difficulties getting established in Europe.

22. Elaine M. Catley's *Sonnet to Norma Piper*: (GA M6340/192)

23. GA M6340/22 Feb 17/34 fr N to Dr P

24. GA M6340/22 Mar 18/34 fr N to Dr P

25. Ibid.

26. Roman numerals were added at the end of the conventional writing of the date to indicate the year of Fascism, or the number of years since the Fascists had come to power in Italy (e.g., XII indicated that 1934 was the 12th year of Fascism).

27. GA M6340/26 May 1/35 fr N to Dr P

28. GA M6340/22 Feb 9/34 fr N to Dr P

29. St. Thomas *Times-Journal* Feb 26/41

30. GA M6340/22 Feb 17/34 fr N to Dr P

31. GA M6340/22 Mar 3/34 fr N to Dr P

32. GA M6340/22 Feb 9/34 fr N to Dr P

33. GA M6340/22 Mar 3/34 fr N to Dr P

34. GA M6340/22 Mar 26/34 fr N to Dr P

35. GA M6340/22 Feb 17/34 fr N to Dr P

36. GA M6340/RCT-132 Int Dunsmore. According to the *Canadian Almanac*, the exchange rates for the mid-1920s were as follows: 1924: 23L/$Cdn; 1925: 25L/$Cdn; 1926: 26.5L/$Cdn.

37. GA M640/RCT-132 Int Dunsmore

38. "Il saggio avventuriero." *Vedetta Fascista*, Apr 13/34 in GA M6340/o.s. Scrapbook, v. 3

39. GA M6340/39 Jul 2/41 fr N to Jack

40. GA M6340/15 Oct 27/55 fr G to RMP

41. GA M6340/109 Jun 28/35 fr Park to G

42. GA M6340/7 Mar 3/34 fr G to N

43. GA M6340/22 Mar 6/34 fr N to G

44. GA M640/RCT-132 Int Dunsmore

45. GA M6340/22 Mar 26/34 fr N to Dr P

46. GA M6340/179

47. GA M6340/32 Dec 8/37 fr N to Dr P

48. GA M6340/22 Mar 26/34 fr N to Dr P

49. Ibid.

50. Ibid. Although no evidence exists to substantiate one of Norma's favourite later anecdotes, it may have been at this gathering of notable musical guests and critics that the soprano Rosina Storchio heard Norma sing the famous aria from *Barber of Seville* and then asked of her neighbour in which language it was being sung. (St. Thomas *Times-Journal* Feb 26/41)

51. GA M6340/22 Mar 26/34 fr N to Dr P

52. GA M6340/22 Apr 24/34 fr N to Dr P

53. GA M6340/22 Apr 13/34 fr N to Dr P

54. Ibid.

55. Ibid.

56. GA M6340/22 Apr 24/34 fr N to Dr P

57. Ibid.

58. GA M6340/22 Apr 13/34 fr N to Dr P

59. GA M6340/22 Apr 24/34 fr N to Dr P

60. GA M6340/22 Apr 1/34 fr N to Dr P

61. GA M6340/25 Apr 28/35 fr N to G

62. GA M6340/26 May 1/35 fr N to G

63. GA M6340/25 Apr 28/35 fr N to G. Norma told her father she drew the idea for their rings from a book, *Lady Betty Across the Water*, borrowed years before from a friend. This potboiler romance written by British authors C. N. and A. M. Williamson was published in Toronto in 1906. Typical of its time, the predictable plot would have appealed to Norma's romantic nature: Lady Betty, younger daughter of an impoverished but noble British family, is sent to America to seek a rich husband but falls in love instead with a man whom she believes to be poor (but who, of course, is revealed at the end to be wealthy and travelling incognito). George and Norma elaborated on the ring described in the Williamsons' story by devising special personal meanings for the small, synthetic stones arranged in their rings as follows: Diamond (purity, strength, steadfastness), Emerald (hope in the future), Amethyst (tender nobility), Ruby (courage), Emerald (faith), Sapphire (true-blue loyalty) and Topaz (the golden whole). The yellow and white gold of the rings represented "the welding of two lives into a perfect whole," and their initials were inscribed in each other's rings. (GA M6340/22 Oct 16/34 fr N to Dr P)

64. GA M6340/12 Mar 15/38 fr G to Amelie

65. Strong-Boag, *Janey Canuck* p 23

66. GA M6340/25 Apr 3/35 fr N to G

67. GA M6340/11, 12 Aug 10/36, Mar 30/38 fr G to Dr P; M6340/34 Dec 28/38 fr N to Dr P

68. GA M6340/27 Jun 8/35 fr N to G

69. GA M6340/30 Nov 28/35 fr N to G

70. GA M6340/28 Jul 5/35 fr N to G

71. GA M6340/25 Apr 9/35 fr N to G

72. GA M6340/218 Oct 6/33 fr Dr P to N

73. GA M6340/30 Oct 5/35 fr N to G

74. GA M6340/9 Jul 23/35 fr G to N

75. George's 1933 passport lists his hair as "grey," but the passport issued in 1967, when he was 85, describes it as "brown." (GA M6340/164)

76. GA M6340/25 Apr 12/35 fr N to G

77. GA M6340/104 Mar 23/38 fr Morlan to G

78. GA M6340/22 Aug 13/34 fr N to Dr P

79. GA M6340/22 Sep 4/34 f fr N to Dr P

80. GA M6340/22 Sep 11/34 fr N to Dr P

81. GA M6340/22, 23 Sep 4, Oct 16/34 fr N to Dr P

82. GA M6340/219 Sep 26/34 fr Dr P to N

83. GA M6340/219 Sep 29/34 fr Dr P to G

84. GA M6340/23 Oct 30/34 fr N to Dr P

85. GA M6340/22 Jun 4/34 fr N to Dr P

86. Int Jack Piper

87. GA M6340/22, 23 Jul 5, Oct 30/34 fr N to Dr P

88. GA M6340/22, 30 Aug 13, Nov 27/34; ca Oct 23/35 fr N to Dr P

89. In July 1934 Norma detailed her monthly expenses for her father: room and board 700L ($58), singing lessons 800L ($67), Italian lessons 140L ($12), scena lessons 120L ($10), piano rental 40L ($3), clothing 130L ($11), incidentals 120L ($10), opera tickets 50L ($4) Total 2,100L ($175). (GA M6340/22 Jul 7/34 fr N to Dr P) NB: Conversions from lire to dollars based on an exchange rate of 12L/$ as reported in the *Canadian Almanac* for 1934.

90. GA M6340/22 Jul 7/34 fr N to Dr P

91. Ibid.

92. GA M6340/22 Aug 17/34 fr N to Dr P

93. GA M6340/23 Oct 7, 18/34 fr N to Dr P

94. GA M6340/23 Oct 18/34 fr N to Dr P

95. GA M6340/23 Oct 7/34 fr N to Dr P
96. GA M6340/23 Oct 18/34 fr N to Dr P. Until the Canadian Citizenship Act of 1947, Canadians were considered British subjects and therefore fully entitled to seek advice and assistance at British embassies abroad.
97. GA M6340/23 Nov 13/34 fr N to G
98. GA M6340/219 Oct 1/34 fr Dr P to N; M6340/117 ca Oct/34 fr Lawrence to Dr P; M6340/23 Nov 13/34 fr N to G
99. GA M6340/27 Jun 9/35 fr N to Dr P; M6340/Jun 11 [ca 1935] fr Dr P to N
100. GA M6340/219 Oct 1/34 fr Dr P to N; M6340/219 Nov/34 fr Dr P to G
101. GA M6340/219 Oct 28/34 fr Dr P to N
102. GA M6340/116 ca Nov/34 fr Jack to Dr P
103. GA M6340/25 Apr 22/35 fr N to G
104. GA M6340/32 Oct 1/37 fr N to Dr P
105. GA M6340/219 Dec 9/34 fr Dr P to N
106. GA M6340/115 Aug 8/41 fr Dick to N. In terms of current dollar values, the Piper family spent roughly 250,000 dollars on Norma's career.
107. GA M6340/25 Apr 7/35 fr N to G
108. GA M6340/27 Jun 23/35 fr N to G
109. GA M6340/24 Mar 23/35 fr N to G
110. GA M6340/29 Aug 13/35 fr N to G
111. GA M6340/22 Jul 6/34 fr N to Dr P
112. GA M6340/22 Jul 8/34 fr N to Dr P
113. GA M6340/22 Aug 17/34 fr N to Dr P
114. GA M6340/24 Mar 23/35 fr N to Dr P
115. GA M6340/23 Nov 11/34 fr N to G; M6340/3 N Diary Jul 4/35
116. GA M6340/28 Jul 15/35 fr N to G; M6340/25 Apr 13/35 fr N to Dr P
117. GA M6340/23 Nov 8/34 fr N to G. Norma probably meant *picchettato*, a quick, smooth series of staccato notes.
118. GA M6340/27 Jun 5/35 fr N to G
119. GA M6340/3 N Diary Apr 8/35, Jul 6/35
120. GA M6340/3 N Diary Apr 8/35
121. GA M6340/23 Nov 29/34 fr N to G
122. GA M6340/27 Jun 5/35 fr N to G
123. GA M6340/26 May 25/35 fr N to G
124. GA M6340/23 Oct 30/34 fr N to Dr P
125. GA M6340/3 N Diary Apr 8/35
126. GA M6340/3 N Diary Jul 4/35
127. GA M6340/23 Nov 13/34 fr N to G
128. GA M6340/23 Nov 9, 23/34 fr N to G
129. GA M6340/7 Nov 7, 9, 16, 18/34 fr G to N
130. GA M6340/7 Nov 2/34 fr G to N; M6340/23 Nov 28/34 fr N to G
131. GA M6340/23 Oct 30/34 fr N to Dr P
132. GA M6340/23 Nov 30/34 fr N to G
133. GA M6340/28 Jul 11/35 fr N to G
134. GA M6340/23 Nov 12/34 fr N to Dr P
135. GA M6340/25, 27 Apr 7, Jun 23/35 fr N to G
136. GA M6340/24 Mar 19/35 fr N to G
137. GA M6340/116 ca Apr/35 fr Jack to N
138. GA M6340/219 ca Mar/35 fr Dr P to G
139. GA M6340/147 May 22/35 fr Vining to Dr P
140. GA M6340/9 Jun 23/35 fr G to N. Grace Moore was an American who had studied in Paris and debuted at the Met in 1928. Although critics were not particularly impressed with her voice, which showed lack of training, she had a "showgirl" figure and "glamorous personality" and was successfully promoted in the 1930s as a "star of stage, screen and radio."

(Tuggle p 211; *New Grove Dictionary* p 461) Also American, Marion Talley generated much excitement with her "brilliant coloratura technique" as a teenager in amateur productions in the early 1920s, but her professional career at the Met in the later 1920s was disappointing (*New Grove* p 638), and she faded from view when Lily Pons (another American, of French birth) "caused a sensation" with her "extremely high coloratura voice" during her debut at the Met in 1931. (*New Grove* p 1059)

141. GA M6340/8 Apr 25/35 fr G to N
142. GA M6340/219 May 2/35 fr Nelson to Johnson
143. GA M6340/219 May 29/35 fr Nelson to Dr P
144. GA M6340/11 Feb 6/36 fr G to C M Cresswell
145. GA M6340/9 May 22/35 fr G to N
146. GA M6340/9 Jun 1/35 fr G to N
147. GA M6340/219 Mar 17/35 fr Dr P to G
148. GA M6340/10 Aug 18, 26/35 fr G to N
149. GA M6340/29 Aug 20/35 fr N to G
150. GA M6340/10 Aug 18/35 fr G to N
151. Ibid.
152. GA M6340/10 Aug 26/35 fr G to N
153. GA M6340/10 Aug 5/35 fr G to N
154. GA M6340/10 Aug 26/35 fr G to N
155. GA M6340/9 Jun 11/35 fr G to N
156. GA M6340/9 Jun 16/35 fr G to N
157. GA M6340/9 Jul 3/35 fr G to N
158. GA M6340/27 Jun 30/35 fr N to G
159. GA M6340/29 Aug 2/35 fr N to G
160. GA M6340/10 Aug 10/35 fr G to N
161. GA M6340/27 Jun 29/35 fr N to G
162. GA M6340/26 May 19/35 fr N to G
163. GA M6340/24 Mar 23/35 fr N to Dr P
164. Pannain p 29; Tuggle pp 7, 8
165. GA M6340/24 Mar 27/35 fr N to G
166. GA M6340/24 Mar 29/35 fr N to Dr P
167. GA M6340/26 May 25/35 fr N to G
168. GA M6340/25 Apr 6/35 fr N to G
169. GA M6340/3 N Diary Apr 8/35
170. GA M6340/25 Apr 6/35 fr N to G
171. GA M6340/27 Jun 6/35 fr N to G
172. Ibid.
173. GA M6340/26 May 14/35 fr N to Dr P
174. GA M6340/219 May 18/35 fr Dr P to N
175. GA M6340/26 May 22/35 fr N to Dr P
176. GA M6340/8, 9 Mar 31, May 3, Jun 14/35 fr G to N
177. GA M6340/26, 27, 30 May 3, Jun 19, Sep 27/35 fr N to G
178. GA M6340/27 Jun 25/35 fr N to G
179. GA M6340/145 Jul 17/35 fr Veronese to G
180. GA M6340/28 Jul 5/35 fr N to G
181. GA M6340/28 Jul 4/35 fr N to Dr P
182. GA M6340/28 Jul 4, 5/35 fr N to G
183. GA M6340/3 N Diary Jul 4/35
184. GA M6340/3 N Diary Jul 6/35
185. GA M6340/28 Jul 7/35 fr N to G
186. GA M6340/28 Jul 13/35 fr N to G; M6340/22 Jul 14/34 fr N to Dr P. Unbeknownst to Norma, conditions at the Met had changed with the Depression. When Johnson became general manager, he was faced with a financial crisis that he resolved by reducing positions,

cutting salaries and shortening the Met's opera season. To compensate for fewer performances, he brought professional opera to the public by introducing weekly radio broadcasts. All of these measures reduced the number of singers required and allowed Johnson the luxury of picking and choosing among first-class artists at home and around the world. (Tuggle pp 7–8)

187. GA M6340/28 Jul 29/35 fr N to G
188. GA M6340/28 Jul 24/35 fr N to G
189. GA M6340/22 Aug 17/34 fr N to Dr P
190. GA M6340/22, 29 Apr 24/34; Aug 14/35 fr N to Dr P
191. GA M6340/29 Aug 13/35 fr N to G
192. GA M6340/29 Aug 5, 13/35 fr N to G
193. GA M6340/31 Jun 21/36 fr N to Dr P. There were many examples: Norma told her father about one California woman who paid 50,000L for a single performance (GA M6340/33 Apr 7/38 fr N to Dr P), and Riccardo Stracciari later told Norma that Amelita Galli-Curci spent 100,000L on her first performance in Italy in 1906. (GA M6340/3 N Diary Apr 22/37)
194. GA M6340/29, 30 Aug 8, Sep 12/35 fr N to G
195. GA M6340/29 Aug 29/35 fr N to G
196. Ibid.
197. GA M6340/29 Aug 5/35 fr N to G
198. GA M6340/27 Jun 20/35 fr N to G
199. GA M6340/29 Aug 8/35 fr N to Dr P
200. GA M6340/30 Sep 3/35 fr N to G
201. GA M6340/29 Aug 20/35 fr N to Dr P
202. GA M6340/30 Sep 3/35 fr N to G
203. GA M6340/29 Aug 8/35 fr N to Dr P
204. GA M6340/30 Sep 3/35 fr N to G; M6340/3 N Diary Sep 5/35
205. GA M6340/3 N Diary Sep 5/35
206. GA M6340/33 Mar 9/38 fr N to Dr P
207. Sat Nt Dec 9/39; *New Grove Dictionary* p 822
208. GA M6340/29, 30 Aug 28, Sep 8/35 fr N to G
209. GA M6340/30 Sep 7/35 fr N to G; M6340/3 N Diary Sep 5/35; M6340/30 Sep 8/35 fr N to Dr P
210. GA M6340/31 Jun 21/36 fr N to Dr P
211. GA M6340/30 Sep 17/35 fr N to G
212. GA M6340/12 Mar 15/38 fr G to Amelie

Chapter 6—Norma and George: Waiting and Hoping, 1935–1939

1. GA M6340/10 Nov 14/35 fr G to Dr P
2. GA M6340/3 N Diary Dec 18/35; M6340/11 Mar 10/36 fr G to Lydia
3. GA M6340/3 N Diary Dec 18/35; Clark p 282. The Pocaterras replaced their original rings quite quickly; diary entries as early as 1937 refer to repairing and replacing specific stones in them.
4. GA M6340/27 Jun 23/35 fr N to G
5. GA M6340/27 Jun 20/35 fr N to G
6. With the luck of good timing, the Fedelis had made a fortune in Canada. They sold out in the Highwood while prices still were high and returned to Italy in 1920 as "rich men." (Sheppard, *Just About Nothing* p 26)
7. Int Pozza
8. GA M6340/219 Oct 28/34 fr Dr P to G
9. GA M6340/23 Oct 30/34 fr N to Dr P
10. GA M6340/49 Jun 17/37 fr Brandli to G
11. GA M6340/24 Mar 29/35 fr N to Dr P
12. GA M6340/220 Oct 8/38 fr Dr P to N
13. GA M6340/47 Nov 14/33 fr RB to Dr P
14. Bennett used his influence several times to help Dick find employment during the

Depression, and he helped Dr Piper to obtain copies of Canadian government documents attesting to George's exemption from military service during the First World War.

15. GA M6340/9 May 4/35 fr G to N
16. Sat Nt Jun 17/39
17. GA M6340/26 May 1/35 fr N to Dr P
18. GA M634026 May 6/35 fr N to Dr P
19. GA M6340/9 May 4/35 fr G to N
20. GA M6340/219 May 8/35 fr Dr P to G
21. GA M6340/12 Mar 15/38 fr G to Amelie
22. GA M6340/31 Jun 21/36 fr N to Dr P
23. GA M6340/25 Apr 12/35 fr N to G; M6340/31 Jun 28, Oct 16/36 fr N to Dr P
24. GA M6340/29 Aug 10/35 fr N to G
25. GA M6340/86 May 23/38 fr Violet to N
26. GA M6340/34 Sep 18/38 fr N to Dr P
27. GA M6340/12 Mar 15/38 fr G to Amelie
28. GA M6340/25 Apr 14/35 fr N to Dr P
29. GA M6340/32 Apr 1/37 fr N to Dr P
30. GA M6340/32, 33 Dec 15/37; Jan 20, Feb 3/38 fr N to Dr P
31. GA M6340/26 May 6/35 fr N to Dr P
32. GA M6340/31 Jul 16/36 fr N to Dr P
33. GA M6340/31 Mar 17/36 fr N to Dr P; CH Mar 5/49; CH Apr 27/57
34. Norma's costumes and operatic accessories were donated to the Glenbow Museum in 1982. Even after years of wear, they were in very good shape, showing only a few repairs and slight modifications. One of the most interesting changes was to the bridal gown worn in *Lucia*. In a letter to her father dated June 25, 1937, Norma described how she substituted the zipper from George's small travelling case for the long row of little buttons and hooks down the back of the costume in order to make her change between scenes go more quickly and smoothly. (GA M6340/32 Jun 25/37 fr N to Dr P)
35. GA M6340/31 Oct 15/36 fr N to Lawrence
36. GA M6340/31 Mar 17/36 fr N to Dr P
37. GW Fall/71
38. GA M6340/32 Oct 1/37 fr N to Dr P
39. Maria Pia, wife of George's nephew Sergio Pozza, was the niece of the prefect, the top civil servant in the province, which included the city of Milan. As "the highest State authority ... [and] direct representative of the central government," the prefect dispensed patronage and exercised wide powers over all aspects of local political, economic and social life. (Clark p 235)
40. GA M6340/29 Aug 13/35 fr N to G
41. Bianconi and Pestelli p 195
42. GA M6340/29 Aug 13/35 fr N to G
43. Bianconi and Pestelli pp 197–99
44. GA M6340/23 Oct 7/34 fr N to Dr P
45. GA M6340/25 Apr 6/35 fr N to G
46. GA M6340/27 Jun 25/35 fr N to G
47. GA M6340/192 Notes
48. GA M6340/24 Mar 28/35 fr N to G
49. GA M6340/219 nd ca Mar/35 fr Dr P to N
50. GA M6340/3 N Diary Jun 24/35
51. GA M6340/9 Jul 6/35 fr G to N
52. GA M6340/32 Dec 22/37 fr N to Lawrence
53. GA M6340/31 Sep 12/36 fr N to Dr P
54. GA M6340/32 Oct 1/37 fr N to Dr P
55. GA M6340/30 Sep 24/35 fr N to Dr P
56. GA M6340/172 Publicity
57. GA M6340/31 Dec 17/36 fr N to Dr P

58. GA M6340/32 Apr 1/37 fr N to Dr P. Complete with her stage makeup and other accessories, Norma's makeup case was donated to the Glenbow Museum in 1982.

59. GA M6340/32 Apr 24/37 fr N to Dr P

60. GA M6340/32 May/37 fr N to Dr P

61. GA M6340/172 Publicity

62. GA M6340/32 Jul 15/37 fr N to Dr P

63. GA M6340/32 Oct 1/37 fr N to Dr P

64. GA M6340/34 Sep 25/38 fr N to Dr P

65. GA M6340/33 Mar 29/38 fr N to Jack

66. GA M6340/29 Aug 20/35 fr N to Dr P

67. GA M6340/172 Publicity

68. GA M6340/32 Apr 1/37 fr N to Dr P

69. GA M6340/19 nd [ca 1937] fr N to Lattimore

70. GA M6340/33 Apr 4/38 fr N to Lawrence

71. GA M6340/32 Dec 8/37 fr N to Dr P

72. Ibid.

73. GA M6340/32 Oct 26/37 fr N to Dr P

74. Although her CV claimed that she knew the roles for nearly a dozen operas, Norma's actual stage experience was limited to five of them, and during her five years in Italy, she performed in fewer than four dozen staged operas: 15 times in *The Barber of Seville*, 11 in *Rigoletto*, 9 in *Lucia*, 3 in *Don Pasquale*, twice in *L'Elisir d'Amore* and only once in *La Sonnambula*.

75. GA M6340/32 Sep 23/37 fr N to Dr P

76. Rosselli pp 124–126

77. GA M6340/32 Feb 10/37 fr N to Dr P

78. GA M6340/35 nd [ca May/39] fr N to Dr P. Born in Quebec in 1847, Emma Albani was the first Canadian-born artist to achieve international fame. Blessed with "an exceptionally beautiful voice," during her four-decade career she toured Canada a number of times and was one of the stars of Covent Garden during the 1870s to 1890s. (*Encyclopedia of Music* 1992 pp 12–13)

79. GA M6340/220 Jul 28/38 fr Dr P to N and G

80. GA M6340/219 Sep /36 [1937] fr Dr P to N

81. GA M6340/31 Jul 16/36 fr N to Dr P

82. GA M6340/220 Apr 19/39 fr Dr P to N and G

83. GA M6340/32 [ca Oct 5/37] fr N to Dr P

84. GA M6340/116 Nov 9/37 fr Jack to N

85. GA M6340/32 Dec 6/37 fr N to Jack

86. GA M6340/34 Jul 5/38 fr N to Dr P

87. GA M6340/32 Dec 6/37 fr N to Jack

88. GA M6340/116 Dec 17/36 fr Jack to Dr P

89. GA M6340/11 Jan 15/37 fr G to Dr P

90. GA M6340/11 Sep 29/36 fr G to Dr P

91. GA M6340/32 Oct 1/37 fr N to Dr P

92. GA M6340/33 Mar 9, Jun 10/38 fr N to Dr P

93. BCA MS-2762/1/14 Feb 12/37fr G to RMP

94. GA M6340/32 Aug 4/37 fr N to Dr P

95. GA M6340/34 Sep 18/38 fr N to Dr P

96. GA M6340/116 Nov 24/38 fr Jack to Isabel

97. GA M6340/34 Jul 21/38 fr N to Dr P

98. GA M6340/219 Dec 12/37 fr Dr P to N and G

99. GA M6340/220 Jan 9, Feb 5/39 fr Dr P to N and G

100. The Edmonton Grads generally were acknowledged to be the best women's basketball team in the world during the 1920s and '30s. On July 29, 1936, Page and the Grads played an exhibition game in Milan during their tour of European cities prior to competing at the Berlin Olympics. (*Edmonton Bulletin* Jul 20, Jul 29/36)

101. BCA MS-2762/1/14 Apr 19/38 fr G to RMP
102. GA M6340/35 May 30/39 fr N to Dr P
103. GA M6340/34 Jul 5/38 fr N to Dr P
104. GA M6340/32 Dec 8/37 fr N to Dr P
105. GA M6340/22 Jun 4/34 fr N to Dr P
106. GA M6340/30 Sep 21/35 fr N to G
107. Clark p 247
108. GA M6340/12 Jul 12/38 fr G to Dr P
109. BCA MS-2762/1/14 Apr 12/37 fr G to RMP
110. GA M6340/111 Mar 14/39 fr RMP to G
111. Ibid.
112. GA M6340/111 Jan 27/37 fr RMP to G
113. GA M6340/111 May 26/40 fr RMP to G
114. GA M6340/12 Jul 12/38 fr G to Dr P
115. Ibid.
116. GA M6340/23 Oct 5/34 fr N to Dr P
117. GA M6340/3 N Diary Oct 2/35
118. GA M6340/25, 27, 31 Apr 22, Jun 9/35; Jul 16/36 fr N to Dr P
119. GA M6340/3 N Diary Mar 7/37. Although Mussolini had the support of a fearsome, quasi-military force known as the Black Shirts, George's purchase in no way indicated an identification with this body. Over time, the wearing of a black shirt at public events had become a sort of uniform, symbolic of the wearer's nationalism and support for the fascist government. Even those who were ambivalent about government direction or Mussolini's leadership could avoid persecution by wearing this symbol. Since Norma was entirely dependent on government favour for opportunities to sing, it seems likely that George bought a black shirt as much to ingratiate himself with government officials as to show support for the political system. (Corresp Gennaro Nov 10/02)
120. GA M6340/34 Aug 14/38 fr N to Dr P
121. GA M6340/32 Apr 1/37 fr N to Dr P
122. Clark pp 247, 257–8
123. GA M6340/12 Sep 26/38 fr G to Dr P
124. GA M6340/36 nd ca Jul/39 fr N to Dr P
125. *Encyclopedia of Music* 1992 p 1399; GA M6340/220 Jan 4/39 fr Dr P to N and G
126. GA M6340/220 Nov 23/38 fr Dr P to N
127. GA M6340/47 May 16, Jun 7/39 fr RB to N
128. GA M6340/35 May 30/39 fr N to Dr P
129. GA M6340/33 Feb 14/38 fr N to Dr P
130. GA M6340/34 Dec 6/38 fr N to Dr P
131. Ibid. Even had the Glyndbourne been interested in using Norma for this tour, she would not have reached North America this way because world events intervened in 1939. Most of the famous cultural organizations from Europe that had intended to participate in the World's Fair decided not to chance crossing the Atlantic Ocean, and by June 1939 many of the cultural events planned for the fair had been cancelled. (Sat Nt Jun 17/39)
132. GA M6340/33 Feb 25/38 fr N to Dr P
133. Ibid.
134. GA M6340/12 Mar 7/38 fr G to Dr P
135. GA M6340/33 Apr 7/38 fr N to Dr P; M6340/33 Mar 1/38 fr N to Legge
136. GA M6340/33 Jun 5/38 fr N to Dr P
137. Ibid.
138. GA M6340/33 Apr 7/38 fr N to Dr P
139. GA M6340/33 Jun 5/38 fr N to Dr P
140. GA M6340/33 May 23/38 fr N to Dr P
141. GA M6340/34 Sep 18/38 fr N to Dr P
142. GA M6340/3 N Diary Jul 28/38

143. Ibid.
144. Ibid.
145. M6340/33 Mar 22/38 fr N to Dr P
146. GA M6340/3 N Diary Apr 8/35
147. Int Pozza
148. GA M6340/34 Sep 18/38 fr N to Dr P
149. GA M6340/33 Apr 7/38 fr N to Dr P. Although Lina Pagliughi's "unimpressive stage presence was a hindrance to her theatrical career," she had a 30-year singing career that included performances at La Scala and Covent Garden and many successful recordings. (*New Grove Dictionary* p 822) Norma reported that Pagliughi's was the singing voice used in 1939 in the Italian version of Disney's *Snow White*. (GA M6340/35 Jan 22/39 fr N to Dr P)
150. GA M6340/34 Jul 5/38 fr N to Dr P
151. GA M6340/220 [Nov] 21/38 fr Dr P to N and G
152. GA M6340/34 Sep 18/38 fr N to Dr P
153. GA M6340/116 Feb 15/39 fr Jack to N
154. GA M6340/35 May 1/39 fr N to Dr P
155. GA M6340/220 Feb 22/39 fr Dr P to N and G
156. GA M6340/35 May 17/39 fr N to Dr P
157. GA M6340/35 May 1/39 fr N to Dr P
158. GA M6340/36 Jul 1/39 fr N to Dr P
159. GA M6340/36 Jul 1, 8/39 fr N to Dr P
160. GA M6340/36 Jul 9/39 fr N to Dr P
161. Ibid.
162. Ibid.
163. GA M6340/36 Aug 17/39 fr N to Dr P
164. GA M6340/36 Aug 9/39 fr N to Dr P
165. GA M6340/36 Aug 28/39 fr N to Dr P
166. Ibid.
167. GA M6340/36 Aug 31/39 fr N to Dr P
168. Ibid.
169. GA M6340/12 Jul 31/39 fr G to Dr P
170. GA M6340/36 Aug 5/39 fr N to Dr P
171. GA M6340/220 Sep 8/39 fr Dr P to N and G
172. GA M6340/36 Sep 3/39 fr N to Dr P
173. Dawson, CH Jul 23/79
174. GA M6340/35 May 1/39 fr N to Dr P
175. GA M6340/12 Sep 6/39 fr G to Dr P
176. GA M6340/13 Jun 8/40 fr G to RMP
177. GA M6340/36 Sep 14/39 fr N to Dr P. With war looming, ticket prices were inflated. By way of comparison, Norma had paid 174 dollars for a stateroom in 1934; the Pocaterras later claimed that it cost them 750 dollars to leave Italy. They arrived at this figure by including all the costs incurred from September 1 to 18 (an additional 200 dollars): their flight to Switzerland, living there for a week, returning to Milan to wind up their affairs and travelling by train to Trieste to board their ship.
178. GA M6340/36 Sep 10, 14/39 fr N to Dr P
179. GA M6340/36 Sep 3, 14/39 fr N to Dr P
180. GA M6340/36 Sep 10, 14/39 fr N to Dr P
181. CH Oct 13/39
182. GA M640/RCT-132 Int Dunsmore
183. CH Oct 13/39

Chapter 7 — Norma and George: On the Highwood, 1939–1941

1. GA M6340/12 Oct 1/39 fr G to Dr P. It seems possible that Irving Hollinrake was the mysterious Canadian friend who cabled George the American money needed to buy tickets on

the *Vulcania*. It was to his attention and address that Norma directed her father and brothers to send money to help the Pocaterras get re-established once they reached North America, and visiting Hollinrake certainly seemed to be George's first priority on returning to Canada.

2. GA M6340/36 Oct 7/39 fr N to G

3. GA M6340/36 Oct 14/39 fr N to G

4. GA M6340/36 Oct 9/39 fr N to G

5. Ibid.

6. GA M6340/40 Oct 10/69 fr N to Harry Strom

7. GA M6340/17 Mar 10/61 fr G to Soledad and Maurice [D'Allaire]

8. GA M6340/116 Jun 13/41 fr Jack to N

9. GA M6340/39 Jul 2/41 fr N to Jack

10. GA M6340/116 Nov 23/39 fr Jack to N

11. GA M6340/39 Jul 2/41 fr N to Jack. Isabelle Burnada, born Isabelle Boyer de la Giroday, was a mezzo-soprano from Vancouver whose talent so impressed Calgary businessman and senator Patrick Burns that he sponsored her studies in Paris and Milan for six years during the 1920s. Her professional name was derived from the names "Burns" and "Canada." (*Encyclopedia of Music* 1992 p 178) Norma seems to have misremembered the value of the senator's contributions; Dr Piper actually told her that Burns' investment in the singer had been 40,000 dollars. (GA M6340/217 Oct 10/30 fr Dr P to N)

12. GA M6340/115 Aug 8/41 fr Dick to N

13. GA M6340/37 Jun 12/40 fr N to Lawrence

14. GA M6340/115 Aug 8/41 fr Dick to N

15. GA M6340/115 Jun 18/41 fr Dick to N

16. GA M6340/115 Aug 8/41 fr Dick to N

17. GA M6340/37 Jun 12/40 fr N to Lawrence

18. GA M6340/117 nd [1940] fr Lawrence to N

19. GA M6340/13 Feb 20/41 fr G to N

20. GA M6340/117 Jun 30/41 fr Lawrence to N

21. GA M6340/115 Jun 17/41 fr Dick to N

22. Although all four siblings inherited money from childless Uncle Richard in 1926 and Aunt Susie in 1933, Dick received an extra portion (6,000 dollars) because of his early ties with Richard and Min Piper. Of all the siblings, only Jack inherited from Uncle Jack Piper (5,000 dollars), possibly because of his name but also because a farm injury to his hand at an early age had made his future seem less secure to his concerned uncle. (GA M6340/27 Jun 11/35 fr N to G) As promised, Dr Piper redressed the situation in his own will with an extra bequest for Lawrence (5,000 dollars).

23. GA M6340/115 Jun 18/41 fr Dick to N

24. GA M6340/116 Jun 13/41 fr Jack to N

25. GA M6340/117 Aug 7/41 fr Lawrence to N

26. GA M6340/47 Dec 14/39 fr RB to N

27. GA M6340/3 N Diary Dec 29/39

28. GA M6340/217 Aug 12/30 fr Dr P to N

29. Troyer p 51; *The Crazy Twenties* p 70

30. GA M6340/37 Jun 12/40 fr N to Lawrence

31. GA M6340/104 Mar 3/39 fr Morlan to G

32. GA M6340/37 Jun 12/40 fr N to Lawrence

33. GA M6340/172 Publicity

34. GA M6340/3 N Diary May 23/40

35. GA M6340/3 N Diary May 21/40

36. GA M6340/37 Jun 12/40 fr N to Lawrence; M6340/40 Feb 11/48 fr N to Mrs Belyea [given name unknown]

37. Sat Nt Oct 28/39

38. CH Oct 11/40

39. GA M6340/37 Jun 12/40 fr N to Lawrence

40. GA M6340/40 Dec 1/47 fr N to G
41. GA M6340/1 G Diary Dec 29/51
42. GA M6340/37 Jun 12/40 fr N to Lawrence
43. GA M6340/36 Oct 11/39 fr N to Nelyon Dewson
44. GA M6340/36 Sep 3/39 fr N to Dr P
45. Ibid.
46. GA M6340/3 N Diary Jun 8/40
47. GA M6340/37 Jul 5/40 fr N to G
48. GA M6340/3 N Diary Jul 8/40
49. GA M6340/3 N Diary Jul 9/40
50. Tuggle p 8
51. GA M6340/13 Jul 11/40 fr G to Sibley
52. Ibid.
53. GA M6340/62 Jul 27/40 fr Charlesworth to N
54. CH Aug 20/40
55. GW Fall/71; GA M6470 Sierra Club (Int N)
56. GA M6340/38 Jan 26/41 fr N to G
57. GA M6340/3 N Diary Nov 7/40
58. GA M6340/3 N Diary Sep 9/40
59. GA M6340/3 N Diary Oct 11/40
60. GA M6340/3 N Diary Aug 29, Oct 7/40
61. GA M6340/179
62. CH Dec 13/40
63. GA M6340/38 Jan 27/41 fr N to G
64. GA M6340/109 Jan 17/41 fr Park to G
65. GA M6340/38 Jan 28/41 fr N to G. As a leader of the Canadian musical community,
MacMillan had spoken and written extensively about the negative impact of the strongly pro-
American bias of the concert-going public and had asserted the importance of nurturing and
employing superior Canadian talent. (MacMillan p 36) Consequently, under his direction the
Toronto Symphony Orchestra was known to have a policy of presenting notable Canadian
artists. (Sat Nt Nov 4/39) That he did not make an effort to use Norma implies that he may not
have been as impressed with her voice as he led her to believe.
66. GA M6340/38 Feb 3/41 fr N to G
67. *London Free Press* Feb 4/41
68. GA M6340/38 Feb 3/41 fr N to G
69. GA M6340/38 Feb 11/41 fr N to G
70. GA M6340/38 Feb 19/41 fr N to G
71. GA M6340/13 Feb 27/41 fr G to N
72. GA M6340/38 Mar 1/41 fr N to G
73. GA M6340/38 Jan 31/41 fr N to G
74. GA M6340/38 Jan 28, Feb 5, Feb 11/41 fr N to G
75. GA M6340/13 Mar 13/41 fr G to N
76. GA M6340/13 Jan 25/41 fr G to N
77. GA M6340/13 Mar 15/41 fr G to N
78. GA M6340/11 ca Feb/40 fr G to RMP
79. GA M6340/111 May 26/40 fr G to RMP
80. Fanella p 45
81. Ibid.
82. GA M6340/13 Jan 28/41 fr G to RMP
83. GA M6340/13 Feb 1/41 fr G to RMP
84. GA M6340/38 Jan 28, Feb 10/41 fr N to G
85. GA M6340/38 Mar 6/41 fr N to G; M6340/13 Mar 11, 13/41 fr G to N
86. GA M6340/13 Jul 9/41 fr G to Morlan
87. GA M6340/38 Feb 21/41 fr N to G

88. GA M6340/38 Mar 12/41 fr N to G
89. GA M6340/38 Feb 14/41 fr N to G
90. Ibid.
91. GA M6340/38 Feb 18/41 fr N to G
92. Ibid.
93. Ibid.; Sat Nt Sep 23/39
94. GA M6340/38 Mar 5/41 fr N to G
95. GA M6340/13 Mar 11/41 fr G to N
96. GA M6340/38 Mar 6/41 fr N to G
97. GA M6340/38 Mar 10/41 fr N to G
98. GA M6340/38 Mar 6, Mar 5/41 fr N to G
99. GA M6340/38 Mar 8/41 fr N to G
100. GA M6340/49 Apr 3/41 fr Brandli to N
101. *Toronto Daily Star* Mar 18/41
102. BCA MS-2762/1/14 Apr 12/37 fr G to RMP
103. GA M6340/13 Jun 7/41 fr G to Kellogg
104. GA M6340/39 May 28/41 fr N to Dick
105. GA M6340/RCT-207 Int with N by Tom Gooden, 1978
106. GA M6340/100 Feb 7/[41] fr Mather to G
107. GA M6340/38 Feb 5/41 fr N to G
108. GA M6340/13 Feb 11, Feb 21/41 fr G to N
109. GA M6340/38 Feb 18/41 fr N to G
110. Peach, CH Jan 12/85
111. GA M6340/148 nd [c1941] fr Boese to N
112. GA M6340/92 Jul 14 [1941] fr Moore to N
113. GA M6340/92 Aug 3/41 fr Moore to N
114. GA M6340/39 Oct 24/41 fr N to G
115. GA M6340/145 Oct 24/41 fr Middlemass to G
116. GA M6340/39 Oct 22/41 fr N to G
117. GA M6340/39 Oct 29/41 fr N to G; *Daily Province* Oct 23/41
119. GA M6340/49 Apr 3/41 fr Brandli to N. Maria Brandli de Bevec outlived her husband by many years, dying in 1971 at age 83.
119. GA M6340/49 Jul 17/41 fr Brandli to N
120. GA M6340/39 Oct 24/41 fr N to G
121. Ibid.
122. GA M6340/39 Oct 28/41 fr N to G
123. GA M6340/39 Oct 24/41 fr N to G

Chapter 8—Norma and George: Valnorma, 1941–1955

1. GA M6340/13 Jul 9/41 fr G to Morlan
2. GA M6340/181 Son of Mtns pp 49–54
3. This scheme first had been suggested to Norma when she boarded with the Tearneys in Toronto the preceding spring. Mr. Tearney, who worked for Molson's Bank for a number of years, had strongly advised Norma against selling her Royalite shares with prices so low, but he suggested they might be used as collateral for a bank loan to fund their property development. (GA M6340/38 Feb 15/41 fr N to G)
4. Patterson, *Far Pastures* p 185
5. GA M6340/14 Feb 14/46 fr G to Sibley
6. GA M6340/181 Son of Mtns p 72
7. GA M6340/13 Dec 19/40 fr G to Hobart A Dowler
8. Int Butters
9. GA M6340/181 Son of Mtns pp 77–78
10. GA M6340/192

11. GA M6340/181 Son of Mtns pp 55a–59a

12. Ints Macleod, Butters

13. Int Butters

14. CH Dec 12/36

15. CH Jan 15/42

16. Albn May 6/43

17. *Banff Crag and Canyon* Sep 27/78

18. CH Sep 5/42

19. A promotional article for ARMTA in 1949 helps to explain Norma's inclusion. Headed "Teachers Must Pass Stiff Examinations," the article outlines all the normally stringent qualifications for ARMTA membership, and then states that enrolment also may be granted "to such as have satisfied … an examining body of their fitness to teach." (Albn Mar 15/49)

20. GA M6364/3 ARMTA

21. In October 1945 George told Donald Read, the young American tenor who had performed the male lead in *Countess Maritza*, that they were considering mounting *La Sonnambula* the next year and that Norma would sing the female lead, but nothing seems to have come of this plan. (GA M6340/14 Oct 2/45 fr G to Donald [Read])

22. Cochrane and Area Historical Society p 343

23. GA M6340/40 Oct 10/69 fr N to Harry Strom

24. GA M6340/181 Son of Mtns pp 87–91. In the 30 years between this incident and its recording in "Son of the Mountains," the Pocaterras must have misremembered the name of the train. *The Imperial Limited* was the premier Canadian train in the pre-First World War period and into the 1920s, but its daily transcontinental runs through Calgary had been discontinued in the early 1930s. The train that stopped for Norma and George in the early 1940s must have been its successor, *The Dominion*. (Turner, passim)

25. GA M6340/14 Oct 2/45 fr G to Donald [Read]

26. GA M6340/3 N Diary Feb 28/35

27. GA M6340/14 Sep 15/48 fr G to Friends [Mathers]

28. Ibid.

29. Tivy, CH Jul 16/83

30. Int Millers

31. Int Brown

32. Reid, Albn Mar 1/76

33. Mount Royal College Yearbook 1942–43

34. Oliver p 114

35. Int Paterson

36. GA M6340/14 Sep 15/48 fr G to Friends [Mathers]

37. GA M6340/15 Sep 19/52 fr G to Mrs Mather

38. Int Paterson

39. Int Macleod

40. GA M6340/148 Oct 3/45 fr Carlyle to N

41. Ints Paterson, Griffin, Brown

42. Int Paterson

43. Int Griffin

44. Int Paterson

45. Ints Griffin, Brown, Paterson

46. GA M6340/14 Mar 8/47 fr G to Frds [Homer and Lea ---- (surname unknown)]

47. Ibid.

48. GA M6340/14 May 24/46 fr G to Dick [Wright]

49. GA M6340/14 nd [ca 1946] fr G to Dick [Wright]

50. GA M6340/14 May 24/46 fr G to Dick [Wright]

51. GA M6340/14 Mar 8/47 fr G to Frds [Homer & Lea ---- (surname unknown)]

52. Tivy, CH Jul 16/83; Reid, Albn Mar 1/7

53. GA M6340/148 Apr 2/49 fr Toole to N

54. CH Nov 23/50

55. CH Mar 31/49

56. Apparently George was very angry one time when the *Herald*'s music reviewer, Jamie Portman, made several negative comments about Norma's voice in his column (in the late 1950s or early 1960s, when it became noticeable that she was losing her top notes). The Pocaterras were friends of the critic's in-laws and, in George's old-fashioned view, felt this personal connection should have guaranteed loyalty and a more sympathetic review. (Int Musselwhite)

57. Int Hamilton

58. Int Macleod

59. GA M6340/14 Mar 21/46 fr G to N

60. GA M6340/14 May 24/46 fr G to Dick [Wright]

61. GA M6340/14 Jan 10/46 fr G to Dick [Wright]

62. GA M6340/40 Nov 11/47 fr N to G

63. GA M6340/40 Dec 9/47 fr N to Mr and Mrs Mather

64. GA M6340/14 Mar 8/48 fr G to Friends [Mathers]

65. GA M6340/14 Apr 24/47 fr G to Mrs Mather and Ernest

66. Ibid.

67. GA M6340/14 Oct 17/47 fr G to Friends [Mathers]

68. GA M6340/14 Jun 24/48 fr G to Campbell

69. GA M6340/14 Oct 12/49 fr G to Friends [Mathers]

70. GA M6340/14 nd [ca Jan/48] fr G to RMP

71. GA M6340/14 Dec 27/47 fr G to Sibley

72. CH Jul 9/49

73. GA M6340/14 Mar 14/46 fr G to Amos

74. GA M6340/14 Oct 17/47 fr G to Friends [Mathers]

75. GA M6340/14 Sep 15/48 fr G to Friends [Mathers]

76. GA M6340/14 Mar 30/48 fr G to Doctor [Morlan]

77. GA M6340/15 Mar 12/52 fr G to Mrs Mather

78. GA M6340/15 Jan 22/53 fr G to Friends [Mathers]

79. Plot summary of movie *Saskatchewan* taken from AMC-TV website: http://www.amctv.com/show/detail?CID=10244-1-CST.

80. Albn, Sep 5/53

81. CH May 10/59

82. GA M6340/15 Dec 1/55 fr G to Danciger

83. GA M6340/15 Jun 23/54 fr G to Fred McGuinness

84. According to "Son of the Mountains": "In the movie, an Indian scout comes out from the woods and sees the tracks of the Mounties' horses who had just passed that way. He calls to his companions, still in the woods, 'Nay-dam-yah-bin-o, Oon-jah-bow' ('They have gone this way. Hurry up.') The director tried several Indian's [sic] voices to say those words, but they did not register well. Then he said, 'George, how about you saying those words?' George did and the 'take' was perfect." (pp 93–94)

85. GA M6340/146 Oct 19/53 fr Walsh to G

86. "Ranch Flicker Talk: Saskatchewan" by movie editor Robert Cummings, in GA M6340/o.s. Scrapbook, v. 3

87. GA M6340/1 G Diary Sep 18/53

88. GA M6340/146 Jun 4/59 fr sec, Knights of the Round Table, Calgary, to G

89. GA M6340/16 Feb 7/59 fr G to Doctor [Morlan]

90. GA M6340/15 Dec 9/54 fr G to Friends [Mathers]

91. GA M6340/16 Jun 14/60 fr G to Doctor [Morlan]

92. GA M6340/17 Oct 22/63 fr G to RMP

93. GA M6340/17 Mar 19/63 fr G to RMP

94. GA M6340/178 G Address to HSA

95. BCA MS-2762/1/14 Apr 25/56 fr G to RMP

96. GA M6340/14 nd [ca Jan/48] fr G to RMP
97. GA M6340/16 Jan 11/56 fr G to Doctor [Morlan]
98. GA M6340/18 Jan 26/65 fr G to Amelie
99. GA M6340/100 Feb 13/50 fr Dorothy Mather to G and N
100. GA M6340/15 Mar 3/50 fr G to Friends [Mathers]
101. GA M6340/15 Oct 18/55 fr G to Friends [Mathers]
102. GA M6340/105 Apr 6/55 fr Ramsay to N
103. GA M6340/105 Jun 24/55 fr Mount Royal College to N

Chapter 9—Norma and George: Studio Years, 1955–1972

1. GA M6340/208 Notebooks
2. The Pocaterras carried two mortgages on the Glengarry house, which they purchased with only 3,000 dollars down on March 1, 1955. They also arranged two private loans, one with the McIntoshes and one with Norma's old friend Bessie Campbell, who allowed them to pay off at least part of their debt in monthly deliveries of produce such as eggs and honey. (GA M6340/155)
3. Int Michael Piper
4. GA M6340/17 Feb 9/60 fr G to Julio Pocaterra Montel
5. Ints Butters, Macleod
6. Ints Brown, Wilson One student recalled that whenever George returned from an outing in the car, even if he was aware that she was teaching, he would lean on the horn until Norma ran outside to open the garage door for him.
7. Int Patterson
8. Int Jack Piper
9. GA M6340/15 Oct 18/55 fr G to Friends [Mathers]
10. In a short history of this piano prepared for Sophie Kok, who purchased it from her former teacher in 1982, Norma relayed the instrument's background as far as she knew it. Made of rosewood, with a "beautiful design of inlaid precious woods," apparently it had been commissioned by Steinway and built by Heintzman for display at the 1912 Toronto Exhibition. That year, wealthy Calgarian Jack Dallas reputedly paid 3,500 dollars to acquire it for his new home in Banff. By 1955 it was in Calgary and no longer playable because of several broken keys. In fact, when the Pocaterras first saw it, its face was against the wall where it sat wedged tightly behind a sofa. It was located for the Pocaterras by the well-known Calgary piano tuner Cal Musselwhite, who restored and tuned it so that it recovered its original "magnificent action and tone." (Int Kok)
11. Int Kok. The same photograph was used for a portrait of Norma painted in miniature on ivory by the Italian artist Maria Joli Fedeli, who visited Calgary in 1964. (GA M6340/2 G Diary Jun 5, 12 Nov 25/64)
12. Int Musselwhite. In 1953 the Calgary Kiwanis Club took over sponsorship and administration of the annual competition organized by the Calgary branch of the Alberta Musical Festival Association. Since that date the event has been known as the Calgary Kiwanis Music Festival.
13. Int Jones
14. Int Woodward
15. Int Henker
16. GW Fall/71
17. Int Eve Ford
18. Ints Jones, Musselwhite
19. Morley, Albn Jun 28/63
20. Int Henker. Mrs Mauchline, the official pianist at the Golden Age Club after 1954, was considered by some to be "one of the finest accompanists in Western Canada." (Morley, Albn Jun 28/63)
21. GA M6340/4 N Diary Oct 14/72
22. GA M6340/4 N Diary Oct 5/74

23. GA M6340/4 N Diary Mar 13/75
24. GA M6340/4 N Diary May 4/73
25. GA M6340/179; Int Brown
26. Int Brown
27. Ints Miller, Munn
28. Int Musselwhite
29. Ints Miller, Munn
30. GA M6340/1 G Diary May 1/51; Apr 22/53; Mar 30/55
31. CH Jun 4/51
32. GA M6340/2 G Diary Apr 24, 25, 27/61
33. GA M6340/2 G Diary Mar 25, 26/65
34. Int Jones
35. Int Musselwhite
36. GA M6340/1 G Diary Sep 6/55
37. GA M6340/2 G Diary Sep 21/68
38. GA M6340/2 G Diary Jun 17/64
39. GA M6340/17 Sep 5/61 fr G to RMP
40. GA M6340/16 Jan 1/56 fr G to Doctor [Morlan]
41. GA M6340/18 Sep 3/66 fr G to Ed and Marguerite ---- [surname unknown]
42. GA M6340/1 G Diary May 21/59
43. GA M6340/15 Oct 29/54 fr G to Jones
44. GA M6340/16 Apr 25/56 fr G to RMP
45. GA M6340/1 G Diary Sep 26/58
46. Int Musselwhite
47. GA M6340/14 Oct 9/46 fr G to RMP
48. GA M6340/138 Feb 12/61 fr Amelie to G
49. M6340/40 Feb 20/61 fr N to Amelie
50. Int Julia Piper
51. Albn Aug 5/64. As of April 2006, the scale model of the Buffalo Head Ranch was still in storage in the artifact collection of the Canadian Museum of Civilization. (Corresp Laflamme)
52. GA M6340/18 May 24/65 fr G to RMP
53. GA M6340/17 Mar 19/63 fr G to RMP
54. Int De Paoli
55. Fanella p 58
56. Although there were several Italian Canadian social and benevolent clubs active in Calgary prior to the Second World War (Fanella p 43), there is no evidence that George ever held membership in any but the Italian Canadian Club, formed in 1952.
57. Fanella pp 42–44. Rebaudengo was also head of the Fascio, a fascist party in Calgary during the 1920s and 1930s that probably functioned more as a social club than an active political organization. Although George demonstrated interest in fascism while in Italy during the latter half of the 1930s, there is no evidence that he belonged to the Calgary Fascio. His friendship with Rebaudengo appears to date from the post-war period.
58. GA M6340/18 Jan 25/67 fr G to Amelie; GA M6340/o.s. Scrapbook, v. 3
59. GA M6340/181 Son of Mtns pp 98–99; GA M6340/o.s. Scrapbook, v. 3
60. Who's Who in Alberta pp 343–44
61. GA M6340/17 Nov 11/63 fr G to Betty McIntosh
62. GA M6340/40 Aug 22/69 fr N to Strom
63. GA M6340/4 G Diary Sep 20/70
64. GA M6340/207
65. GA M6340/40 Sep 24/72 fr N to Harry Monahan
66. GA M6340/4 N Diary Feb 28/72
67. GA M6340/4 N Diary Mar 17/72
68. Ibid.
69. GA M6340/4 N Diary Feb 11/72

70. In 1981, the Rose Bowl was replaced by a keeper plaque of the same name, which in turn was replaced in 1990 by a medal known as the George Pocaterra Medal. (Corresp Quinton)

Chapter 10 — Norma: Alone Again, 1972–1983

1. GA M6340/4 N Diary Dec 10/72
2. GA M6340/180
3. Alta Dept of Energy website: http://www.energy.gov.ab.ca/457.asp
4. GA M6340/4 N Diary Oct 4/72
5. CH Sep 2/78
6. GA M6340/4, 5 N Diary Apr 7, Jun 27/74, Apr 22/79
7. GA M6340/4, 5 N Diary Jan 1/73; Oct 25/74; May 2/79
8. Officially, the competitor winning this scholarship was the one who received the highest mark in the class Folk Songs, Traditional Airs and Sea Shanties. (Corresp Quinton)
9. Over the years, the Calgary Kiwanis Music Festival streamlined its award system. As a result, in 2002 the following were awarded: the George W. Pocaterra Medal (adjudicator's choice from the male opera class), the George W. Pocaterra Memorial Scholarship of 100 dollars (highest mark for French or Italian art song), the Norma Piper Pocaterra Memorial Scholarship of 200 dollars (for male oratorio) and another Pocaterra scholarship of 100 dollars (for the 19-and-under concert or recital class). (Corresp Quinton)
10. Dawson, CH Jul 23/79
11. Martin, CH Sep 2/78
12. GW Fall/71
13. Reid, Albn Mar 1/76
14. GA M640/RCT-132 Int Dunsmore
15. GA M6340/4 N Diary Apr 10/74
16. GA M6340/5 N Diary May 1, Sep 28/76
17. Ints Michael Piper, Shirley Piper; GA M6340/4 N Diary Dec 25/74
18. GA M6340/4 N Diary Jul 11/75
19. GA M6340/5 N Diary Jul 16, 22/76
20. George actually called Elpoca Mountain "Paul," after Paul Amos. Its sister mountain, which they called "George," is now known as Gap Mountain. In 1984 Paul Amos's contribution to the exploration of the area was finally recognized with the designation of Spotted Wolf Creek. Appropriately, this stream is a companion to Pocaterra Creek. (Corresp Daffern Feb1/05)
21. *Banff Crag and Canyon* Sep 27/78
22. GA M6340/2 G Diary Sep 7/62
23. GA M6340/5 N Diary Jan 25, 26/78
24. Int Hamilton
25. Ints MacKinnons, Chinneck. In addition to her enthusiastic support as a member, "booster" and subscriber, Norma provided the association with much-appreciated ongoing financial support during her lifetime and a generous bequest in her will. The Southern Alberta Opera Association became the Calgary Opera Association in 1983.
26. Int Macleod
27. Int Michael Piper
28. Norma's grave at Burnsland Cemetery is located in Section N Block 05 Lot 011. There is no headstone.
29. Int Leier. Their seats are located at Orchestra, Centre, Row P, Seats 12 (Norma) and 13 (George).
30. Tivy, CH Jul 16/83
31. GA M6340/25 Apr 3/35 fr N to G
32. Dawson, CH Jul 23/79

Epilogue

1. Corresp Daffern Dec 13/04
2. Corresp Daffern Feb 1/05. During the 1960s and '70s, Piper Creek was known as Elpoca Creek, but that changed when the name "Elpoca" was officially adopted in 1978 for a creek on the other side of Elpoca Mountain.
3. Corresp Daffern Feb 1/05. Regretting that she was not more specific in her original naming of the creek, Gillean is considering revising her book references to read "Norma Piper Creek." Once this name comes into common usage, the official name may be modified, thereby satisfying Norma's many admirers by making her identification with the area more obvious and complete.

References
Unpublished

Primary Documents

Alberta Registered Music Teachers Association, Calgary Branch fonds, 1935–1999. Glenbow Archives.
Calgary Musical Club fonds, 1915–1963. Glenbow Archives.
Canadian Club of Calgary fonds, 1910–2002. Glenbow Archives.
Edwin Fenwick fonds, British Columbia Archives (MS-93-6227).
1881 Census: Westminster Township, Middlesex County, Ontario. Index. www.familysearch.org.
1871 Census: Westminster Township, Middlesex County, Ontario. Index. Library and Archives Canada.
1861 Census: Westminster Township, Middlesex County, Ontario. Index. London and Middlesex County Branch, Ontario Genealogical Society.
Emigration Service Fund, 1843–1854: Miscellaneous Accounts. Department of Finance. Library and Archives Canada.
George and Norma Piper Pocaterra fonds, 1848–1979. Glenbow Archives (M 6340).
John Haddin fonds, 1910–1961. Glenbow Archives.
Mary Shortt fonds, 1929–1973. Glenbow Archives.
Pocaterra, George William. Last Will and Testament. June 3, 1957. Alberta Justice, Clerk's Office.
Pocaterra, Norma Mill. Last Will and Testament. July 13, 1980. Alberta Justice, Clerk's Office.
Prime Ministers' fonds: Richard Bedford Bennett: Requests for Letters of Introduction: Norma Piper to A. B. Muddiman. Library and Archives Canada.
Raymond M. Patterson fonds, 1918–1984, British Columbia Archives.
Rotary Club of Calgary fonds, 1916–1987. Glenbow Archives.
Scottsville Cemetery, Westminster Township. Listing. London and Middlesex County Branch, Ontario Genealogical Society.
Sierra Club of Alberta fonds, 1973–1993. Glenbow Archives.
Susan Henker fonds, ca 1959–1969. Glenbow Archives.

Correspondence

Colby, Jo-Anne. CPR Archives. Correspondence with JH. September 10, 2002.
Daffern, Gillean. Correspondence with JH. December 13, 2004, February 1, 2005.
Dale, Anne C. Faculty of Dentistry, University of Toronto. Correspondence with JH. March 15, 2002.
Gennaro, Valeria. Correspondence with JH. February 4, November 10, 2002.
Laflamme, Annie. Canadian Museum of Civilization. Correspondence with JH. November 12, November 26, 2002, April 18, 2006.
McClelland, Arthur, David McCord, and Sarah Morton. London Room, London Public Library. Correspondence with JH. December 24, 2001; January 6, February 22, December 18, 2002; February 8, 2005.

Middlesex Land Registry Office, London, Ontario. Correspondence with JH. February 2003.
Ontario Genealogical Society, Elgin Branch. Correspondence with JH. February 2003.
Piper, Jack and Julia. Correspondence with JH. November 30, 2001.
Quinton, Donna. Calgary Kiwanis Music Festival. Correspondence with JH. November 4, 2002.
Strachwitz, Dr Moritz Graf. Deutsches Adelsarchiv Marburg. Correspondence with JH. March 9, 2005.

Interviews

Baumgart, Adolf. Interview with DF. June 18, 1992.
Brown, Lois Callaway. Interview with JH. November 18, 2002.
Butters, Donna. Interview with JH. November 18, 2001.
Chinneck, Doreen. Interview with JH. September 12, 2001.
Cook, Averil. Interview with JH. December 5, 2002.
Dempsey, Hugh A. Interview with JH. November 27, 2002.
De Paoli, Louis. Interview with DF. March 16, 1994.
Duncan, Cleone. Interview with JH. April 25, 2004.
Ford, Eve Zacharias. Interview with JH. January 26, 2005.
Ford, Phyllis Chapman Clarke. Interview with JH. August 16, 2003.
Griffin, Shirley Flock. Interview with JH. November 18, 2001.
Hamilton, Molly Blanchfield. Interview with JH. October 19, 2001.
Hawley, Dorothy. Interview with JH. September 14, 2001.
Henker, Susan. Interview with JH. January 14, 2003.
Jackson, Dale. Interview with JH. February 7, 2005.
Jones, Sylvia. Interview with JH. September 27, 2001.
Kok, Sophie. Interview with JH. September 12, 2001.
Leier, Laurie. Interview with JH. October 17, 2002.
Lorieau, Maurice. Interview with JH. December 5, 2002.
MacKinnon, Jamie and Betty. Interview with JH. December 1, 2001.
Macleod, Faye. Interview with JH and DF. November 10, 2001.
McMillan, Melody Wilson. Interview with JH. October 4, 2001.
Miller, Frances and Gary. Interview with JH. July 10, 2001.
Munn, Sandra. Interview with JH. July 30, 2001.
Musselwhite, Florence. Interviews with JH. August 27, September 17, 2001.
Page, P. K. Interview with DF. November 7, 1995.
Paterson, Leona. Interview with JH. February 5, 2002.
Patterson, Marigold. Interviews with DF. July 12, 1991; November 2, 1995.
Perkins, Marilyn. Interview with JH. March 7, 2002.
Piper, Jack and Julia. Interviews with JH. September 24, October 8, November 25, 2001.
Piper, Michael. Interview with JH. September 24, 2001.
Piper, Shirley. Interview with JH. September 18, 2001.
Pozza, Guido. Interview with JH. April 15, 2002.
Wilson, Lil. Interview with JH. October 2, 2001.
Winans, Eleanor Carlyle. Interview with JH. April 29, 2004.
Woodward, Susan Milner. Interview with JH. October 5, 2001.

Theses

Kennedy, Norman John. 1952. The Growth and Development of Music in Calgary. Unpublished MA thesis, University of Alberta.
Mawhood, Rhonda. 1991. Images of Feminine Beauty in Advertisements for Beauty Products, English Canada, 1901–1941. Unpublished MA thesis, McGill University.
Oliver, Kathleen E. 1992. Splendid Circles: Women's Clubs in Calgary, 1912–30. Unpublished MA thesis, University of Calgary.
Philip, Catherine Ross. 1975. The Women of Calgary and District, 1875–1914. Unpublished MA thesis, University of Calgary.

Published

Books

Alberta in the 20th Century: Vol 2: The Birth of the Province. 1992. Edmonton: United Western Communications.

Alberta Registered Music Teachers Association, Calgary Branch. 1985. *ARMTA Calgary Branch 50th Anniversary, 1935–1985.*

Bianconi, Lorenzo and Giorgio Pestelli, eds. 1998. *Opera Production and its Resources.* Chicago: University of Chicago Press.

Braithwaite, Max. [ca 1977] *The Hungry Thirties, 1930/1940.* Toronto: Natural Science of Canada Ltd.

The Canadian Almanac. 1925–1939. Toronto: Copp, Clark and Co. Ltd.

Canadian Federation of Music Teachers' Associations. 1959. *Twelfth Biennial Convention, Canadian Federation of Music Teachers' Associations: July 1–4, 1959, Jubilee Auditorium, Calgary, Alberta.*

Canadian Who's Who. 1936-1937, 1948, 1964-1966. Downsview, ON: University of Toronto Press.

Chicago City Directory. 1928–1929. Chicago: D.B. Cooke and Co.

Chiniki Research Team. 1987. *Ozade-Mnotha Wapta Makochi: Stoney Place Names.* Prepared for the Chiniki Band Council.

Clark, Martin. 1996. *Modern Italy, 1871–1995.* 2nd edition. New York: Addison Wesley Longman Ltd.

Cochrane and Area Historical Society. [ca 1977] *Big Hill Country: Cochrane and Area.*

Colpitts, George. [ca 1991] *History of the Highwood River.* High River, AB: Highwood Restoration and Conservation Association.

The Crazy Twenties, 1920/1930. [ca 1978] Toronto: Natural Science of Canada Ltd.

Cummins Map Co. *Cummins Rural Directory Map: Alberta.* Winnipeg: Cummins Map Co. [ca 1918].

Dempsey, Hugh A. [ca 1994] Calgary, Spirit of the West: A History. Calgary: Glenbow Museum and Fifth House.

East Longview Historical Society. 1973. *Tales and Trails: A History of Longview and Surrounding Area, 1900-1972.* Calgary: Tales and Trails History Book Society.

Fanella, Antonella. 2000. *With Heart and Soul: Calgary's Italian Community.* Calgary: University of Calgary Press.

Foran, Maxwell. 1978. *Calgary: An Illustrated History.* Toronto: J. Lorimer and National Museum of Man, National Museum of Canada.

Ford, Clifford. [ca 1982] *Canada's Music: An Historical Survey.* Agincourt, ON: GLC Publishers.

Fraser, Sylvia, ed. [ca 1997] *A Woman's Place: Seventy Years in the Lives of Canadian Women.* Toronto: Key Porter Books.

Gray, James H. [ca 1991] *R. B. Bennett: The Calgary Years.* Toronto: University of Toronto Press.

Gray, James H. [ca 1975] *The Roar of the Twenties.* Toronto: Macmillan of Canada.

High River Pioneers and Old Timers' Association. 1960. *Leaves from the Medicine Tree.* Lethbridge, AB: *Lethbridge Herald.*

Illustrated Historical Atlas of Middlesex County, Ontario. 1878. Toronto: H. R. Page and Co.

Kallmann, Helmut, Gilles Potvin and Kenneth Winters, eds. [1992?] *Encyclopedia of Music in Canada.* 2nd ed. Toronto: University of Toronto Press.

Kimbell, David R. B. [ca 1991] *Italian Opera.* Cambridge, UK: Cambridge University Press.

London City Directories. 1901–1918. Hamilton: Vernon.

MacLean, H. R. [1987?] *History of Dentistry in Alberta, 1880-1980.* Edmonton: Alberta Dental Association.

Mount Royal College. 1942–1955. *The Varshicom* [yearbook].

The New Grove Dictionary of Opera. 1992. Grove's Dictionaries of Music.

Patterson, Raymond M. 1961. *The Buffalo Head.* New York: W. Sloane Associates.

------. *Far Pastures.* [ca 1963]. Sidney, B.C.: Gray's Publishing.

Prentice, Alison et al. [ca 1988] *Canadian Women: A History.* Toronto: Harcourt Brace Jovanovich Canada.

Rosselli, John. [ca 1984] *The Opera Industry in Italy from Cimarosa to Verdi: The Role of the Impresario.* Cambridge, UK: Cambridge University Press.

Sheppard, Bert. 1977. *Just About Nothing: the Hardest Part of Doing Nothing is Knowing When to Quit.* Calgary: McAra Printing.

Sheppard, Bert. 1988. *Spitzee Days.* 2nd ed. High River, AB: Museum of the Highwood.

Strong-Boag, Veronica Jane. 1994. *"Janey Canuck": Women in Canada, 1919–1939.* Ottawa: Canadian Historical Association.

------. [ca 1993] *The New Day Recalled: Lives of Girls and Women in English Canada, 1919–1939.* Rev. ed. Toronto: Copp Clark Pitman.

Thompson, John Herd. [ca 1985] *Canada, 1922–1939: Decades of Discord.* Toronto: McClelland and Stewart.

Troyer, Warren. [ca 1982] *The Sound and the Fury: An Anecdotal History of Canadian Broadcasting.* Toronto, ON: Personal Library.

Tuggle, Robert T. [ca 1983] *The Golden Age of Opera.* New York: Holt, Rinehart and Winston.

Turner, Robert D. 1987. *West of the Great Divide: An Illustrated History of the Canadian Pacific Railway in British Columbia 1880–1986.* Victoria: Sono Nis Press.

Waite, P. B. 1992. *The Loner: Three Sketches of the Personal Life and Ideas of R. B. Bennett, 1870–1947.* Toronto: University of Toronto Press.

Wetherell, Donald Grant. 1990. *Useful Pleasures: The Shaping of Leisure in Alberta, 1896–1945.* Edmonton: Alberta Culture and Multiculturalism.

Who's Who in Alberta. 1969. 1st ed. Saskatoon, SK: Lyone Publications.

Who's Who in Canada. 1940–1941. Markham, ON: International Press Publications.

Who's Who in Chicago and Vicinity: The Book of Chicagoans. 1931. Chicago: The A. S. Marquis Co.

Youngstown and District Historical Society. 1984. *Youngstown Memories Across the Years, 1909–1983.* Youngstown, AB: The society.

Articles—Signed

Brennan, Brian. 1995. Operato's Spirit Still Lives On. *Calgary Herald.* October 14.

Brewer, Alice. 1931. Vancouver correspondent. *Music and Musicians* [Seattle]. October.

Charlesworth, Hector. 1941. Among the Musicians. Saturday Night. January 11; February 8.

------. Canadian Wins in Opera. 1939. *Saturday Night.* September 23.

------. The Problem of Musical Refugees. 1939. *Saturday Night.* July 8.

------. Wartime Tastes in Music. 1939. *Saturday Night.* September 23.

Dawson, Eric. 1979. War Killed Norma Pocaterra's Career, But No Bitterness Lingers. *Calgary Herald.* July 23.

MacMillan, Ernest. 1936. Problems of Music in Canada. *Yearbook of the Arts in Canada.* Toronto: Macmillan.

Martin, Don. 1978. War Quashed Calgary Woman's Career on World Opera Stages. *Calgary Herald.* September 2.

Morley, Frank S. 1963. Truly Great Voice. *Albertan.* June 28.

Pannain, Guido. 1956. "Italian Opera from 'Falstaff' to Today." *Fifty Years of Opera and Ballet in Italy.* Carmine Siniscalco, ed.

Peach, Jack. 1985. Baritone's Scrapbooks Reveal Rich Cultural Past. *Calgary Herald.* January 12.

Pocaterra, George W. 1963. Among the Nomadic Stoneys. *Alberta Historical Review,* Vol 11, No 3, Summer.

------. 1949. Indian Place Names Known Only to Few Historians. *Calgary Herald.* July 9.

------. 1932. The Last Buffalo Hunt, as told by a Stony Chief. *Calgary Herald.* January 23.

------. 1932. Lone Warrior Defies Tribe for Revenge. *Calgary Herald.* October 22.

Primrose, Tom. 1961. Will 'Gold Strike' Close Old Legend? *Albertan.* November 8.

Reid, Eva. 1976. Eavesdrop with Eva Reid. *Albertan.* March 1.

Schuck, Paula. 2000. Women's Unpaid Labour at Heart of City's Social Conscience: They Were Home-makers, Mothers and Philanthropists, Who Laid the Foundation of London's Social and Community Organizations. *London Free Press.* January 1.

Smith, Catherine Munn. 2000. J. Frank Moodie: The Man and the Mine. *Alberta History,* Vol 48,

No 2, Spring.

Snow, Kathleen M. 1994. Cultural Life in Calgary in the Twentieth Century. *Centennial City: Calgary 1894–1994*. Donald Smith and Henry Klassen, eds.

Starr, M. 1971. Norma Piper: She Sings the Songs of Life. *Canadian Golden West*. Fall.

Tivy, Patrick. 1983. Farewell to a Celebrated Singer. *Calgary Herald*. July 16.

Articles—Unsigned

Albertan. 1925. Where Calgary Surpasses London. December 12.

------. 1931. Society Notes. February 21, 24, 28; March 6.

------. 1931. Spot West of Nanton May Be Lost El Dorado. February 12.

------. 1953. Strange Characters Have Invaded Banff. September 5.

Calgary Herald. 1925. London Old Boys Elect Dr Piper. November 14, 1925.

------. 1925. London Old Boys Plan Turkey Feed. November 21.

------. 1939. Dr W. A. Piper Dies at Home; Here 21 Years. October 17.

------. 1939. Italy Peaceful but Switzerland Full of Rumours. October 13.

------. 1940. Norma Piper Delights Audience of Airmen. December 13.

------. 1940. Ten New Artists Named for Met. October 11.

------. 1942. Norma Piper Recital Distinct Success. January 15.

------. 1942. Norma Piper to Sing Here on Wednesday. January 10.

------. 1945. Enthusiastic Audience Sees Pleasing Operetta. May 11.

------. 1945. Mount Royal College Conservatory of Music. September 8.

------. 1947. Chamber Music Concert Sunday. November 22.

------. 1949. Norma Piper Concert Will Aid Kerby Fund. March 25.

------. 1949. Song Recital Reveals Excellent Technique. March 31.

------. 1950. Norma Piper Delights Audience with Arias. November 23.

------. 1959. Indian Authority Describes Movie Work with Film Star. June 10.

------. 1983. Calgary Loses Fervent Backer of the Opera. July 12.

------. 1983. Obituary. July 11.

------. Society Notes. February 20, 1931; October 13, 1939; August 20, 1940.

Crag and Canyon [Banff]. 1978. George Pocaterra Honoured. September 27.

Edmonton Journal. 1931. Search for Gold Lures Hundreds on Barren Trail. February 16.

Glenbow [magazine]. 1982. Museum Acquires Pocaterra Collection. September/October.

London Free Press. 1908. Obituary. December 22.

------. 1936. Acclaimed Former London Girl Now Singing in Milan. December 12.

------. 1941. Former London Girl, Grand Opera Star in Italy, Home Again by Fortunes of War. January 31.

------. 1941. Norma Piper is Charming Artist. February 4.

------. 1941. Norma Piper Sings at her Former School. February 6.

------. 1941. Opera Singer Comes "Home." January 31.

Sunday Province [Vancouver]. 1931. Young Singer is Heard in Recital. September 13.

Websites

http://www.amctv.com/show/detail?CID=10244-1-CST

http://www.energy.gov.ab.ca/457.asp

Index

318

The Authors

Jennifer Hamblin has an MA in history from McMaster University and a Master of Library Science from the University of Toronto. She works as a reference librarian at the Glenbow Museum and lives with her family in Calgary.

David Finch has an MA in history from the University of Calgary. He works as a consulting historian and has authored a number of books including "R. M. Patterson: A Life of Great Adventure." He lives with his family in Calgary.